# DR DOBSON ANSWERS YOUR QUESTIONS

# Dr Dobson

## *Answers Your Questions*

**JAMES DOBSON**

KINGSWAY PUBLICATIONS
EASTBOURNE

First published in the USA by
Tyndale House Publishers, Wheaton, Illinois

First British edition 1983



ISBNs 0 86065 225 4 (cased)
0 86065 226 2 (paperback)

The publishers wish to express their gratitude to Hodder & Stoughton Limited for permission to reproduce material based on and quoted from *Straight Talk to Men and their Wives*, *Emotions: Can You Trust Them?* and *Hide or Seek*.

Printed in Great Britain for
KINGSWAY PUBLICATIONS LTD
Lottbridge Drove, Eastbourne, E. Sussex BN23 6NT by
Richard Clay (The Chaucer Press) Ltd,
Bungay, Suffolk

*Acknowledgments*
It is with gratitude that I hereby acknowledge the assistance of four women who contributed significantly to the production of this book. They are *Virginia Muir,* Managing Editor for Tyndale House Publishers, who assembled original material from my prior writings and recordings; *Dee Otte,* my Administrative Assistant, who kept the wheels turning when they would otherwise have ground to a halt; *Teresa Kvisler,* who typed and collated the final manuscript; and, of course, my beloved wife, *Shirley,* who is an active partner in everything I do. Without the encouragement and dedication of these four members of the "team", a half finished manuscript would remain hopelessly buried beneath a mountain of paper on my desk.

This book is affectionately dedicated to the professional colleagues and staff members who help me direct the activities of our non-profit ministry, Focus on the Family. David McQuiston, Gil Moegerle, Peb Jackson, and seventy other co-workers and friends are deeply devoted to the principles and values expressed throughout this book.

It is entirely appropriate, therefore, that I take this opportunity to thank them for their diligent efforts to preserve the institution of the family.

## *A Word from the Publisher*

James Dobson has become widely respected in the United Kingdom for his ministry through books and the film series *Focus on the Family*. In his home country, the United States, he carries on his work through TV and radio as well. The following article, entitled "Focus on the Family", is taken from the American publication *The Saturday Evening Post*, and gives a glimpse of the wider sphere into which Dr Dobson's help and encouragement are now moving.

# FOCUS ON THE FAMILY

*Author James Dobson calls upon his deeply ingrained Judeo-Christian values to connect the family of the '80s with the principles of "discipline, love, self-esteem, loyalty and fidelity."*

*CHARLES W. PHILLIPS* *

Credit a man with eight best-selling books, give him a radio show on 197 stations, put him in a film series to be viewed by 10 million people and book him on shows with Donahue and Tom Snyder and that same man is an instant celebrity . . . a full-fledged personality. Unless his name is Dr. James Dobson.

A tall, handsome man who is both dignified and downhome, tough but sympathetic, Dobson only recently is achieving fame beyond Christian circles. Thanks to a swing back to conservatism, his family-first philosophy is suddenly in vogue, his traditional values are suddenly acceptable, his ideas are suddenly in season.

Depending on who's counting, Dobson wears at least seven—no, make that eight—hats. Sometimes, in the course of a day he switches from one to another so smoothly, so adroitly, so often, that he might add quick-change artist to the list of vocations separated by commas after the Ph.D. in his name. Answering to the labels of father, husband, associate clinical professor of pediatrics at the University of Southern California School of Medicine, psychologist, author, radio and TV personality and speaker, Dobson manages a balancing act in the Flying Wallenda tradition. The trick, he has learned, is to maintain priorities and never let one role dominate at the expense of the others. At this, too, he succeeds.

The immensity of his influence in the areas of child and family psychology has been likened to that of Dr. Benjamin Spock of twenty years ago, although the similarity ends there. Dobson is a politically conservative, back-to-basics disciplinarian who believes in spoiling the rod to spare the child

---

*Reprinted from *The Saturday Evening Post,* a division of the Benjamin Franklin Literary and Medical Society, Inc. © 1982.

and who practices at home what he preaches on film, in books and around the lecture circuit.

"First and foremost, I'm a committed Christian," he explains. "I was raised in a Christian home, and those values are ingrained deeply within me. Most of what I teach is an outgrowth of traditional Christian concepts with regard to the family and home. I get a great deal of satisfaction in feeling used by God in the lives of people. I don't find my work stressful at all; in fact, I'm having the time of my life. The most difficult aspect is trying to keep it all under control and not let my professional identity interfere with my roles as father and husband."

It was this inevitable tug between his private and professional lives that helped convince him in 1979 to put his Focus on the Family seminar on tape. The seminar, usually offered in person by Dobson over a one-day or two-day period, centers on such topics as Christian fathering, preparing for adolescence, building self-esteem and the conflict of wills between parent and child. When the film idea was first presented by Word Publishers of Waco, Texas, he argued that surely no one would sit through seven one-hour films and watch a man stand in front of an audience and talk about traditional values and discipline. Reluctantly, he agreed to the project and admits today that his worst fears have been proven "dead wrong."

"The film series was actually a method of coping with so many demands on my time," he recalls. "I was getting anywhere from 500 to 1,000 speaking requests a year and was accepting about six per month. That might not sound like much until you realize most talks and seminars take place on weekends. Put that way, I wasn't with my children enough. I began to feel I was losing out on something. The films allowed me to stay home and yet get the message out."

The tapes, usually shown over a seven-week period or in succession over seven days, not only had immediate impact but have shown staying power. Marketing executives at Word say some 10 million people have already viewed the films at a clip of 100,000 persons per week. Most of the screenings are at local churches—more than 20,000 at latest count—but a variety of other organizations, including members of NFL teams, PTAs and military installation personnel, also have viewed them.

The format of the films is simple. In the fall of 1978, Dobson was scheduled to deliver his much-in-demand Focus on the Family seminar to 3,000 persons jammed into Laurie

Auditorium in San Antonio. Special guests included wife Shirley, mother Myrtle and a film crew assigned to videotape the entire Friday night and all-day Saturday sessions. Except for the opening sequences and a few closeups of the audience, the films' visual content is limited to Dobson at the podium or occasionally at the large onstage chalkboard. Surprisingly, each of the one-hour segments passes quickly, thanks to Dobson's well-documented research, relaxed delivery and frequent anecdotes. He draws on his experience as the father of a sixteen-year-old daughter and eleven-year-old son and his years as associate clinical professor of pediatrics at the University of Southern California School of Medicine. He recalls his daughter's first slumber party, when he, as an observer, quickly recognized the popularity pecking order of the girls in attendance. Using such memories as a base, he spins off into discussions of peer pressure and the importance of having a positive self-image. Recollections of his son's "terrible twos" serve as a springboard for talks about headstrong toddlers and strong-willed adolescents.

"If I have a motive in what I'm doing, it's nothing more ambitious than to connect the family in the '80s with the wisdom of the Judeo-Christian ethic—the traditional wisdom that's been with us for thousands of years," he explains. "The principles haven't changed, and they still work. I'm referring to discipline, love, self-esteem, loyalty and fidelity between husband and wife and commitment within the family. These aren't new ideas; I've never said I created anything new. That's why I have confidence in what I'm saying, because I didn't originate it—it existed long before I was born. All I've attempted to do is to take the wisdom that's been with us for thousands of years and put it in a package that people find interesting and entertaining. Hopefully, it captures their imagination and provides the motivation to do what they probably already knew was right."

Part of the interesting, entertaining package is the Dobson family itself. Although Dobson stoutly occupies the role of lone breadwinner and protective head of the household, he's hardly a throwback to the Neanderthal man who demanded submission and dragged the little woman around by her topknot. Dobson's done his share of diapering and dishes and marvels at wife Shirley, a former teacher, for her easy superiority at the art of homemaking. Their relationship is a solid, warm partnership based on respect.

"We've been married twenty years, and she is literally my best friend. If I had one evening to spend with any personality on earth, I'd spend it with Shirley. We have a great deal in common, and it's a testimonial to the power of love that I could be with anybody for twenty years and still find that person interesting, but she affects me that way."

Although his lectures are amply sprinkled with descriptive tales from the Dobson family archives, he's careful to stop short of relocating Shirley, Danae and Ryan from their comfortably private California home to life in a fishbowl. He discovered the danger of overexposure one weekend when Ryan accompanied him to a speaking engagement and was pressed for an autograph. The bewildered five-year-old responded, "But I can't even write." From that point onward, the subject of Dad's work has been low-keyed at home. The children seldom listen to his daily radio broadcasts (now aired on 197 stations), rarely watch him on television and are not preoccupied with the flourishing ministry that attracts some 4,500 letters to his office each day.

In spite of his image as Superdad, he feels no undue pressure to rear two perfect, "textbook" children. Observers might look to the Dobsons as model parents with model offspring, but Dobson draws a more realistic picture.

"My kids are healthy, seemingly happy and get along well in school. But these principles I teach don't need Danae and Ryan to prove them valid. They'll be valid even if I fail as a father. They existed before I came along, and they'll be here after I leave. God doesn't need me to prove what he said about the family is right. Even if everything goes to pieces at my house—and I pray it doesn't—the principles will still be true."

And they'll be true fifty years from now, long after the era of permissiveness, the "me" generation and the do-your-own-thing life style have gone the route of other fads, believes Dobson. The pendulum has swung back to traditional values, he says, and although the family unit is in real trouble, luckily, people recognize the threat, are looking for answers and are hungry for the kind of self-help information he provides.

"The most dangerous threat to family life is one seldom mentioned," says Dobson. "We can talk about alcoholism, drug abuse or infidelity, but a more common threat is the simple matter of overcommitment. I'm talking about the husband and wife who are too exhausted to take walks together, understand one another, meet each other's needs, have time for play, have time for children, have time for devotions. The husband often moonlights to maintain some standard of living; the wife works and tries to oversee the home; everyone is on the brink of exhaustion. I see that as the quickest route to the destruction of the family, and it can happen so easily.

"Sure, we have to make a living, but there's more to overcommitment than that. Why do we have to have a standard of living that we didn't have thirty years ago? I think we're sacrificing things that are absolutely irreplaceable. Things like relationship with the family, the loving interaction between husband and wife, parent and child. When you lie on your deathbed and look back over your life, you won't remember the new automobile, the new couch or the neighborhood you lived in. You'll remember who loved you, who cared for you and where you fit into somebody's life. If those things matter then, they should matter now, and we ought to live like they do."

Some people might find dealing with other families' problems discouraging, but Dobson sees it as fulfilling. He's a man of principle and those principles are the heart of his message.

"They work when people live by them rather than allowing their own needs to dominate everyone else in the family. At one point, people were taught to scream for their rights. This is disastrous when it's applied to the national level. What works best is when I say to you, 'I care about you as much as I care about myself. Your needs are my needs.' That's what makes life worth living. It's not when I clench my fists and grit my teeth and set out to get my own way."

Dobson's way is quieter, and it's winning converts every time he presents his case on a talk show, at a seminar, through a film or another book.

"I find it tremendously exciting to have an opportunity to express creativity in figuring out where people's needs are and where the hurts are and how to help them. I don't see myself as a crusader trying to change the world by myself, but I can do what I can. I can do my part."

# CONTENTS

Introduction 15
1 Life in the Family 19
2 Spiritual Training of Children 39
3 Education of Children 61
4 Learning Problems in Childhood 73
5 Sex Education at Home and School 89
6 The Discipline of Infants and Toddlers 97
7 Understanding the Role of Discipline 113
8 The "How To" of Discipline 131
9 Spankings: When, How, and Why 151
10 The Source of Self-Esteem in Children 163
11 Developing Self-Esteem in Children 177
12 Parental Overprotection 201
13 Sibling Rivalry 215
14 Teaching Children to Be Responsible 227
15 Hyperactivity in Children 245
16 Coping with Adolescence 257
17 Questions from Adolescents 281
18 Self-Esteem in Adulthood 299

19 A Christian Perspective on Anger 313
20 Romantic Love 325
21 Conflict in Marriage 331
22 The Homemaker 349
23 Depression in Women 365
24 Understanding Premenstrual Tension 375
25 Coping with Menopause 385
26 Male and Female Uniqueness 403
27 The Meaning of Masculinity 413
28 Adult Sexuality 429
29 Homosexuality 449
30 Television and Violence 455
31 Understanding Guilt 463
32 Interpretation of Impressions 475
33 Mid-Life and Beyond 491
34 Dr. Dobson Talks about Families 497
Final Comment 505
Notes 509
Question Index 513

# INTRODUCTION

During the summer of 1981, my family joined two others on a white water rafting trip down the beautiful Rogue River in Oregon. Those three days of churning water and blistering sun turned out to be one of the most exciting experiences of our lives . . . and perhaps my last! Just before departing on the journey I was told by our host, Dr. Richard Hosley, that "the river is always boss." Forty-eight hours later I learned what he meant.

Rather than floating on the raft for fifty miles in relative serenity and safety, I chose to paddle along behind in a plastic eight-foot canoe. And on the second afternoon, I insisted on rowing into the most treacherous part of the river. It was a bad decision.

Ahead lay a section of water known as the "Coffeepot," so named because the narrowing of the rock-walled banks created an unpredictable, bubbling current that had been known to suck small boats below the surface without warning. In fact, one unfortunate raftsman drowned in that area last summer. Nevertheless, I paddled toward the rapids with confidence (and blissful ignorance).

I seemed to be handling the task quite well for the first few moments, before everything suddenly came unraveled. I was hit unexpectedly by the backwash flowing over a large rock and was unceremoniously thrown into the turbulent water. It seemed like an eternity before I came to the surface, only to find breathing impossible. A bandana that had been around my neck was now plastered across my mouth and was held there by my glasses. By the time I clawed free and gasped for air, another wave hit me in the face, sending half the river into my lungs. I came up coughing and sputtering before taking another unscheduled trip below the surface. By then I was desperate for air and keenly aware that the Coffeepot was only twenty-five yards downstream!

A kind of panic gripped me that I had not experienced since childhood! Although my life jacket probably guaranteed my survival, I definitely considered the possibility that I was drowning. My family and friends watched helplessly from the raft as I bobbed through the rapids into the narrowest section of the river.

Through incredible rowing skill, Dr. Hosley managed to "hold" the raft until I could float alongside and grab the rope that rims the upper exterior structure. Then, as we were thrown from one side of the river to another, I pulled my feet up and sprang off the rocks and into the raft, avoiding a crushing blow against the vertical walls of the bank. I can assure you that I rode for several miles in the safety of the raft before moving a muscle!

The only lasting casualty of the experience is a matter of collegiate pride. Dr. Hosley was wearing a shirt with his beloved Stanford University named across the front. It survived the trip. But somewhere on the bottom of the Rogue River in shame and dishonor lies a watersoaked hat bearing the logo of the University of Southern California. It was a sad moment in the historic rivalry between the two alma maters!

After the crisis had passed, I reflected on the utter helplessness I had felt as the river's toy. My life was totally out of control and nothing could be taken for granted, not even a breath of air. Then my thoughts turned to the similar panic that is expressed so often in my counseling practice and in letters that are sent to my office. I currently receive thousands of letters per day, many of which reflect the same helplessness and lack of control I felt in the Rogue River. In fact, the analogy to "drowning" is certainly appropriate in this context; anxious people often use that precise term to describe the experience of being inundated by the events of life. Either they or their loved ones are involved in drug abuse, infidelity, alcoholism, divorce, physical disabilities, mental illness, adolescent rebellion, or low self-esteem. And immediately downstream are even greater dangers and threats.

Not all of the people who express this kind of anxiety are adults who have had time to mature and perceive life from a grown-up perspective. Some are children and adolescents who are trying to cope with problems in the best way possible. And for many today, their only alternative seems to be the ultimate self-hatred of suicide. Consider the following letter I received last year from a bewildered young man whom I'll call Roger.

> Dear Dr. Dobson:
>
> Hi, I'm 11 years old. I'm going in 6th grade. I just got done reading your book, "Preparing for Adolescence." I want you to know it helped me.
>
> When I was in 5th grade I was going with this girl. She broke up with me. *I had family problems.* [Italics mine.] So I tried to hang myself. Well I got a really bad pain in my neck. Then I got to where I couldn't breathe. I realized I wanted to live. So I yanked the noose off. And now God and I are struggling together.
>
> Love,
> Roger
>
> P.S. I didn't go into drugs and I never will. I have been asked but I say no. Some people respect me, others think I'm chicken. I don't care.

Each desperate letter of this nature that I receive represents thousands of individuals with similar problems who do not bother to write. And at the core of their vast reservoir of misery lies the great common denominator of turmoil within the family. (Note Roger's vague reference to his problems at home. One can imagine its pivotal role in his attempted suicide.) The American family is experiencing an unprecedented period of disintegration which threatens the entire superstructure of our society, and we simply *must* take whatever steps are necessary to insure its integrity.

The urgency of this mission has become the predominant passion of my professional life. My greatest desire is to serve the God of my fathers by contributing to the stability and harmony of individual families in every way possible. If I can prevent just *one* child from experiencing the nightmare of parental conflict and divorce and custody hearings and wretching emotional pain, then my life will not have been lived in vain. If I can snatch a *single* fellow traveler from the turbulent waters that threaten to take him under, then there is purpose and meaning to my work. If I can lead but one lost human being to the personhood of Jesus Christ—the giver of life itself—then I need no other justification for my earthly existence.

That brings us to the book you are about to read, which is a product of the mission I've described. In this instance, however, our purpose has not been to deal with the great crises of life. Rather, our focus has been on the common questions relating to the institutions of marriage and parenthood. The philosophy underlying the recommendations offered is based on the best psychological information now available, in keeping with the commandments and values provided by the Creator Himself.

Finally, I should explain that not all of the material presented herein is unique to this book. I have drawn literally from my previous writings and recordings by condensing larger discussions into more succinct replies. Portions of seven earlier books are represented in this volume, beginning with *Dare to Discipline* and concluding with *Straight Talk to Men and Their Wives.* Our purpose has been to extract frequently asked questions and answers which heretofore were "buried" deep within the original publications. Then by adding to that material and providing an index to the issues discussed, I believe we have provided specific approaches to real problems.

I hope you find this book helpful, whether you are currently gasping for air or floating high above the rapids. Thanks for your interest in our work, and may God continue to bless your home.

*James Dobson, Ph.D.*
Associate Clinical Professor of Pediatrics
USC School of Medicine

SECTION 1

# LIFE IN THE FAMILY

**I'm afraid I'm not ready to raise the baby I bore last month. Sure, I understand how to feed and bathe and diaper him. But I'm uncertain about the future. What should be the objective of my relationship with him? Can you give me a foundational philosophy that will guide my parenting efforts during my child's first four years of life?**

Your question reminds me of a friend who flew his single-engine airplane toward a small country airport some years ago. He arrived as the sun had dropped behind a mountain at the close of the day, and by the time he maneuvered into a position to land, he could not see the hazy field below. He had no lights on his plane and there was no one on duty at the airport. He circled the runway for another attempt to land, but the darkness had then become even more impenetrable. For two hours he flew his plane around and around in the blackness of the night, knowing that he faced certain death when his fuel was expended. Then, as greater panic gripped him, a miracle occurred. Someone on the ground heard the continuing drone of his engine and realized his predicament. That merciful man drove his car back and forth on the runway to show my friend the location of the airstrip, and then let his lights cast their beam from the far end while the plane landed.

I think of that story whenever I am coming down at night in a commercial airliner. As I look ahead, I can see the green lights bordering the runway which tell the captain where to direct the plane. If it stays between those lighted boundaries, all will be well. There is safety in that illuminated zone, but disaster lies to the left or right.

As new parents, we need clearly marked boundaries telling us where to steer the family ship. We require some guiding *principles*, as you requested, which will help us raise our children in safety and health.

Toward that end, let me provide two distinct messages which must be conveyed to every child during his first forty-eight months. These concepts are of great significance in my approach to parenthood, and can be thought of as beacons or guiding lights. They are:

1. "I love you more than you can possibly understand. You are precious to me and I thank God every day that He lets me raise you!"

2. "Because I love you, I must teach you to obey me. That is the only way I can take care of you and protect you from things that might hurt you. Let's read what the Bible tells us: 'Children, obey your parents, for this is what God wants you to do' (Eph. 6:1)." This is an abbreviated answer to a very important and complex question, but perhaps it will give you a place to begin formulating your *own* philosophy of parenting.[1]

**Can you give us a guideline for how much work children should be given to do?**

There should be a healthy balance between work and play. Many farm children of the past had daily chores that made life pretty difficult. Early in the morning and again after school they would feed the pigs, gather the eggs, milk the cows, and bring in the wood. Little time was reserved for fun, and childhood became a pretty drab experience. That was an extreme position and I certainly don't favor its return. However, contrast that level with its opposite, recommended by some modern behaviorists who recommend that we not even ask our children to water the lawn or let out the cat. According to this recommendation, Junior should be allowed to lie on his overfed stomach watching six or eight hours of worthless television while his schoolwork gathers dust in the corner. Both extremes, as usual, are harmful to the child. The logical middle ground can be found by giving the child an exposure to responsibility and work, but preserving time for his play and fun. The amount of time devoted to each activity should vary with the age of the ·hild, gradually requiring more work as he grows older.[2]

**Should parents force a child to eat?**
No. I am no expert in nutrition, but I believe a normal child's appetite is governed by the amount of food he needs. He will get hungry when he needs nourishment. However, I do believe the parent should carefully guard that appetite, making sure that he satisfies it with the foods his body requires. A bit of sugar in the afternoon can make him disinterested in his dinner. Or he may sit down at the table and fill his stomach with juice or one item on his plate. Thus, it may be necessary to give him one kind of food at a time, beginning with iron-rich meat and other protein, followed by the less important items. Once he is satisfied, I can see no value in forcing him to continue eating. Incidentally, the parent should know that a child's appetite often drops off rapidly between two and three years of age. This occurs because his time of maximum growth rate has subsided, and his need for food is reduced.[3]

**What do you think of the phrase "Children should be seen and not heard"?**
That statement reveals a profound ignorance of children and their needs. I can't imagine how any loving adult could raise a vulnerable little boy or girl by that philosophy. Children are like clocks, they must be allowed to run![4]

**Would you go so far as to apologize to a child if you felt you had been in the wrong?**
I certainly would—and indeed, I have. A few years ago I was burdened with pressing responsibilities which made me fatigued and irritable. One particular evening I was especially grouchy and short-tempered with my ten-year-old daughter. I knew I was not being fair, but was simply too tired to correct my manner. Through the course of the evening, I blamed Danae for things that were not her fault and upset her needlessly several times. After going to bed, I felt bad about the way I had behaved and I decided to apologize the next morning. After a good night of sleep and a tasty breakfast, I felt much more optimistic about life. I approached my daughter before she left for school and said, "Danae, I'm sure you know that daddies are not perfect human beings. We get tired and irritable just like other people, and there are times when we are not proud of the way we

behave. I know I wasn't fair with you last night. I was terribly grouchy, and I want you to forgive me."

Danae put her arms around me and shocked me down to my toes. She said, "I knew you were going to have to apologize, Daddy, and it's OK; I forgive you."

Can there be any doubt that children are often more aware of the struggles between generations than are their busy, harassed parents?[5]

**I am very disappointed with the way my four-year-old is developing. If the present trends continue, he will be a failure as an adult. Is it possible to forecast a child's future character and personality traits from this early age?**

Probably not. Rene Voeltzel said, "We must not look too soon in the child for the person he will later become." I agree. It is unfair and damaging to judge him too soon. Be patient and give your little fellow time to mature. Work gently on the traits that concern you the most, but, by all means, allow him the privilege of being a child. He will be one for such a brief moment, anyway.[6]

**How do you feel about having a family council, where each member of the family has an equal vote on the decisions affecting the entire family?**

It's a good idea to let each member of the family know that the others value his viewpoint and opinion. Most important decisions should be shared within the group because that is an excellent way to build fidelity and family loyalty. However, the equal vote idea is carrying the concept too far; an eight-year-old should not have the same influence that his mother and father have in making decisions. It should be clear to everyone that the parents are the benevolent captains of the ship.[7]

**Should I punish my son for bed-wetting?**

Absolutely not! It is never appropriate to punish a child for any involuntary action. To punish someone for something he simply cannot avoid doing is to set him up for serious problems.

Of course, if you have reason to think that your son is awake and simply lies there in bed and urinates because he is too lazy to get up and go to the bathroom, that is another matter. However, true enuresis is totally involuntary.[8]

**Can you offer any advice for dealing with recurring bed-wetting in a six-year-old boy?**
Enuresis can produce emotional and social distress for the older child. Thus, it is wise to help him conquer the problem as soon as possible. I would recommend that you make use of a buzzer device that emits a loud noise when your boy urinates at night. Sears, Roebuck and Co. sells a unit called a Wee Alert, which I have found effective *when used properly* for children four years of age and older.

Bed-wetting occurs in most cases as a result of very sound sleep, which makes it difficult, if not impossible, for the child to learn nighttime control on his own. His mind does not respond to the signal reflex action that ordinarily awakens a lighter sleeper. Fortunately, that reflex action can be trained or conditioned to awaken even a deep sleeper in most instances.

The Wee Alert system produces a very irritating sound when urination occurs at night. The child has been instructed to awaken one parent (determining which one can create some interesting marital arguments) who must place him in a tub of cool water or splash cold water on his face. Both alternatives are unpleasant, of course, but are essential to the success of the program. The child is told that this is *not* a form of punishment for wetting the bed. It is necessary to help him break the habit so he can invite friends to spend the night and he can go to other homes, as well. The cold water awakens the child fully and gives him a reason not to want to repeat the experience. It is a form of aversive conditioning, such as is used to help break the habit of smoking. Later, the relaxation immediately prior to urination is associated with the unpleasantness of the bell and the cold water. When that connection is made, urinary control is mastered.

This procedure may take from four to eight weeks to conquer bed-wetting, but success can occur much more quickly in some cases. My own son remained dry the third night we used the equipment. As indicated in the Wee Alert instructions, it is unnecessary to restrict liquids, get the child up at night, use punishment, etc. None of these standard procedures communicate with the unconscious mind during periods of deep, dreamy sleep. The Wee Alert system apparently does.

(Please note that I did not invent the Wee Alert system and receive no compensation from Sears for recommending this product. I merely suggest the device because it usually works.)

Another successful system is called a Nite-Train-r. It can be ordered from Nite-Train-r, P. O. Box 282, Newberg, OR 97132.[9]

**My wife and I are extremely busy during this period of our lives. My job takes me on the road several days a week, and my wife has become very successful as a real estate agent. Quite honestly, we are not able to spend much time with our three children, but we give them our undivided attention when we are together. My wife and I wish we had more family time, but we take comfort in knowing that it's not the quantity of time between parent and child that really matters; it's the quality of that time that makes the difference. Would you agree with that statement?**

There is a grain of truth in most popular notions, and this one is no exception. We can all agree that there is no benefit in being with our children seven days a week if we are angry, oppressive, unnurturing and capricious with them. But from that point forward, the quantity versus quality issue runs aground. Simply stated, *that dichotomy will not be tolerated in any other area of our lives; why do we apply it only to children?* Let me illustrate.

Let's suppose you are very hungry, having eaten nothing all day. You select the best restaurant in your city and ask the waiter for the finest steak on his menu. He replies that the filet mignon is the house favorite, and you order it charcoal-broiled, medium rare. The waiter returns twenty minutes later with the fare and sets it before you. There in the center of a large plate is a lonely piece of meat, one inch square, flanked by a single bit of potato.

You complain vigorously to the waiter, "Is this what you call a steak dinner?"

He then replies, "Sir, how can you criticize us before you taste that meat? I have brought you one square inch of the finest steak money can buy. It is cooked to perfection, salted with care, and served while hot. In fact, I doubt if you could get a better piece of meat anywhere in the city. I'll admit that the serving is small, but after all, sir, everyone knows that it isn't the quantity that matters; it's the quality that counts in steak dinners."

"Nonsense!" you reply, and I certainly agree. You see, the subtlety of this simple phrase is that it puts two necessary virtues in opposition to one another and invites us to choose between them. If quantity and quality are worthwhile ingredients in family relationships, then why not give our kids *both?* It is insufficient to toss our "hungry" children an occasional bite of steak, even if it is prime, corn-fed filet mignon.

Without meaning any disrespect to you for asking this question, my concern is that the quantity-versus-quality cliche has become, perhaps, a rationalization for giving our kids *neither!* This phrase has been bandied about by over-committed and harassed parents who feel guilty about the lack of time they spend with their children. Their boys and girls are parked at child care centers during the day and with baby-sitters at night, leaving little time for traditional parenting activities. And to handle the discomfort of neglecting their children, Mom and Dad cling to a catch phrase that makes it seem so healthy and proper: "Well, you know, it's not the *quantity* of time that matters, it's the *quality* of your togetherness that counts." I maintain that this convenient generalization simply won't hold water.[10]

**If it were possible to put a speedometer on a particular style of living, our family would consistently break the sound barrier. We're all so incredibly busy that we hardly have any home life at all. What effect does this breathless pace have on a family, and especially on kids?**

The inevitable loser from this life in the fast lane is the little guy who is leaning against the wall with his hands in the pockets of his blue jeans. He misses his father during the long days and tags around after him at night, saying, "Play ball, Dad!" But Dad is pooped. Besides, he has a briefcase full of work to be done. Mom had promised to take him to the park this afternoon, but then she had to go to that Women's Auxiliary meeting at the last minute. The lad gets the message—his folks are busy again. So he drifts into the family room and watches two hours of pointless cartoons and reruns on television.

Children just don't fit into a "to do" list very well. It takes time to be an effective parent when children are small. It takes time to introduce them to good books—it takes time to fly kites and play punch ball and put together jigsaw puzzles. It takes time to listen, once more, to the skinned-knee episode and talk about the bird with the broken wing. These are the building blocks of esteem, held together with the mortar of love. But they seldom materialize amidst busy timetables. Instead, crowded lives produce fatigue—and fatigue produces irritability—and irritability produces indifference—and indifference can be interpreted by the child as a lack of genuine affection and personal esteem.

As the commercial says, "Slow down, America!" What is your rush, anyway? Don't you know your children will be gone so quickly and you will have nothing but blurred memories of those years when they needed you? I'm not suggesting that we invest our entire adult lives into the next generation, nor must everyone become parents. But once those children are here, they had better fit into our schedule somewhere.[11]

**My family lives together under one roof and we share the same last name. But we don't "feel" like a family. We're so rushed and stressed by the routine pressures of living that I sometimes feel I hardly know my wife and kids. How can I begin to put a sense of togetherness into this harried household? How do *you* put meaningful activities into your family?**

I've written and spoken extensively on the dangers of overcommitment and "routine panic," and I will not repeat that warning here, except to say that you should make a concerted effort to slow the pace at which your family is running. Beyond that advice, however, I would emphasize the importance of creating special *traditions* in your home. By traditions I'm referring to those recurring events and behaviors that are anticipated, especially by children, as times of closeness and fellowship between loved ones.

For example, one of the most important holiday traditions in our family centers around food. Each year during Thanksgiving and Christmas, the women prepare tremendous meals, involving the traditional holiday menu of turkey and all that goes with it. A great favorite is a fruit dish called ambrosia, containing sectioned oranges and peeled grapes. The family peels the grapes together the night before Thanksgiving.

The Thanksgiving and Christmas holidays are wonderful experiences for all of us. There's laughter and warm family interaction through the day. We look forward to that festive season, not just for the food, but for what happens between loved ones who convene.

We not only attempt to serve traditional Thanksgiving and Christmas meals, but we try to have specific foods on each holiday throughout the year. On New Year's Day, for reasons which I cannot explain, we enjoy a southern meal of pinto beans cooked at least eight hours with large chunks of lean ham, served with cornbread and little onions. It's so good! On July 4th we invite thirty or more friends and serve barbecued hamburgers and baked beans in the backyard. This has become a prelude to the fireworks display.

Obviously, many of our traditions (but not all) focus on the enjoyable activity of eating together. Another example occurs immediately *prior* to the Thanksgiving dinner. After the food is on the table and family members are seated, I read a passage of Scripture and Shirley tells the story of the Pilgrims who thanked God for helping them survive the ravages of winter. Then each person is given two kernels of Indian corn to symbolize the blessings he or she is most thankful for that year. A basket is passed and every member drops in the corn while sharing their two richest blessings from God during that year. Our expressions of thankfulness inevitably involve people—children and grandparents and other loved ones. As the basket moves around the table, tears of appreciation and love are evident on many faces. It is one of the most beautiful moments of the year.

This brings me back to the question about harried homes. The great value of traditions is that they give a family a sense of identity and belonging. All of us desperately need to feel that we're not just part of a busy cluster of people living together in a house, but we're a living, breathing family that's conscious of our uniqueness, our character, and our heritage. That feeling is the only antidote for the loneliness and isolation that characterize so many homes today.

**I know that for the sake of my marriage and my family I should not overcommit myself. But what do I do with the guilt feelings I have when I neglect worthwhile things, especially with regard to my duties in the church?**

I think God wants us to exercise common sense in the assignments we accept—even those involving worthwhile causes. Inevitably, this judgment will require us to decline some responsibilities in order to maintain a balance between work, recreation, family activities, exercise, devotions, etc. If too many good activities are attempted, other good objectives will be sacrificed. That is like installing a new sprinkler system in a yard and putting too many outlets on the line. When that occurs, *nothing* is watered properly.

I'm reminded, also, of a magazine advertisement that explained how Gallo Wines are produced. It contained a message that is relevant to this discussion. I had not previously known that grape farmers not only prune dead branches from their vines, but they also eliminate a certain amount of the fruit-producing branches. In other words, they sacrifice some of the crop so that what fruit is left will be better. Do you see the relevance to our lives today?

Notice these Bible verses from John 15:1, 2:

> I am the true Vine, and my Father is the Gardener. He lops off every branch that doesn't produce and he prunes those branches that bear fruit for even larger crops.

It is necessary in the Christian life to eliminate some good things from your schedule so that the other things you do are done better. That is the best way to achieve better quality in the good activities that remain. But let me add a warning that this objective can easily become a rationalization for carrying no responsibility in the church or bearing no burden for the needs of others. That is certainly not a justifiable position to take.[12]

**We are not able financially to take long car trips or get into expensive hobbies, like skiing. Could you suggest some simple traditions that will appeal to small children?**
You don't have to spend a lot of money to preserve meaningful family life. Children love daily routine activities of the simplest kind. They enjoy hearing the same stories a thousand times over, and they'll laugh at the same jokes until you're ready to climb the wall from repeating them. You can turn the routine chores of living into times of warmth and closeness if you give a little thought to them. The key is *repetition*, which conveys the feeling of tradition.

Let me give an example. When my family was younger I attempted as often as possible to put the children to bed in the evening. By that time of night, my wife was exhausted and she appreciated the help. It also guaranteed me at least fifteen to twenty minutes with the kids no matter how busy I had been that day.

The responsibility included diapering Ryan during the first three years of his life. (It took him a while to overcome that requirement, as it does with all children.) I figured if I had to put a diaper on a squirming toddler, I might as well turn the activity into something that would be fun for both of us. So we played a little game each night. I would talk to the pins as I was diapering my son. I would say, "Pins, don't stick him; I don't really think you ought to stick him. See, he's being still; he's not wiggling around. Tonight you don't have to stick him; maybe tomorrow night, but don't stick him tonight." Ryan loved the game! He'd listen quietly, his eyes as big as half dollars. If he wiggled too much and kept me from getting his diapers on, I would scrape the point of the pin gently on his leg, not enough to hurt, but enough to make him aware of it. He'd look up at me and say, "Those mean ol' pins sticked me, Daddy!" We would both grin. And every night Ryan would say without fail, "Talk to the pins, Daddy!" It was something we did together, turning a routine activity into something of pleasure between a father and his toddler.

I'm reminded of what Howard Hendricks said when his children were grown. He asked them what they most enjoyed about their childhood—the vacations they had taken, the parks they had visited, and all the moments that they had enjoyed together. Their answer surprised him. What they appreciated most were the times when he had gotten down on the floor and fought with them!

My daughter felt the same way when she was young. She would rather fight with me than go to Disneyland or the zoo! After we had had a tussle that left me exhausted, she always thanked me for fighting with her. For some reason, kids love that wild activity. (Mothers hate it.) There's a kind of informal love that transpires in a playful romp that doesn't occur any other way.

I also like the idea of reserving one night a week for oral reading with the family. Sometimes that's difficult to accomplish with children of varying ages, but if your sons and daughters are clustered in age, I think it's a great activity. You can read *Tom Sawyer* and other books that have been so popular down through the ages. The idea is to read *together* as a family.

In short, I believe many Americans have forgotten the value of characteristics and activities which identify the families as unique and different. This benefit was beautifully illustrated by the stage play *Fiddler on the Roof*. What gave the violinist his stability and balance on his precarious perch? It was *tradition*—which told every person who he was. I want to give that same heritage to my children.[13]

**Can these traditions be useful in teaching spiritual values as well?**

They certainly can. In fact, by far the most *important* traditions are those that help instill Christian principles and elements of the Judeo-Christian heritage in our children. This gives a boy or girl an additional sense of history and of his/her place in it. If you asked me to indicate *who I am* today, my answer would reflect the Christian values and teachings that I learned as a child. Those understandings began even before I could talk.

Thus, a vital fringe benefit of Christianity is the tremendous sense of identity that grows out of knowing Jesus Christ. Each child can be made aware, beyond a shadow of doubt, that he is a personal creation of God. He can know that the Creator has a plan for his life and that Jesus died for him. I'm convinced that there is no greater sense of self-esteem and personal worth than the personal awareness that comes from deeply ingrained spiritual values. This understanding answers the important questions of life, including "Who am I?" "Who loves me?" "Where am I going?" and "What is the purpose of life?" Only Christ can provide the answers to these questions which give meaning to this earthly experience.

**What would you do if your eighteen-year-old son decided to become a social dropout and run away from home?**

It is difficult for anyone to know exactly how he would face a given crisis, but I can tell you what I think would be the best reaction under those circumstances. Without nagging and whining, I would hope to influence the boy to change his mind before he made a mistake. If he could not be dissuaded, I would have to let him go. It is not wise for parents to be too demanding and authoritative with an older teenager; they may force him to defy their authority just to prove his independence and adulthood. Besides this, if they pound on the table, wring their hands, and scream at their wayward son, he will not feel the full responsibility for his own behavior. When Mom and Dad are too emotionally involved with him, he can expect them to bail him out if he runs into trouble. I think it is much wiser to treat the late adolescent like an adult; he's more likely to act like one if he is given the status offered to other adults. The appropriate parental reaction should be: "John, you know I feel you are making a choice that will haunt you for many years. I want you to sit down with me and we will analyze the pros and cons; then the final decision will be yours. I will not stand in your way." John knows that the responsibility is on his shoulders. Beginning in middle adolescence, parents should give a child more and more responsibility each year, so that when he gets beyond their control he will no longer need it.

The Gospel of St. Luke contains an amazingly relevant story of a young dropout. It is commonly known as the parable of the prodigal son. Read the story in Luke 15 and then note that it contains several important messages that are highly relevant to our day. First, the father did not try to locate his son and drag him home. The boy was apparently old enough to make his own decision and the father allowed him the privilege of determining his course.

Second, the father did not come to his rescue during the financial stress that followed. He didn't send money. There were no well-meaning church groups that helped support his folly. Note in verses 16 and 17, "No one gave him anything . . . he finally came to his senses" (TLB). Perhaps we sometimes keep our children from coming to their senses by preventing them from feeling the consequences of their own mistakes. When a teenager gets a speeding citation, *he* should pay for it. When he wrecks his car, *he* should have it fixed. When he gets suspended from school, *he* should take the consequences without parental protests to the school. He will learn from these adversities. The parent who is too quick to bail his child out of difficulty may be doing him a disservice.

Third, the father welcomed his son home without belittling him or demanding reparations. He didn't say, "I told you you'd make a mess of things!" or "You've embarrassed your mom and me to death. Everyone is talking about what a terrible son we've raised!" Instead, he revealed the depth of his love by saying, "He was lost and is found!"[14]

**I want to ask you a very personal question. Your books deal with practical aspects of everyday living. They offer solutions and suggestions for handling the typical frustrations and problems of parenthood and marriage. But that makes me wonder about your own family. Does your home always run smoothly? Do you ever feel like a failure as a father? And if so, how do you deal with self-doubt and recrimination?**

I have been asked this question many times, although the answer should surprise no one. Shirley and I experience the same frustrations and pressures that others face. Our behavior is not always exemplary, nor is that of our children. And our household can become very hectic at times.

Perhaps I can best illustrate my reply by describing the day we now refer to as "Black Sunday." For some reason, the Sabbath can be the most frustrating day of the week for us, especially during the morning hours. I've found that other parents also experience tensions during the "get 'em ready for church" routine. But Black Sunday was especially chaotic. We began that day by getting up too late, meaning everyone had to rush to get to church on time. That produced emotional pressure, especially for Shirley and me. Then there was the matter of the spilt milk at breakfast and the black shoe polish on the floor. And, of course, Ryan got dressed first, enabling him to slip out the back door and get himself dirty from head to toe. It was necessary to take him down to the skin and start over with clean clothes once more. Instead of handling these irritants as they arose, we began criticizing one another and hurling accusations back and forth. At least one spanking was delivered, as I recall, and another three or four were promised. Yes, it was a day to be remembered (or forgotten). Finally, four harried people managed to stumble into church, ready for a great spiritual blessing, no doubt. There's no pastor in the world who could have moved us on that morning.

I felt guilty throughout the day for the strident tone of our home on that Black Sunday. Sure, our children shared the blame, but they were merely responding to our disorganization. Shirley and I had overslept, and that's where the conflict originated.

After the evening service, I called the family together around the kitchen table. I began by describing the kind of day we had had, and asked each person to forgive me for my part in it. Furthermore, I said that I thought we should give each member of the family an opportunity to say whatever he or she was feeling inside.

Ryan was given the first shot, and he fired it at his mother. "You've been a real grouch today, Mom!" he said with feeling. "You've blamed me for everything I've done all day long."

Danae then poured out her hostilities and frustrations. Finally, Shirley and I had an opportunity to explain the tensions that had caused our overreaction.

It was a valuable time of ventilation and honesty that drew us together once more. We then had prayer as a family and asked the Lord to help us live and work together in love and harmony.

My point is that *every* family has moments when they violate all the rules—even departing from the Christian principles by which they have lived. Fatigue itself can damage all the high ideals which have been recommended to parents in seminars and books and sermons. The important question is, how do mothers and fathers reestablish friendship within their families when the storm has passed? Open, nonthreatening discussion offers one solution to that situation.

Returning to the question, let's acknowledge that a psychologist can no more prevent all emotional distress for his family than a physician can circumvent disease in his. We live in an imperfect world which inflicts struggles on us all. Nevertheless, biblical principles offer the most healthy approach to family living—even turning stress to our advantage. (Someday I'll tell you about Black Monday.)[15]

**Our financial problems are getting more frustrating every day. Do you have any suggestions?**

There are thousands of books available for those who want to gain control of their monetary resources, and I am no authority on that subject. Thus, my comments on this topic will be brief and to the point. My one contribution is in opposition to the lust for more and more things—leading us to buy that which we neither need nor can afford.

Though I can make no claim to wealth, I have tasted most of the things Americans hunger for: new cars, an attractive home, and gadgets and devices which promise to set us free. Looking at those materialistic possessions from the other side of the cash register, I can tell you that they don't deliver the satisfaction they advertise! On the contrary, I have found great wisdom in the adage, "That which you own will eventually own you!" How true that is. Having surrendered my hard-earned dollars for a new object only obligates me to maintain and protect it; instead of its contributing to my pleasure, I must spend my precious Saturdays oiling it, mowing it, painting it, repairing it, cleaning it, or calling the Salvation Army to haul it off. The time I might have invested in worthwhile family activities is spent in slavery to a depreciating piece of junk.

Let me ask you to recall *the* most worthless, unnecessary expenditure you have made in the last year. Perhaps it was an electric can opener which now sits in the garage, or a suit of clothes which will never be worn. Do you realize that this item was not purchased with your money; it was bought with your time which you traded for money? In effect, you swapped a certain proportion of your alloted days on earth for that piece of junk which now clutters your home. Furthermore, no power on earth could retrieve the time which you squandered on its purchase. It is gone forever. We are investing our lives in worthless materialism, both in the original expenditures and on subsequent upkeep and maintenance.

Do I sound a bit preachy in this discourse? Perhaps it is because I am condemning my own way of life. I am sick of the tyranny of things! But I'm also addressing the "have nots," those multitudes who are depressed because they own so little. How many women today are depressed because they lack something which either wasn't invented or wasn't fashionable fifty years ago? How many families are discontented with their two-bedroom house, when it would have been considered entirely adequate in the 1800s? How many men will have heart attacks this year from striving to achieve an ever-increasing salary? How many families will court financial ruin just to keep up with the Joneses, and then find to their dismay that the Joneses have refinanced and are ahead again?

The utter folly of materialism was dramatically emphasized during my most recent trip to England. As I toured the museums and historical buildings, I was struck by what I called "empty castles." Standing there in the lonely fog were the edifices constructed by proud men who thought they owned them. But where are those men today? All are gone and most are forgotten. The hollow castles they left behind stand as monuments to the physical vulnerability and impermanence of the men who built them. Not one has survived to claim his possession. As Jesus said of the rich fool who was about to die and leave his wealth, "Then whose shall those things be, which thou hast provided?" (Luke 12:20 KJV)

May I say with the strongest conviction that I want to leave more than "empty castles" behind me when I die. At forty-five years of age, I realize how rapidly my life is passing before my eyes. Time is like a well-greased string which slides through my taut fingers. I've tried vainly to hold it or even slow its pace, but it only accelerates year by year. Just as surely as the past twenty years evaporated so quickly, the next three or four decades will soon be gone. So there is no better time than now for me (and you) to assess the values which are worthy of my time and effort. Having made that evaluation, I have concluded that the accumulation of wealth, even if I could achieve it, is an insufficient reason for living. When I reach the end of my days, a moment or two from now, I must look backward on something more meaningful than the pursuit of houses and land and machines and stocks and bonds. Nor is fame of any lasting benefit. I will consider my earthly existence to have been wasted unless I can recall a loving family, a consistent investment in the lives of people, and an earnest attempt to serve the God who made me. Nothing else makes much sense, and certainly nothing else is worthy of my agitation! How about you?[16]

**Considering how difficult it is to be good parents, why should anyone want to have children? Is it worth it?**
Parenthood is costly and complex, no doubt about that. I'm reminded of a woman with seven rambunctious children who boarded a Los Angeles bus and sat in the seat behind me. Her hair was a mess and the black circles under her eyes revealed a state of utter exhaustion. As she stumbled past me with her wiggling tribe, I asked, "Do all those children belong to you, or is this some kind of picnic?"

She looked at me through squinted eyes and said, "They're all mine, and believe me, it's no picnic!"

The woman is right. Parenthood is no job for sissies. Am I suggesting, then, that newly married couples should remain childless? Certainly not! The family that loves children and wants to experience the thrill of procreation should not be frightened by the challenge of parenthood. Speaking from my own perspective as a father, there has been no greater moment in my life than when I gazed into the eyes of my infant daughter, and five years later, my son. What could be more exciting than seeing those tiny human beings begin to blossom and grow and learn and love? And what reward could be more meaningful than having my little boy or girl climb onto my lap as I sit by the fire, hug my neck, and whisper, "I love you, Dad."

Oh, yes, children are expensive, but they're worth the price. Besides, nothing worth having comes cheap.[17]

SECTION 2

# SPIRITUAL TRAINING OF CHILDREN

**Should a child be allowed to "decide for himself" on matters related to his concept of God? Aren't we forcing our religion down his throat when we tell him what he must believe?**

Let me answer that question with an illustration from nature. A little gosling (baby goose) has a peculiar characteristic that is relevant at this point. Shortly after he hatches from his shell he will become attached, or "imprinted," to the first thing that he sees moving near him. From that time forward, he will follow that particular object when it moves in his vicinity. Ordinarily, he becomes imprinted to the mother goose who was on hand to hatch the new generation. If she is removed, however, the gosling will settle for any mobile substitute, whether alive or not. In fact, a gosling will become most easily attached to a blue football bladder, dragged by on a string. A week later, he'll fall in line behind the bladder as it scoots by him. Time is the critical factor in this process. The gosling is vulnerable to imprinting for only a few seconds after he hatches from the shell; if that opportunity is lost, it cannot be regained later. In other words, there is a critical, brief period in the life of a gosling when this instinctual learning is possible.

There is also a critical period when certain kinds of instruction are possible in the life of the child. Although humans have no instincts (only drives, reflexes, urges, etc.), there is a brief period during childhood when youngsters are vulnerable to religious training. Their concepts of right and wrong, which Freud called the superego, are formulated during this time, and their view of God begins to solidify. As in the case of the gosling, the opportunity of that period must be seized when it is available. Leaders of the Catholic Church have been widely quoted as saying, "Give us a child until he is seven years old and we'll have him for life"; their affirmation is usually correct, because permanent attitudes can be instilled during these seven vulnerable years. Unfortunately, however, the opposite is also true. The absence or misapplication of instruction through that prime-time period may place a severe limitation on the depth of the child's later devotion to God. When parents say they are going to withhold indoctrination from their small child, allowing him to "decide for himself," they are almost guaranteeing that he will "decide" in the negative. If a parent wants his child to have a meaningful faith, he must give up any misguided attempts at objectivity. The child listens closely to discover just how much his parent believes what he is preaching; any indecision or ethical confusion from the parent is likely to be magnified in the child.[1]

**My wife and I have bedtime prayer with our child each night, and he goes to Sunday school and church every week. Still, I don't feel that this is enough to ensure his religious development. What more can I do to foster his spiritual growth at this time when his attention span is so limited?**

The answer was provided by Moses as he wrote more than 4,000 years ago in the book of Deuteronomy: "You must teach them [the principles and commandments of God] to your children and talk about them when you are at home or out for a walk; at bedtime and the first thing in the morning. Tie them to your finger, wear them on your forehead, and write them on the doorposts of your house!" (Deut. 6:7-9 TLB). In other words, we can't instill these attitudes during a brief bedtime prayer, or during formalized training sessions. We must *live* them from morning to night. They should be reinforced during our casual conversation, being punctuated with illustrations, demonstrations, compliments, and chastisement. This teaching task is, I believe, *the* most important assignment God has given to us as parents.[2]

**It is difficult for us to have meaningful devotions as a family because our young children seem so bored and uninvolved. They yawn and squirm and giggle while we**

**are reading from the Bible. On the other hand, we feel it is important to teach them to pray and study God's Word. Can you help us deal with this dilemma?**
The one key word to family devotions is *brevity*. Children can't be expected to comprehend and appreciate lengthy adult spiritual activities. Four or five minutes devoted to one or two Bible verses, followed by a short prayer, usually represents the limits of attention during the preschool years. To force young children to comprehend eternal truths in an eternal devotional can be eternally dangerous.[3]

**How is the concept of God established in the mind of the child?**
It is a well-known fact that a child identifies his parents with God, whether or not the adults want that role. While yielding to their loving leadership, for example, children are also learning to yield to the benevolent leadership of God Himself.

We have the responsibility of reflecting the two aspects of divine nature to the next generation. First, our Heavenly Father is a God of unlimited love, and our children must become acquainted with His mercy and tenderness through our own love toward them. But make no mistake about it, our Lord is also the possessor of majestic authority! The universe is ordered by a supreme Lord who requires obedience from His children and has warned them that "the wages of sin is death." To show our little ones love without authority is as serious a distortion of God's nature as to reveal an iron-fisted authority without love.[4]

**What is the most critical period in the spiritual training of young children?**
I believe the fifth year of a child's life is the most critical. Up to that time, he believes in God because his parents tell him it is the thing to do. At about five or six years of age he comes to a fork in the road: either he begins to reach out and accept the concept as his own, or he does not. At that point, he may "buy it" and put his feet down onto a more solid foundation—or he may start to doubt it, laying the basis for rejection.

I certainly don't mean to imply that parents should wait until the child is five or six to begin spiritual training. Nor are subsequent years unimportant. But I am convinced that our most diligent efforts in the home, and our best teachers in

Sunday school, ought to be applied to the child of five or six years. There are crucial crossroads after that, but this is the first important one.[5]

**Many people believe that children are basically "good," and only learn to do wrong from their parents and culture. Do you agree?**

If they mean that all children are worthy and deserving of our love and respect, I certainly do agree. But if they believe that children are by nature unselfish, giving, and sinless before God, I must disagree. I wish that assessment of human nature were accurate, but it contradicts scriptural understandings. Jeremiah wrote: "The heart is deceitful above all things, and desperately wicked: who can know it?" (Jer. 17:9 KJV). Jeremiah's inspired insight into human nature is validated by the sordid history of mankind. The path of civilization is blotted by murder, war, rape, and plundering from the time of Adam forward. This record of evil makes it difficult to hold to the pollyannish view that children are pure and holy at birth and merely learn to do wrong from their misguided parents. Surely during the past 6,000 years, there must have been at least *one* generation for whom parents did things right. Yet greed, lust, and selfishness have characterized us all. Is this nature also evident in children? King David thought so, for he confessed, ". . . in sin did my mother conceive me" (Psa. 51:5 KJV).

What meaningful difference, then, is made by the distinction between the two views of children? Practically everything, in fact. Parents who believe all toddlers are infused with goodness and sunshine are urged to get out of the way and let their pleasant nature unfold. On the other hand, parents who recognize the inevitable internal war between good and evil will do their best to influence the child's choices—to shape his will and provide a solid spiritual foundation. They acknowledge the dangers of adult defiance as expressed in 1 Samuel 15:23—"For rebellion is as bad as the sin of witchcraft, and stubbornness is as bad as worshiping idols" (TLB).[6]

**Parents have been commanded in the Bible to "train up a child in the way he should go." But this poses a critical question: What way should he go? If the first seven years**

**represent the "prime time" for religious training, what should be taught during this period? What experiences should be included? What values should be emphasized?** You've asked an excellent question. It is my strong belief that a child should be exposed to a carefully conceived, systematic program of religious training. Yet we are much too haphazard about this matter. Perhaps we would hit the mark more often if we more clearly recognized the precise target.

Listed below is a "Checklist for Spiritual Training"—a set of targets at which to aim. Many of the items require maturity which children lack, and we should not try to make adult Christians out of our immature youngsters. But we can gently urge them toward these goals—these targets—during the impressionable years of childhood.

Essentially, the five scriptural concepts which follow should be consciously taught, providing the foundation on which all future doctrine and faith will rest. I encourage every Christian parent to evaluate his child's understanding of these five areas:

CONCEPT I: "And thou shalt love the Lord thy God with all thy heart" (Mark 12:30 KJV).

1. Is your child learning of the love of God through the love, tenderness, and mercy of his parents? (most important)
2. Is he learning to talk about the Lord, and to include Him in his thoughts and plans?
3. Is he learning to turn to Jesus for help whenever he is frightened or anxious or lonely?
4. Is he learning to read the Bible?
5. Is he learning to pray?
6. Is he learning the meaning of faith and trust?
7. Is he learning the joy of the Christian way of life?
8. Is he learning the beauty of Jesus' birth and death?

CONCEPT II: "Thou shalt love thy neighbor as thyself" (Mark 12:31 KJV).

1. Is he learning to understand and empathize with the feelings of others?
2. Is he learning not to be selfish and demanding?
3. Is he learning to share?
4. Is he learning not to gossip and criticize others?
5. Is he learning to accept himself?

CONCEPT III: "Teach me to do thy will; for thou art my God" (Psa. 143:10 KJV).

1. Is he learning to obey his parents as preparation for later obedience to God? (most important)
2. Is he learning to behave properly in church—God's house?
3. Is he learning a healthy appreciation for both aspects of God's nature: love and justice?
4. Is he learning that there are many forms of benevolent authority outside himself to which he must submit?
5. Is he learning the meaning of sin and its inevitable consequences?

CONCEPT IV: "Fear God, and keep his commandments: for this is the whole duty of man" (Eccl. 12:13 KJV).

1. Is he learning to be truthful and honest?
2. Is he learning to keep the Sabbath day holy?
3. Is he learning the relative insignificance of materialism?
4. Is he learning the meaning of the Christian family, and the faithfulness to it which God intends?
5. Is he learning to follow the dictates of his own conscience?

CONCEPT V: "But the fruit of the Spirit is . . . self-control" (Gal. 5:22, 23 RSV).

1. Is he learning to give a portion of his allowance (and other money) to God?
2. Is he learning to control his impulses?
3. Is he learning to work and carry responsibility?
4. Is he learning the vast difference between self-worth and egotistical pride?
5. Is he learning to bow in reverence before the God of the universe?

In summary, your child's first seven years should prepare him to say, at the age of accountability, "Here I am, Lord, send me!"[7]

**My four-year-old frequently comes running home in tears because she has been hit by one of her little friends. I have taught her that it is not right to hit others, but now they are making life miserable for my little girl. As a Christian parent, what should I tell her about defending herself?**

You were wise to teach your daughter not to hit and hurt others, but self-defense is another matter. Children can be unmerciful in their torment of a defenseless child. When youngsters play together, they each want to have the best toys and determine the ground rules to their own advantage. If they find they can predominate by simply flinging a well-aimed fist at the nose of their playmate, someone is likely to get hurt. I'm sure there are Christians who disagree with me on this issue, but I believe you should teach your child to defend herself when attacked. Later, she can be taught to "turn the other cheek," which even mature adults find difficult to implement.

I recently consulted with a mother who was worried about her small daughter's inability to protect herself from aggression. There was one child in their neighborhood who would crack three-year-old Ann in the face at the slightest provocation. This little bully, named Joan, was very small and feminine, but she never felt the sting of retaliation because Ann had been taught not to fight back. I recommended that Ann's mother tell her to return Joan's attack if Joan hits first. Several days later the mother heard a loud altercation outside, followed by a brief scuffle. Then Joan began crying and went home. Ann walked casually into the house with her hands in her pockets, and explained, "Joan socked me so I had to help her remember not to hit me again." Ann had efficiently returned an eye for an eye and a tooth for a tooth. She and Joan have played together much more peacefully since that time.

Generally speaking, a parent should emphasize the foolishness of fighting. But to force a child to stand passively while being clobbered is to leave him at the mercy of his cold-blooded peers.[8]

**Do you think children between five and ten should be allowed to listen to rock music on the radio?**

No. Rock music is an expression of an adolescent culture. The words of teenagers' songs deal with dating, broken hearts, drug usage and luv-luv-luv. This is just what you don't want your seven-year-old thinking about. Instead, his world of excitement should consist of adventure books, Disney-type productions, and family activities—camping, fishing, sporting events, games, etc.

On the other hand, it is unwise to appear dictatorial and oppressive in such matters. I would suggest that you keep your preteen so involved with wholesome activities that he does not need to dream of the days to come.[9]

**How can I help my child develop wholesome, accepting attitudes toward people of other racial and ethnic groups?**
There is no substitute for parental modeling of the attitudes we wish to teach. Someone wrote, "The footsteps a child follows are most likely to be the ones his parents thought they covered up." It is true. Our children are watching us carefully, and they instinctively imitate our behavior. Therefore, we can hardly expect them to be kind to all of God's children if we are prejudiced and rejecting. Likewise, we will be unable to teach appreciativeness if we never say, "please" or "thank you" at home or abroad. We will not produce honest children if we teach them to lie to the bill collector on the phone by saying, "Dad's not home." In these matters, our boys and girls instantly discern the gap between what we say and what we do. And of the two choices, they usually identify with our behavior and ignore our empty proclamations.[10]

**I'm trying to raise and train two boys without the help of a husband and father, and I'm not handling the assignment very well. Shouldn't the church be doing something to help me as a single parent?**
Yes, it is clearly the task of the church to assist you with your parenting responsibilities. This requirement is implicit in Jesus' commandment that we love and support the needy in all walks of life. He said, "Inasmuch as ye have done it unto the least of these, my brethren, ye have done it unto me." If Jesus meant these words, and He obviously did, then our effort on behalf of a fatherless or motherless child is seen by the Creator of the universe as a direct service to Himself!

But the commandment to Christians is more explicitly stated in James 1:27: "The Christian who is pure and without fault, from God the Father's point of view, is the one who takes care of orphans and widows, and who remains true to the Lord" (TLB).

These Scriptures make it clear that we Christians are going to be held accountable for how well we reach out to those in need. The men of the church should take fatherless boys to the park, showing them how to throw a ball or catch a Frisbee. They should look for opportunities to reshingle or repaint a single mother's house, or do those repair jobs that she would find difficult to do even if she were not carrying heavy work responsibilities. And she might be in need of cash when her children are small. The biblical assignment is clear: wherever the need exists, it should be met by Christian men of the church![11]

**My husband and I are missionaries and have recently been assigned to a remote area of Colombia. Our ministry will be with an Indian culture which can only be reached by horseback or on foot. My concern is for our children, ages seven and nine, and their educational future. There are no schools near our new location, of course, and the nearest boarding facility will be more than 200 miles away. Because of the cost of travel, we would only be able to see them through the summers and perhaps at one other time during the year. Although I could teach them the academic subjects required between now and high school years, they obviously need social contact with their peers and we don't want to deprive them of those experiences. Would you recommend keeping them with us, or sending them away to school?**

"What will we do with the children?" That is often the most difficult question missionaries must answer. I don't propose to have final solutions to this thorny problem, although I do have some definite views on the subject. I've dealt with the children of missionaries, many of whom had become bitter and resentful of the sacrifices they were required to make. They were deprived of a secure home at a critical stage in their development and experienced deep emotional wounds in the process. Consequently, adolescent rebellion was common among these angry young people who resented their parents and the God who sent them abroad.

Based on these observations, it is my firm conviction that the family unit of missionaries should remain intact, if at all possible. I cannot overemphasize the importance of parental support and love during the formative years of life. A child's sense of security and well-being is primarily rooted in the stability of his home and family. Therefore, he is certain to be shaken by separation not only from his parents, but also from his friends and the familiar surroundings of his own culture. He suddenly finds himself in a lonely dormitory in a foreign land where he may face rejection and pressures that threaten to overwhelm him. I can think of no better method of producing emotional (and spiritual) problems in a vulnerable child!

My friend Dr. Paul Cunningham expressed a similar view during a conference on family life. His comments were recorded by a court reporter and are quoted below, with Dr. Cunningham's permission:

> I am married to a missionary's daughter who at the age of five and a half was sent to boarding school in Africa, where she saw her parents about three times a year. This represents the most severe kind of sacrifice that a missionary has to face. I have had the privilege of ministering to the children of missionaries, and I think it can be safely said, and I want to say this very carefully, that those children who have had this experience often never fully recover from it.
>
> My wife, for example, was "put down" when she was in the school because of the strong anti-American sentiment there. She was the only American in her school. We're not talking about a child of ten or twelve years old, but only six. All in all, it has made her a tremendously strong person, and I doubt if she would have been all that she is to me and to our children had she not had those tough experiences. But at the same time, were she not from strong English stock with tremendous gifts and graces, I don't know . . . maybe she would not have survived, because others haven't.
>
> I can't feel that this is a good policy at this point to make this the only answer for these families . . . to separate tender little children from their parents. I know of one situation, for example, where the children have to take a long ride in a riverboat to see their parents; I'm talking about little children. It's a trip of several hours to their mission compound. Their mother says goodbye to them in the fall, and she does not see them for many months because of the expense of traveling. They could be taken by helicopter instead of the riverboat ride, but they don't have the money. We must do something to assist people like this, whatever the cost.

Dr. Cunningham and I agree that the true issue may actually be one of priorities. Meaningful family involvement outranks educational considerations by a wide margin, in my view. Furthermore, contact with parents during the early years is even more important than contact with peers. And finally, even missionaries (who have been called to a life of sacrifice and service) must reserve some of their resources for their own families. After all, a lifetime of successes on a foreign field will be rather pale and insignificant to those who lose their own children.[12]

**My wife and I disagree strongly about the role of materialism in the lives of our kids. She feels that we should give them the toys and games that we never had as kids. At Christmas time, we stack gifts knee-deep around the tree, and then spend the next six months trying to pay for all the stuff we have bought. And, of course, the grandparents lavish gifts on our children throughout the year. I feel this is a mistake, even if we could afford to do what we are doing. What is your view on materialism in the life of a child?**

I also have concerns about giving kids too many things, which often reflects our inability to say "no" to them. During the hardships of the Great Depression, it was very simple for parents to tell their children that they couldn't afford to buy them everything they wanted; Dad could barely keep bread on the table. But in opulent times, the parental task becomes more difficult. It takes considerably more courage to say, "No, I won't buy you Baby-Blow-Her-Nose," than it did to say, "I'm sorry, but you know we can't afford to buy that doll." The child's lust for expensive toys is carefully generated through millions of dollars spent on TV advertising by toy manufacturers. Their commercials are skillfully made so that the toys look like full-sized copies of their real counterparts: jet airplanes, robot monsters, and automatic rifles. The little buyer sits open-mouthed in utter fascination. Five minutes later he begins a campaign that will eventually cost his dad $14.95 plus batteries and tax. The trouble is, Dad probably *can* afford to buy the new item, if not with cash, at least with his magic credit card. And when three other children on the block get the coveted toys, Mom and Dad begin to feel the pressure, and even the guilt. They feel selfish because they have indulged themselves for similar luxuries. Suppose the parents are courageous enough to resist the child's urging; he is not blocked—grandparents are notoriously easy to "con." Even if the child is unsuccessful in getting his parents or grandparents to buy what he wants, there is an annual foolproof resource: Santa Claus! When Junior asks Santa to bring him something, his parents are in an inescapable trap. What can they say, "Santa can't afford it"? Is Santa going to forget and disappoint him? No, the toy will be on Santa's sleigh.

Some would ask, "And why not? Why shouldn't we let our children enjoy the fruits of our good times?" Certainly I would not deny the child a reasonable quantity of the things he craves. But many American children are inundated with excesses that work toward their detriment. It has been said that prosperity offers a greater test of character than does adversity, and I'm inclined to agree. There are few conditions that inhibit a sense of appreciation more than for a child to feel he is entitled to whatever he wants, whenever he wants it. It is enlightening to watch as a child tears open stacks of presents at his birthday party or perhaps at Christmas time. One after another, the expensive contents are tossed aside with little more than a glance. The child's mother is made uneasy by this lack of enthusiasm and appreciation, so she says, "Oh, Marvin! Look what it is! It's a little tape recorder! What do you say to Grandmother? Give Grandmother a big hug. Did you hear me, Marvin? Go give Grams a big hug and kiss." Marvin may or may not choose to make the proper noises to Grandmother. His lack of exuberance results from the fact that prizes which are won cheaply are of little value, regardless of the cost to the original purchaser.

There is another reason that the child should be denied some of the things he thinks he wants. Although it sounds paradoxical, you actually cheat him of pleasure when you give him too much. A classic example of this saturation principle is evident in my household each year during the Thanksgiving season. Our family is blessed with several of the greatest cooks who ever ruled a kitchen, and several times a year they do their "thing." The traditional Thanksgiving dinner consists of turkey, dressing, cranberries, mashed potatoes, sweet potatoes, peas, home-made hot rolls, two kinds of salad, and six or eight other dishes. Our behavior at this table is disgraceful, but wonderful. Everyone eats until he is uncomfortable, not saving room for dessert. Then the apple pie, pound cake, and fresh ambrosia are brought to the table. It just doesn't seem possible that we could eat another bite, yet somehow we do. Finally, taut family members begin to stagger away from their plates, looking for a place to fall. Later, about three o'clock in the afternoon, the internal pressure begins to subside, and someone passes the candy around. As the usual time for the evening meal arrives, no one is hungry, yet we've come to expect three meals a day. Turkey and roll sandwiches are constructed and consumed, followed by another helping of pie. By this time, everyone is a bit blank-eyed, absent-mindedly eating what they neither want nor enjoy. This ridiculous ritual continues for two or three days, until the thought of food becomes disgusting. Whereas eating ordinarily offers one of life's greatest pleasures, it loses its thrill when the appetite for food is satiated.

Pleasure occurs when an intense need is satisfied. If there is no need, there is no pleasure. A glass of water is worth more than gold to a man dying of thirst. The analogy to children should be obvious. If you never allow a child to want something, he never enjoys the pleasure of receiving it. If you buy him a tricycle before he can walk, and a bicycle before he can ride, and a car before he can drive, and a diamond ring before he knows the value of money, he accepts these gifts with little pleasure and less appreciation. How unfortunate that such a child never had the chance to long for something, dreaming about it at night and plotting for it by day. He might have even gotten desperate enough to work for it. The same possession that brought a yawn could have been a trophy and a treasure. I suggest that you and your wife allow your child the thrill of temporary deprivation; it's more fun and much less expensive.[13]

**How can I teach my children Christian attitudes toward possessions and money?**

This is accomplished not only with words, but also by the way you handle your own resources.

It is interesting to me that Jesus had more to say in the Bible about money than any other subject, which emphasizes the importance of this topic for my family and yours. He made it clear that there is a direct relationship between great riches and spiritual poverty, as we are witnessing in America today. Accordingly, it is my belief that excessive materialism in parents has the power to inflict enormous spiritual damage on our sons and daughters. If they see that we care more about things than people . . . if they perceive that we have sought to buy their love as a guilt reducer . . . if they recognize the hollowness of our Christian testimony when it is accompanied by stinginess with God . . . the result is often cynicism and disbelief. And more important, when they observe Dad working fifteen hours a day to capture ever more of this world's goods, they know where his treasure is. Seeing is believing.[14]

**We've heard a lot about war toys. Do you think they are damaging to children?**

Kids have been playing cowboys and Indians and other combat games for hundreds of years, and I'm inclined to feel that the current worry is unfounded. Young boys, particularly, live in a feminine world; they're with their mothers far more than their dads. The teachers of the nursery school, kindergarten, and elementary school are likely to be women. Their Sunday school teachers are probably female, too. In this sugar and spice world, I think it is healthy for boys to identify with masculine models, even if the setting involves combat. Two boys can "shoot" each other without emotional arousal. "Bang! Bang! You're dead," they shout.

On the other hand, parents should limit the amount of violence and killing their children view on television and in the movies. The technology of audio-visual electronics has become tremendously effective, and can be far more stimulating and damaging. Measurable physiological changes occur while a child is watching a violent movie; the pulse rate quickens, eyes dilate, hands sweat, the mouth goes dry, and breathing accelerates. If repeated often, the emotional impact of this experience should be obvious.[15]

**My husband and I are distressed because our teenager seems to be rejecting her Christian beliefs. She was saved at an early age and in the past has shown a real love for the Lord. My inclination is to panic, but before I do, can you offer a word of encouragement?**

A small child is told what to think during his formative years. He is subjected to all the attitudes, biases, and beliefs of his parents, which is right and proper. They are fulfilling their God-given responsibility to guide and train him. However, there must come a moment when all of these concepts and ideas are examined by the individual, and either adopted as true or rejected as false. If that personal evaluation never comes, then the adolescent fails to span the gap between "What I've been told" versus "What I believe." This is one of the most important bridges leading from childhood to adulthood.

It is common, then, for a teenager to question the veracity of the indoctrination he has received. He may ask himself, "Is there really a God? Does He know me? Do I believe in the values my parents have taught? Do I want what they want for my life? Have they misled me in any way? Does my experience contradict what I've been taught?" For a period of years beginning during adolescence and continuing into the twenties, this intensive self-examination is conducted.

This process is especially distressing to parents who must sit on the sidelines and watch everything they have taught being scrutinized and questioned. It will be less painful, however, if both generations realize that the soul-searching is a normal, necessary part of growing up.[16]

**At what age should a child be given more freedom of choice regarding his religious beliefs and practices?**
After the middle adolescent years (thirteen to sixteen years), some children resent being told exactly what to believe; they do not want religion "forced down their throats," and should be given more and more autonomy in what they believe. But if the early exposure has been properly conducted, they will have an inner mainstay to steady them. That early indoctrination, then, is the key to the spiritual attitudes they will carry into adulthood.

Despite this need to take a softer approach to spiritual training as the child moves through adolescence, it is *still* appropriate for parents to establish and enforce a Christian standard of behavior in their homes. Therefore, I *would* require my seventeen-year-old to attend church with the family. He should be told, "As long as you are under this roof, we will worship God together as a family. I can't control what you think. That's your business. But I have promised the Lord that we will honor Him in this home, and that includes 'remembering the Sabbath to keep it holy.' "[17]

**You've indicated that seven deaths have occurred in your family during the past eighteen months. We have also had several tragic losses in our family in recent years. My**

**wife died when our children were five, eight, and nine. I found it very difficult to explain death to them during that time. Can you offer some guidelines regarding how a parent can help his children cope with the stark reality of death—especially when it strikes within the immediate family?**

Some years ago, I attended a funeral at the Inglewood Cemetery-Mortuary in Inglewood, California. While there, I picked up a brochure written by the president of the mortuary, John M. McKinley. Mr. McKinley had been in the funeral business for fifteen years before writing this valuable pamphlet entitled "If It Happens to Your Child." He gave me permission to reproduce the content here in answer to your question:

> I knew Tommy's parents because they lived in the neighborhood and attended the same church. But I knew Tommy especially well because he was one of the liveliest, happiest five-year-olds it had ever been my pleasure to meet. It was a shock, therefore, when his mother became a client of mine at the death of her husband.
>
> As a doctor must learn to protect himself from the suffering of his patients, so a funeral director must protect himself from grief. During the course of the average year I come in direct contact with several thousand men and women who have experienced a shattering loss, and if I did not isolate myself from their emotions, my job would be impossible. But I have not been able to isolate myself from the children.
>
> "I don't know what I would have done if I had not had Tommy," his mother told me when I visited her in her home the morning she called me. "He has been such a little man—hasn't cried, and is doing everything he can do to take his daddy's place." And it was true. Tommy was standing just as he imagined a man would stand, not crying, and doing his best to take his daddy's place.
>
> I knew it was wrong. I knew I should tell her so—that Tommy was not a man; that he needed to cry; that he needed comfort probably far more than she. But I am not a psychologist, and I said nothing.
>
> In the two years since then I have watched Tommy. The joy has not come back in his face, and it is clear even to my layman's mind that he is an emotionally sick child. I am sure it began when his mother, unknowingly, made it

difficult—impossible—for him to express his grief, and placed on him an obligation he could not fulfill; that of "taking daddy's place."

There have been few examples so clear cut as Tommy's, but I have seen so much that made me wince, and I have been asked so often: "What should I tell Mary?" or Paul, or Jim, that I finally decided to do something about it. I went to the experts, the men who know how a child should be treated at such moments of tragedy, and I asked them to lay down some guidelines that parents could understand and follow. I talked to several psychologists and psychiatrists and pediatricians, but principally to Dr. A. I. Duvall, a psychiatrist, and Dr. James Gardner, a child psychologist. Translated into my layman's language, here is the gist of what I learned.

—When a child, like any other human being, experiences a deeply painful loss, not only should he be permitted to cry; he should be encouraged to cry until the need for tears is gone. He should be comforted while the tears are flowing, but the words "Don't cry" should be stricken from the language.

—The need to cry may be recurrent for several days, or at widening intervals, several months; but when the need is felt, no effort should be made to dam the tears. Instead, it should be made clear that it is good to cry, and not "babyish" or "sissy" or anything to be ashamed of.

—At times, the child may need to be alone with his grief, and if this feeling comes, it should be respected. But otherwise physical contact and comfort will be almost as healing as the tears.

—The child should be told the truth; that death is final. "Mommy has gone on a vacation" or "Daddy has gone on a trip" only adds to the confusion and delays the inevitable. Children—particularly young children—have a very imperfect time sense. If "Mommy has gone on a vacation," they are going to expect her back this afternoon or tomorrow. And when tomorrow and tomorrow comes and she does not reappear, not only will the hurt be repeated endlessly, but the child will lose faith in the surviving parent just at the time when faith and trust are needed most. It is hard to say "never" when you know it will make the tears flow harder, but it is the kindest word in the long run.

—It is not necessary to explain death to a young child. It may even be harmful to try. To the five-year-old, "death" is absence, and explanations may only confuse him. If he has seen a dead bird or a dead pet, it may be helpful to make a comparison, but the important fact which the child must accept is absence. If he can be helped to accept the fact that father or mother or brother or sister is gone and will never return, then through questions and observations he will gradually build his own picture of "death" and its meaning.

—A child should not be unduly shielded from the physical appearance and fact of death. If a father dies, the child should be permitted to see the body, so that with his own eyes he can see the changes, the stillness, the difference between the vital strength which was "daddy" and this inanimate mask which is not "daddy" at all. Seeing with his own eyes will help.

—A child should be protected, however, from any mass demonstrations of grief, as from a large group of mourners at a funeral. Rather, the child should be taken in privately before the funeral to say goodbye.

—If the child is very young—say two to five or six—great care should be used in explaining death in terms which are meaningful to adults, but which may be very puzzling to children. For example, to say that "Mommy has gone to Heaven" may make perfect sense to a religious bereaved father, but it may leave a five-year-old wondering why Mommy has deserted him. At that answer, "Heaven" is simply a far place, and he will not be able to understand why his mother stays there instead of coming home to take care of him.

—Along with tears, a child is quite likely to feel sharp resentment, even anger at the dead parent, or the brother or sister who has "gone." This feeling is the result of the child's conviction that he has been deserted. If this feeling does arise, the child should be permitted to express it freely, just as in the case of tears.

—More common, and frequently more unsettling to a child, is his guilt feelings when a death occurs. If he has been angry at his sister, and the sister dies, he is likely to think it is his fault, that his anger killed her. Or if his mother dies, and he is not told honestly and simply what has happened, he is likely to believe that his misbehavior drove her away. Guilt feelings in young children, reinforced

> by death, can lead to neurotic patterns which last throughout life.
>
> But if a child is encouraged to cry until the need for tears is gone; if he is comforted enough; if he is told the simple truth; if he is permitted to see for himself the difference between death and life; if his resentment or guilt is handled in the same straightforward way as his tears, his sense of loss will still be great, but he will overcome it.
>
> There is a positive side, too. If death is treated as a natural part of human experience, it is much easier for a loved one to live in memory. When the initial impact of grief is gone, it is a natural thing to remember and re-tell stories which evoke vivid recollections of the personality and habits which made the loved one a special person. Children take great delight in this, for in their rich world of imagination they can make the absent one live again. Such reminiscing does not renew or increase their sorrow. To the extent that it makes them free to remember, the cause for sorrow is removed.

Mr. McKinley's advice is excellent, as far as it goes. However, it has not included any references to the Christian message, which provides the *only* satisfactory answer to death. Obviously, I disagree with Mr. McKinley's reservations about heaven. We can say, "Your mother is gone for now, but thank God we'll be together again on the other side!" How comforting for a grieving child to know that a family reunion will someday occur from which there will never be another separation! I recommend that Christian parents begin acquainting their children with the gift of eternal life long before they have need of this understanding.[18]

# SECTION 3

# EDUCATION OF CHILDREN

**I've read that it is possible to teach four-year-old children to read. Should I be working on this with my child?**

If a preschooler is particularly sharp and if he can learn to read without feeling undue adult pressure, it might be advantageous to teach him this skill. Those are big "if's," however. Few parents can work with their own children without showing frustration over natural failures. It's like teaching your wife to drive: risky, at best—disastrous at worst. Besides this limitation, learning should be programmed at the age when it is most needed. Why invest unending effort in teaching a child to read when he has not yet learned to cross the street, or tie his shoes, or count to ten, or answer the telephone? It seems foolish to get panicky over preschool reading, as such. The best policy is to provide your children with many interesting books and materials, to read to them and answer their questions, and then to let nature take its unobstructed course.[1]

**Some educators have said we should eliminate report cards and academic marks. Do you think this is a good idea?**

No, academic marks are valuable for students in the third grade or higher. They serve as a form of reinforcement—as a reward for the child who has achieved in school and as a nudge to the youngster who hasn't. It is important, though, that marks be used properly; they have the power to create or to destroy motivation. Through the elementary years and in the required courses of high school, a child's grades should be based on what he does with what he has. In other words, we should grade according to ability. A slow child should be able to succeed in school just as certainly as a gifted youngster. If he struggles and sweats to achieve, he should be rewarded with a symbol of accomplishment even if his work falls short of an absolute standard. By the same token, the gifted child should not be given an A just because he is smart enough to excel without working.

*Our primary purpose in grading during the elementary and junior high school years should be to reward academic effort.* On the other hand, college preparation courses in high school must be graded on an absolute standard. An A in chemistry or Latin is accepted by college admission boards as a symbol of excellence, and high school teachers must preserve that meaning. But then, Slow Joe and his friends need not be in those difficult courses.[2]

**Do you ever favor removing a child from one school and transferring him to another?**

Yes, there are times when a change of schools—or even a change of teachers within a school—can be in the child's best interest. Educators are reluctant to approve these transfers, for obvious reasons, although the possibility should be considered when the situation warrants. For example, there are occasions when a young student runs into social problems that can be resolved best by giving him a "clean start" somewhere else. Furthermore, schools vary tremendously in their difficulty; some are located in higher socioeconomic areas where a majority of the children are much more intelligent than would ordinarily be expected. The mean IQ in schools of this nature may fall between 115-120. What happens, then, to a child with average ability in such a setting? Although he might have competed successfully in an ordinary school, he is in the lower 15 percent at Einstein Elementary. My point is this: success is not absolute, it is relative. A child does not ask, "How am I doing?" but rather, "How am I doing compared to everyone else?" Little Johnny may grow up thinking he is a dummy when he would have been an intellectual leader in a less competitive setting. Thus, if a child is floundering in one academic environment, for *whatever* reason, the solution might involve a transfer to a more suitable classroom.[3]

**Do you think religion should be taught in the public schools?**

Not as a particular doctrine or dogma. The right of parents to select their child's religious orientation must be protected and no teacher or administrator should be allowed to contradict what the child has been taught at home. On the other hand, the vast majority of Americans do profess a belief in God. I would like to see this unnamed God acknowledged in the classroom. The Supreme Court decision banning nonspecific school prayer (or even silent prayer) is an extreme measure, and I regret it. The tiny minority of children from atheistic homes could easily be protected by the school during prayerful moments.

Incidentally, it is interesting to me that the courts have absolutely prohibited even silent prayer in the classroom, yet the Congress of the United States begins its session every day with spoken prayer. Likewise, the Supreme Court ruled in 1981 that schools could not even post the Ten Commandments on their bulletin boards, yet those same biblical directives are inscribed on the walls of the Supreme Court building! What does that tell us about the wisdom of our judges in establishing moral policy for the nation?[4]

**I have observed that elementary school and junior high school students, even high schoolers, tend to admire the more strict teachers. Why is this true?**

Yes, the teachers who maintain order *are* often the most respected members of the faculties, provided they aren't mean and grouchy. A teacher who can control a class without being oppressive is almost always loved by her students. One reason is that there is safety in order. When a class is out of control, particularly at the elemenatary school level, the children are afraid of each other. If the teacher can't make the class behave, how can she prevent a bully from doing his thing? How can she keep the students from ridiculing one of its less able members? Children are not very fair and understanding with each other, and they feel good about having a strong teacher who is.

Second, children love justice. When someone has violated a rule, they want immediate retribution. They admire the teacher who can enforce an equitable legal system, and they find great comfort in reasonable social rules. By contract, the teacher who does not control her class inevitably allows crime to pay, violating something basic in the value system of children.

Third, children admire strict teachers because chaos is nerve-racking. Screaming and hitting and wiggling are fun for about ten minutes; then the confusion begins to get tiresome and irritating.

I have smiled in amusement many times as second- and third-grade children astutely evaluated the relative disciplinary skills of their teachers. They know how a class should be conducted. I only wish all of their teachers were equally aware of this important attribute.

**I am a teacher in junior high school, and there are five separate classes that come to my room to be taught science each day. My biggest problem is getting these students to bring books, paper, and pencils to class with them. I can lend them the equipment they need, but I never get it back. What do you suggest?**

I faced an identical problem the years I taught in junior high school, and finally reached a solution which is based on the certainty that young people will cooperate if it is to *their* advantage to do so. After begging and pleading and exhorting them unsuccessfully, I announced one morning that I was no longer concerned about whether they brought their pencils and books to class. I had twenty extra books and several boxes of sharpened pencils which they could borrow. If they forgot to bring these materials, all they had to do was ask for a loan. I would not gnash my teeth or get red in the face; they would find me willing to share my resources. However, there was to be one hitch: the borrowing student would have to forfeit his seat for that one-hour class. He would have to stand by his chair while I was teaching, and if any written work was required, he had to lean over his desk from a standing position. As might be imagined, the students were less than ecstatic about this prospect. I smiled to myself and saw them racing around before class, trying to borrow a book or pencil. I did not have to enforce the standing rule very often because the issue had become the pupils' campaign rather than mine. Once a week, or so, a student would have to spend the hour in a vertical position, but that youngster made certain he did not blunder into the same situation twice.

The principle has broader applicability: give children maximum reason to *want* to comply with your wishes. Your anger is the *least* effective of all possible reasons.[5]

**Do you think it would be useful to reinstate the traditional rules and regulations in the schools, such as dress codes, guidelines on hair length, and good grooming?**
While I agree with the viewpoint that hair style and similar matters of momentary fashion are not worthy of concern in themselves, *adherence to a standard is an important element of discipline.* It is a great mistake to require *nothing* of children—to place no demands on their behavior. Whether a high school girl wears slacks or a dress is not of earthshaking importance, although it *is* significant that she be required to adhere to a few reasonable rules. If one examines the secret of success behind a championship football team, a magnificent orchestra, or a successful business, the principal ingredient is invariably discipline. How inaccurate is the belief that self-control is maximized in an environment which places no obligations on its children. How foolish is the assumption that self-discipline is a product of self-indulgence. *Reasonable* rules and standards are an important part of any educational system, in my view.[6]

**I am a teacher of a wild fifth-grade class. In it are two or three kids who are driving me crazy. Can you offer some tips that will help me gain control?**
Perhaps so. Let me offer these suggestions. First decide what is motivating the disruptive behavior: it takes no great social scientist to recognize that the loud mouths are usually seeking the attention of the group. For them, anonymity is the most painful experience imaginable. The ideal prescription is to extinguish their attention-getting behavior and then meet their need for gaining acceptance by less noisy means. I worked with a giddy little sixth grader named Larry whose mouth never shut. He perpetually disrupted the tranquility of his class, setting up a constant barrage of silliness, wise remarks, and horseplay. His teacher and I constructed an isolated area in a remote corner of the schoolroom; from that spot he could see nothing but his teacher and the front of the room. Thereafter, Larry was sentenced to a week in the isolation booth whenever he chose to be disruptive, which effectively eliminated the supporting reinforcement. Certainly, he could still act silly behind the screen, but he could not see the effect he was having on his peers. Besides this limitation, each outburst lengthened

his lonely isolation. Larry spent one entire month in relative solitude before the extinction was finalized. When he rejoined society, his teacher immediately began to reward his cooperation. He was given the high status jobs (messenger, sergeant-at-arms, etc.) and praised for the improvement he had made. The results were remarkable.

Some school districts have implemented a more structured form of "extinction" for their worst behavioral problems (that is, the behavior is extinguished, not the children!). The students who are seemingly incapable of classroom cooperation are assigned to special classes, consisting of twelve to fifteen students. These youngsters are then placed on a program called "systematic exclusion." The parents are informed that the only way their child can remain in a public school is for them to come and get him if they are called during the school day. The child is then told that he can come to school each morning, but the moment he breaks one of the well-defined rules, he will be sent home. He might be ejected for pushing other pupils in the line at 9:01 A.M. Or he may make it until 1:15 or later before dismissal occurs. There are no second chances, although the child is free to return at the start of school the following morning. Despite the traditional belief that children hate school, most of them hate staying home even more. Daytime television gets pretty monotonous, particularly under the hostile eye of a mom who had to interrupt her activities to come get her wayward son. Disruptive behavior is very quickly extinguished under this controlled setting. It just isn't profitable for the student to challenge the system. Positive reinforcement in the form of verbal and material rewards are then generously applied for the child's attempts to learn and study. I worked with one child in a behavior modification classroom who was termed the most disruptive child ever seen at a major Los Angeles neuro-psychiatric hospital. After four months in this controlled setting, he was able to attend a regular class in the public schools.

All that is required to use this principle of extinction in a particular classroom is a little creativity and the administrative authority to improvise.[7]

**It is my understanding that we forget 80 percent of everything we learn in three months' time and a higher percentage is forgotten as time passes. Why, then, should**

**we put children through the agony of learning? Why is mental exercise needed if the effort is so inefficient?**

Your question reflects the viewpoint of the old progressive education theorists. They wanted the school curriculum to be nothing more than "life adjustment." They placed a low priority on intellectual discipline for the reasons you mentioned. Even some college professors have adopted this "no content" philosophy, reasoning that the material learned by students today may be obsolete tomorrow, so why ask them to learn it? I strongly disagree with this approach to education. There are at least five reasons why learning is important, even if a high incidence of forgetting and obsolescence do take place:

(1) Perhaps the most important function of school, apart from teaching the basic literary and mathematical skills, is to foster self-discipline and self-control. The good student learns to sit for long hours, follow directions, carry out assignments and channel his mental faculties. Homework, itself, is relatively unnecessary as an educational tool, but it is valuable as an instrument of discipline. Since adult life often requires self-sacrifice, sweat, and devotion to causes, the school should play a role in shaping a child's capacity to handle this future responsibility. Certainly, play is important in a child's life too. He should not work all the time; the home and school should provide a healthy balance between discipline and play.

(2) Learning is important because we are *changed* by what we learn, even if the facts are later forgotten. No college graduate could remember everything he learned in school, yet he is a very different person for having gone to college. Learning produces alterations in values, attitudes, and concepts which do not fade in time. (3) Even if the learned material cannot be recalled, the individual knows the facts exist and where he can find them. If we asked a complicated question of an uneducated man, he would be likely to give a definite, unqualified response. The same question would probably be answered more cautiously by a man with a doctor's degree; he would say, "Well, there are several ways to look at it." He knows the matter is more complex than it appears, even if he doesn't have the full answer. (4) We don't forget 100 percent of what we learn. The most important facts take their place in our permanent memory for future use. The human brain is capable of storing 2 billion bits of data in a lifetime; education is the process of filling that memory bank with useful information. (5) Old learning makes new learning easier. Each mental exercise gives us more

associative cues with which to link future ideas and concepts.

I wish there were an easier, more efficient process for shaping human minds than the slow, painful experience of education. I'm afraid we'll have to depend on this old-fashioned approach until a "learning pill" is developed.[8]

**The children who attend our church tend to be rather wild, and consequently, the classes are chaotic. Is this characteristic of most church school programs?**

I'm afraid so, and it is a matter for concern. It has been my strong conviction that the church should support the family in its attempt to implement biblical principles in the home. This is especially true with reference to the teaching of respect for authority. This is not an easy time to be a parent because authority has eroded drastically in our society. Therefore, mothers and fathers who are trying to teach respect and responsibility to their children, as the Bible prescribes, need all the help they can get, particularly from the church.

But in my opinion, most churches fail miserably at this point. There is no aspect of the church mission that I feel is weaker or more ineffective than discipline in the Sunday school. Parents who have struggled to maintain order and respect all week send their kids off to church on Sunday morning, and what happens? They are permitted to throw erasers and shoot paper wads and swing on the light fixtures. I'm not referring to any one denomination. I've seen it happen in almost all of them. In fact, I think I was one of those eraser throwers in my day.[9]

**Why do you think our Sunday schools are so lax and permissive, and what can we do about it?**

Teachers are volunteers who may not know how to handle kids. But more often, they are afraid of irritating sensitive parents. They don't feel they have a right to teach children to respect God's house. If they try, they might anger Mama Bear and lose the entire family. I'm not recommending that we punish children in Sunday school, of course. But there are ways to maintain order among children, once we decide that it is important to us. Training sessions can help teachers do a better job. Pastors can back up Sunday school workers. Disruptive children can be assigned to a one-on-one relationship with a teacher for a time, etc. My concern is that we can't seem to agree that discipline has a place in the church schools program. In its absence, the chaos that results is an insult to God and to the meaning of worship. You can't reach *any* educational objective in an atmosphere of chaos and confusion. It is impossible to teach students when they don't even hear you.[10]

# SECTION 4

# LEARNING PROBLEMS IN CHILDHOOD

**We have a one-year-old daughter and we want to raise her right. I've heard that parents can increase the mental abilities of their children if they stimulate them properly during the early years. Is this accurate, and if so, how can I accomplish this with my baby?**

Recent research indicates that parents *can* increase the intellectual capability of their children. This conclusion was one of the most important findings derived from a ten-year study of children between eight and eighteen months of age. This investigation, known as Harvard University's Preschool Project, was guided by Dr. Burton L. White and a team of fifteen researchers between 1965 and 1975. They studied young children intensely during this period, hoping to discover which experiences in the early years of life contribute to the development of a healthy, intelligent human being. The conclusions from this exhaustive effort are summarized below, as reported originally in the *APA Monitor.*

1. It is increasingly clear that the origins of human competence are to be found in a critical period of development between eight and eighteen months of age. The child's experiences during these brief months do more to influence future intellectual competence than any time before or after.
2. The single most important environmental factor in the life of the child is his mother. "She is on the hook," said Dr. White, and carries more influence on her child's experiences than any other person or circumstance.
3. The amount of *live* language directed to a child

(not to be confused with television, radio, or overheard conversations) is vital to his development of fundamental linguistic, intellectual, and social skills. The researchers concluded, "Providing a rich social life for a twelve- to fifteen-month-old child is the best thing you can do to guarantee a good mind."

4. Those children who are given free access to living areas of their homes progressed much faster than those whose movements are restricted.
5. The nuclear family is the most important educational delivery system. If we are going to produce capable, healthy children, it will be by strengthening family units and by improving the interactions that occur within them.
6. The best parents were those who excelled at three key functions:
   (1) They were superb designers and organizers of their children's environments.
   (2) They permitted their children to interrupt them for brief thirty-second episodes, during which personal consultation, comfort, information, and enthusiasm were exchanged.
   (3) "THEY WERE FIRM DISCIPLINARIANS WHILE SIMULTANEOUSLY SHOWING GREAT AFFECTION FOR THEIR CHILDREN." (I couldn't have said it better myself.)[1]

These six conclusions are exciting to me, for I find within them an affirmation and validation of the scriptural concepts to which I have devoted my entire professional life: discipline with love; the dedication of mothers during the early years; the value of raising children; the stability of the family, etc. It is obvious that the Creator of the universe is best able to tell us how to raise children, and He has done just that through His holy Word.

Do you want to help your children reach the maximum potential that lies within them? Then raise them according to the precepts and values given to us in the Scriptures.[2]

**My six-year-old son has always been an energetic child with some of the symptoms of hyperactivity. He has a short attention span and flits from one activity to another. I took him to a pediatrician who said he was not actually hyperactive, in the medical sense, and should**

**not be given medication for this mild problem. However, he's beginning to have learning problems in school because he can't stay in his seat and concentrate on his lessons. What should I do?**
It is likely that your son is immature in comparison with his peers, a child we have traditionally called a "late bloomer." If so, he could profit from being retained in the first grade next year. If his birthday is between December 1 and July 1, I would definitely ask the school guidance office to advise you on this possibility. If that service is not available, you should have him examined for educational readiness by a child development specialist (child psychologist, pediatrician, neurologist, etc.). Retaining an immature boy during his early school career (kindergarten or first grade) can give him a great social and academic advantage throughout the remaining years of elementary school. However, it is very important to help him "save face" with his peers. If possible, he should change schools for at least a year to avoid embarrassing questions and ridicule from his former classmates.

Let me state my recommendation in broader terms for other parents of preschool children. The age of the child is the *worst* criterion on which to base a decision regarding when to begin a school career. That determination should be made according to specific neurologic, social, psychologic and pediatric variables. And for boys, who average six months behind girls of comparable age in maturity, it is even more important to consider his readiness to learn.

Finally, I agree with the perspective of Dr. Raymond Moore and Dorothy Moore regarding the value of postponing formalized education for *all* children. Writing in their excellent book, *Home Grown Kids* (Word Publishers), they provide irrefutable evidence to indicate that children who are kept at home until even eight or nine years of age, when finally enrolled in school, typically catch and pass their age mates within a few months. Furthermore, they are less vulnerable to the whims of the group and show long-term qualities of independence and leadership. Keeping children at home in the early elementary school years is an idea whose time has come. If further information is desired, I suggest that you read the Moores' interesting book on this subject.[3]

**Can the late bloomer who is *not* retained or held out of school be expected to catch up with his class academically after he has matured physically?**
Usually not. If the problem were simply a physical phenomenon, the slow maturing child could be expected to gain on his early developing friends. However, emotional factors are invariably tangled in this difficulty. A child's self-concept is amazingly simple to damage but exceedingly difficult to reconstruct. Once a child begins to think of himself as stupid, incapable, ignorant, and foolish, the concept is not easily eliminated. If he is unable to function as required in the early academic setting, he is compressed in the vise-like jaws of the school and the home; the conflict is often deeply ingrained.[4]

**If age is such a poor factor to use in determining classroom readiness, why do schools use it exclusively to indicate when a child will enter kindergarten?**
Because it is so convenient. Parents can plan for the definite beginning of school when their child reaches six years of age. School officials can survey their districts and know how many first graders they will have the following year. If an eight-year-old moves into the district in October, the administrator knows with certainty that the child belongs in the second grade, and so on. The use of chronological age as a criterion for school entrance is great for everybody—except the late bloomer.[5]

**We have a six-year-old son who is also a late bloomer, and he is having trouble learning to read. Can you explain the link between his immaturity and this perplexing learning problem?**
It is likely that your late bloomer has not yet completed a vital neurologic process involving an organic substance called myelin. At birth, the nervous system of the body is not insulated. That is why an infant is unable to reach out and grasp an object; the electrical command or impulse is lost on its journey from the brain to the hand. Gradually, a whitish substance (myelin) begins to coat the nerve fibers, allowing controlled muscular action to occur. Myelinization typically proceeds from the head downward and from the center of the body outward. In other words, a child can control the movement

of his head and neck before the rest of his body. Control of the shoulder precedes the elbow, which precedes the wrist, which precedes the large muscles in the hands, which precedes small muscle coordination of the fingers. This explains why elementary school children are taught block letter printing before they learn cursive writing; the broad strokes and lines are less dependent on minute finger control than the flowing curves of mature penmanship.

Since visual apparatus in humans is usually the last neural mechanism to be myelinated, your immature child may not have undergone this necessary developmental process by his present age of six years. Therefore, such a child who is extremely immature and uncoordinated may be neurologically unprepared for the intellectual tasks of reading and writing. Reading, particularly, is a highly complex neurological process. The visual stimulus must be relayed to the brain without distortion, where it should be interpreted and retained in the memory. Not all six-year-old children are equipped to perform this task. Unfortunately, however, our culture permits few exceptions or deviations from the established timetable. A six-year-old must learn to read or he will face the emotional consequences of failure.[6]

**My child is having great trouble in school again this year. The psychologist said he is a "slow learner," and will probably always struggle academically. Please tell me what a "slow learner" is.**

A slow learner is a child who has difficulty learning in school, and usually scores between 70 and 90 on tests of intelligence. These individuals comprise more than 20 percent of the total population. In many ways, the school children in this category face some serious challenges in their classroom. Of particular concern are the individuals with IQs in the lower range of the slow learner classification (70 to 80) who are virtually destined to have difficulties in school. No special education is available for them in most schools, although they are not appreciably different from the borderline retarded students. A "retarded" child with an IQ of 70 would probably qualify for the highly specialized and expensive educational program, including a smaller class, a specially trained teacher, audio-visual aids and a "no fail" policy. By contrast, a slow learning child with an IQ of 80 would usually receive no such advantages. He must compete in regular classes against the full range of students who are more capable than he. The concept of competition implies winners and losers; it is the slow learner who usually "loses."[7]

**What causes a child to be a slow learner?**

There are many hereditary, environmental, and physical factors which contribute to one's intellect, and it is difficult to isolate the particular influences. In some cases, however, accumulating evidence seems to indicate that dull normal intelligence and even borderline retardation can be caused by a lack of intellectual stimulation in the child's very early years. There appears to be a critical period during the first three to four years when the potential for intellectual growth must be seized. If the opportunity is missed, the child may never reach the capacity which had originally been available to him. The slow learning child can be one who has not heard adult language regularly; he has not been provided with interesting books and puzzles to occupy his sensory apparatus; he has not been taken to the zoo, the airport, or other exciting places; he has grown up with a minimum of daily training and guidance from adults. The lack of stimulation available to such a child may result in the failure of enzyme systems to develop properly in the brain.[8]

**You said the slow learning child faces some special challenges at school. What, specifically, are those hurdles for him?**

He is the child who "would if he could—but he can't." He will rarely, if ever, get the thrill of earning a "hundred" on his spelling test. He is the last child chosen in any academic game or contest. He often has the least sympathy from his teachers. He is no more successful in social activities than he is in academic pursuits, and the other children often reject him openly. Like the late bloomer, the slow learner gradually develops a crushing image of failure that distorts his self-concept and damages his ego. A colleague of mine overheard two intellectually handicapped students discussing their prospects with girls; one said, "I do OK until they find out I'm a retard." Obviously, this child was keenly aware of his diminished status. What better way is there to assassinate self-confidence in our children than to place 20 percent of them in a situation where excellence is impossible to achieve, where inadequacy is the daily routine, and where inferiority is a living reality? It is not surprising that such a child may become a mischievous tormentor in the third grade, a bully in the sixth, a loudmouth in junior high, and a dropout-delinquent in high school.[9]

**Is retention in the same grade advisable for any child, other than the late bloomer? How about the slow learner?** There are some students who profit from a second year in the same grade level. The best guideline regarding failure to promote is this: retain the child for whom something will be *different* next year. A child who is sick for seven months in one academic year might profit from another run-through when he is healthy. And again, the late bloomer should be held back in kindergarten (or the first grade at the latest) to place him with youngsters of comparable development. For the slow learner, however, nothing will be changed. If he was failing the fourth grade in June, he will continue to fail the fourth grade in September. It is not often realized that the curricular content of each grade level is very similar to the year before and the year after. The same concepts are taught year after year; the students in each grade are taken a little farther, but much of the time is spent in review. The arithmetical methods of addition and subtraction, for example, are taught in the primary years, but considerable work is done on these tasks in the sixth grade, too. Nouns and verbs are taught repeatedly for several years.

Thus, the most unjustifiable reason for retention is to give the slow learner another year of exposure to easier concepts. He will not do better the second time around! Nor is there much magic in summer school. Some parents hope that a six-week program in July and August will accomplish what was impossible in the ten months between September and June. They are often disappointed.[10]

**If retention and summer school do not solve the problem of the slow learner, what can be done for these children?** Let me offer three suggestions that can tip the scales in favor of the slow learning child with learning problems.

1. *Teach him to read, even if a one-to-one teacher-student ratio is required* (and it probably will be). Nearly every child can learn to read, but many boys and girls have difficulty if taught

only in large groups. Their minds wander and they do not ask questions as readily. Certainly, it would be expensive for the school to support an additional number of remedial reading teachers, but I can think of no expenditure that would be more helpful. Special techniques, teaching machines and individual reinforcement can be successful in teaching reading—the most basic of all academic skills—to the children who are least likely to learn without individual attention. This assistance should not be delayed until the fourth or fifth grades or in junior high. By those late dates the child has already endured the indignities of failure.

Many school districts have implemented creative programs to focus on reading problems. One such program, the "ungraded primary," eliminates the distinctions between students in the first three grades. Instead of grouping children by age, they are combined according to reading skill. Good readers in the first, second, and third grade may occupy the same classes. Poor readers are also grouped together. This procedure takes the sting out of retention and allows children to profit from the benefits of homogeneous grouping. Another system is called the "split reading" program. In this method, the better half of the readers in a given class arrive at school thirty minutes early to be taught reading. The poorer half of the readers remain a half-hour later each evening for the same purpose. There are many such programs which have been devised to teach reading more effectively. And of course, parents who are concerned about their child's basic academic skills may wish to seek tutorial assistancc to supplement these school programs.

Let me state it more explicitly: *It is absolutely critical to your child's self-concept that he learn to read early in his school career, and if professional educators can't do the job, someone else must!*

2. *Remember that success breeds success.* The best motivation for a slow learner is to know that he is succeeding. If the adults in his life show confidence in him, he will be more likely to have confidence in himself. In fact, most humans share this same characteristic. We tend to act the way we think other people "see" us. This reality was made clear to me when I joined the National Guard. I had recently graduated from college and chose to enlist for an extended period of reserve military experience rather than to serve two years of active duty. I was immediately packed up and put on a bus for Fort Ord, California, to undergo a six-month clerical training program.

Contrary to the recruiting posters, this exciting new career opportunity was not a matter of personal choice; it was selected for me. Nevertheless, the next six months were spent learning the fascinating world of military forms, typing, and filing. One hundred eighty-three days later I returned to the local National Guard unit with this newly acquired knowledge available for usage. Surprisingly, I was not welcomed back with any overwhelming degree of enthusiasm. Everyone knows that privates are stupid. *All* privates are stupid. I was a private, so it stood to reason that there was thickness between my ears. With the exception of a few other stupid privates, I was outranked by the whole world. Everybody from the privates-first-class to the colonel anticipated ignorant behavior from me, and to my amazement, their expectation proved accurate. The first assignment given, following six months of clerical training, was to type a simple letter in two copies. After investing twenty-five minutes of concentrated effort at the typewriter, I realized that the carbon paper was inserted upside down. Reverse lettering was smudged all over the back of the main copy, which did not exactly overwhelm the first sergeant with gratitude. Similar complex procedures, like marching "in step," were strangely difficult to perform. From today's perspective, it is clear that my performance was consistent with my image. Likewise, many children who fail in school are merely doing what they think others expect of them. Our reputation with our peers is a very influential force in our lives.

Finally, the slow learner needs individual attention in all of his academic work, which can only be given by teachers who have relatively small classes. He also needs access to audio-visual approaches to learning, including the latest in computer technology. The inordinate expense of such programs is a reality we must face in view of the current financial crisis in the schools, but for the slow learner, his program is dependent on receiving an enriched experience that does not often occur in the traditional classroom.[11]

**Do slow learners and mentally retarded children have the same needs for esteem that others have?**

Sometimes I wish they didn't, but their needs are no different. During a portion of my training at Lanternman State Hospital, Pomona, California, I was impressed by the vast need for love shown by some of the most retarded patients. There were times when I would step into the door of a children's ward and forty or more severely retarded youngsters would rush toward me screaming, "Daddy! Daddy! Daddy!" They would push and shove around my legs with their arms extended upward, making it difficult to avoid falling. Their deep longings to be loved simply couldn't be satisfied in the group experiences of hospital life, despite the exceptionally high quality of Lanternman.

The need for esteem has led me to favor a current trend in education, whereby borderline mentally retarded children are given special assistance *in* their regular classrooms without segregating them in special classes. The stigma of being a "retard," as they call themselves, is no less insulting for a ten-year-old than it would be for you or me.[12]

**I have heard the term "classic underachiever" applied to children—will you define that concept for me?**
The underachiever is a student who is unsuccessful in school *despite* his ability to do the work. He may have an IQ of 120 or better, yet earn D's and F's on his report card. If possible, underachieving children are even more numerous and less understood than slow learners or late bloomers. The confusion is related to the fact that *two* specific ingredients are necessary to produce academic excellence, yet the second is often overlooked. First *intellectual ability* must be there. But mental capacity is insufficient by itself. *Self-discipline* is also required. An able child may or may not have the self-control necessary to bear down day after day on something he considers painful and difficult. Furthermore, intelligence and self-discipline are frequently *not* correlated. We often see a child having one without the other.[13]

**What solution would you offer for the problem of underachievers?**
I have dealt with more than 500 underachievers and have come to the conclusion that there are only two functional solutions to this syndrome. The first is certainly no panacea: parents can become so involved in schoolwork that the child has no choice but to do the job. To make this possible, the school must expend additional effort to communicate assignments and progress to

parents—Junior is certainly not going to carry the message! Adolescents, particularly, will confound the communication between school and home as much as possible. In one of the high schools where I served, for example, students had a twenty-minute "homeroom" session each day. This time was used for the flag salute, council meetings, announcements, and related matters. Very little opportunity for studying occurred there, yet each day, hundreds of parents were told that all homework was finished during that session. The naive parents were led to believe that the homeroom period was a two-hour block of concentrated effort.

Parents must know what goes on in school if they want to reinforce their child's academic responsibilities. They should provide support in areas where self-discipline is needed. The evening study period should be highly structured—routine hours and a minimum of interferences. To do this, parents must know what was assigned and how the finished product should look. Finally, negative attitudes should be withheld from the learning situation. Berating and criticizing an underachiever do not make him work harder.

I must hasten to say that this procedure is not an easy solution. It rarely works for more than a week or two, since many parents also lack the required self-discipline to continue the program. And when they quit, so does Junior! There must be a better way, and I believe there is.

An underachiever often thrives under a system of immediate reinforcement.[14] If he is not challenged by personal satisfaction and motivators usually generated in the classroom, he must be fed some artificial incentives in the form of rewards applied to small units of behavior. Instead of gifts or other desirable objectives being offered to the child for earning an A in English at the end of the semester, he should be given ten cents for each properly diagrammed sentence.

The use of immediate reinforcement serves the same function as a starter on a car! You can't drive very far with it, but it gets the engine going much easier than pushing. For the idealist who objects to the use of the extrinsic motivation (which is often inaccurately called a bribe), I would ask this question: "What alternative do we have, other than to let the child grow out of his problem?"[15]

**My child has a visual-perceptual problem that makes it hard for him to read. I understand his difficulty. But he brings home F's and D's in most of his classes, and I know that will limit his opportunities in life. What should be the attitude of a parent toward a child who fails year after year?**

Obviously, tutorial assistance and special instruction should be provided, if possible. Beyond that, however, I would strongly suggest that academic achievement be de-emphasized at home.

Requiring a visually handicapped child or a slow learner to compete academically is like forcing a polio victim to run the hundred yard dash. Imagine a mother and father standing disapprovingly at the end of the track, berating their crippled child as he hobbles across the finish line in last place.

"Why don't you run faster, son?" his mother asks with obvious displeasure.

"I don't think you really care whether you win or lose," says his embarrassed father.

How can this lad explain that his legs will not carry him as fast as those of his peers? All he knows is that the other sprinters run past him to the cheering of the crowd. But who would expect a crippled child to win a race against healthy peers? No one, simply because his handicap is obvious. Everyone can see it.

Unfortunately, the child with a learning deficit is not so well understood. His academic failure is more difficult to understand and may be attributed to laziness, mischievousness, or deliberate defiance. Consequently, he experiences pressures to do the impossible. And one of the most serious threats to emotional health occurs when a child faces demands that he cannot satisfy.

Let me restate the preceding viewpoint in its most concise terms: I believe in academic excellence. I want to maximize every ounce of intellectual potential which a child possesses. I don't believe in letting him behave irresponsibly simply because he doesn't choose to work. Without question, there is a lasting benefit to be derived from educational discipline.

But, on the other hand, some things in life are more important than academic excellence, and self-esteem is one of them. A child can survive, if he must, without knowing a noun from a verb. But if he doesn't have some measure of self-confidence and personal respect, he won't have a chance in life.

I want to assert my conviction that the child who is

unequipped to prosper in the traditional educational setting is not inferior to his peers. He possesses the same degree of human worth and dignity as the intellectual young superstar. It is a foolish cultural distortion that causes us to evaluate the worth of children according to the abilities and physical features they may (or may not) possess.

Every child is of equal worth in the sight of God, and that is good enough for me. Thus, if my little boy or girl can't be successful in one environment, we'll just look for another. Any loving parent would do the same.[16]

*Author's note:* For a discussion of learning problems associated with visual-perceptual difficulties, see the section devoted to the topic, "Hyperactivity in Children."

# SECTION 5

# SEX EDUCATION AT HOME AND SCHOOL

**When do children begin to develop a sexual nature? Does this occur suddenly during puberty?**

No, it occurs long before puberty. Perhaps the most important scientific fact suggested by Freud was his observation that children are not asexual. He stated that sexual gratification begins in the cradle and is first associated with feeding. Behavior during childhood is influenced considerably by sexual curiosity and interest, although the happy hormones do not take full charge until early adolescence. It is not uncommon for a four-year-old to be fascinated by nudity and the sexual apparatus of boys versus girls. This is an important time in the forming of sexual attitudes; parents should be careful not to express shock and extreme disapproval of this kind of curiosity, although they are entitled to inhibit overt sexual activity between children. It is believed that many sexual problems begin as a result of inappropriate training during early childhood.[1]

**Who should teach children about sex and when should that instruction begin?**

For those parents who are able to handle the instructional process correctly, the responsibility for sex education should be retained in the home. There is a growing trend for all aspects of education to be taken from the hands of parents (or the role is deliberately forfeited by them). This is unwise. Particularly in the matter of sex education, the best approach is one that begins in early childhood and extends through the years, according to a policy of openness, frankness, and honesty. Only parents can provide this lifetime training.

The child's needs for information and guidance can rarely be met in one massive conversation provided by reluctant parents as their child approaches adolescence. Nor does a concentrated formal educational program outside the home offer the same advantages derived from a *gradual* enlightenment that begins during the third or fourth year of life and reaches a culmination shortly before puberty.[2]

**Neither my husband nor I feel comfortable about discussing sex with our children. He thinks the school should supply the information they need, but I feel that it is our responsibility. Must I force myself to talk about this difficult subject?**
Despite the desirability of sex education being handled by highly skilled parents, we have to face the fact that many families feel as you do. They are admittedly unqualified and reluctant to do the job. Their own sexual inhibitions make it extremely difficult for them to handle the task with poise and tact. For families such as yours which cannot teach their children the details of human reproduction, there must be outside agencies that will assist them in this important function. It is my firm conviction that the Christian church is in the best position to provide that support for its members, since it is free to teach not only the anatomy and physiology of reproduction, but also the *morality and responsibility* of sex. Unfortunately, most churches are also reluctant to accept the assignment, leaving the public schools as the only remaining resource.[3]

**Do you believe in the "double standard," whereby girls are expected to remain virgins while boys are free to experiment sexually?**
I most certainly do not. There is no such distinction found in the Bible, which must be the standard by which morality is measured. Sin is sin, whether committed by males or females.

**We've been very slow getting around to sex education in our family. In fact, our child is eleven now, and we haven't given her any specific instructions. Is it too late, or is there still time to prepare her for adolescence?**

Your situation is not ideal, of course, but you should do your best to help your daughter understand what the next few years will bring. Parents should usually plan to end their instructional program before their child enters puberty (the time of rapid sexual development in early adolescence). Puberty usually begins between ten and twelve years of age for girls and between twelve and fourteen for boys. Once this developmental period is entered, teenagers are typically embarrassed by discussions of sex with their parents. Adolescents usually resent adult intrusion during this time, preferring to have the subject of sex ignored at home. We should respect their wishes. We are given but a single decade to provide the proper understanding of human sexuality; after that foundation has been constructed, we can only serve as resources to whom the child can turn if he chooses.[4]

**What should I talk about when I discuss sex with my preteenager?**

In preparing yourself for these discussions, it may be helpful to review the checklist of ten subjects cited below. You should have a good notion of what you will say about each of these topics:

1. The role of intercourse in marriage
2. Male and female anatomy and physiology
3. Pregnancy and the birth process
4. Nocturnal emission ("wet dreams")
5. Masturbation
6. Guilt and sexual fantasy
7. Menstruation
8. Morality and responsibility in sex
9. Venereal disease
10. Secondary sex characteristics which will be brought about by glandular changes—pubic hair, general sexual development, increasing interest in sex, etc.[5]

**How do you feel about sex education in the public schools, as it is typically handled?**

For the children of Christian families or others with firm convictions about moral behavior, an acceptable sex education program must consist of two elements. First the anatomy and physiology of reproduction should be taught. Second, moral attitudes and responsibilities related to sex must be discussed.

*These components should never be separated as long as the issue of morality is considered important!* Sexual sophistication without sexual responsibility is sexual disaster! To explain all the mechanics of reproduction without teaching the proper attitudes and controls is like giving a child a loaded gun without showing him how to use it. Nevertheless, this second responsibility is often omitted or minimized in the public school setting.

Despite their wish to avoid the issue of morality, teachers of sex education find it almost impossible to remain neutral on the subject. Students will not allow them to conceal their viewpoint. "But what do you think about premarital intercourse, Mr. Burgess?" If Mr. Burgess refuses to answer this question, he has inadvertently told the students that there is no definite right or wrong involved. By not taking a stand for morality he has endorsed promiscuity. The issue appears arbitrary to his students, rendering it more likely that their intense biological desires will get satisfied.

I would like to stress the fact that I am not opposed to sex education in the public schools—provided both elements of the subject are presented properly. However, I don't want my children taught sex technology by a teacher who is either neutral or misinformed about the consequences of immorality. It would be preferable that Junior would learn his concepts in the streets than for a teacher to stand before his class, having all the dignity and authority invested in him by the school and society, and tell his impressionable students that traditional morality is either unnecessary or unhealthy. Unless the schools are prepared to take a definite position in favor of sexual responsibility (and perhaps the social climate prevents their doing so), some other agency should assist concerned parents in the provision of sex education for their children. As indicated earlier, churches could easily provide this service for society. The YMCA, YWCA, or other social institutions might also be helpful at this point. Perhaps there is no objective that is more important to the future of our nation than the teaching of moral discipline to the most recent generation of Americans.[6]

**A recent book for parents contends that good sex education will reduce the incidence of promiscuity and sexual irresponsibility among teenagers. Do you agree?**
Of course not. Teenagers are sexually better informed today

than at any time in human history, although the traditional boy-girl game seems to be as popular as ever. The assumption that physiologic information will inhibit sexual activity is about as foolish as thinking an overweight glutton can be helped by understanding the biologic process of eating. I am in favor of proper sex education for other reasons—but I have no illusions about its unique power to install responsibility in adolescents. Morality, if it is valued, must be approached directly, rather than through the back doors of anatomy and physiology. Of much greater potency is a lifelong demonstration of morality in all its forms by parents whose very lives reveal their fidelity and commitment to one another and to Jesus Christ.[7]

**How do you feel about the teaching of traditional male and female roles to children? Do you think boys should be made to do girls' work, and vice versa?**
The trend toward the blending of masculine and feminine roles is well ingrained in America at this time. Women smoke cigars and wear pants. Men splash perfume and don jewelry. There is little sexual identity seen in their hair length, manner, interests, or occupations, and the trend is ever more in this direction. Such similarity between men and women causes great confusion in the minds of children with regard to their own sex-role identity. They have no distinct models to imitate and are left to grope for the appropriate behavior and attitudes.

Therefore, I *firmly* believe in the value of teaching traditional male and female roles during the early years. To remove this prescribed behavior for a child is to further damage his sense of identity, which needs all the help it can get. The masculine and feminine roles are taught through clothing, close identification with the parent of the same sex, and, to some degree, through the kind of work required, and in the selection of toys provided for play. I am not suggesting that we panic over tomboy tendencies in our girls or that we demand he-man behavior from our boys. Nor is it unacceptable for a boy to wash the dishes or a girl to clean the garage. We should, on the other hand, gently nudge our children in the direction of their appropriate sex roles.[8]

**Many American colleges and universities are permitting men and women to live in coeducational dormitories, often rooming side by side. Others now allow unrestricted**

**visiting hours by members of the opposite sex. Do you think this promotes more healthy attitudes toward sex?** It certainly promotes more sex, and some people think that's healthy. The advocates of cohabitation try to tell us that young men and women can live together without doing what comes naturally. That is nonsense. The sex drive is one of the strongest forces in human nature, and Joe College is notoriously weak in suppressing it. I would prefer that the supporters of coeducational dormitories admit that morality is not very important to them. If morality is something we value, then we should at least give it a wobbly-legged chance to survive. The sharing of collegiate bedrooms hardly takes us in that direction.[9]

# SECTION 6

# THE DISCIPLINE OF INFANTS AND TODDLERS

**Some psychologists, especially the behaviorists, believe that children are born as "blank slates," being devoid of personality until they interact with their environments. Do you agree?**

No. I am now certain that the personalities of newborns vary tremendously, even before parental and environmental influence is exercised. Every mother of two or more children will affirm that each of her infants had a different personality—a different "feel"—from the first time they were held. Numerous authorities in the field of child development now agree that these complex little creatures called babies are far from "blank slates" when they enter the world. One important study by Chess, Thomas, and Birch revealed nine kinds of behaviors in which babies differ from one another. These differences tend to persist into later life and include level of activity, responsiveness, distractibility, and moodiness, among others.

Another newborn characteristic (not mentioned by Chess) is most interesting to me and relates to a feature which can be called "strength of the will." Some children seem to be born with an easygoing, compliant attitude toward external authority. As infants they don't cry very often and they sleep through the night from the second week and they goo at the grandparents and they smile while being diapered and they're very patient when dinner is overdue. During later childhood, they love to keep their rooms clean and they especially like to do their homework and they can entertain themselves for hours. There aren't many of these supercompliant children, I'm afraid, but they are known to exist in some households (not my own).

Just as surely as some children are naturally compliant, there are others who seem to be defiant upon exit from the womb. They come into the world smoking a cigar and yelling about the temperature in the delivery room and the incompetence of the nursing staff and the way things are run by the administrator of the hospital. They expect meals to be served the instant they are ordered, and they demand every moment of mother's time. As the months unfold, their expression of willfulness becomes even more apparent, the winds reaching hurricane force during toddlerhood.

The expression of the will, whether compliant or defiant, is only one of an infinite number of ways children differ at birth. And how foolish of us to have thought otherwise. If God can make every snowflake unique, and every grain of sand at the beach is different from its counterparts, then why would the Creator stamp out children as though they were manufactured by Henry Ford? Hardly! Every one of us as human beings is known to the Creator apart from every other human on earth. And I'm thankful that we are![1]

**If children differ in temperament at the moment of birth, then is it reasonable to conclude that some babies are more difficult to care for than others?**

There *are* easy babies and there are difficult babies! Some seem determined to dismantle the homes into which they were born; they sleep cozily during the day and then howl in protest all night; they get colic and spit up the vilest stuff on their clothes (usually on the way to church); they control their internal plumbing until you hand them to strangers, and then let it blast. Instead of cuddling into the fold of the arms when being held, they stiffen rigidly in search of freedom. And to be honest, a mother may find herself leaning sockeyed over a vibrating crib at 3:00 A.M., asking the eternal question, "Is this what my life has come down to?" A few days earlier she was wondering, "Will he survive?" Now she is asking, "Will *I* survive?"

But believe it or not, both generations will probably recover and this disruptive beginning will be nothing but a dim memory for the parents in such a brief moment. And from that demanding tyrant will grow a thinking, loving human being with an eternal soul and a special place in the heart of the Creator. To the exhausted and harassed new mother, let me say, "Hang tough! You are doing *the* most important job in the universe."[2]

**What kind of discipline is appropriate for my six-month-old son?**

No *direct* discipline is necessary for a child under seven months of age, regardless of behavior or circumstances. Many parents do not agree, and find themselves "swatting" a child of six months for wiggling while being diapered or for crying in the midnight hours. This is a serious mistake. A baby is incapable of comprehending his "offense" or associating it with the resulting punishment. At this early age he needs to be held, loved, and most important, to hear a soothing human voice. He should be fed when hungry and kept clean and dry and warm. In essence, it is probable that the foundation for emotional and physical health is laid during this first six-month period, which should be characterized by security, affection, and warmth.[3]

**I have a very fussy eight-month-old baby who cries whenever I put her down. My pediatrician says she is healthy and that she cries just because she wants me to hold her all the time. I do give her a lot of attention, but I simply can't keep her on my lap all day long. How can I make her less fussy?**

The crying of infants is an important form of communication. Through their tears we learn of their hunger, fatigue, discomfort, or diaper disaster. Thus, it is important to listen to those calls for help and interpret them accordingly. On the other hand, your pediatrician is right. It *is* possible to create a fussy, demanding baby by rushing to pick her up every time she utters a whimper or sigh. Infants are fully capable of learning to manipulate their parents through a process called reinforcement, whereby any behavior that produces a pleasant result will tend to recur. Thus, a healthy baby can keep his mother hopping around his nursery twelve hours a day (or night) by simply forcing air past his sandpaper larynx. To avoid this consequence, it is important to strike a balance between giving your baby the attention she needs and establishing her as a tiny dictator. Don't be afraid to let her cry a reasonable period of time (which is thought to be healthy for the lungs), although it is necessary to listen to the tone of her voice for the difference between random discontent and genuine distress. Most mothers learn to recognize this distinction in time.

I used to stand out of sight at the doorway of my daughter's nursery for four or five minutes, awaiting a momentary lull in the crying before going to her crib. By so doing, I reinforced the pauses rather than the tears. You might try the same approach.

Perhaps it would be helpful to illustrate this point by including a letter which reached my desk recently.

> Dear Dr. Dobson:
>
> The reason I'm writing is this: The Lord has blessed us so much I should be full of joy. But I have been depressed for about ten months now. I don't know whether to turn to a pastor, a doctor, a psychologist, a nutritionist, or a chiropractor!
>
> Last September the Lord gave us a beautiful baby boy. He is just wonderful. He is cute and he is smart and he is strong. We just can't help but love him. But he has been very demanding. The thing that made it hardest for me was last month Jena was taking some college classes two nights a week, and I took care of Rolf. He cried and sobbed the whole time and eventually cried himself to sleep. Then I would either hold him because he would awaken and continue crying, or if I did get to lay him down, I wouldn't make any noise because I was afraid I would wake him up.
>
> I am used to being able to pay bills, work on the budget, read and file mail, answer letters, type lists, etc., in the evening. But all this must be postponed to a time when Jena is here.
>
> That's why it has been such a depressing time for me. I just can't handle all that crying. It is probably worse because Jena is breast feeding Rolf. That wakes me up too, and I get very tired and am having a great deal of trouble getting up in the morning to go to work. Now I have started getting sick very easily.
>
> I love our baby a lot and wouldn't trade him for anything in the world, but I don't understand why I'm so depressed. Sure Jena gets tired too because we can't seem to get Rolf to go down for the night before 11 or 12 midnight and he wakes up twice in every night.
>
> Another thing that has been a constant struggle is leaving Rolf in the nursery at church. He isn't content to be away from us very long so the workers end up having to track Jena down almost every week. We hardly ever get to be together for the worship service. And this has been going on for ten months!

We have all the things we would ever dream of at our age — our own neat little house in a good neighborhood, a good job that I enjoy, and not least of all, our life in Christ.

I have no reason to be depressed and to be so tired all the time. I come home from work so exhausted that I'm in no frame of mind to take Rolf out of his mother's hair so she can fix dinner. He hangs on her all the time. I just don't know how she stands it. She must have a higher tolerance to frustration than I do.

If you have any insights as to what we should do, please let me know. Thanks, and God bless you!

Chuck

It is difficult to believe that a ten-month-old baby could take complete charge of two mature adults and mold them to suit his fancy, but that is precisely what Rolf is doing. He fits the pattern of an extremely strong-willed baby who has already learned how to manipulate his parents to achieve his purposes. If they put him to bed or even set him down, if they leave him in the nursery, if they turn their backs on him for a moment—he screams in protest. And being peace-loving parents with great needs for solitude and tranquility, they jump to satisfy Rolf's noisy demands before he gets agitated. In so doing, they "reinforce" his tearful behavior and guarantee its continuation.

I would recommend that Chuck and Jena feed and diaper Rolfie, then proceed to let him cry himself to sleep at about 7:00 P.M. every evening for a week. As this little fellow becomes convinced that the exhausting work of continuous crying is not going to accomplish his objectives, the behavior will disappear. Likewise, they should give him plenty of love and attention and then go about their duties and activities. Rolf will get the message in time.

On the other hand, if Rolfie is, as I suspect, a bona fide strong-willed child, his parents can anticipate a few hundred-thousand more struggles on other battlefields in the years to come.[4]

**Please describe the best approach to the discipline of a one-year-old child.**

Many children will begin to test the authority of their parents during the second seven-month period. The confrontations will be minor and infrequent before the first birthday, yet the beginnings of future struggles can be seen. My own daughter, for example, challenged her mother for the first time when she was nine months old. My wife was waxing the kitchen floor when Danae crawled to the edge of the linoleum. Shirley said, "No, Danae," gesturing to the child not to enter the kitchen. Since our daughter began talking very early, she clearly understood the meaning of the word *no*. Nevertheless, she crawled straight onto the sticky wax. Shirley picked her up and set her down in the doorway, while saying, "No" more firmly. Not to be discouraged, Danae again scrambled onto the newly mopped floor. My wife took her back, saying, "No" even more strongly as she put her down. Seven times this process was repeated until Danae finally yielded and crawled away in tears. As far as we can recall, that was the first direct collision of wills between my daughter and wife. Many more were to follow.

How does a parent discipline a one-year-old? Very carefully and gently! A child at this age is extremely easy to distract and divert. Rather than jerking a wrist watch from his hands, show him a brightly colored alternative—and then be prepared to catch the watch when it falls. When unavoidable confrontations do occur, as with Danae on the waxy floor, win them by firm persistence but not by punishment. Again, don't be afraid of the child's tears, which can become a potent weapon to avoid naptime or bedtime or diapertime. Have the courage to lead the child without being harsh or mean or gruff.

Compared to the months that are to follow, the period around one year of age is usually a tranquil, smooth-functioning time in a child's life.[5]

**Are the "terrible twos" really so terrible?**

It has been said that all human beings can be classified into two broad categories: those who would vote "yes" to the various propositions of life, and those who would be inclined to vote "no." I can tell you with confidence that each toddler around the world would definitely cast a negative vote! If there is one word that characterizes the period between fifteen and twenty-four months of age, it is *no!* No, he doesn't want to eat his cereal. No, he doesn't want to play with his dump truck. No, he doesn't want to take his bath. And you can be sure, no, he doesn't want to go to bed anytime at all. It is easy to see why this period of life has been called "the first adolescence," because of the negatives, conflict, and defiance of the age.

Perhaps the most frustrating aspect of the "terrible twos" is the tendency of kids to spill things, destroy things, eat horrible things, fall off things, flush things, kill things, and get into things. They also have a knack for doing embarrassing things, like sneezing on a nearby man at a lunch counter. During these toddler years, any unexplained silence of more than thirty seconds can throw an adult into a sudden state of panic. What mother has not had the thrill of opening the bedroom door, only to find Tony Tornado covered with lipstick from the top of his pink head to the carpet on which he stands? On the wall is his own artistic creation with a red handprint in the center, and throughout the room is the aroma of Chanel No. 5 with which he has anointed his baby brother. Wouldn't it be interesting to hold a national convention sometime, bringing together all the mothers who have experienced that exact trauma?

The picture sounds bleak, and, admittedly, there are times when a little toddler can dismantle the peace and tranquility of a home. (My son Ryan loved to blow bubbles in the dog's water dish—a game which still horrifies me.) However, with all of its struggles, there is no more thrilling time of life than this period of dynamic blossoming and unfolding. New words are being learned daily, and the cute verbal expressions of that age will be remembered for half a century. It is a time of excitement over fairy stories and Santa Claus and furry puppy dogs. And most important, it is a precious time of loving and warmth that will scurry by all too quickly. There are millions of older parents today with grown children who would give all they possess to relive those bubbly days with their toddlers.[6]

**It is already obvious that we have an extremely defiant child who has demanded his own way since the day he was born. I think we have disciplined and trained him as well as possible, but he still opposes any boundaries or limits we try to set on him. Can you tell me why *I* feel so guilty and defeated, even though I know I've been a good parent?**
Your guilt is very common among parents of strong-willed children, and for good reason. You are engaged in an all-out tug of war which leaves you frustrated and fatigued. No one told you that parenthood would be this difficult, and you blame yourself

for the tension that arises. You and your husband had planned to be such loving and effective parents, reading fairy stories to your pajama-clad angels by the fireplace. But reality has turned out to be quite different, and that difference is depressing to you.

Furthermore, I have found that the parents of compliant children don't understand their friends with defiant youngsters. They intensify guilt and anxiety by implying, "If you would raise your kids the way I do it, you wouldn't be having those awful problems." May I emphasize to both groups that the willful child can be difficult to control even when his parents handle him with great skill and dedication.

**Our twenty-four-month-old son is not yet toilet trained, although my mother-in-law feels he should be under control now. Should we spank him for using his pants instead of the potty?**
No. Tell your mother-in-law to cool down a bit. It is entirely possible that your child *can't* control himself at this age. The last thing you want to do is spank a two-year-old for an offense which he can't comprehend. If I had to err on this matter, it would be in the direction of being too late with my demands, rather than too early. Furthermore, the best approach to potty training is with rewards rather than with punishment. Give him a sucker (or sugarless candy) for performing properly. When you've proved that he can comply, then you can hold him responsible in the future.[7]

**I get very upset because my two-year-old boy will not sit still and be quiet in church. He knows he's not supposed to be noisy, but he hits his toys on the pew and sometimes talks out loud. Should I spank him for being disruptive?**
Your question reveals a rather poor understanding of the nature of toddlers. Most two-year-olds can no more fold their hands and sit still in church and listen to the sermon than they could swim the Atlantic Ocean. They squirm and churn and burn because they *must*. You just can't hold a toddler down. All their waking hours are spent in activity, and that's normal for this stage of development. So I do not recommend that your child be punished for this behavior. I think he should be left in the church nursery where he can shake the foundations without

disturbing the worship service. If there is no nursery, I suggest, if it is possible from a financial point of view, that he be left at home with a sitter until he is at least three years of age.[8]

**At what age could you expect a child to sit quietly in church?**
The ability to sit quietly in church is a gradually developing example of self-control. He will learn it in small increments during the first few years of his life. I would expect that perhaps by four years of age he should be able to control his activity and sit in church without making any loud disturbance, even if he is drawing or coloring or looking at books. By the time he is five he should be ready to sit through the service without dropping things, waving his arms around, etc. But even at that age, punishment for noise is inappropriate except in instances of deliberate and willful defiance.[9]

**I have to spank my toddler most frequently for touching the china and expensive trinkets which decorate our home. How can I make her leave these breakable things alone?**
I caution parents not to punish toddlers for behavior which is natural and necessary to learning and development. Exploration of their environment, for example, is of great importance to intellectual stimulation. You and I as adults will look at a crystal trinket and obtain whatever information we seek from that visual inspection. A toddler, however, will expose it to all of her senses. She will pick it up, taste it, smell it, wave it in the air, pound it on the wall, throw it across the room, and listen to the pretty sound that it makes when shattering. By that process she learns a bit about gravity, rough versus smooth surfaces, the brittle nature of glass, and some startling things about mother's anger.

I am not suggesting that your child be allowed to destroy your home and all of its contents. Neither is it right to expect her to keep her hands to herself. Parents should remove those items that are fragile or particularly dangerous, and then strew the child's path with fascinating objects of all types. Permit her to explore everything possible and do not ever punish her for touching something that she *did not know was off limits*, regardless of its value. With respect to dangerous items, such as electric plugs and stoves, as well as a few untouchable objects, such as the knobs on the television set, it is possible and necessary to teach and enforce the command, "Don't touch!" After making it clear what is expected, a thump on the fingers or slap on the hands will usually discourage repeat episodes.[10]

**When, then, should the toddler be subjected to mild punishment?**

When he openly defies his parents' spoken commands! If he runs the other way when called—if he slams his milk on the floor—if he screams and throws a tantrum at bedtime—if he hits his friends—these are the forms of unacceptable behavior which should be discouraged. Even in these situations, however, all-out spankings are not often required to eliminate the response. A firm thump or a rap on the fingers will convey the same message just as convincingly. Spankings should be reserved for moments of greatest antagonism during later years.

I feel it is important to stress this point: the toddler years are critical to the child's future attitude toward authority. He should be patiently taught to obey without being expected to behave like an adult.[11]

**My three-year-old daughter, Nancy, plays unpleasant games with me in grocery stores. She runs when I call her and makes demands for candy and gum and cupcakes. When I refuse, she throws the most embarrassing temper tantrums you can imagine. I don't want to punish her in front of all those people, and she knows it. What should I do?**

If there are sanctuaries where the usual rules and restrictions do not apply, then your children will behave differently in those protected zones than elsewhere. I would suggest that you have a talk with Nancy on the next trip to the market. Tell her exactly what you expect, and make it clear that you mean business. Then when the same behavior occurs, take her to the car or behind the building and do what you would have done at home. She'll get the message.

In the absence of this kind of away-from-home parental leadership, some children become extremely obnoxious and defiant, especially in public places. Perhaps the best example was a ten-year-old boy named Robert, who was a patient of my good friend Dr. William Slonecker. Dr. Slonecker said his pediatric staff dreaded the days when Robert was scheduled for an office visit. He literally attacked the clinic, grabbing instruments and files and telephones. His passive mother could do little more than shake her head in bewilderment.

During one physical examination, Dr. Slonecker observed severe cavities in Robert's teeth and knew that the boy must be referred to a local dentist. But who would be given the honor? A referral like Robert could mean the end of a professional friendship. Dr. Slonecker eventually decided to send him to an older dentist who reportedly understood children. The confrontation that followed now stands as one of the classic moments in the history of human conflict.

Robert arrived in the dentist's office, prepared for battle.

"Get into the chair, young man," said the doctor.

"No chance!" replied the boy.

"Son, I told you to climb onto the chair, and that's what I intend for you to do," said the dentist.

Robert stared at his opponent for a moment and then replied, "If you make me get in that chair, I will take off all my clothes."

The dentist calmly said, "Son, take 'em off."

The boy forthwith removed his shirt, undershirt, shoes and socks, and then looked up in defiance.

"All right, son," said the dentist. "Now get on the chair."

"You didn't hear me," sputtered Robert. "I said if you make me get on that chair I will take off *all* my clothes."

"Son, take 'em off," replied the man.

Robert proceeded to remove his pants and shorts, finally standing totally naked before the dentist and his assistant.

"Now, son, get into the chair," said the doctor.

Robert did as he was told, and sat cooperatively through the entire procedure. When the cavities were drilled and filled, he was instructed to step down from the chair.

"Give me my clothes now," said the boy.

"I'm sorry," replied the dentist. "Tell your mother that we're going to keep your clothes tonight. She can pick them up tomorrow."

Can you comprehend the shock Robert's mother received when the door to the waiting room opened, and there stood her pink son, as naked as the day he was born? The room was filled with patients, but Robert and his mom walked past them and into the hall. They went down a public elevator and into the parking lot, ignoring the snickers of onlookers.

The next day, Robert's mother returned to retrieve his clothes, and asked to have a word with the dentist. However, she did not come to protest. These were her sentiments: "You don't know how much I appreciate what happened here yesterday. You see, Robert has been blackmailing me about his clothes for years. Whenever we are in a public place, such as a grocery store, he makes unreasonable demands of me. If I don't immediately buy him what he wants, he threatens to take off all his clothes. You are the first person who has called his bluff, doctor, and the impact on Robert has been incredible!"[12]

**I know you recommend that spanking should be relatively infrequent during toddler years. What is another disciplinary technique for a child this age who has been disobedient?**

One possible approach is to require the boy or girl to sit in a chair and think about what he has done. Most children of this age are bursting with energy and absolutely hate to spend ten dull minutes with their wiggly posteriors glued to a chair. To some individuals, this form of punishment can be even more effective that a spanking, and is remembered longer.[13]

**What can I do if Johnny, my three-year-old, refuses to stay in bed at night? He climbs right out while I'm standing there telling him to stay put!**

The parent who cannot require a toddler to stay on a chair or in his bed is not yet in command of the child. There is no better time than now to change the relationship.

I would suggest that the youngster be placed in bed and given a little speech, such as, "Johnny, this time Mommie means business. Are you listening to me? *Do not* get out of this bed. Do you understand me?" Then when Johnny's feet touch the floor, give him one swat on the legs with a small switch. Put the switch on his dresser where he can see it, and promise him one more stroke if he gets up again. Walk confidently out of the room without further comment. If he rebounds again, fulfill your promise and offer the same warning if he doesn't stay in bed. Repeat the episode until Johnny acknowledges that you are the boss. Then hug him, tell him you love him, and remind him how important it is for him to get his rest so that he won't be sick, etc. Your purpose in this painful exercise (painful for both parties) is not only to keep li'l John in bed, but to confirm your leadership in his mind. It is my opinion that too many American parents lack the courage to win this kind of confrontation and are off-balance and defensive ever after. Dr. Benjamin Spock wrote in 1974, "Inability to be firm is, to my mind, the commonest problem of parents in America today." I agree.[14]

---

**We have an adopted child who came to us when he was two years old. He was so abused during those first couple of years that my husband and I cannot let ourselves punish him, even when he deserves it. We also feel we don't have the right to discipline him, since we are not his real parents. Are we doing right?**

I'm afraid you are making a mistake commonly committed by the parents of adopted children. They pity their youngsters too much to control them. They feel that life has already been too harsh with the little ones, and they must not make things worse by disciplining them. As you indicated, there is often the feeling that they do not have the right to make demands on their adopted children. These guilt-laden attitudes can lead to unfortunate consequences. Transplanted children have the same needs for guidance and discipline as those remaining with their biological parents. One of the surest ways to make a child feel insecure is to treat him as though he is different—unusual—brittle. If the parents view him as an unfortunate waif to be shielded, he will see himself that way too.

Parents of sick and deformed children are also likely to find discipline harder to implement. A child with a withered arm or some nonfatal illness can become a little terror, simply because the usual behavioral boundaries are not established by his parents. It must be remembered that the need to be controlled and governed is almost universal in childhood; this need is not eliminated by other problems and difficulties in life. In some cases, the desire for boundaries is maximized by other troubles, for it is through loving control that parents express personal worth to a child.[15]

SECTION 7

# UNDER-STANDING THE ROLE OF DISCIPLINE

**Why is there so much confusion on the subject of discipline today? Is it really that difficult to raise our children properly?**

Parents are confused because they have been taught an illogical, unworkable approach to child management by many professionals who ought to know better. Child development authorities have muddied the water with permissive philosophies which contradict the very nature of children. Let me cite an example. *Growing Pains* is a question-and-answer book for parents, published by the American Academy of Pediatrics (a division of the American Medical Association). The following question written by a parent is quoted in the book, along with the answer provided by the pediatrician.

> CHILD SLAMS DOOR IN PARENT'S FACE
>
> Q. What does one do when an angry child slams a door in one's face?
>
> A. Step back. Then do nothing until you have reason to believe that the child's anger has cooled off. Trying to reason with an angry person is like hitting your head against a stone wall.
>
> When the child is in a good mood, explain to him how dangerous door-slamming can be. Go so far as to give him a description of how a person can lose a finger from a slammed door. Several talks of this sort are generally enough to cure a door-slammer.

How inadequate is this reply, from my point of view. The writer failed to recognize that the door-slamming behavior was *not* the real issue in this situation. To the contrary, the child was demonstrating his defiance of parental authority, and for *that* he should have been held accountable. Instead, the parent is told to wait until the child is in a good mood (which could be next Thursday), and then talk about the dangers of door-slamming. It seems clear that the child was begging his mom to accept his challenge, but she was in the other room counting to ten and keeping cool. And let's all wish her lots of luck on the next encounter.

As I've stated, the great givers of parental advice have failed to offer a course of action to be applied in response to willful defiance. In the situation described above, for example, what is Mom supposed to do until Junior cools off? What if he is breaking furniture and writing on the back of that slammed door? What if he calls her dirty names and whacks his little sister across the mouth? You see, the *only* tool given to Mom by the writer, above, is postponed *reason*. And as every mother knows, reason is practically worthless in response to anger and disrespect.

Nature has provided a wonderfully padded place for use in moments of haughty defiance, and I wish the disciplinary "experts" were less confused as to its proper purpose.[1]

**Permissiveness is a relative term. Please describe its meaning to you.**

When I use the term permissiveness, I refer to the absence of effective parental authority, resulting in the lack of boundaries for the child. This word represents childish disrespect, defiance, and the general confusion that occurs in the absence of adult leadership.[2]

**Do you think parents are now beginning to value discipline more? Is the day of permissiveness over?**

Parents who tried extreme permissiveness have seen its failure, for the most part. Unfortunately, those parents will soon be grandparents, and the world will profit little from their experience. What worries me most is the kind of discipline that will be exercised by the generation now reaching young adulthood. Many of these new parents have never seen good discipline exercised. They have had no model. Besides, in many cases they have severed themselves from the best source of information, avowing that anyone over thirty is to be mistrusted. It will be interesting to see what develops from this blind date between mom and baby.[3]

**Is it accurate to say that an undisciplined preschooler will continue to challenge his parents during the latter years of childhood?**
It often occurs that way. When a parent loses the early confrontations with the child, the later conflicts become harder to win. The parent who never wins, who is too weak or too tired or too busy to win, is making a costly mistake that will usually come back to haunt him during the child's adolescence. If you can't make a five-year-old pick up his toys, it is unlikely that you will exercise any impressive degree of control during his adolescence, the most defiant time of life. It is important to understand that adolescence is a condensation or composite of all the training and behavior that has gone before. Any unsettled matter in the first twelve years is likely to fester and erupt during adolescence. Therefore, the proper time to begin disarming the teenage time-bomb is twelve years before it arrives.[4]

**My first year as a teacher was a disaster. I loved the students as though they were my own children, but they totally rejected that affection. I simply couldn't control them. Since then, I've learned that children can't accept love until they have tested the strength and courage of their teachers. Why do you think this is true?**
I don't know. But every competent teacher will verify the fact that respect for authority must precede the acceptance of love. Those teachers who try to spread love in September and discipline the following January are destined for trouble. It won't work. (That's why I have recommended—half seriously—that teachers not smile 'til Thanksgiving!)

Perhaps the most frustrating experience of my professional career occurred when I was asked to speak to a group of college students who were majoring in education. The year was 1971, when permissive philosophies were rampant . . . especially on college campuses. Most of these men and women were in their final year of preparation, and would soon be teaching in their own classrooms. The distress that I felt came from my inability to convince these idealistic young people of the principle you have observed. They really believed that they could pour out love to their students and be granted instant respect from these rebels who had been at war with everyone. I felt empathy for the new teachers who would soon find themselves in the jungles of inner city schools, alone and afraid. They were bound to get their "love" thrown back in their startled faces, just as you did. *Students simply cannot accept a teacher's love until they know that the giver is worthy of their respect.*

You might be interested to know that I have made the same observation in other areas of life, including man's relationship with God. Remember that He revealed His majesty and wrath and justice through the Old Testament before we were permitted to observe Jesus' incomparable love in the New Testament. It would appear that respect must precede loving relationships in all areas of life.[5]

**Some parents feel guilty about demanding respect from their children, because it could be an underhanded way of making themselves feel powerful and important. What do you think?**

I disagree. It is most important that a child respect his parents, because that relationship provides the basis for his attitude toward all other people. His view of parental authority becomes the cornerstone for his later outlook on school authority, police and law, the people with whom he will eventually live and work, and for society in general.

Another equally important reason for maintaining parental respect is that if you want your child to accept your values when he reaches his teen years, then you must be worthy of his respect during his younger days.

When a child can successfully defy his parents during his first fifteen years, laughing in their faces and stubbornly flouting their authority, he develops a natural contempt for them. "Stupid old Mom and Dad! I've got them wound around my little finger. Sure they love me, but I really think they're afraid of me." A child may not utter these words, but he feels them each time he outsmarts his adult companions and wins the confrontations and battles. Later he is likely to demonstrate his disrespect in a more open matter. His parents are not deserving of his respect, and he does not want to identify with anything they represent. He rejects every vestige of their philosophy.

This factor is important for Christian parents who wish to sell their concept of God to their children. They must first sell themselves. If they are not worthy of respect, then neither is their religion or their morals, or their government, or their country, or any of their values. This becomes the "generation gap" at its most basic level. The chasm does not develop from a failure to communicate; we're speaking approximately the same language. Mark Twain once said about the Bible, "It's not the things I don't understand that bother me; it's the things I do!" Likewise, our difficulties between generations result more from what we *do* understand in our communication than in our confusion with words. The conflict between generations occurs because of a breakdown in mutual respect, and it bears many painful consequences.[6]

**You place great stress on the child being taught to respect the authority of the parents. But does that coin have two sides? Don't parents have an equal responsibility to show respect for their children?**

They certainly do! A mother cannot require her child to treat her with dignity if she will not do the same for him. She should be gentle with his ego, never belittling him or embarrassing him in front of his friends. Punishment should be administered away from the curious eyes of gloating onlookers. The child should not be laughed at unmercifully. His strong feelings and requests, even if foolish, should be given an honest appraisal. He should feel that his parents "really *do* care about me." Self-esteem is the most fragile attribute in human nature; it can be damaged by very minor incidents and its reconstruction is often difficult to engineer. A father who is sarcastic and biting in his criticism of children cannot expect to receive genuine respect in return. His offspring might fear him enough to conceal their contempt, but revenge will often erupt in late adolescence.[7]

**What goes through the mind of a child when he is openly defying the wishes of his parent?**

Children are usually aware of the contest of wills between generations, and that is precisely why the parental response is so important. When a child behaves in ways that are disrespectful or harmful to himself or others, his hidden purpose is often to verify the stability of the boundaries. This testing has much the same function as a policeman who turns doorknobs at places of business after dark. Though he tries to open doors, he hopes they are locked and secure. Likewise, a child who assaults the loving authority of his parents is greatly reassured when their leadership holds firm and confident. He finds his greatest security in a structured environment where the rights of other people (and his own) are protected by definite boundaries.[8]

**Could you explain further why *security* for the child is related to parental discipline and structure? It just doesn't add up for me. I guess I've been influenced by the psychologists and writers who stress the importance of children growing up in an atmosphere of freedom and democracy in the home.**

After working with children for twenty-one years, I couldn't be more convinced that they draw confidence from knowing where their boundaries are and who intends to enforce them. Perhaps an illustration will make this more clear. Imagine yourself driving a car over the Royal Gorge in Colorado. The bridge is suspended hundreds of feet above the canyon floor, and as a first-time traveler, you are tense as you drive across. (I knew one little fellow who was so awed by the view over the side of the bridge that he said, "Wow, Daddy. If you fell off of here it'd kill you constantly!") Now suppose that there were no guardrails on the side of the bridge; where would you steer the car? Right down the middle of the road! Even though you don't plan to hit those protective walls along the side, you feel more secure just knowing they are there.

The analogy to children has been demonstrated empirically. During the early days of the progressive education movement, one enthusiastic theorist decided to take down the chain-link fence that surrounded the nursery school yard. He thought the children would feel more freedom of movement without that visible barrier surrounding them. When the fence was removed, however, the boys and girls huddled near the center of the play yard. Not only did they not wander away, they didn't even venture to the edge of the grounds.

There is a security in defined limits. When the home atmosphere is as it should be, the child lives in utter safety. He never gets in trouble unless he deliberately asks for it, and as long as he stays within the limits, there is mirth and freedom and acceptance. If this is what is meant by "democracy" in the home, then I favor it. If it means the absence of boundaries, or that each child sets his own boundaries, then I'm inalterably opposed to it.[9]

---

**Everyone tells me that children love justice and law and order. If that's true, why doesn't my little son respond better to me when I talk reasonably with him about his misbehavior? Why do I have to resort to some form of punishment to make him listen to me?**

The answer is found in a curious value system of children which respects strength and courage (when combined with love). What better explanation can be given for the popularity of the mythical Superman and Captain Marvel and Wonder Woman in the folklore of children? Why else do children proclaim, "My dad can beat up your dad"? (One child replied to that statement, "That's nothing, my *mom* can beat up my dad, too!")

You see, boys and girls care about the issue of "who's toughest." Whenever a youngster moves into a new neighborhood or a new school district, he usually has to fight (either verbally or physically) to establish himself in the hierarchy of strength. Anyone who understands children knows that there is a "top dog" in every group, and there is a poor little defeated pup at the bottom of the heap. And every child between those extremes knows where he stands in relation to the others.

This respect for strength and courage also makes children want to know how "tough" their leaders are. They will occasionally disobey parental instructions for the precise purpose of testing the determination of those in charge. Thus, whether you are a parent or grandparent or Boy Scout leader or bus driver or Brownie leader or a schoolteacher, I can guarantee that sooner or later, one of the children under your authority will clench his little fist and challenge your leadership.

This defiant game, called "Challenge the Chief," can be played with surprising skill by very young children. A father told me of taking his three-year-old daughter to a basketball game. The child was, of course, interested in everything in the gym except the athletic contest. The father permitted her to roam free and climb on the bleachers, but he set up definite limits regarding how far she could stray. He took her by the hand and walked with her to a stripe painted on the gym floor. "You can play all around the building, Janie, but don't go past this line," he instructed her. He had no sooner returned to his seat than the toddler scurried in the direction of the forbidden territory. She stopped at the border for a moment, then flashed a grin over her shoulder to her father, and deliberately placed one foot over the line as if to say, "Whacha gonna do about it?" Virtually every parent the world over has been asked the same question at one time or another.

The entire human race is afflicted with this tendency toward willful defiance. God told Adam and Eve that they could eat anything in the Garden of Eden except the forbidden fruit. Yet they challenged the authority of the Almighty by deliberately disobeying His commandment. Perhaps this tendency toward self-will is the essence of "original sin" which has infiltrated the human family. It certainly explains why I place such stress on the proper response to willful defiance during childhood, for that rebellion can plant the seeds of personal disaster. The thorny weed which it produces may grow into a tangled briar patch during the troubled days of adolescence.

When a parent refuses to accept his child's defiant challenge, something changes in their relationship. The youngster begins to look at his mother and father with disrespect; they are unworthy of his allegiance. More important, he wonders why they would let him do such harmful things if they really loved him. The ultimate paradox of childhood is that boys and girls want to be led by their parents, but insist that their mothers and fathers earn the right to lead them.[10]

**Isn't it our goal to produce children with *self*-discipline and *self*-reliance? If so, how does your approach to *external* discipline by parents get translated into internal control?**

You've asked a provocative question, but one that reveals a misunderstanding of children, I believe. There are many authorities who suggest that parents not discipline their children for the reason implied by your question: they want their kids to discipline themselves. But since young people lack the maturity to generate that self-control, they stumble through childhood without experiencing *either* internal or external discipline. Thus, they enter adult life having never completed an unpleasant assignment, or accepted an order that they disliked, or yielded to the leadership of their elders. Can we expect such a person to exercise self-discipline in young adulthood? I think not. He doesn't even know the meaning of the word.

My concept is that parents should introduce their child to discipline and self-control by the use of external influences when he is young. By being required to behave responsibly, he gains valuable experience in controlling his own impulses and resources. Then as he grows into the teen years, the transfer of responsibility is made year by year from the shoulders of the parent directly to the child. He is no longer forced to do what he has learned during earlier years. To illustrate, a child should be *required* to keep his room relatively neat when he is young. Then somewhere during the midteens, his own self-discipline should take over and provide the motivation to continue the task. If it does not, the parent should close the door and let him live in a dump, if necessary.[11]

**I have been hearing about "Parent Effectiveness Training" classes offered in various parts of the country. What do you think of them?**

Dr. Thomas Gordon is the creator of this program, which has become very widespread. There are more than 8,000 P. E.T. classes in operation throughout the country. These sessions offer some worthwhile suggestions in the area of listening skills, in the use of parent-child negotiation, and in the cultivation of parental tolerance.

Nevertheless, it is my view that the great flaws in Tom Gordon's philosophy far outweigh the benefits. They are: (1) his failure to understand the proper role of authority in the home; (2) his humanistic viewpoint which teaches that children are born innately "good," and then learn to do wrong; (3) his tendency to weaken parental resolve to instill spiritual principles systematically during a child's "teachable" years.[12]

(For a complete discussion of the Parent Effectiveness Training program, see *The Strong-Willed Child*, Chapter 7.)

**I would like to compare your approach to discipline with that of Dr. Tom Gordon. He often cites an illustration of a child who puts his feet on an expensive item of living room furniture. His parents become irritated at this gesture and order him to take his dirty shoes from the chair or table. Gordon then shows how much more politely those parents would have handled the same indiscretion if the offender had been an adult guest. They might have cautiously asked him to remove his shoes, but would certainly not have felt it necessary to discipline or criticize the visitor. Dr. Gordon then asks, "Aren't children people, too? Why don't we treat them with the same respect that we do our adult friends?" Would you comment on this example?**

I have heard Dr. Gordon relate the same illustration and feel that it contains both truth and distortion. If his point is that we need to exercise greater kindness and respect in dealing with our children, then I certainly agree. However, to equate children with adult visitors in the home is an error in reasoning. I do not bear *any* responsibility for teaching proper manners and courtesy to my guests; I certainly do have that obligation on behalf of my children. Furthermore, the illustration implies that children and adults think and act identically, and have the same needs. They don't. A child often behaves offensively for the precise purpose of testing the courage of his parents. He wants them to establish firm boundaries. By contrast, a guest who puts his feet on a coffee table is more likely to be acting through ignorance or insensitivity.

More important, this illustration cleverly redefines the traditional parental relationship with children. Instead of bearing direct responsibility for training and teaching and leading them, Mom and Dad have become cautious co-equals who can only hope their independent little "guests" will gradually get the message.

No, our children are not casual guests in our home. They have been loaned to us temporarily for the purpose of loving them and instilling a foundation of values on which their future lives will be built. And we will be accountable through eternity for the way we discharge that responsibility.[13]

**Dr. Gordon and others condemn the use of parental "power" which he defines as being synonymous with parental authority. Do you also equate the meaning of these two words?**

No, and that is a major distinction between Dr. Gordon's view of proper parenting and my own. It would appear from his writings that he views all authority as a form of unethical oppression. In my opinion, the two concepts are as different as love and hate. Parental power can be defined as a hostile form of manipulation in order to satisfy selfish adult purposes. As such, it disregards the best interests of the little child on whom it tramples, and produces a relationship of fear and intimidation. Drill instructors in the Marine Corps have been known to depend on this form of power to indoctrinate their beleaguered recruits.

Proper authority, by contrast, is defined as loving *leadership.* Without decision-makers and others who agree to follow, there is inevitable chaos and confusion and disorder in human relationships. Loving authority is the glue that holds social orders together, and it is absolutely necessary for the healthy functioning of a family.

There are times when I say to my child, "Ryan, you are tired because you were up too late last night. I want you to brush your teeth right now and put on your pajamas." My words may sound like a suggestion, but Ryan would be wise to remember who's making it. If that is parental power, according to Dr. Gordon's definition, then so be it. I do not always have time to negotiate, nor do I feel obligated in every instance to struggle for compromise. I have the *authority* to do what I think is in Ryan's best interest, and there are times when I expect him not to negotiate, but to *obey.* And, of critical importance, his learning to yield to my loving leadership is excellent training for his later submission to the loving authority of God. This is very different from the use of vicious and hostile power, resulting from the fact that I outweigh him.[14]

**How about Gordon's suggested use of "I" messages versus "you" messages?**

There is substantial truth in the basic idea. "I" messages can request change or improvement without being offensive: "Diane, it embarrasses me when our neighbors see your messy room. I wish you would straighten it." By contrast, "you" messages often attack the personhood of the recipient and put him on the defensive: "Why don't you keep your stuff picked up? So help me, Diane, you get sloppier and more irresponsible every day!" I agree with Dr. Gordon that the first method of communicating is usually superior to the second, and there is wisdom in his recommendation.

However, let's suppose I have taken my four-year-old son, Dale, to the market where he breaks all known rules. He throws a temper tantrum because I won't buy him a balloon, and he hits the daughter of another customer, and grabs a handful of gum at the checkout stand. When I get darlin' Dale outside the store there is little doubt that he is going to hear a few "you" messages—such as, "When *you* get home, young man, *you* are going to have *your* bottom tanned!"

From my perspective, again, there are few occasions in the life of a parent when he speaks not as an equal or a comrade or a pal, but as an *authority*. And in those circumstances, an occasional "you" message will fit the circumstances better than an expression of personal frustration by the parent.[15]

**Dr. Gordon said parents cannot know what is in the best interest of their children. Do you claim to make weighty decisions on behalf of your kids with unshakable confidence? How do you know that what you're doing will ultimately be healthy for them?**

It is certain that I will make mistakes and errors as a parent. My human frailties are impossible to hide and my children occasionally fall victim to those imperfections. But I cannot abandon my responsibilities to provide leadership simply because I lack infinite wisdom and insight. Besides, I do have more experience and a better perspective on which to base those decisions than my children possess at this time. I've *been* where they're going.

Perhaps a crude example would be illustrative. My daughter has a pet hamster (uncreatively named Hammy) who has a passion for freedom. He spends a portion of every night gnawing on the metal bars of his cage and forcing his head through the trap door. Recently I sat watching Hammy busily trying to escape. But I was not the only one observing the furry little creature. Sitting in the shadows a few feet away was old Sigmund, our dachshund. His erect ears, squinted eyes, and panting tongue betrayed his sinister thoughts. Siggie was thinking, "Come on, baby, break through to freedom! Bite those bars, Hambone, and I'll give you a thrill like you've never experienced!"

How interesting, I thought, that the hamster's greatest desire would bring him instant and violent death if he should be so unfortunate to achieve it. Hammy simply lacked the perspective to realize the folly of his wishes. The application to human experience was too striking to be missed and I shook my head silently as the animal drama spoke to me. There are occasions when the longings and desires of our children would be harmful or disastrous if granted. They would choose midnight bedtime hours and no schoolwork and endless cartoons on television and chocolate sundaes by the dozen. And in later years, they might not see the harm of drug abuse and premarital sex and a life of uninterrupted fun and games. Like Hammy, they lack the "perspective" to observe the dangers which lurk in the shadows. Alas, many young people are "devoured" before they even know that they have made a fatal mistake.

Then my thoughts meandered a bit farther to my own relationship with God and the requests I submit to Him in personal prayer. I wondered how many times I had asked Him to open the door on my "cage," not appreciating the security it was providing. I resolved to accept His negative answers with greater submission in the future.

Returning to the question, let me repeat that my decisions on behalf of my children do not reflect infinite wisdom. They do, however, emanate from love and an intense desire to do the best I can. Beyond that, the ultimate outcome is committed to God virtually every day of my life.[16]

**My mother and father were harsh disciplinarians when I was a child, and I was afraid of them both. My cousin, on the other hand, was raised in a home with very few rules. She was a spoiled brat then and is still selfish today. Would you compare these two approaches to child rearing—the authoritarian and the permissive homes—and describe their effects on children?**

They are equally harmful to children, in my view. On the side of harshness, a child suffers the humiliation of total domination. The atmosphere at home is icy and rigid, and he lives in constant fear of punishment. He is unable to make his own decisions and his personality is squelched beneath the hob-nailed boot of parental power. Lasting characteristics of dependency, hostility and even psychosis can emerge from this overbearing oppression. The opposite approach, ultimate permissiveness, is equally tragic. In this setting, the child is his own master from his earliest babyhood. He thinks the world revolves around his heady empire, and he often has utter contempt and disrespect for those closest to him. Anarchy and chaos reign in his home and his mother is often the most nervous, frustrated woman on her block. When the child is young, his mother is stranded at home because she is too embarrassed to take her little devil anywhere. He later finds it difficult to yield to outside symbols of authority, such as teachers, police, ministers or even God.

To repeat, both extremes of authority are disastrous for the well being of a child. There is safety only in the middle ground, which is sometimes difficult for parents to locate.[17]

**You have said that your philosophy of discipline (and of family advice in general) was drawn from the Scriptures. On what references do you base your views, and especially your understanding of the will and the spirit?** The dual responsibility assigned to parents appears repeatedly in the Scriptures, but is addressed most clearly in two passages:

> SHAPING THE WILL
> He [the father] must have proper authority in his own household, and be able to control and command the respect of his children (1 Tim. 3:4, 5 Phillips).
>
> PRESERVING THE SPIRIT
> Children, the right thing for you to do is to obey your parents as those whom the Lord has set over you. The first commandment to contain a promise was: "Honour thy father and thy mother that it may be well with thee, and that thou mayest live long on the earth." *Fathers, don't over-correct your children or make it difficult for them to obey the commandment. Bring them up with Christian teaching in Christian discipline* (Eph. 6:1-4 Phillips, emphasis added).

It is significant that this second Scripture instructs children to obey their parents but is followed immediately by admonitions to fathers regarding the limits of discipline. We see an identical pattern in Colossians 3:20, 21:

> Children, obey your parents in everything, for this pleases the Lord. Fathers, do not provoke your children, lest they become discouraged (RSV).

Another favorite Scripture of mine makes it clear that a parent's relationship with his child should be modeled after God's relationship with man. In its ultimate beauty, that interaction is characterized by abundant love—a love unparalleled in tenderness and mercy. This same love leads the benevolent father to guide, correct—and even bring some pain to the child when it is necessary for his eventual good.

> "My son, do not regard lightly the discipline of the Lord, nor lose courage when you are punished by him. For the Lord disciplines him whom he loves [Note: Discipline and love work hand in hand; one being a function of the other], and chastises every son whom he receives." It is for discipline that you have to endure. God is treating you as sons; for what son is there whom his father does not discipline? If you are left without discipline, in which all have participated, then you are illegitimate children and not sons. Besides this, we have had earthly fathers to discipline us and we respected them. [Note: the relationship between discipline and respect was recognized more than 2,000 years ago.] For the moment all discipline seems painful rather than pleasant; later it yields the peaceful fruit of righteousness to those who have been trained by it (Heb. 12:5-9, 11 RSV).

The Book of Proverbs is replete with similar instructions to parents regarding the importance of authority and discipline. Let me quote a few examples:

> Foolishness is bound in the heart of a child; but the rod of correction shall drive it far from him (Prov. 22:15 KJV).
>
> Withhold not correction from the child: for if thou beatest him with the rod, he shall not die. Thou shalt beat him with the rod, and shalt deliver his soul from hell (Prov. 23:13, 14 KJV).
>
> He that spareth his rod hateth his son: but he that loveth him chasteneth him betimes (Prov. 13:24 KJV).
>
> The rod and reproof give wisdom: but a child left to himself bringeth his mother to shame (Prov. 29:15 KJV).
>
> Correct thy son, and he shall give thee rest; yea, he shall give delight unto thy soul (Prov. 29:17 KJV).

Why is parental authority so vigorously supported throughout the Bible? Is it simply catering to the whims of oppressive, power-hungry adults, as some modern educators surmise? No, the leadership of parents plays a significant role in the development of a child! By learning to yield to the loving authority (leadership) of his parents, a child learns to submit to other forms of authority which will confront him later in life. The way he sees his parents' leadership sets the tone for his eventual relationships with his teachers, school principal, police, neighbors, and employers. These forms of authority are necessary to healthy human relationships. Without respect for leadership, there is anarchy, chaos, and confusion for everyone concerned. And ultimately, of course, respect of earthly authority teaches children to yield to the benevolent authority of God Himself.

On this and other relevant issues, the Bible offers a consistent foundation on which to build an effective philosophy of parent-child relationships. It is my belief that we have departed from the standard which was clearly outlined in both the Old and New Testaments, and that deviation is costing us a heavy toll in the form of social turmoil. Self-control, human kindness, respect, and peacefulness can again be manifest in America if we will return to this ultimate resource in our homes and schools.[18]

SECTION 8

# THE "HOW TO" OF DISCIPLINE

**Philosophically, I recognize the need to take charge of my kids. But that isn't enough to help me discipline properly. Give me a step by step set of instructions that will help me do the job correctly.**

All right, let me outline six broad guidelines that I think you'll be able to apply. These principles represent the essence of my philosophy of discipline.

*First: Define the boundaries before they are enforced.* The most important step in any disciplinary procedure is to establish reasonable expectations and boundaries *in advance.* The child should know what is and what is not acceptable behavior *before* he is held responsible for those rules. This precondition will eliminate the overwhelming sense of injustice that a youngster feels when he is slapped or punished for his accidents, mistakes, and blunders. If you haven't defined it—don't enforce it!

*Second: When defiantly challenged, respond with confident decisiveness.* Once a child understands what is expected, he should then be held accountable for behaving accordingly. That sounds easy, but as we have seen, most children will assault the authority of their elders and challenge their right to lead. In a moment of rebellion, a little child will consider his parents' wishes and defiantly choose to disobey. Like a military general before a battle, he will calculate the potential risk, marshal his forces, and attack the enemy with guns blazing. When that nose-to-nose confrontation occurs between generations, it is *extremely* important for the adult to win decisively and confidently. The child has made it clear that he's looking for a fight, and his parents would be wise not to disappoint him! *Nothing* is more destructive to parental leadership than for a mother or father to disintegrate during that struggle. When the parent consistently loses those battles, resorting to tears and screaming and other evidence of frustration, some dramatic changes take place in the way they are "seen" by their children. Instead of being secure and confident leaders, they become spineless jellyfish who are unworthy of respect or allegiance.

*Third: Distinguish between willful defiance and childish irresponsibility.* A child should not be spanked for behavior that is not willfully defiant. When he forgets to feed the dog or make his bed or take out the trash—when he leaves your tennis racket outside in the rain or loses his bicycle—remember that these behaviors are typical of childhood. It is, more than likely, the mechanism by which an immature mind is protected from adult anxieties and pressures. Be gentle as you teach him to do better. If he fails to respond to your patient instruction, it then becomes appropriate to administer some well-defined consequences (he may have to work to pay for the item he abused or be deprived of its use, etc.). However, childish irresponsibility is very different from willful defiance, and should be handled more patiently.

*Fourth: Reassure and teach after the confrontation is over.* After a time of conflict during which the parent has demonstrated his right to lead (particularly if it resulted in tears for the child), the youngster between two and seven (or older) may want to be loved and reassured. By all means, open your arms and let him come! Hold him close and tell him of your love. Rock him gently and let him know, again, why he was punished and how he can avoid the trouble next time. This moment of communication builds love, fidelity, and family unity. And for the Christian family, it is extremely important to pray with the child at that time, admitting to God that we have *all* sinned and no one is perfect. Divine forgiveness is a marvelous experience, even for a very young child.

*Fifth: Avoid impossible demands.* Be absolutely sure that your child is *capable* of delivering what you require. Never punish him for wetting the bed involuntarily or for not becoming potty-trained by one year of age, or for doing poorly in school when he is incapable of academic success. These impossible demands put the child in an unresolvable conflict: there is no way out. That condition brings inevitable damage to human emotional apparatus.

*Sixth: Let love be your guide!* A relationship that is

characterized by genuine love and affection is likely to be a healthy one, even though some parental mistakes and errors are inevitable.[1]

**I want to control and lead my strong-willed child properly, but I'm afraid I'll break his spirit and damage his emotions in some way. How can I deal with his misbehavior without hurting his self-concept?**

I sense that you do not have a clear understanding of the difference between breaking the *spirit* of a child, and shaping his *will*. The human spirit, as I have defined it, relates to the self-esteem or the personal worth that a child feels. As such, it is exceedingly fragile at *all* ages and must be handled with care. You as a parent correctly assume that you can damage your child's spirit quite easily . . . by ridicule, disrespect, threats to withdraw love, and by verbal rejection. *Anything* that depreciates his self-esteem can be costly to his spirit.

However, while the spirit is brittle and must be treated gently, the will is made of steel. It is one of the few intellectual components which arrives full strength at the moment of birth. In a recent issue of *Psychology Today*, this heading described the research findings from a study of infancy: "A baby knows who he is before he has language to tell us so. He reaches deliberately for control of his environment, especially his parents." This scientific disclosure would bring no new revelation to the parents of a strong-willed infant. They have walked the floor with him in the wee small hours, listening to this tiny dictator as he made his wants and wishes abundantly clear.

Later, a defiant toddler can become so angry that he is capable of holding his breath until he loses consciousness. Anyone who has ever witnessed this full measure of willful defiance has been shocked by its power. One headstrong three-year-old recently refused to obey a direct command from her mother, saying, "You're just my *mommie*, you know!" Another mere mommie wrote me that she found herself in a similar confrontation with her three-year-old son over something that she wanted him to eat. He was so enraged by her insistence that he refused to eat or drink *anything* for two full days. He became weak and lethargic, but steadfastly held his ground. The mother was worried and guilt-ridden, as might be expected. Finally, in desperation, the father looked the child in the eyes and convinced him that he was going to receive a well deserved spanking if he didn't eat his dinner. With that maneuver, the contest was over. The toddler surrendered. He began to consume everything he could get his hands on, and virtually emptied the refrigerator.

Now tell me, please, why have so few child development authorities recognized this willful defiance? Why have they written so little about it? My guess is that the acknowledgment of childish imperfection would not fit neatly with the humanistic notion that little people are infused with sunshine and goodness, and merely "learn" the meaning of evil. To those who hold that rosy view I can only say, "Take another look!"

Returning to your question, your objective as a parent is to shape the will of your child while leaving his spirit intact.[2]

**Then how can I do that? How can I shape my nine-year-old son's will without damaging his spirit?**

It is accomplished by establishing reasonable boundaries and enforcing them with love, but by avoiding any implication that the child is unwanted, unnecessary, foolish, ugly, dumb, a burden, an embarrassment, or a disastrous mistake. Any accusation that assaults the worth of a child in this way can be costly, such as "You are so dumb!" Or, "Why can't you make decent grades in school like your sister?" Or, "You have been a pain in the neck ever since the day you were born!"

Rather, I would suggest that you respond decisively the next time your son behaves in a blatantly disruptive or defiant manner. There should be no screaming or derogatory accusations, although he should soon know that you mean what you say. He should probably be given a spanking and sent to bed an hour or two early. The following morning you should discuss the issue rationally, reassuring him of your continuing love, and then start over. Most rebellious preteenagers respond beautifully to this one-two punch of love and consistent discipline. It's an unbeatable combination.[3]

**My wife and I have a strong-willed child who is incredibly difficult to handle. I honestly believe we are doing our job about as well as any parents would do, yet she still breaks the rules and challenges our authority. I guess I need**

**some encouragement. First, tell me if an especially strong-willed kid *can* be made to smile and give and work and cooperate. If so, *how* is that accomplished? And second, what is my daughter's future? I see trouble ahead, but don't know if that gloomy forecast is justified.** There is no question about it. A willful child such as yours can be difficult to control even when her parents handle her with great skill and dedication. It may take several years to bring her to a point of relative obedience and cooperation within the family unit. While this training program is in progress, it is important not to panic. Don't try to complete the transformation overnight. Treat your child with sincere love and dignity, but require her to follow your leadership. Choose carefully the matters which are worthy of confrontation, then accept her challenge on those issues and *win* decisively. Reward every positive, cooperative gesture she makes by offering your attention, affection, and verbal praise. Then take two aspirin and call me in the morning.

Concerning that second half of your question, I must admit that your daughter, *if not properly disciplined*, would be in a "high risk" category for antisocial behavior later in life. Such a child is more likely to challenge her teachers in school and question the values she has been taught and shake her fist in the faces of those who would lead her. I believe that youngster is more inclined toward sexual promiscuity and drug abuse and academic difficulties. This is not an inevitable prediction, of course, because the complexities of human personality make it impossible to forecast behavior with complete accuracy.

On the other hand, these dangers I have described are greatly minimized by parents who actively seek to shape the will of the children during the early years. That's why the future of your daughter is not a negative one. It is my belief that a strong-willed child like yours typically possesses more character and has greater potential for a productive life than her compliant counterpart. The key to reaching that potential is to gain a measure of control of the child's will and then, at the appropriate moment, transfer that control to the individual as she approaches the end of adolescence.

Sounds easy, doesn't it? It's a tough assignment, but God will help you accomplish it.[4]

**You have described the nature of willfully defiant behavior and how parents should handle it. But does all unpleasant behavior result from this deliberate misbehavior?**

No. Disobedience can be very different in origin from the "challenging" response I've been describing. A child's antagonism and negativism may emanate from frustration, disappointment, fatigue, illness, or rejection, and therefore must be interpreted as a warning signal to be heeded. Perhaps the toughest task in parenthood is to recognize the difference between these behavioral messages. A child's resistant behavior always contains a message to his parents which they must decode before responding.

For example, he may be saying, "I feel unloved now that I'm stuck with that yelling baby brother. Mom used to care for me; now nobody wants me. I hate everybody." When this kind of message underlies the rebellion, the parents should move quickly to pacify its cause. When a two-year-old screams and cries at bedtime, one must ascertain what he is communicating. If he is genuinely frightened by the blackness of his room, the appropriate response should be quite different than if he is merely protesting about having to go nighty-night. The art of good parenthood revolves around the interpretation of behavior.[5]

**My six-year-old has suddenly become sassy and disrespectful in his manner at home. He told me to "buzz off" when I asked him to take out the trash, and he calls me names when he gets angry. I feel it is important to permit this emotional outlet, so I haven't suppressed it. Do you agree?**

I couldn't disagree more strongly. Your son is aware of his sudden defiance, and he's waiting to see how far you will let him go. This kind of behavior, if unchecked, will continue to deteriorate day by day, producing a more profound disrespect with each encounter. If you don't discourage it, you can expect some wild experiences during the adolescent years to come. Thus, the behavior for which punishment is most necessary is that involving a direct assault on the leadership and personhood of the parent (or teacher), especially when the child obviously knows he shouldn't be acting that way.

With regard to the ventilation of anger, it is possible to let a child express his strongest feelings without being insulting or disrespectful. A tearful charge, "You weren't fair with me and you embarrassed me in front of my friends," should be accepted and responded to quietly and earnestly. But a parent should never permit a child to say, "You are so stupid and I wish you would leave me alone!" The first statement is a genuine expression of frustration based on a specific issue; the second is an attack on the dignity and authority of the parent. In my opinion, the latter is damaging to both generations and should be inhibited.[6]

**How should I respond if my child says, "I hate you!" when he is angry?**

If my child screamed his hatred at me *for the first time* in a moment of red-faced anger, I would probably wait until his passion had cooled and then convey this message in a loving and sincere manner: "Charlie, I know you were very upset earlier today when we had our disagreement, and I think we should talk about what you are feeling. *All* children get angry at their parents now and then, especially when they feel unfairly treated. I understand your frustration and I'm sorry we got into such a hassle. But that does not excuse you for saying, 'I hate you!' You'll learn that no matter how upset I become over something you've done, I'll *never* tell you that I hate you. And I can't permit you to talk that way to me. When people love each other, as you and I do, they don't want to hurt one another. It hurt me for you to say that you hated me, just as you would be hurt if I said something like that to you. You can, however, tell me what angers you, and I will listen carefully. If I am wrong, I will do my best to change the things you dislike. So I want you to understand that you are free to say *anything* you wish to me as always, even if your feelings are not very pleasant. But you will never be permitted to scream and call names and throw temper tantrums. If you behave in those childish ways, I will have to punish you. Is there anything you need to say to me now? (If not, then put your arms around my neck because I love you!)"

My purpose would be to permit the ventilation of negative feelings without encouraging violent, disrespectful, manipulative behavior.[7]

**What is the most common error made by parents in disciplining their children?**

In my opinion, it is the inappropriate use of *anger* in attempting to control boys and girls. There is no more ineffective method of influencing human beings (of all ages) than the use of irritation and anger. Nevertheless, *most* adults rely primarily on their own emotional response to secure the cooperation of children. One teacher said on a national television program, "I like being a professional educator, but I hate the daily task of teaching. My children are so unruly that I have to stay mad at them all the time just to control the classroom." How utterly frustrating to be required to be mean and angry as part of a routine assignment, year in and year out. Yet many teachers (and parents) know of no other way to lead children. Believe me, it is exhausting and it doesn't work!

Consider your *own* motivational system. Suppose you are driving your automobile home from work this evening, and you exceed the speed limit by forty miles per hour. Standing on the street corner is a lone policeman who has not been given the means to arrest you. He has no squad car or motorcycle; he wears no badge, carries no gun, and can write no tickets. All he is commissioned to do is stand on the curb and scream insults as you speed past. Would you slow down just because he shakes his fist in protest? Of course not! You might wave to him as you streak by. His anger would achieve little except to make him appear comical and foolish.

On the other hand, nothing influences the way Mr. Motorist drives more than occasionally seeing a black and white vehicle in hot pursuit with nineteen red lights flashing in the rear view mirror. When his car is brought to a stop, a dignified, courteous patrolman approaches the driver's window. He is six foot nine, has a voice like the Lone Ranger, and carries a sawed-off shotgun on each hip. "Sir," he says firmly but politely, "our radar unit indicates you were traveling sixty-five miles per hour in a twenty-five mile per hour zone. May I see your driver's license please?" He opens his leatherbound book of citations and leans toward you. He has revealed no hostility and offers no criticisms, yet you immediately go to pieces. You fumble nervously to locate the small document in your wallet. (The one with the horrible Polaroid picture.) Why are your hands moist and your mouth dry? Why is your heart thumping in your throat? Because the course of *action* that John Law is about to take is notoriously unpleasant. Alas, it is his *action* which dramatically affects your future driving habits.

Disciplinary *action* influences behavior; anger does not. As a matter of fact, I am convinced that adult anger produces a destructive kind of disrespect in the minds of our children. They perceive that our frustration is caused by our inability to control the situation. We represent justice to them, yet we're on the verge of tears as we flail the air with our hands and shout empty threats and warnings. Let me ask: Would *you* respect a superior court judge who behaved that emotionally in administering legal justice? Certainly not. This is why the judicial system is carefully controlled to appear objective, rational, and dignified.

I am not recommending that parents and teachers conceal their legitimate emotions from their children. I am not suggesting that we be like bland and unresponsive robots who hold everything inside. There are times when our boys and girls become insulting or disobedient and our irritation is entirely appropriate. In fact, it *should* be revealed, or else we appear phony and unreal. My point is merely that anger often becomes a *tool* used consciously for the purpose of influencing behavior. It is ineffective and can be damaging to the relationship between generations.[8]

**What place should fear occupy in a child's attitude toward his mother or father?**

There is a narrow difference between acceptable, healthy "awe" and destructive fear. A child should have a general apprehension about the consequences of defying his parent. By contrast, he should not lie awake at night worrying about parental harshness or hostility. Perhaps a crude example will illustrate the difference between these aspects of fear. A busy highway can be a dangerous place to take a walk. In fact, it would be suicidal to stroll down the fast lane of a freeway at 6:00 P.M. on any Friday. I would not be so foolish as to get my exercise in that manner because I have a healthy fear of fast-moving automobiles. As long as I don't behave ridiculously, I have no cause for alarm. I am unthreatened by this source of danger because it only reacts to my willful defiance. I want my child to view me with the same healthy regard. As long as he does not choose to challenge me, openly and willfully, he lives in total safety. He need not duck and flinch when I suddenly scratch my eyebrow. He should have no fear that I will ridicule him or treat him unkindly. He can enjoy complete security and safety—until he chooses to defy me. Then he'll have to face the consequences. This concept of fear, which is better labeled "awe" or "respect," is modeled after God's relationship with man. "Fear of God is the beginning of wisdom," we are taught. He is a God of justice, and at the same time, a God of infinite love and mercy. These attributes are complementary, and should be represented to a lesser degree in our homes.[9]

**I have an especially defiant five-year-old son, and I'm doing my best to cope with the assignment of shaping his will. But to be honest with you, I suffer from great feelings of guilt and self-doubt most of the time. Lately, I have been depressed over the constant tug of war I'm in with this kid. Do other parents of strong-willed children feel the same?**

Yes, many do. One of the problems is that parents have been told by the "experts" that managing children is duck-soup for those who do it right. That leaves them with intense self-condemnation when things don't work that smoothly in their homes. No one told them that parenthood would be this difficult, and they blame themselves for the tension that arises. They had planned to be such loving and effective parents, reading fairy stories to their pajama-clad angels by the fireplace. The difference between life as it is and life as it ought to be is a frightening and distressing bit of reality.

I'm glad that you were able to verbalize your feelings of guilt and depression. That is important. In response, let me give you three assurances that will help you: (1) It *isn't* all your fault, (2) It won't always be so difficult, (3) You're probably doing a much better job than you think. Hang in there. Your strong-willed child will someday be a stalwart, respectable, hard-working citizen who's only source of depression will emanate from conflict with his own strong-willed child.[10]

**I find it easier to say "no" to my children than to say "yes," even when I don't feel strongly about the permission they are seeking. I wonder why I automatically respond so negatively.**

It is easy to fall into the habit of saying "no" to our kids.

"No, you can't go outside."

"No, you can't have a cookie."
"No, you can't use the telephone."
"No, you can't spend the night with a friend."

We parents could have answered affirmatively to all of these requests, but chose almost automatically to respond in the negative. Why? Because we didn't take time to stop and think about the consequences; because the activity could cause us more work or strain; because there could be danger in the request; because our children ask for a thousand favors a day and we find it convenient to refuse them all.

While every child needs to be acquainted with denial of some of his more extravagant wishes, there is also a need for parents to consider each request on its own merit. There are so many necessary "no's" in life that we should say "yes" whenever we can.

Dr. Fitzhugh Dodson extended this idea in his book *How to Father*, saying that your child "needs time with you when you are not demanding anything from him, time when the two of you are mutually enjoying yourselves." I agree![11]

**The children in our neighborhood are bratty with one another and disrespectful with adults. This upsets me, but I don't know what to do about it. I don't feel I have a right to discipline the children of my neighbors. How can I deal with this?**

Parents in a neighborhood *must* learn to talk to each other about their kids, but that takes some doing! There is no quicker way to anger one mother than for another woman to criticize her precious cub. It is a delicate subject, indeed. That's why the typical neighborhood is like yours, providing little "feedback" to parents in regard to the behavior of their children. The kids know there are no lines of communication between adults and they take advantage of the barrier. What each block needs is a mother who has the courage to say, "I want to be told what my child does when he is beyond his own yard. If he is a brat with other children, I would like to know it. If he is disrespectful with adults, please mention it to me. I will not consider it tattling and I won't resent your coming to me. I hope I can share my insights regarding your children, too. None of our sons and daughters is perfect, and we'll know better how to teach them if we can talk openly to each other as adults."[12]

**My husband and I are divorced, so I have to handle all the discipline of the children myself. How does this change the recommendations you've made about discipline in the home?**

Not at all. The principles of good discipline remain the same, regardless of the family setting. The procedures do become somewhat harder for one parent, like yourself, to implement, since you have no one to support you when the children become defiant. You have to play the role of father *and* mother, which is not easily done. Nevertheless, children do not make allowances for your handicap. You must demand their respect or you will not receive it.[13]

**My little girl is sometimes sugar-sweet, and other times she is unbearably irritating. How can I get her out of a bad mood when she has not really done anything to deserve punishment?**

I would suggest that you take her in your arms and talk to her in this manner: "I don't know whether you've noticed it or not, but you have two 'personalities.' A personality is a way of acting and talking and behaving. One of your personalities is sweet and loving. No one could possibly be more lovable and happy when this personality is in control. It likes to work and look for ways to make the rest of the family happy. And all you have to do is press a little red button, 'ding,' and out comes the other personality. It is cranky and noisy and silly. It wants to fight with your brother and disobey your mom. It gets up grouchy in the morning and complains throughout the day.

"Now, I know that you can press the button for the neat personality or you can call up the mean one. Sometimes it takes some punishment to make you press the right button. If you keep on pressing the wrong one, like you have been today, then I'm going to make you uncomfortable, one way or the other. I'm tired of that cranky character and I want to see the grinny one. Can we make a deal?"

When discipline becomes a game, as in a conversation such as this, then you've achieved your purpose without conflict and animosity.[14]

**Our six-year-old is extremely negative and disagreeable. He makes the entire family miserable and our attempts to discipline him have been ineffective. He just happens to have a sour disposition. How should we deal with him?**
The objective with such a child is to define the needed changes and then reinforce those improvements when they occur. Unfortunately, attitudes are abstractions that a six-year-old may not fully understand, and you need a system that will clarify the "target" in his mind. Toward this end, I have developed an Attitude Chart (see illustration) which translates these subtle mannerisms into concrete mathematical terms. Please note: This system which follows would *not* be appropriate for the child who merely has a bad day, or displays temporary unpleasantness associated with illness, fatigue, or environmental circumstances. Rather, it is a remedial tool to help change persistently negative and disrespectful attitudes by making the child conscious of his problem.

The Attitude Chart should be prepared and then reproduced, since a separate sheet will be needed every day. Place an X in the appropriate square for each category, and then add the total points "earned" by bedtime. Although this nightly evaluation process has the appearance of being objective to a child, it is obvious that the parent can influence the outcome by considering it in advance (it's called cheating). Mom or Dad may want Junior to receive eighteen points on the first night, barely missing the punishment but realizing he must stretch the following day. I must emphasize, however, that the system will fail miserably if a naughty child does not receive the punishment he deserves, or if he hustles to improve but does not obtain the family fun he was promised. This approach is nothing more than a method of applying reward and punishment to attitudes in a way that children can understand and remember.

For the child who does not fully comprehend the concept of numbers, it might be helpful to plot the daily totals on a cumulative graph, such as the one provided below.

I don't expect everyone to appreciate this system or to apply it at home. In fact, parents of compliant, happy children will be puzzled as to why it would ever be needed. However, the mothers and fathers of sullen, ill-tempered children will comprehend more quickly. Take it or leave it, as the situation warrants.[15]

## MY ATTITUDE CHART

______________
DATE

| | 1 EXCELLENT | 2 GOOD | 3 OKAY | 4 BAD | 5 TERRIBLE |
|---|---|---|---|---|---|
| My Attitude Toward Mother | | | | | |
| My Attitude Toward Dad | | | | | |
| My Attitude Toward Sister | | | | | |
| My Attitude Toward Friends | | | | | |
| My Attitude Toward Work | | | | | |
| My Attitude At Bedtime | | | | | |

TOTAL POINTS ____________

## CONSEQUENCES

| | |
|---|---|
| 6–9 POINTS | The family will do something fun together. |
| 10–18 POINTS | Nothing happens, good or bad. |
| 19–20 POINTS | I have to stay in my room for one hour. |
| 21–22 POINTS | I get one swat with belt. |
| 23+ POINTS | I get two swats with belt. |

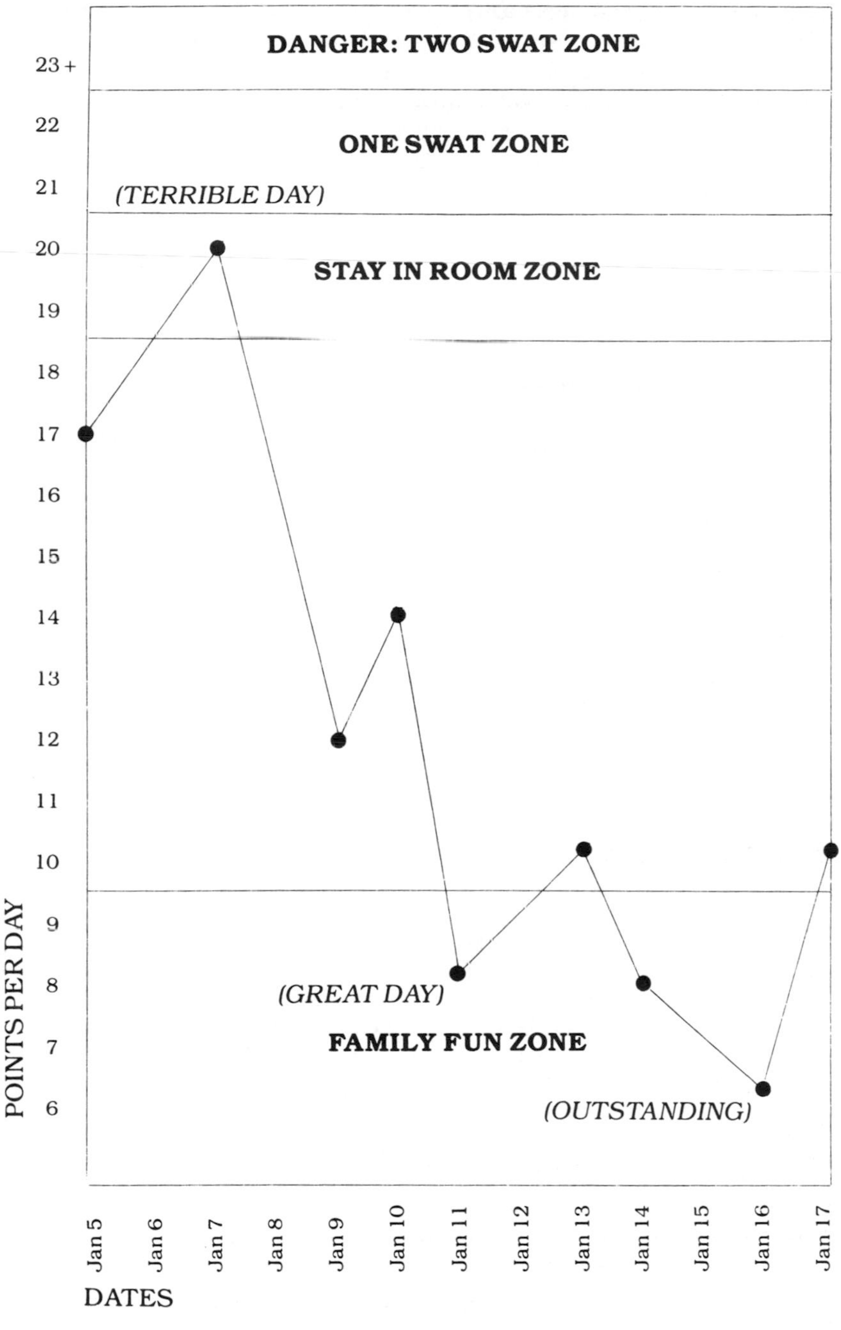

DANGER: TWO SWAT ZONE
ONE SWAT ZONE
(TERRIBLE DAY)
STAY IN ROOM ZONE
(GREAT DAY)
FAMILY FUN ZONE
(OUTSTANDING)
POINTS PER DAY
23 +
22
21
20
19
18
17
16
15
14
13
12
11
10
9
8
7
6
Jan 5
Jan 6
Jan 7
Jan 8
Jan 9
Jan 10
Jan 11
Jan 12
Jan 13
Jan 14
Jan 15
Jan 16
Jan 17
DATES

**My four-year-old son came into the house and told me he had seen a lion in the backyard. He was not trying to be funny. He really tried to convince me that this lie was true and became quite upset when I didn't believe him. I want him to be an honest and truthful person. Should I have spanked him?**
Definitely not. There is a *very* thin line between fantasy and reality in the mind of a preschool child, and he often confuses the two. This occurred when I took my son to Disneyland at three years of age. He was absolutely terrified by the wolf who stalked around with the three pigs. Ryan took one look at those sharp, jagged teeth and screamed in terror. I have a priceless motion picture of him scrambling for the safety of his mother's arms. After we returned home, I told Ryan there was a "very nice man" inside the wolf suit, who wouldn't hurt anyone. My son was so relieved by that news that he needed to hear it repeatedly.

He would say, "Dad?"

"What, Ryan?"

"Tell me 'bout that nice man!"

You see, Ryan was not able to distinguish between the fantasy character and a genuine threat to his health and safety. I would guess your son's lion story was a product of the same kind of confusion. He may well have believed that a lion was in the backyard. Thus, you would have been wise to play along with the game while making it perfectly clear that you didn't believe the story. You could have said, "My! My! A lion in the backyard. I sure hope he is a friendly old cat. Now, Billy, please wash your hands and come eat lunch."[16]

**At times I feel that I am overreacting to insignificant issues and at other times I fail to respond to an act of deliberate defiance. How can I know when to ignore a misbehavior and when to confront my child?**
The ability to "read" your child's thoughts and feelings is a skill that can be learned by the mother and father who take the time to study the behavior of their kids. Ultimately, the key to competent parenthood is in being able to get behind the eyes of your child, seeing what he sees and feeling what he feels. When he is lonely, he needs your company. When he is defiant, he needs your help in controlling his impulses. When he is afraid, he needs the security of your embrace. When he is curious, he

needs your patient instruction. When he is happy, he needs to share his laughter and joy with those he loves.

Thus, the parent who learns to comprehend his child's feelings is in a position to respond appropriately and meet the needs that are apparent. And at this point, raising healthy children becomes a highly developed art, requiring the greatest wisdom, patience, devotion and love that God has given to us. The Apostle Paul called the Christian life a "reasonable service." We parents would do well to apply that same standard to the behavior of our children.

SECTION 9

# SPANKINGS: WHEN, HOW, AND WHY

**As an advocate of spankings as a disciplinary tool, don't you worry about the possibility that you might be contributing to the incidence of child abuse in this country?**

Yes, I do worry about that. One of my great frustrations in teaching parents has been the difficulty in conveying a *balanced* environment, wherein discipline is evident when necessary, but where it is matched by patience and respect and affection. Let it never be said that I favor the "slap 'em across the mouth" approach to authoritarianism. That hostile manner wounds the spirit and inflicts permanent scars on the psyche.

*No* subject distresses me more than the phenomenon of child abuse which is so prevalent in America today. There are children all across the country, even while I write, who are suffering untold miseries at the hands of their parents. Some of these pitiful little tots are brought to our hospital in every imaginable condition. They have been burned and bruised and broken and their little minds are permanently warped by the awful circumstances into which they were born.

Every professional who works with hurt children has to learn to cope with his own empathy. I have gained a measure of control over my own emotions; however, I have never been able to observe a battered child without feeling a literal agony within my chest. Diseased children suffer, of course, but most of them experience some degree of parental love which provides an emotional undergirding. But battered children suffer physically *and* emotionally. For them, no one cares. No one understands. There is no one to whom the longings can be expressed. They cannot escape. They cannot explain why they are hated. And many of them are too young to develop defense mechanisms or even call for help.

I dealt this spring with an eight-year-old girl who had been sexually assaulted repeatedly by her alcoholic father since she was fifteen months of age. What an immeasurable tragedy! Another child in Los Angeles was blinded by his mother, who destroyed his eyes with a razor blade. Can you imagine going through life knowing that your handicap resulted from a deliberate act by your own mother? Another small child in our city was pushed from a car on a crowded freeway and left clinging to the chain link divider for eight or nine hours. Another child's feet were held to a hot iron as punishment.

Just recently, a radio news summary broadcast through my office intercom told of finding a ten-year-old girl hanging by her heels in her parents' garage. These kinds of horror stories are all too familiar to those of us who work with children. In fact, it is highly probable that some youngster within a mile or two of your house is experiencing destructive abuse in one manner or another. Brian G. Fraser, attorney for the National Center for Prevention and Treatment of Child Abuse and Neglect, has written: "Child abuse . . . once thought to be primarily a problem of the poor and down-trodden . . . occurs in every segment of society and may be the country's leading cause of death in children."

The last thing on earth that I want to do is to provide a rationalization and justification for such parental oppression. Let me say it again: I don't believe in harsh, inflexible discipline, even when it is well intentioned. Children must be given room to breathe and grow and love. But there are also threatening circumstances at the permissive end of the spectrum, and many parents fall into one trap in an earnest attempt to avoid the other. These dual dangers were beautifully described by Marguerite and Willard Beecher, writing in their book *Parents on the Run:*[1]

> The adult-centered home of yesteryear made parents the masters and children their slaves. The child-centered home of today has made parents the slaves and children the masters. There is no true cooperation in any master-slave relationship, and therefore no democracy. Neither the restrictive-authoritative technique of rearing children nor the newer "anything goes" technique develop the genius within the individual, because neither trains him to be self-reliant . . . .

> Children reared under arbitrary rules become either spineless automatons or bitter revolutionaries who waste their lives in conflict with those around them. But children who know no law higher than their own passing fancy become trapped by their own appetites. In either case, they are slaves. The former are enslaved by leaders on whom they depend to tell them what to do, and the latter are enslaved by the pawnbroker. Neither are [sic] capable of maintaining society on any decent basis. A lifetime of unhappiness may be avoided if the twig is bent so the tree will not incline in either of these mistaken directions.[2]

**There is so much controversy now over the use of corporal punishment (spanking) that I would like to hear your rationale for the use of this approach. Specifically, what do you say to those who believe corporal punishment teaches children to hit and hurt others?**

I debated a psychologist who held that view, on the Phil Donahue television show a few years ago. Let me quote from a comment attributed to Dr. John Valusek by *Parade Magazine*.

> "The way to stop violence in America is to stop spanking children," argues psychologist John Valusek. In a speech to the Utah Association for Mental Health some weeks ago, Valusek declared that parental spanking promotes the thesis that violence against others is acceptable.
>
> "Spanking is the first half-inch on the yardstick of violence," said Valusek. "It is followed by hitting and ultimately by rape, murder, and assassination. The modeling behavior that occurs at home sets the stage: 'I will resort to violence when I don't know what else to do.' "[3]

How ridiculous it seems to blame America's obsession with violence on the disciplinary efforts of loving parents! This conclusion is especially foolish in view of the bloody fare offered to our children on television each day. The average sixteen-year-old has watched 18,000 murders during his formative years, including a daily bombardment of knifings, shootings, hangings, decapitations, and general dismemberment. Thus, it does seem strange that the psychological wizards of our day search elsewhere for the cause of brutality—and eventually point the finger of blame at the parents who are diligently training our future responsible citizens. Yet this is the kind of "press" that has been given in recent years to parents who believe in spanking their disobedient children.

Opposition to corporal punishment can be summarized by four common arguments, all of them based on error and misunderstanding. The first is represented by Dr. Valusek's statement, and assumes that spankings teach children to hit and hurt others. It depicts corporal punishment as a hostile physical attack by an angry parent whose purpose is to damage or inflict harm on his little victim. Admittedly, that kind of violence does occur regularly between generations and is tremendously destructive to children. However, corporal punishment in the hands of a loving parent is altogether different in purpose and practice. It is a teaching tool by which harmful behavior is inhibited, rather than a wrathful attempt by one person to damage another. One is an act of love; the other is an act of hostility, and they are as different as night and day.

I responded to Dr. Valusek's argument in my previous book, *Hide or Seek*, showing the place of minor pain in teaching children to behave responsibly:

> Those same specialists also say that a spanking teaches your child to hit others, making him a more violent person. Nonsense! If your child has ever bumped his arm against a hot stove, you can bet he'll never deliberately do that again. He does not become a more violent person because the stove burnt him. In fact, he learned a valuable lesson from the pain. Similarly, when he falls out of his high chair or smashes his finger in the door or is bitten by a grumpy dog, he learns about the physical dangers in his world. These bumps and bruises throughout childhood are nature's way of teaching him that the physical world around him must be respected. They do not damage his self-esteem. They do not make him vicious. They merely acquaint him with reality. In like manner, an appropriate spanking from a loving parent in a moment of defiance provides the same service. It tells him there are not only physical dangers to be avoided, but he must steer clear of some social traps as well (selfishness, defiance, dishonesty, unprovoked aggression, etc.).[4]

The second rationale against corporal punishment can also be found in Dr. Valusek's concluding sentence, "I will resort to violence (spankings) when I don't know what else to do." Do you see the subtlety of this quotation? It characterizes a spanking as an absolute last resort—as the final act of exasperation and frustration. As such, it comes on the heels of screaming, threatening, hand-wringing, and buckets of tears. Even those authorities who recommend corporal punishment often fall into this trap, suggesting that it be applied only when all else has failed. I couldn't disagree more strongly.

A spanking is to be reserved for use in response to willful defiance, *whenever it occurs.* Period! It is much more effective to apply it early in the conflict, while the parent's emotional apparatus is still under control, than after ninety minutes of scratching and clawing. In fact, child abuse is more likely to occur when a little youngster is permitted to irritate and agitate and sass and disobey and pout for hours, until finally the parent's anger reaches a point of explosion where anything can happen (and often does). Professionals like Dr. Valusek have inadvertently contributed to violence against children, in my view, because they have stripped parents of the right to correct children's routine behavior problems while they are of minor irritation. Then when these small frustrations accumulate, the parent does (as Valusek said) "resort to violence when he doesn't know what else to do."

The third common argument against spanking comes from the findings of animal psychology. If a mouse is running in a maze, he will learn much faster if the experimenter rewards his correct turns with food than he will if his incorrect choices are punished with a mild electric shock. From this and similar studies has come the incredible assumption that punishment has little influence on human behavior. But human beings are not mice, and it is naive to equate them simplistically. Obviously, a child is capable of rebellious and defiant attitudes which have no relevance to a puzzled mouse sitting at a crossroads in a maze. I agree that it would not help boys and girls learn to read by shocking them for each mispronounced word. On the other hand, deliberate disobedience involves the child's perception of parental authority and his obligations to accept it (whereas the mouse does not even know the experimenter exists).

If punishment doesn't influence human behavior, then why is the issuance of speeding citations by police so effective in controlling traffic on a busy street? Why, then, do homeowners rush to get their tax payments in the mail to avoid a 6 percent penalty for being late? If punishment has no power, then why does a well-deserved spanking often turn a sullen little troublemaker into a sweet and loving angel? Rat psychology notwithstanding, both reward and punishment play an important role in shaping human behavior, and neither should be discounted. Leonardo da Vinci hadn't heard about the mouse in the maze when he wrote, "He who does not punish evil commands it to be done!"

The fourth argument against the judicious practice of spanking comes from those who see it as damaging to the dignity and self-worth of the child. Suffice it to say at this point that a child is fully capable of discerning whether his parent is conveying love or hatred. This is why the youngster who knows he deserves a spanking appears almost relieved when it finally comes. Rather than being insulted by the discipline, he understands its purpose and appreciates the control it gives him over his own impulses.

This childish comprehension was beautifully illustrated by a father who told me of a time when his five-year-old son was disobeying in a restaurant. This lad was sassing his mother, flipping water on his younger brother, and deliberately making a nuisance of himself. After four warnings went unheeded, the father took his son by the arm and marched him to the parking lot where he proceeded to administer a spanking. Watching this episode was a meddling woman who had followed them out of the restaurant and into the parking lot. When the punishment began, she shook her finger at the father and screamed, "Leave that boy alone! Turn him loose! If you don't stop I'm going to call the police!" The five-year-old, who had been crying and jumping, immediately stopped yelling and said to his father in surprise, "What's wrong with that woman, Dad?" He understood the purpose for the discipline, even if the "rescuer" didn't. I only wish that Dr. Valusek and his contemporaries were as perceptive as this child.

Let me hasten to emphasize that corporal punishment is not the only tool for use in shaping the will, nor is it appropriate at all ages and for all situations. The wise parent must understand the physical and emotional characteristics of each stage in childhood, and then fit the discipline to a boy's or girl's individual needs.[5]

**Can you provide some "ground-rules" for the use of corporal punishment for strong-willed toddlers?**

Mild spankings can begin between fifteen and eighteen months of age. They should be relatively infrequent, and must be reserved for clear defiance, not childish irresponsibility. A heavy hand of authority during this period causes the child to suppress his need to experiment and test his environment, which can have long lasting consequences. The toddler should be taught to obey and yield to parental leadership, but that end result will not be accomplished overnight.

When spankings occur, they should be administered with a neutral object; that is, with a small switch or belt, but rarely with the hand. I have always felt that the hand should be seen by the child as an object of love rather than an instrument of punishment. Furthermore, if a parent commonly slaps a youngster when he is not expecting to be hit, then he will probably duck and flinch whenever Father suddenly scratches his ear. And, of course, a slap in the face can reposition the nose or do permanent damage to the ears or jaw. If all spankings are administered with a neutral object, applied where intended, then the child need never fear that he will suddenly be chastised for some accidental indiscretion. (There are exceptions to this rule, such as when a child's hands are slapped or thumped for reaching for a stove or other dangerous object.)

Should a spanking hurt? Yes, or else it will have no influence. A swat on the behind through three layers of wet diapers simply conveys no urgent message. However, a small amount of pain for a young child goes a long way; it is certainly not necessary to lash or "whip" him. Two or three stinging strokes on the legs or bottom with a switch are usually sufficient to emphasize the point, "You must obey me." And finally, it is important to spank *immediately* after the offense, or not at all. A toddler's memory is not sufficiently developed to permit even a ten-minute delay in the administration of justice. Then after the episode is over and the tears have subsided, the child might want to be held and reassured by his mother or father. By all means, let him come. Embrace him in the security of your loving arms. Rock him softly. Tell him how much you love him and why he must "mind his mommie." This moment can be the most important event in the entire day. And for the Christian family, it is extremely important to pray with the child at that time, admitting to God we have *all* sinned and no one is perfect. Divine forgiveness is a marvelous experience, even for a very young child.[6]

**How long do you think a child should be allowed to cry after being punished or spanked? Is there a limit?**
Yes, I believe there should be a limit. As long as the tears represent a genuine release of emotion, they should be permitted to fall. But crying quickly changes from inner sobbing to an exterior weapon. It becomes a tool of protest to punish the enemy. Real crying usually lasts two minutes or less, but may continue for five. After that point, the child is merely complaining, and the change can be recognized in the tone and intensity of his voice. I would require him to stop the protest crying, usually by offering him a little more of whatever caused the original tears. For the younger child, the crying can easily be stopped by getting him interested in something else.[7]

**I have spanked my children for their disobedience and it didn't seem to help. Does this approach fail with some children?**
Children are so tremendously variable that it is sometimes hard to believe that they are all members of the same human family. Some children can be crushed with nothing more than a stern look; others seem to require strong and even painful disciplinary measures to make a vivid impression. This difference usually results from the degree to which a child needs adult approval and acceptance. The primary parental task is to get behind the eyes of the child, thereby tailoring the discipline to his unique perception.

In a direct answer to your question, it is not this individual variation that causes spanking to be ineffectual in most cases. When disciplinary measures fail, it is usually because of fundamental errors in their application. It is possible for twice the amount of punishment to yield half the results. I have made a study of situations where the parent has told me that the child ignores the spankings he receives, going back to violate the same rule. There are four basic reasons for the lack of success:

1. The most recurring problem results from infrequent, whimsical punishment. Half the time the child is not punished for a particular act of defiance; the other half of the time he is held accountable for it. Children need to know the certainty of justice.

2. The child may be more strong-willed than the parent, and they both know it. If he can outlast a temporary onslaught, he has won a major battle, eliminating punishment as a tool in the

parent's repertoire. Even though Mom spanks him, he wins the battle by defying her again. The solution to this situation is obvious: outlast him; win, even if it takes a repeated measure. The experience will be painful for both participants, but the benefits will come tomorrow and tomorrow and tomorrow.

3. The parent suddenly decides to employ this form of punishment after doing nothing for a year or two prior to that time. It takes a child a while to respond to a new procedure in this manner, and the parent might get discouraged during the adjustment period.

4. The spanking may be too gentle. If it doesn't hurt, it isn't worth avoiding next time. A slap with the hand on the bottom of a multi-diapered thirty-month-old is not a deterrent to anything. It isn't necessary to beat a child, certainly, but he should be able to "feel" the message.

There *are* some children for whom spankings do not work. Notably, I've seen hyperactive children who are greatly agitated by any response which excites their nervous system. In these and related cases, other forms of discipline must be applied.[8]

**Is my ten-year-old too old to be spanked?**
Physical punishment should be relatively infrequent during the period immediately prior to adolescence. Of course, some strong-willed children absolutely demand to be spanked, and their wishes should be granted. However, the compliant youngster should have experienced his last woodshed experience by the end of his first decade (or even four years earlier).[9]

**I would like to hear your views about disciplining a teenager, especially since you say spanking him is neither wise nor productive.**
Your only tool of discipline is to manipulate your teenager's environmental circumstances in moments of confrontation. You have the keys to the family automobile and can allow your son or daughter to use it (or be chauffeured in it). You may grant or withhold privileges, including permission to go to a party. You control the family purse and can choose to share it or loan it or dole it or close it. And you can "ground" your adolescent or deny him the use of the telephone or television for awhile.

Now obviously, these are not very influential "motivators,"

and are at times totally inadequate for the situation at hand. After we have appealed to reason and cooperation and family loyalty, all that remains are relatively weak methods of "punishment." We can only link behavior of our kids with desirable and undesirable consequences and hope the connection will be of sufficient influence to elicit their cooperation.

If that sounds pretty wobbly-legged, let me admit what I am implying: a willful, angry sixteen-year-old boy or girl *can* win a confrontation with his or her parents today, if worst comes to worst. The law leans ever more in the direction of emancipation of the teenager. He can leave home in many areas and avoid being returned. He can drink and smoke pot and break many other civil laws before he is punished by society. His girl friend can obtain birth control pills in many states without her parents' knowledge or permission. And if that fails, she can slip into a clinic for an unannounced abortion. Very few "adult" privileges and vices can be denied a teenager who has the passion for independence and a will to fight.

How different was the situation when Billy-Joe was raised on the farm in days of old, living perhaps eight or ten miles by horseback from the home of his nearest contemporary. His dad, Farmer Brown, impressed by his own authority, could "talk sense" to his rebellious boy without the interference of outside pressures. There is no doubt that it was much easier for father and son to come to terms while siting on a plow at the far end of Forgotten Field.

But today, every spark of adolcscent discontent is fanned into a smoldering flame. The grab for the teen dollar has become big business, with enticing magazines, record companies, radio, television, and concert entrepreneurs to cater to each youthful whim. And, of course, masses of high school students congregate idly in the city and patronize those obliging companies. They have become a force to be considered.

Unless teenagers have an inner tug toward cooperation and responsibility, the situation can get nasty very quickly. But where does that voice of restraint originate? It has been my contention that the early years of childhood are vital to the establishment of respect between generations. Without that kind of foundation—without a touch of awe in the child's perception of his parent—then the balance of power and control is definitely shifted toward the younger combatant. I would be doing a disservice to my readers if I implied otherwise.[10]

SECTION 10

# THE SOURCE OF SELF-ESTEEM IN CHILDREN

**Why are feelings of inadequacy and inferiority so prevalent among people of all ages at this time?**

The current epidemic of self-doubt has resulted from a totally unjust and unnecessary system of evaluating human worth now prevalent in our society. Not everyone is seen as worthy; not everyone is accepted. Instead, we reserve our praise and admiration for a select few who have been blessed from birth with the characteristics we value most highly. It is a vicious system, and we, as parents, must counterbalance its impact.

It seems that human worth in our society is carefully reserved for those who meet certain rigid specifications. The beautiful people are born with it; those who are highly intelligent are likely to find approval; superstar athletes are usually respected. But no one is considered valuable just because he *is!* Social acceptability is awarded rather carefully, making certain to exclude those who are unqualified.[1]

**When you speak of "rigid specifications" on which human worth is evaluated, what characteristics rank the highest to us?**

At the top of the list of the most highly respected and valued attributes in our culture is *physical attractiveness.* Those who happen to have it are often honored and even feared; those who do not may be disrespected and rejected through no fault of their own. Though it seems incredibly unfair, this measure of human worth is evident from the earliest moments of life, when an attractive infant is considered more valuable than a homely one. For this reason, it is not uncommon for a mother to be very depressed shortly after the birth of her first baby. She knew that most newborns are rather ungamely, but she hadn't expected such a disaster! In fact, she had secretly hoped to give birth to a grinning, winking, blinking six-week-old Gerber baby, having four front teeth and rosy, pink cheeks. Instead, they hand her a red, toothless, bald, prune-faced, screaming little creature whom she often wants to send back. You see, the personal worth of that one-day-old infant is actually doubted by his parents.

As the child grows, his value as a person will be assessed not only by his parents, but also by those outside his home. Beauty contests offering scholarships and prizes for gorgeous babies are now common, as if the attractive child didn't already have enough advantages awaiting him in life. This distorted system of evaluating human worth can be seen in a thousand examples. You may recall the tragic incident that occurred in Chicago during the sixties, when eight student nurses were viciously murdered. The following day, a commentator was discussing the violent event on the radio, and he said, "The thing that makes this tragedy much worse is that all eight of these girls were so attractive!" In other words, the girls were more valuable human beings because of their beauty, making their loss more tragic. If one accepts that statement, then the opposite is also true: the murders would have been less tragic if homely girls were involved. The conclusion, as written by George Orwell, is inescapable: "All [people] are equal, but some [people] are more equal than others."

My point is that from the earliest experience of life, a child begins to learn the social importance of physical beauty. The values of his society cannot be kept from his little ears, and many adults do not even try to conceal their bias.[2]

**How do feelings of inferiority get started? It seems as though I've always felt inadequate, but I can't remember where it all began.**

You don't remember it because your self-doubt originated during your earliest days of conscious existence. A little child is born with an irrepressible inclination to question his own worth; it is as "natural" as his urge to walk and talk. At first, it is a primitive assessment of his place in the home, and then it extends outward to his early social contacts beyond the front door. These initial impressions of who he is have a profound effect on his developing personality, particularly if the experiences are painful. It is not uncommon for a prekindergartener to have concluded already that he is terribly ugly, incredibly dumb, unloved, unneeded, foolish, or strange.

These early feelings of inadequacy may remain relatively tranquil and subdued during the elementary school years. They lurk just below the conscious mind and are never far from awareness. But the child with the greatest self-doubts constantly "accumulates" evidence of his inferiority during these middle years. Each failure is recorded in vivid detail. Every unkind remark is inscribed in his memory. Rejection and ridicule scratch and nick his delicate ego all through the "quiet" years. Then it happens! He enters adolescence and his world explodes from within. All of the accumulated evidence is resurrected and propelled into his conscious mind with volcanic forcefulness. He will deal with that experience for the rest of his life. Have you done the same?[3]

**Why do people seem to be more conscious of their physical flaws and inadequacies now than in the past? What accounts for the "epidemic" of inferiority which you described?**

I believe this tremendous emphasis on physical attractiveness is a by-product of the sexual revolution going on around us. Our society has been erotically supercharged since the mid-sixties when the traditional moral standards and restraints began to collapse. Television, radio, magazines, movies, billboards, literature and clothing all reflect this unparalleled fascination with sensuality of various sorts. Now obviously, when sex becomes all-important in a society, as we are witnessing, then each person's sex appeal and charm take on new social significance. Simply stated, the more steamed up a culture becomes over sex, the more it will reward beauty and punish ugliness.

It is my view that the increased sensuality in America during the seventies and eighties is generating a higher incidence of emotional casualties among people who are intensely aware of their inability to compete in the flirtatious game. If beauty represents the necessary currency (the gold coin of worth), then they are undeniably bankrupt. And sadly, the most vulnerable victims of this foolish measure of human worth are the little children who are too young to understand, too immature to compensate, and too crushed to fight back.[4]

**I understand how society evaluates the worth of a child on the basis of his physical attractiveness. But how does *he* learn of that assessment so early? By what mechanism does this cultural attitude get transmitted to preschool kids?**

They can hardly miss it in the world around them. It's a dull child who fails to notice that the ugly do not win Miss America contests; the ugly do not become cheerleaders; the ugly seldom star in movies; the ugly may not get married; the ugly have fewer friends; the ugly are less desirable! Furthermore, in examining the traditional literature of childhood, I am amazed to see how many of the age-old stories center around physical attractiveness in one form or another. Consider these examples:

*The Ugly Duckling.* Here is a familiar story about an unhappy little bird who was rejected by the better-looking ducks. The ugly duckling was disturbed by his grotesque appearance. Fortunately for him, however, he had a beautiful swan inside which surfaced in young adulthood. (The story does not mention the ugly duckling who grew up to be an ugly duck!) How many children wait patiently for their beautiful swan to appear, seeing things go from bad to worse during adolescence?

*Rudolph the Red-Nosed Reindeer.* Rudolph had a weird nose which caused him to be rejected by his fellow reindeer. This story has nothing to do with reindeer; it has everything to do with children. This is how they treat the physically peculiar. They are rejected and ridiculed. The only way the world's "Rudolphs" can gain acceptance is to perform some miraculous feat, symbolized by the gallant sleigh ride in the snowstorm.

*Dumbo the Elephant.* Dumbo was ridiculed for having big floppy ears, until he used them to fly. The theme is remarkably similar to the plight of poor Rudolph. It appears repeatedly in the literature of the young because of its common occurrence in the lives of children themselves.

*Snow White and the Seven Dwarfs.* The evil queen asked the fateful question, "Mirror, mirror on the wall, who's the fairest of them all?" I am still awed by the crassness of her question considering all of the possibilities to which a magic mirror might respond! Yet the motivation behind her request is clear: the fairest of them all was the most noble, worthy person in the land. Perhaps she still reigns.

*Cinderella.* The primary difference between Cinderella and her two wicked stepsisters was a matter of beauty. Any illustrated story of Cinderella will reveal that fact. Sure,

Cinderella was ragged and uncombed, but the basic ingredient was there. It wasn't the pumpkin and the mice that shook up the prince when Cinderella arrived at the ball. You can bet she was a pretty little thing.

My point is that we are incredibly effective in teaching very young children the importance of personal beauty. *All* children learn it shortly after babyhood! We could do no better if our best educators convened to design a fool proof instructional system.[5]

**What role do teachers play in emphasizing the importance of physical attractiveness?**

Unfortunately, teachers are products of the same society which molds the values and attitudes of everyone else. They are often repelled by the physically unattractive child and drawn to the cutie.

Two researchers, Ellen Berscheid and Elaine Walster, published their startling findings in a classic article, "Beauty and the Best," in *Psychology Today* (March 1972). Consider the impact of these biases against the homely youngster.

1. Evidence seems to include that academic grades given to students are influenced by the attractiveness of the child.
2. When shown a set of children's pictures and asked to identify the child who probably created the classroom disturbance (or some similar act of misconduct), adults were likely to select an unattractive child as the offender. Likewise, the ugly child was thought to be more dishonest than his cute peer.
3. According to the findings of Karen Dion, the way an adult handles a discipline problem is related to the attractiveness of the child. In other words, the *same* misbehavior is likely to be handled more permissively for the cute youngster and more severely for his ugly classmate.
4. Most important (and correlating with my observations), the impact of physical attractiveness is well established in nursery school! Cute little three-year-olds already enjoy greater popularity among their peers. And unfortunately, certain physical features, such as fatness, are already recognized and disliked at this tender age.[6]

**What are the prospects for the very pretty or handsome child? Does he usually have smooth sailing all the way?** He has some remarkable advantages, as I have described. He is much more likely to accept himself and enjoy the benefits of self-confidence. However, he also faces some unique problems which the homely child never experiences. Beauty in our society is power, and power can be dangerous in immature hands. A fourteen-year-old nymphet, for example, who is prematurely curved and rounded in all the right places may be pursued vigorously by males who would exploit her beauty. As she becomes more conscious of her flirtatious power, she is sometimes urged toward promiscuity. Furthermore, women who have been coveted physically since early childhood, such as Marilyn Monroe or Brigitte Bardot, may become bitter and disillusioned by the depersonalization of body worship.

Research also indicates some interesting consequences in regard to marital stability for the "beautiful people." In one important study, the more attractive college girls were found to be less happily married twenty-five years later. It is apparently difficult to reserve the "power" of sex for one mate, ignoring the ego gratification which awaits outside the marriage bonds. And finally, the more attractive a person is in his youth, the more painful is the aging process.

My point is this: the measurement of worth on a scale of beauty is wrong, often damaging both the "haves" and the "have-nots."[7]

**What do teenagers most often dislike about themselves?** In a classic study by E. A. Douvan, titled *Adolescent Girls*, nearly 2,000 girls from eleven to eighteen years of age were asked, "What would you most like to change about yourself if you could . . . your looks, your personality, or your life?" Fifty-nine percent mentioned some aspect of their physical appearance. (Only 4 percent desired greater ability.) The most common personal dissatisfaction for both boys and girls concerns facial defects, primarily skin problems. In a later study by H. V. Cobb, children in grades four to fourteen were asked to complete the sentence, "I wish I were": The majority of the boys answered "taller" and the girls answered "smaller." Certainly, there is a great volume of scientific evidence to document children's preoccupation and dissatisfaction with their own physical characteristics.[8]

**You referred to a "system" of evaluating human worth in our culture, beginning with the most important attribute of physical attractiveness. What ranks second in significance?**
It is the presence of intelligence, as expressed in scholastic aptitude. When the birth of a firstborn child is eminent, his parents pray that he will be normal . . . that is, "average." But from that moment on, average will not be good enough. Their child must excel. He must succeed. He must triumph. He must be the first of his age to walk or talk or ride a tricycle. He must earn a stunning report card and amaze his teachers with his wit and wisdom. He must star in Little League, and later he must be the quarterback or the senior class president or the valedictorian. His sister must be the cheerleader or the soloist or the homecoming queen. Throughout the formative years of childhood, his parents give him the same message day after day: "We're counting on you to do something fantastic, son, now don't disappoint us!"

According to Martha Weinman Lear, author of *The Child Worshippers,* the younger generation is our most reliable status symbol. Middle-class parents vigorously compete with each other in raising the best-dressed, best-fed, best-educated, best-mannered, best-medicated, best-cultured, and best-adjusted child on the block. The hopes, dreams, and ambitions of an entire family sometimes rest on the shoulders of an immature child. And in this atmosphere of fierce competition, the parent who produces an intellectually gifted child is clearly holding the winning sweepstakes ticket. As Lear says, "By the present line of thinking all children deserve the very best except the [intellectually] gifted, who deserve even better."

Unfortunately, exceptional children are just that—exceptions. Seldom does a five-year-old memorize the King James Version of the Bible, or play chess blindfolded, or compose symphonies in the Mozart manner. To the contrary, the vast majority of our children are not dazzlingly brilliant, extremely witty, highly coordinated, tremendously talented, or universally popular! They are just plain kids with oversized needs to be loved and accepted as they are. Thus, the stage is set for unrealistic pressure on the younger generation and considerable disappointment for their parents.[9]

**You have stated that a majority of children emerge from the school systems with the conviction that they are unintelligent and stupid. Would you explain why this attack on self-worth affects so many kids today?**

There are five large groups of children who consistently fail in the classroom, leading them (and their parents) to conclude that they are incapable. These broad categories are as follows:

1. *The slow learner.* This is the child who lacks an aptitude for academic work. He tries to do the assignments but nothing turns out right. He has difficulty learning to read in the first grade. He doesn't understand science. He rarely receives a "happy face" for doing things properly, and *never* has his teacher written "Nice work!" on his paper. He is the only child in the room who won't get a gold star on his spelling chart. And he is probably going to be retained in the same grade at least once, which convinces him of his stupidity!

2. *The semiliterate child.* This is the child in whose home two languages are spoken, but he has learned neither of them very well. Thus, he is not "bilingual"—he is semiliterate. He may be so incapable of expressing himself that he rarely makes a sound unless compelled to talk. His progress in an English school will be an uphill struggle throughout his childhood.

3. *The underachiever.* This is the child who is bright but unself-disciplined and unmotivated to work. His school assignments are usually late, missing, sloppy, or foolish, leading him to draw the same weary conclusion: "I'm dumb!"

4. *The culturally deprived child.* This is a youngster from an impoverished neighborhood. He has never visited a zoo, ridden on a plane, or been fishing. His daddy's identity is a mystery and his mother works long hours to support five little children. His vocabulary is minuscule, except for an astounding array of slang words, and he has no place to read or study at home. He *knows* he isn't going to make it in school, and this fact is already influencing his personal evaluation.

5. *The late bloomer.* This is the immature child (usually a boy) who starts school before he is ready and experiences early failure. Though he may catch up in maturity later, his lack of school success may handicap him throughout his school career.

*It is appalling to recognize that the children in these five categories actually outnumber those students who feel successful in school!*[10]

**It is obvious that you think the attitudes and reactions of parents play a key role in the self-esteem of children.**
Children are extremely vulnerable to the subtle attitude of their parents. That's why adults must learn to guard what they say in the presence of their children. How many times, following a speaking engagement, have I been consulted by a mother regarding a particular problem her child is having. As Mom describes the gritty details, I notice that the subject of all this conversation is standing about a yard behind her. His ears are ten feet tall as he listens to a candid description of all his faults. The child may remember that conversation for a lifetime.

It is clear that parents often convey disrespect to a child whom they genuinely love. For example, Mom may become tense and nervous when little Jimmy speaks to guests or outsiders. She butts in to explain what he is trying to say or laughs nervously when his remarks sound foolish. When someone asks him a direct question, she interrupts and answers for him. She reveals her frustration when she is trying to comb his hair or make him "look nice" for an important event. He knows she thinks it is an impossible assignment. If he is to spend a weekend away from the family, she gives him an extended lecture on how to avoid making a fool of himself. These subtle behaviors are signals to the child that his mother doesn't trust him with her image—that he must be supervised closely to avoid embarrassing the whole family. He reads disrespect in her manner, though it is framed in genuine love.

My point is that parents should be sensitive to the self-concept of their children, being especially mindful of matters pertaining to physical attractiveness or intelligence of the kids. These are two primary "soft spots" where boys and girls are most vulnerable.[11]

**What are some of the factors that hinder parents from building their child's self-esteem?**
In a very real sense, we parents are products of the society whose values I have condemned. We have systematically been taught to worship beauty and brains, as everyone else, and so have our grandmommas and grandpoppas and uncles and aunts and cousins and neighbors. We all want superchildren who will amaze the world. Let's face it, folks: We have met the enemy, and it is *us*. Often the greatest damage is unintentionally inflicted right in the home, which should be the child's

sanctuary and fortress. Furthermore, I have observed in working with parents that their *own* feelings of inferiority make it difficult for them to accept gross imperfections in their children. They don't intend to reject their sons and daughters, and they work hard to conceal these inner thoughts. But their "damaged" child symbolizes their own personal inadequacies and failures. Thus, it takes a very mature parent to look down upon an ugly child, or one who is clearly deficient in mentality, and say, "Not only do I love you, little one, but I recognize your immeasurable worth as a human being."

The first step in overcoming this bias is to examine your own feelings—even being willing to expose those guilt-laden attitudes which may have been unconscious heretofore. Are you secretly disappointed because your child is so ordinary? Have you rejected him, at times, because of his lack of appeal and charm? Do you think he is dumb and stupid? Was he born during a difficult time, imposing financial and physical stress on the family? Did you want a girl instead of a boy? Or a boy instead of a girl? Was this child conceived out of wedlock, forcing an unwanted marriage? Do you resent the freedom you lost when he came or the demands he places on your time and effort? Does he embarrass you by being either too loud and rambunctious or too inward and withdrawn?

Quite obviously, you can't teach a child to respect himself when you dislike him for reasons of your own! By examining your inner-most feelings, perhaps with the help of an understanding counselor or doctor, you *can* make room in your heart as a loving parent for your less-than-perfect youngster. After all, what right do we have to demand superchildren when we are so ordinary ourselves![12]

**You have talked about the attributes or characteristics which are most highly valued in the Western culture. But what is the source of self-esteem itself?**

Feelings of self-worth and acceptance, which provide the cornerstone of a healthy personality, can be obtained from only *one* source. It cannot be bought or manufactured. Self-esteem is only generated by what we see reflected about ourselves in the eyes of other people or in the eyes of God. In other words, evidence of our worthiness must be generated *outside* of ourselves. It is only when others respect us that we respect ourselves. It is only when others love us that we love ourselves.

It is only when others find us pleasant and desirable and worthy that we come to terms with our own egos. Occasionally, a person is created with such towering self-confidence that he doesn't seem to need the acceptance of other people, but he is indeed a rare bird. The vast majority of us are dependent on our associates for emotional sustenance each day. What does this say, then, about those who exist in a state of perpetual isolation, being deprived of loving, caring human contact year after year? Such people are virtually certain to experience feelings of worthlessness, accompanied by deep depression and despair.[13]

**You say beauty and intelligence are the most critical factors in shaping self-esteem and confidence. What other influences contribute to the child's level of self-confidence?**

Let me list some of the more common variables that relate to self-worth in our culture:

1. Parents have a remarkable power to preserve or damage the self-esteem of a child. Their manner either conveys respect and love or disappointment and disinterest.
2. Older siblings can crush the confidence of a younger, weaker child. The little one can never run as fast, or fight as well, or achieve as much as his big brothers and sisters. And if his words are perpetually matters of scorn, he can easily conclude that he is foolish and incapable.
3. Early social blunders and mistakes are sometimes extremely painful, being remembered throughout a lifetime.
4. Financial hardship, depriving a child of the clothes and lifestyle of his peers, can cause a child to feel inferior. It is not the poverty, itself, which does the damage. Rather, it is the relative comparison with others. It is possible to feel deprived when you are truly rich by the world's standards. Incidentally, money is probably the third most important source of self-esteem in our culture. In the materialistic eyes of society, for example, a pimply-faced teenager on a bicycle is somehow considered less worthy than a pimply-faced teenager in a Datsun 280Z.
5. Disease, even when unapparent, may represent the child's "inner flaw." A cardiac condition, or other disorder, which forces Mom to nag and beg him to slow down can convince a child that he is brittle and defective.
6. A child who has been raised in a protected environment, such as a farm or a foreign missionary outpost, may be

embarrassed by his underdeveloped social skills. His tendency is to pull inward in shy withdrawal.

7. Embarrassing family characteristics, such as having an alcoholic father or a mentally retarded sibling, can produce feelings of inferiority through close identification with the disrespected relatives.

Unfortunately, this list could be almost endless. In working with the problem of inadequacy, I have drawn this conclusion: whereas a child can lose self-esteem in a thousand ways, the careful reconstruction of his personal worth is usually a slow, difficult process.

**You have convinced me that beauty, brains, and materialism are false values that demoralize the self-esteem of kids. But what will take their place? What values do you suggest that I teach to my children?**

I believe *the* most valuable contribution a parent can make to his child is to instill in him a genuine faith in God. What greater ego satisfaction could there be than knowing that the Creator of the universe is acquainted with me, personally? That He values me more than the possessions of the entire world; that He understands my fears and my anxieties; that He reaches out to me in immeasurable love when no one else cares; that His only Son, Jesus, actually gave His life for me; that He can turn my liabilities into assets and my emptiness into fullness; that a better life follows this one, where the present handicaps and inadequacies will all be eliminated—where earthly pain and suffering will be no more than a dim memory! What a beautiful philosophy with which to "clothe" your tender child. What a fantastic message of hope and encouragement for the broken teenager who has been crushed by life's circumstances. This is self-esteem at its richest, not dependent on the whims of birth or social judgment, or the cult of the superchild, but on divine decree.[14]

# SECTION 11

# DEVELOPING SELF-ESTEEM IN CHILDREN

**I have a nine-year-old daughter who lacks confidence and self-respect. What can I do to help her?**

One of the most productive means of instilling self-confidence is to teach methods by which the child can compensate. *Compensation* occurs when the individual counterbalances his weaknesses by capitalizing on his strengths. It is our job as parents to help our children find those strengths and learn to exploit them for all the self-satisfaction they will yield. And this brings us to a very important concept to be grasped: Inferiority can either crush and paralyze an individual, or it can provide tremendous emotional energy which powers every kind of success and achievement. Remember that the same boiling water that hardens the egg will soften the carrot. Everything depends on the individual's *reaction* to stressful circumstances.

The question is, will your daughter collapse under the weight of inferiority, or will she use her emotional needs to supercharge her initiative and drive? The answer may depend on the direction you can provide in identifying compensatory skills. Perhaps she can establish her niche in music—many children do. Maybe she can develop her artistic talent, or learn to write or cultivate mechanical skills, or learn to cook or raise rabbits for fun and profit. Regardless of what the choice is, the key is to start her down that road early . . . right now! There is nothing more risky than sending a teenager into the storms of adolescence with no skills, no unique knowledge, no means of compensating. When this occurs, her ego is stark naked. She cannot say, "I may not be the most popular student in school, but I am the best trumpet player in the band!" Her only source of self-esteem comes from the acceptance of other students—and their love is notoriously fickle.[1]

**Can you explain the process of compensation in greater detail? How does it relate to feelings of low self-esteem?** The unconscious reasoning of a compensater goes like this:

> I refuse to be drowned in a sea of inferiority. I can achieve adequacy through success if I work hard at it. Therefore, I will pour all my energy into basketball (or painting, or sewing, or politics, or graduate school, or gardening, or motherhood, or salesmanship, or Wall Street—or for a child, elementary school, or piano playing, or baton-twirling or football).

This kind of compensation provides the emotional energy for virtually every kind of successful human behavior, as described earlier. In a famous study by Victor and Mildred Goertzel, entitled *Cradles of Eminence*, the home backgrounds of four hundred highly successful people were investigated. These four hundred subjects were individuals who had made it to the top. They were men and women whose names you would recognize as brilliant or outstanding in their respective fields (Churchill, Gandhi, F. D. Roosevelt, Schweitzer, Einstein, Freud, etc.). The intensive investigation into their early home lives yielded some surprising findings:

1. Three-fourths of the children [were] troubled—by poverty; by a broken home; by rejecting, over-possessive, estranged, or dominating parents; by financial ups and downs; by physical handicaps; or by parental dissatisfaction over the children's school failures or vocational choices.
2. Seventy-four of eighty-five writers of fiction or drama and sixteen of twenty poets [came] from homes where, as children, they saw tense psychological dramas played out by their parents.
3. Handicaps such as blindness; deafness; being crippled, sickly, homely, undersized, or overweight; or having a speech defect [occurred] in the childhoods of over one-fourth of the sample.

It seems very apparent that the need to compensate for their disadvantages was a major factor in their struggle for personal achievement. It may even have been *the* determining factor.

There have been thousands, perhaps millions, of inadequate persons who used compensation to achieve esteem and confidence. Perhaps the most classic illustration is seen in the life of Eleanor Roosevelt, the former First Lady. Being orphaned at ten, she underwent a childhood of utter anguish. She was very homely and never felt she really belonged to anybody. According to Victor Wilson, Newhouse News Service, "She was a rather humorless introvert, a young woman unbelievably shy, unable to overcome her personal insecurity and with a conviction of her own inadequacy." The world knows, however, that Mrs. Roosevelt did rise above her emotional shackles. As Wilson said, ". . . from some inner wellspring, Mrs. Roosevelt summoned a tough, unyielding courage, tempered by remarkable self-control and self-discipline . . . ." That "inner wellspring" has another appropriate name: compensation!

Obviously, one's *attitude* toward a handicap determines its impact on his life. It has become popular to blame adverse circumstances for irresponsible behavior; i.e., poverty *causes* crime, broken homes *produce* juvenile delinquents, a sick society imposes drug addiction on its youth. This fallacious reasoning removes all responsibility from the shoulders of the individual. The excuse is hollow. We must each decide what we will do with inner inferiority or outer hardship.

Admittedly, it requires courage to triumph despite unfavorable odds. Compensation takes guts, for some much more than others. The easier path is to wallow in self-pity—to freak-out on drugs—to hate the world—to run—to withdraw—to compromise. Regardless of the ultimate course of action, however, the choice is ours alone and no one can remove it from us. Hardship does not *determine* our behavior, but it clearly influences it.

Parents can and should open the door to responsible "choices" by giving their children the means by which to compensate, beginning during their middle childhood years.[2]

**What is the *best* source of compensation for boys in this culture, especially for the kid who is "hurting" inside?**
Because of the status athletes have in today's high schools, I believe this avenue of compensation should be explored by the parents of "high risk" boys. If a child is reasonably coordinated, he can be taught to play basketball, football, tennis, track, or golf. I have seen some of the most homely adolescents who were highly respected for helping Thomas Jefferson High School win

the championship. As stated before, the key to athletic excellence is to give Junior an early start. We do not hesitate to provide piano lessons for our eight-year-olds; why should we not give basketball training at the same age?[3]

**My son is not athletically inclined. How can I as a parent decide what skill my son should develop? Shouldn't that choice be left to him?**

Many parents feel they do not have the right to force a choice of this nature on their child. They sit back in the hopes that he will make it for himself. However, most children are remarkably unself-disciplined. It is always difficult to learn a new skill—particularly during the initial stages. There is no fun to be derived from total failure, which is the typical feeling in the beginning. Thus, the child never learns those important skills which he will need so badly later on. I recommend that you, his parent, make a careful assessment of his areas of strength. Then select a skill where you believe the greatest possibilities for success lie. Once this selection is made, see to it that he gets through the first stage. Reward him, push him, threaten him, beg him—bribe him if necessary—but make him learn it. If you discover later that you've made a mistake, back up and start over on something else. But don't let inertia keep you from teaching something emotionally useful to your offspring! Does this form of coercion impinge upon the freedom of the child to choose for himself? Perhaps, but so does making him eat properly, keep himself clean, and go to bed at a reasonable hour. It is, as they say, in the child's best interest.[4]

**What happens when a child is so different from the group that he cannot compete, no matter how hard he tries?**

That dead-end street is most often responsible for attempts at self-destruction. I am reminded of a sad little girl named Lily, an eighth-grader who was referred to me for psychological counselling. She opened the door to my office and stood with eyes cast down. Underneath several layers of powder and make-up, her face was completely aglow with infected acne. Lily had done her best to bury the inflammation, but she had not been successful. She weighed about eighty-five pounds and was a physical wreck from head to toe. She sat down without raising her eyes to mine, lacking the confidence to face me. I didn't need to ask what was troubling her. Life had dealt her a devastating blow, and she was bitter, angry, broken, and deeply hurt. The teenager who reaches this point of despair can see no tomorrow. He has no hope. He can't think of anything else. He knows he is repulsive and disgusting. He would like to crawl in a hole, but there is no place to hide. Running away won't help, nor will crying change anything. Too often he chooses suicide as the only way out.

Lily gave me little time to work. The following morning she staggered into the school office and announced that she had internalized everything in the family medicine cabinet. We labored feverishly to retrieve the medication and finally succeeded on the way to the hospital. Lily survived physically, but her self-esteem and confidence had died years earlier. The scars on her sad face symbolized the wounds on her adolescent heart.

Obviously, the inability to gain social acceptance is not merely an uncomfortable feeling among the young; such lack of self-esteem can actually extinguish the desire to go on living. Parents and teachers must be taught to recognize the early symptoms of personal despair during the tender, pliable years of childhood, and more importantly, what they can do about it.[5]

**I know children can be hateful and mean, especially to the handicapped child or one who is "different." This seems terribly destructive to kids who are especially vulnerable to ridicule. Do you agree that adults are responsible to intercede when a child is being attacked by his peers?**

I certainly do and I am well aware of the danger you described. In fact, I lived it. When I was approximately eight years old, I attended a Sunday school class as a regular member. One morning a visitor entered our class and sat down. His name was Fred, and I can still see his face. More important, I can still see Fred's ears. They were curved in the shape of a reversed C, and protruded noticeably. I was fascinated by the shape of Fred's unusual ears because they reminded me of jeep fenders (we were deep into World War II at the time). Without thinking of Fred's feelings, I pointed out his strange feature to my friends, who all thought Jeep Fenders was a terribly funny name for a boy with bent ears. Fred seemed to think it was funny, too, and he chuckled along with the rest of us. Suddenly, Fred stopped laughing. He jumped to his feet, red in the face (and ears), and rushed to the door crying. He bolted into the hall and ran from the building. Fred never returned to our class.

I remember my shock over Fred's violent and unexpected reaction. You see, I had *no* idea that I was embarrassing him by my little joke. I was a sensitive kid and often defended the underdog, even when I was a youngster. I would *never* have hurt a visitor on purpose—and that is precisely my point. Looking back on the episode, I hold my teachers and my parents responsible for that event. They should have told me what it feels like to be laughed at . . . especially for something different about your body. My mother, who was very wise with children, has since admitted that she should have taught me to feel for others. And as for the Sunday school leaders, I don't remember what their curriculum consisted of at that time, but what better content could they have presented than the *real* meaning of the commandment, "Love thy neighbor as thyself"?[6]

**You implied that the "middle child" has greater problems with low self-esteem than other members of the family. Maybe that explains why my second son has never been a confident person.**

Low self-esteem can become a problem for any human being, regardless of birth order or age. However, the middle child does sometimes find it more difficult to establish his identity within the family. He enjoys neither the status of the eldest nor the attention given to the baby. Furthermore, he is likely to be born at a busy period in the life of his parents, and especially his mother. Then when he reaches the toddler years, his precious territory is invaded by a cute little newborn who steals Mama from him. Is it any wonder that he often asks, "Who am I and where is my place in life?"[7]

**What can I do to help my middle child, who suffers from low self-esteem?**

I would recommend that parents take steps to insure the identity of *all* their children, but especially the child in the middle. That can be accomplished by occasionally relating to each boy or girl as individuals, rather than merely as members of the group. Let me offer two suggestions that may serve as examples that well illustrate what I mean.

1. It is meaningful for Dad to "date" each child, *one at a time*, every four or five weeks. The other kids should not be told where they are going until it is revealed by the boy or girl in retrospect. They can play miniature golf, go bowling, play basketball, eat tacos or pizza, or visit a skating rink. The choice should be made by the child whose turn has arrived.

2. Ask each offspring to design his own flag, which can be sewn in canvas or cloth. That flag is then flown in the front yard on the child's "special" days, including birthdays, after he has received an A in school, when he scores a goal in soccer, or hits a home run in baseball, and so forth.

There are other ways to accomplish the same purpose. The target, again, is to plan activities that emphasize one child's individuality apart from his identity within the group.[8]

**My son is an outstanding gymnast. His high school coach says he has more natural ability than anyone he's ever seen. Yet, when he is being judged in a competitive meet, he does terribly! Why does he fail during the most important moments?**

If your son thinks of himself as a failure, his performance will probably match his low self-image when the chips are down. In the same way, there are many excellent golfers in the PGA tour who make a satisfactory living in tournament play, but they never win. They consistently place second, third, sixth, or tenth. Whenever it looks like they might come in first, they "choke" at the last minute and let someone else win. It is not that they want to fail; rather, they don't "see" themselves as winners, and their performance merely reflects this image.

I talked recently with a concert pianist of outstanding talent who has resolved never to play in public again. She knows she is blessed with remarkable talent, but believes she is a loser in every other regard. Consequently, when she plays the piano on stage, her mistakes and errors make her sound like a beginner. Each time this mortifying experience has occurred, she has become more convinced of her own unworthiness in *every* area. She has now withdrawn into the secluded, quiet, talentless world of have-nots.

There is no question about it: a lack of self-confidence can completely immobilize a talented person, simply through the threat of failure.[9]

**Is this true of mental ability, too? My twelve-year-old was asked to recite a poem at a school function the other day, and he went completely blank in front of the crowd. I know he knew the poem perfectly because he said it dozens of times at home. He's a bright child, but he's had this trouble before. Why does his mind "turn off" when he's under pressure?**

It will be helpful to understand an important characteristic of intellectual functioning. Your son's self-confidence, or the lack of it, actually affects the way his brain operates. All of us have experienced the frustration of mental "blocking," which you described. This occurs when a name or fact or idea just won't surface to the conscious mind, even though we *know* it is recorded in the memory. Or suppose we are about to speak to an antagonistic group and our mind suddenly goes blank. This kind of blocking usually occurs (1) when social pressure is great, and (2) when self-confidence is low. Why? *Because emotions affect the efficiency of the human brain.* Unlike a computer, our mental apparatus only functions properly when a delicate biochemical balance exists between the neural cells. This substance makes it possible for a cell to "fire" its electrochemical charge across the gap (synapse) to another cell. It is now known that a sudden emotional reaction can instantly change the nature of that biochemistry, blocking the impulse. This blockage prevents the electrical charge from being relayed and the thought is never generated. This mechanism has profound implications for human behavior; for example, a child who feels inferior and intellectually inadequate often does not even make use of the mental power with which he has been endowed. His lack of confidence produces a disrupting mental interference, and the two go around in an endless cycle of defeat. This is obviously what happened to your son when he "forgot" the poem.[10]

**What can I do to help him?**

Actually, it is not unusual for a twelve-year-old to "choke" in front of a crowd. I once stood before three hundred fellow teenagers with my words stuck in my throat and my mind totally out to lunch. It was a painful experience, but time gradually erased its impact. As your child matures, he will probably overcome the problem, if he can experience a few successes to build his confidence. Anything that raises self-esteem will reduce the frequency of mental blocking for children and adults alike.[11]

**What kind of homes produce children with a high degree of self-confidence? Are there characteristics of the most wholesome families that we can try to emulate?**

Dr. Stanley Coopersmith, associate professor of psychology, University of California, studied 1,738 normal middle-class boys and their families, beginning in the pre-adolescent period and following them through to young manhood. After identifying those boys having the highest self-esteem, he compared their homes and childhood influences with those having a lower sense of self-worth. He found three important characteristics which distinguished them: (1) The high-esteem children were clearly more loved and appreciated at home than were the low-esteem boys. (2) The high-esteem group came from homes where parents had been significantly more strict in their approach to discipline. By contrast, the parents of the low-esteem group had created insecurity and dependence by their permissiveness. Their children were more likely to feel that the rules were not enforced because no one cared enough to get involved. Furthermore, the most successful and independent young men during the latter period of the study were found to have come from homes that demanded the strictest accountability and responsibility. And as could have been predicted, the family ties remained the strongest, not only in the wishy-washy homes, but in the homes where discipline and self-control had been a way of life. (3) The homes of the high-esteem group were also characterized by democracy and openness. Once the boundaries for behavior were established, there was freedom for individual personalities to grow and develop. The boys could express themselves without fear of ridicule, and the overall atmosphere was marked by acceptance and emotional safety.[12]

**I share your concern over the unjust emphasis on beauty and intelligence among children today. That's why we are playing down the importance of those two factors in our home. For example, my son has very crooked teeth, but I**

**tell him that it isn't important what he looks like. What matters is the person inside. Do you agree with this approach?**
Not entirely. A parent who strongly opposes the unfortunate stress currently placed on beauty and brains, as I do, must resolve a difficult philosophical question with regard to his own children. While he recognizes the injustice of this value system, he knows his child is forced to compete in a world which worships those attributes. What should he do, then? Should he help his youngster become as attractive as possible? Should he encourage his "average" child to excel in school? Or would he be wise to de-emphasize these values at home, hoping the boy or girl will learn to live with his/her handicaps?

There are no "scientific" answers to those questions. I can only give you my considered opinion, in reply. Despite the injustice of this system, my child will not be the one to change it. I am obligated to help him compete in his world as best he can. If his ears protrude, I will have them flattened. If his teeth are crooked, I will see that they are straightened. If he flounders academically, I will seek tutorial assistance to pull him out. He and I are allies in his fight for survival, and I will not turn a deaf ear to his needs.

Rick Barry, the former professional basketball star, is a handsome, 6′7″ specimen of health and confidence. Yet as a child he was humiliated and self-conscious about his teeth, even causing him to talk with his hand over his mouth. As he described in the book, *Confessions of a Basketball Gypsy:*

> When my second teeth came in, they came in crooked and two of them were missing in front. Maybe my folks could not afford to have them fixed, or maybe having teeth fixed was not then what it is now. I remember talking to Dad about putting in false teeth in front and wearing braces, which might cut my gums when I exerted myself playing ball. Anyway, I did not have my teeth fixed until I was in college. I was very sensitive about my teeth. I was ashamed to look at myself in the mirror. I used to keep my mouth shut and I'd never smile. I used to keep my hand over my mouth, which muffled my voice and made it hard for people to understand me. I developed this habit of keeping my hand over my mouth, just sort of always resting on my chin, and I couldn't shake it for years afterward.

This kind of discomfort is incredibly painful to a child. That's why I believe it is a parental obligation, within the limits of financial resources, to eradicate the flaws which generate the greatest sensitivity. Dr. Edward Podolsky agrees. He is assistant supervisory psychiatrist at Kings County Hospital in New York City, and recommends that physical deformities be corrected before the child enters first grade, if possible. After that time, peer pressure becomes a major factor in shaping his self-concept.

But we parents must walk a tightrope at this point. While I am helping my child to compete in the world as it is, I must also teach him that its values are temporal and unworthy. Explaining the two contradictory sides of that coin requires considerable skill and tact. How can I urge my daughter to fix her hair neatly and then tell her, "Beauty doesn't matter?" The key is to begin very early to instruct the child on the true values of life: love for all mankind, kindness, integrity, trustworthiness, truthfulness, devotion to God, etc. Physical attractiveness is then described as part of a social game we must play. Since the world is our ball park, we cannot completely ignore the rules of the game. But whether we hit a home run or strike out, we can take comfort in knowing that baseball, itself, is not that important. Herein lies an anchor that can hold a child steady.[13]

**What about good-natured teasing and joking within the family? Is it harmful to laugh and kid each other?**

The most healthy families are those which can laugh together, and I certainly don't think our egos should be so fragile that we all have to walk on cracked eggs around each other. However, even innocent humor can be painful when one child is always the object of the jokes. When one youngster has an embarrassing feature, such as bed-wetting or thumb-sucking or stuttering or a striking physical flaw, the other members of the family should be encouraged to tread softly on the exposed nerves thereabout. And particularly, one should not ridicule a child for his size, whether he is a small boy or a large girl. There is nothing funny about that subject. This is the guiding principle: it is wise not to tease a child about the features he is also defending outside the home. And when he asks for any joke to end, his wishes should be honored.[14]

**My twelve-year-old is embarrassed about the size of her nose. But what I can't understand is that she keeps talking about it to her friends. Should I call this to her attention and advise her *not* to mention this problem?**
One of the most obvious characteristics of a person who feels inferior is that he talks about his deficiencies to anyone who will listen. An overweight person feels compelled to apologize to his companions for ordering a hot fudge sundae. He echoes what he imagines they're thinking: "I'm already fat enough without eating this," he says, scooping up the cherry and syrup with his spoon. Likewise, a woman who thinks she's unintelligent will admit freely, "I am really bad at math; I can hardly add two and two." This kind of self-denigration is not as uncommon as one might think.

While there is no virtue in becoming an image-conscious phony, trying to be something we're not, I believe it is also a mistake to go to the other extreme. While the person is blabbing about all of his ridiculous inadequacies, the listener is formulating a lasting impression of him.

So, I do recommend that you teach a "no-knock" policy to your daughter. She should learn that constant self-criticism can become a bad habit, and it accomplishes nothing. There is a big difference between accepting blame when it is valid and in simply chattering about one's inferiority. Your daughter should know that her friends are probably thinking about their *own* flaws, anyway.[15]

**I want to get my six-year-old daughter ready for some of the esteem problems that will probably occur when she is a teenager. How can I begin bracing her for the social pressure she is likely to face?**
In a sense, all of childhood is a preparation for adolescence and beyond. Mothers and fathers are granted a single decade to lay a foundation of values and attitudes that will help their children cope with the future pressures and problems of adulthood. As such, we would all do well to acquaint our young children with the meaning of self-worth and its preservation, since every human being has to deal with that issue at some point in the life cycle.

This teaching process should begin during the kindergarten years, if not before. For example, when your child meets someone who is too shy to speak or even look at him, you might say, "Why do you suppose Billie is too embarrassed to tell you what he is feeling? Do you think he doesn't have much self-confidence?" (Use the word *confidence* frequently, referring to a kind of courage and belief in one's self.) When your child participates in a school or church program, compliment him for having the confidence to stand in front of a group without hanging his head or thrusting his tongue in his cheek.

Then as the elementary years unfold, begin focusing on the negative side of that important ingredient. Talk openly about feelings of inferiority and what they mean. For example, "Did you notice how David acted so silly in class this morning? He was trying hard to make everyone pay attention to him, wasn't he? Do you have any idea why he needs to be noticed every minute of the day? Maybe it's because David doesn't like himself very much. I think he is trying to force people to like him because he thinks he is disrespected. Why don't you try to make friends with David and help him feel better about himself? Would you like to invite him to spend the night?"

Not only will you help your child "tune in" to the feelings of others through this instruction, but you will also be teaching him to understand his *own* feelings of inadequacy. Each year that passes should bring more explicit understandings about the crisis in worth which comes to everyone. It would be wise to give him an illustration of people who have overcome great feelings of inferiority (such as Eleanor Roosevelt), and ultimately, the *best* examples will come from the struggles of your own adolescent experiences. The goal is to send your pubescent son or daughter into the teen years, armed with four specific concepts: (1) all adolescents go through a time when they don't like themselves very much; (2) most feel ugly and dumb and unliked by their peer group; (3) the worst of this self-doubt will not last very long, although most human beings have to deal with those feelings off and on throughout life; (4) each of us possesses incredible value because we are children of the Creator, who has a specific plan for our lives.

I suppose this strategy appeals to me, not only for its possible contribution to a healthy adolescence, but because it takes us in the direction of human understanding. And how badly that comprehension is needed! I read recently that 80 percent of the people who get fired from their jobs have not failed to perform as required. In other words, they do not lack *technical* skill or abilities. Their dismissal occurs because *they can't get along with people*. They misunderstand the motives of others and respond with belligerence and insubordination. We can minimize that possibility by training our children to "see" others in a truer light, while preserving their own dignity and sense of worth.[16]

**I have heard that you are critical of the "Barbie" products and other teenage role-model dolls of this type. Explain the nature of your concern.**

My objection to Barbie and her companions is on two levels. First, there could be no better method for teaching the worship of beauty and materialism than is done with these luscious dolls. If we intentionally sought to drill our babies on the necessity of growing up rich and gorgeous, we could do no better than has already been done. Did you ever see an ugly Barbie doll? Has she ever had even the slightest imperfection? Of course not! She oozes femininity and sex appeal. Her hair is thick and gleaming—loaded with "body" (whatever in the world that is). Her long, thin legs, curvacious bust, and delicate feet are absolutely perfect. Her airbrushed skin is without flaw or blemish (except for a little statement on her bottom that she was "Made in Hong Kong"). She never gets pimples or blackheads, and there is not an ounce of fat on her pink body. Not only is Barbie one of the beautiful people, but so are all her buddies. Her swinging boyfriend, Ken, is an adolescent composite of Charles Atlas, Rock Hudson, and Clark Kent (mild-mannered reporter for the *Daily Planet*). These idealized models load an emotional time bomb set to explode the moment a real live thirteen-year-old takes her first long look in the mirror. No doubt about it—Barbie she ain't!

Yet it is not the physical perfection of these Barbie dolls (and her many competitors) that concerns me most; of much greater harm are the teenage games that they inspire. Instead of three- and four-year-old boys and girls playing with stuffed animals, balls, cars, trucks, model horses and the traditional memorabilia of childhood, they are now learning to fantasize about life as an adolescent. Ken and Barbie go on dates, learn to dance, drive sports cars, get suntans, take camping trips, exchange marriage vows, and have babies (hopefully in that order). The entire adolescent culture with its emphasis on sexual awareness is illustrated to tiny little girls who ought to be thinking about more childish things. This places our children on an unnatural timetable likely to reach the peak of sexual interest several years before it is due—with all the obvious implications for their social and emotional health.[17]

**My child is often ridiculed and hurt by the other children on our block, and I don't know how to handle the situation. He gets very depressed and comes home crying frequently. How should I respond when this happens?**

When your child has been rejected in this manner, he is badly in need of a friend—and you are elected. Let him talk. Don't try to tell him that it doesn't hurt or that it's silly to be so sensitive. Ask him if he knows what it is that his "friends" don't like. (He may be causing their reaction by dominance, selfishness, or dishonesty.) Be understanding and sympathetic without weeping in mutual despair. As soon as appropriate, involve yourself with him in a game or some other activity which he will enjoy. And finally, set about resolving the underlying cause.

I would suggest that you ask your child to invite one of his school friends to go to the zoo on Saturday (or offer other attractive "bait") and then spend the night at your house. Genuine friendship often grows from such beginnings. Even the hostile children on the block may be more kind when only one of them is invited at a time. Not only can you help your child make friends in this way, but you can observe the social mistakes he is making to drive them away. The information you gain can later be used to help him improve his relationship with others.[18]

**My ten-year-old daughter hates to have her hair in a pigtail because her friends don't wear theirs that way. I have always loved pigtails, ever since I was a little girl. Am I wrong to make her please me by wearing her hair the way I want it?**

Yes, particularly if your daughter feels unnecessarily different and foolish with her friends. Social pressure on the nonconformist is severe, and you should not place your daughter in this uncomfortable position. Closeness between generations comes from the child's knowledge that his parent understands and appreciates his feelings. Your inflexibility on this point reveals a lack of empathy and may bring later resentment.[19]

**We have a four-year-old adopted child, and want to raise him to have a strong awareness of our love for him and of the love of God. What suggestions do you have for us and other parents of adopted children regarding the special needs that will arise?**
The best answer I've found for that question quotes Dr. Milton I. Levine from the publication *Your Child from 2 to 5.*[20] I'll quote from that source and then comment on Dr. Levine's views.

> COMMON-SENSE APPROACHES TO ADOPTION
> Adopting children has become such an accepted practice these days that the quavering question, "Shall I tell him he's adopted?" doesn't even qualify as soap-opera dialogue any more. Most parents realize that telling a youngster from the earliest possible moment provides the only solid foundation for his and their security.
>
> However, as Dr. Milton I. Levine, advisory board member of *2-to-5 World News* and Associate Professor of Pediatrics, New York Hospital—Cornell Medical Center, points out: "Even though adoption is no longer regarded as a shameful secret but rightly as a logical matter of fact, the situation still demands delicacy, understanding, and many common-sense decisions on the part of parents."
>
> Parents should tell the child about his adoption from the time he begins to beg for stories, says Dr. Levine. This will spare the youngster serious shock that can accompany the revelation in later years. Parents might treat the story as a wondrous chapter in the family's history. But the tendency to put off a decision sometimes affects even the best-intentioned adoptive parents. "Let's wait until he's old enough to understand," they may say, and delay the explanation until a basic fact turns into a dark secret. In Dr. Levine's opinion, even five- and six-year-olds are too old to be told without resultant emotional damage. He urges parents to:
>
> 1. Tell the child about his adoption from the moment he is ready to listen to stories.
> 2. Use the word "adopted" in the narrative until it becomes a synonym for "chosen" and "selected" and "wanted."
> 3. Make no attempt to conceal the adoption, even though moving into a new neighborhood might invite concealment.

"Some adoptive parents never seem to outgrow an apologetic attitude based on a feeling that they are merely pinch-hitting for the child's 'own' parents," says Dr. Levine. "For their own mental health, as well as their child's, they must accept the fact that they are, in reality, the youngster's parents. The mother and father who raise a child from infancy, giving him the love and care that enable him to grow freely, *are* the *real* parents; the strangers who produced the baby are merely *biological* parents. The difference can't be stressed strongly enough. By imparting to the child, even unconsciously, an unjustified feeling of loss—a feeling that he *had parents*, but now has substitutes, however loving—these adoptive parents endanger the child's security in his closest relationships and retard his understanding of the true role of parent."

Even professionals are divided over what to tell adopted children about their biological parents, Dr. Levine admits. There are at least three possible approaches, he points out, but not one can qualify as an answer:

1. Tell the child his biological parents are dead.
2. State plainly that the biological parents were unable to care for their baby themselves.
3. Tell the child nothing is known about the biological parents, but that he was secured from an agency dedicated to finding good homes for babies.

"There are pros and cons to all of these solutions," emphasizes Dr. Levine, who prefers the first approach because: "The child who is told that his biological parents are dead is free to love the mother and father he lives with. He won't be tormented by a haunting obligation to search for his biological parents when he's grown.

"Since the possibility of losing one's parents is one of childhood's greatest fears, it is true that the youngster who is told that his biological parents are dead may feel that all parents—including his second set—are pretty impermanent," concedes Dr. Levine. "Nevertheless, I feel that in the long run the child will find it easier to adjust to death than to abandonment. To tell a youngster that his parents gave him up because they were unable to take care of him is to present him with a complete rejection. He cannot comprehend the circumstances which might lead to such an act. But an unwholesome view of himself as an unwanted object, not worth fighting to keep, might be established.

Sex education is another thorny problem for adoptive parents. Any simple, natural explanation of reproduction stresses that a baby is conceived out of his mother's and father's love for each other and their desire to have a child. This explanation is reassuring to other children. But it may, because of the complexity of his situation, cause the adopted child to feel estranged from his adoptive parents, dubious about his own beginnings, and a little out of step with nature in general.

---

I would disagree with Dr. Levine only in reference to comments made about the biological parents. I am unwilling to lie to my child about anything, and would not tell him that his natural parents were dead if that were not true. Sooner or later, he will learn that he has been misled, which could bring the entire adoption story under suspicion.

Instead, I would be inclined to tell the child that very little is known about his biological parents. Several inoffensive and vague possibilities could be offered to him, such as, "We can only guess at the reasons the man and woman could not take care of a baby. They may have been extremely poor and unable to give you the care you needed; or perhaps the woman was sick; or she may not have had a home. We just don't know. But we *do* know that we're thankful that you could come be our son [or daughter], which was one of the greatest gifts God ever gave to us."

Furthermore, I would add three suggestions to Dr. Levine's comments. First, Christian parents should present the adoptive event as a tremendous blessing (as implied above) that brought great excitement to the household. Tell about praying for a child and waiting impatiently for God's answer. Then describe how the news came that the Lord had answered those prayers, and how the whole family thanked Him for His gift of love. Let your child know your delight when you first saw him lying in a crib, and how cute he looked in his blue blanket, etc. Tell him that his adoption was one of the happiest days of your life, and how you raced to the telephone to call all your friends and family members to share the fantastic news. (Again, I'm assuming that these details are true.) Tell him the story of Moses' adoption by Pharaoh's daughter, and how God chose him for a great work with the children of Israel. Look for other, similar illustrations which convey respect and dignity to the adoptee. You see, the child's interpretation of the adoptive event is almost totally dependent on the manner in which it is conveyed during the early years. Most certainly, one does not want to approach the subject sadly, admitting reluctantly that a dark and troublesome secret must now be confessed.

Second, celebrate *two* birthdays with equal gusto each year: the anniversary of his birth, and the anniversary of the day he became your son (or daughter). While other biological children in the family celebrate one birthday, the second hoopla will give the adopted child a compensative edge to offset any differences he might feel relative to his siblings. And use the word "adopted" openly and freely, until it loses its esoteric sting.

Third, when the foundation has been laid and the issue defused, then forget it. Don't constantly remind the child of his uniqueness to the point of foolishness. Mention the matter when it is appropriate, but don't reveal anxiety or tension by constantly throwing adoption in the child's face. Youngsters are amazingly perceptive at "reading" these thinly disguised attitudes.

I believe it is possible, by following these common sense suggestions, to raise an adopted child without psychological trauma or personal insult.[21]

**You have been very critical of the value system in the Western world, which damages our self-concepts and mental health. What important changes could be made in our culture to produce a higher percentage of emotionally healthy children and adults?**

In counseling with neurotic patients, it is apparent that emotional problems usually originate in one of two places (or both): either from an unloving or unnourishing relationship with parents, or from an inability to gain acceptance and respect from peers. In other words, most emotional disorders (except organic illness) can be traced to destructive relationships with people during the first twenty years of life.

Therefore, the most valuable revision would be for adults to begin actively teaching children to love and respect each other (and, of course, to demonstrate that love in their own lives).

Far from manifesting kindness and sensitivity, however, children are often permitted to be terribly brutal and destructive, especially to the handicapped child, the ugly child, the slow-learning child, the uncoordinated child, the foreign child, the minority child, the small or the large child, and the child who is perceived to be different from his peers in even the most insignificant feature. And predictably, the damage inflicted on young victims often reverberates for a lifetime.

Adults should devote their creative energies to the teaching of *love* and *dignity*. And, if necessary, we should *insist* that children approach each other with kindness. Can boys and girls be taught to respect their peers? They certainly can! Young people are naturally more sensitive and empathetic than adults. Their viciousness is a learned response, resulting from the highly competitive and hostile world which their leaders have permitted to develop. In short, children are destructive to the weak and lowly because we adults haven't bothered to teach them to "feel" for one another.

Perhaps an example will help explain my concern. A woman told me recently about her experience as a room mother for her daughter's fourth-grade class. She visited the classroom on Valentine's Day to assist the teacher with the traditional party on that holiday. Valentine's Day can be the most painful day of the year for an unpopular child. Every student *counts* the number of valentines he is given, as a direct measure of his social worth. This mother said the teacher announced that the class was going to play a game which required the formation of boy-girl teams. That was her first mistake, since fourth graders have not yet experienced the happy hormones which draw the sexes together. The moment the teacher instructed the students to select a partner, all the boys immediately laughed and pointed at the homeliest and least respected girl in the room. She was overweight, had protruding teeth, and was too withdrawn even to look anyone in the eye.

"Don't put us with Hazel," they all said in mock terror. "*Anybody* but Hazel! She'll give us a disease! Ugh! Spare us from Horrible Hazel." The mother waited for the teacher (a strong disciplinarian) to rush to the aid of the beleaguered little girl. But to her disappointment, nothing was said to the insulting boys. Instead, the teacher left Hazel to cope with that painful situation in solitude.

Ridicule by one's own sex is distressing, but rejection by the opposite sex is like taking a hatchet to the self-concept. What could this devastated child say in reply? How does an overweight fourth-grade girl defend herself against nine aggressive boys? What response could she make but to blush in mortification and slide foolishly into her chair? This child, whom God loves more than the possessions of the entire world, will never forget that moment (or the teacher who abandoned her in this time of need).

If I had been the teacher of Hazel's class on that fateful Valentine's Day, those mocking, joking boys would have had a fight on their hands. Of course, it would have been better if the embarrassment could have been prevented by discussing the feelings of others from the first day of school. But if the conflict occurred as described, with Hazel's ego suddenly shredded for everyone to see, I would have thrown the full weight of my authority and respect on her side of the battle.

My spontaneous response would have carried this general theme: "Wait just a minute! By what right do any of you boys say such mean, unkind things to Hazel? I want to know which of you is so perfect that the rest of us couldn't make fun of you in some way? I know you all very well. I know about your homes and your school records and some of your personal secrets. Would you like me to share them with the class, so we can all laugh at you the way you just did at Hazel? I could do it! I could make you want to crawl into a hole and disappear. But listen to me! You need not fear. I will *never* embarrass you in that way. Why not? Because it *hurts* to be laughed at by your friends. It hurts even more than a stubbed toe or a cut finger or a bee sting.

"I want to ask those of you who were having such a good time a few minutes ago: Have you ever had a group of children make fun of you in the same way? If you haven't, then brace yourself. Some day it will happen to you, too. Eventually you will say something foolish . . . and they'll point at you and laugh in your face. And when it happens, I want you to remember what happened today."

*(Then addressing the entire class,)* "Let's make sure that we learn something important from what took place here this afternoon. First, we will not be mean to each other in this class. We will laugh together when things are funny, but we will not do it by making one person feel bad. Second, I will *never* intentionally embarrass anyone in this class. You can count on that. Each of you is a child of God. He molded you with His loving hands, and He has said that we all have equal worth as human beings. This means that Suzie is neither better nor worse than Charles or Mary or Brent. Sometimes I think maybe you believe a few of you are more important than others. It isn't true. Every one of you is priceless to God and each of you will

live forever in eternity. That's how valuable you are. God loves every boy and girl in this room, and because of that, I love every one of you. He wants us to be kind to other people, and we're going to be practicing that kindness through the rest of this year."

When a strong, loving teacher comes to the aid of the least respected child in his class, as I've described, something dramatic occurs in the emotional climate of the room. Every child seems to utter an audible sigh of relief. The same thought is bouncing around in many little heads: "If Hazel is safe from ridicule—even overweight Hazel—then I must be safe, too." You see, by defending the least popular child in the room, a teacher is demonstrating (1) that he has no "pets"; (2) that he respects everyone; (3) that he will fight for anyone who is being treated unjustly. Those are three virtues which children value highly, and which contribute to mental health.

And may I suggest to parents, *defend the underdog in your neighborhood*. Let it be known that you have the confidence to speak for the outcast. Explain this philosophy to your neighbors, and try to create an emotional harbor for the little children whose ship has been threatened by a storm of rejection. Don't be afraid to exercise *leadership* on behalf of a youngster who is being mauled. There is no more worthy investment of your time and energy.[22]

# SECTION 12

# PARENTAL OVER-PROTECTION

**Is it possible to love a child too much?**

Not if the love is totally mature and unconditional. However not everything that is called "love" is healthy for a child. Some Americans are excessively child-oriented at this stage in history; many parents have invested all of their hopes, dreams, desires, and ambitions in their youngsters. The natural culmination of this philosophy is overprotection of the next generation. I dealt with one anxious parent who stated that her children were the *only* sources of her satisfaction. During the long summers, she spent most of her time sitting at the front room window, watching her three girls while they played. She feared that they might get hurt or need her assistance, or they might ride their bikes in the street. Her other home responsibilities were ignored, despite her husband's complaints. She did not have time to clean her house or cook meals; guard duty at the front window was her only function. She suffered enormous tensions over the known and unknown threats that could hurt her beloved offspring.

Childhood illness and sudden danger are always difficult for a loving parent to tolerate, but the slightest threat produces unbearable anxiety for the overprotective mom and dad. Not only do they suffer; their child is often a victim, too.[1]

**What happens to a child whose parents are overprotective and fail to assign appropriate responsibility to their child?**

A dependency relationship may develop with far-reaching implications. Such a youngster often falls behind his normal timetable in preparation for ultimate release as a young adult.

As a ten-year-old, he can't make himself do anything unpleasant, since he has never had any experience in handling the difficult. He does not know how to "give" to anyone else, for he has only thought of himself. He finds it hard to make decisions or exercise any kind of self-discipline. A few years later, he will steamroll into adolescence completely unprepared for the freedom and responsibility he will find there. And finally, his future wife is in for some swell surprises which I shudder to contemplate.[2]

**I want to avoid the dependency trap you described, but am not sure how it begins or how to head it off with an infant son. Alert me to the key elements in this process.**
It is probably easier to foster an unhealthy dependency relationship between parent and child than it is to avoid one. Let's examine the mechanism as it often occurs. At the moment of birth, a little child is completely and totally helpless. One forgets just how dependent a newborn is—in fact, I want to forget it, just as soon as possible! That little creature lying in the crib can do nothing for himself: he doesn't roll over, he can't scratch his head, he is unable to verbalize his thoughts, and he won't lift a finger in his own behalf. Consequently, his parents are responsible for meeting his every need. They are his servants, and if they're too slow in meeting his demands, he is equipped with a spine-chilling scream to urge them into action. He bears no obligations whatsoever. He doesn't even have to appreciate their efforts. He won't say "please" or "thank you"; he doesn't apologize for getting them up six times in one night; he even offers no sympathy when at 3:01 A.M. his exhausted mom drives the point of a safety pin through the fleshy part of her thumb (without doubt, the greatest agony in human experience!). In other words, a child begins his life in a state of complete and total dependency on those whose name he bears.

About twenty years later, however, at the other end of childhood, we expect some radical changes to have occurred in that individual. He should then be able to assume the full responsibilities of young adulthood. He is expected to spend his money wisely, hold down a job, be loyal to one woman, support the needs of his family, obey the laws of the land, and be a good citizen. In other words, during the course of childhood, an individual should progress from a position of *no* responsibility to a position of full responsibility. Now, how does little

John-John get from position A to position B? How does this magical transformation of self-discipline take place? There are many self-appointed experts on child raising who seem to feel it all should happen toward the latter end of adolescence, about fifteen minutes before Big John leaves home permanently. Prior to that time, he should be allowed to do whatever he wishes at the moment.

I reject that notion categorically. The best preparation for responsible adulthood is derived from training in responsibility during childhood. This is not to say that the child should be forced to act like an adult. It does mean that he can be encouraged to progress on an orderly timetable of events, carrying the level of responsibility that is appropriate for his age. Shortly after birth, for example, the mother begins transferring responsibilities from her shoulders to those of her infant. Little by little he learns to sleep through the night, hold his own bottle, and reach for what he wants. Later he is potty-trained (hopefully), and he learns to walk and talk. Gradually, as each new skill is mastered, his mother "frees" herself that much more from this servitude.

Each year he should make more of his own decisions than in the prior twelve months; the routine responsibilities of living should fall to his shoulders as he is able to handle them. A seven-year-old, for example, is usually capable of selecting his own clothing for the day. He should be keeping his room straight and making his bed each morning. A nine- or ten-year-old may be carrying more freedom, such as in the choice of television programs to watch (within reason). I am not suggesting that we abdicate parental leadership altogether; rather, I believe we should give conscious thought to the reasonable, orderly transfer of freedom and responsibility, so that we are preparing the child each year for that moment of full independence which must come.[3]

**You wrote in one of your books, "All of life is a preparation for adolescence and beyond." Please explain and elaborate on that statement.**

I was referring, again, to this need to grant independence to children and permit them to make their own decisions. Parents would be wise to remember that the day is fast approaching when the child they have raised will pack his suitcase and leave home, never to return. And as he walks through the door to confront the outside world, he will no longer be accountable to their parental authority and supervision. He can do what he chooses. No one can require him to eat properly, or get his needed rest, or find a job, or live responsibly, or serve God. He will sink or swim on his own.

This sudden independence can be devastating for some individuals who have not been properly prepared for it. But how can a mother and father train sons and daughters so that they won't go wild in the first dizzying months of freedom? How can they equip them for that moment of emancipation?

The best time to begin preparing a child for the ultimate release is during toddlerhood, before a relationship of dependence is established. As Renshaw wrote:

> It may be messier for the child to feed himself; more untidy for him to dress himself; less clean when he attempts to bathe himself; less perfect for him to comb his hair; but unless his mother learns to sit on her hands and allow the child to cry and to try, she will overdo for the child, and independence will be delayed.[4]

This process of granting appropriate independence must continue through the elementary school years. Parents should permit their kids to go to summer camp even though it might be "safer" to keep them at home. Likewise, boys and girls ought to be allowed to spend the night with their friends when invited. They should make their own beds, take care of their animals, and do their homework. When this assignment has been handled properly through the years, a high school senior should be virtually emancipated, even though he still lives with his parents.[5]

**My mother waited on me hand and foot when I was a child, and I would feel guilty if I didn't serve the needs of my kids as well. Do you really think it is in their best interest for me to do less for them?**

I'm not suggesting that you give up mothering and nurturing your children, but it *is* appropriate for you to let them carry the level of responsibility that their age and maturity permits. This point was made by Marguerite and Willard Beecher, writing in their excellent book, *Parents on the Run*. They stated, and I strongly agree, that *the parent must gain his freedom from the child, so that the child can gain his freedom from the parent.*

Think about that for a moment. If you never get free from your child by transferring responsibility to him, then he remains hopelessly bound to you, too! You have knotted each other in a paralyzing interdependency which stifles growth and development.

I admit the difficulty of implementing this policy. Our deep love for our children makes us tremendously vulnerable to their needs. Life inevitably brings pain and sorrow to little people, and we hurt when they hurt. When others ridicule them or laugh at them, when they feel lonely and rejected, when they fail at something important, when they cry in the midnight hours, when physical harm threatens their existence—these are the trials which seem unbearable to those of us who watch from the sidelines. We want to rise like a mighty shield to protect them from life's sting—to hold them snugly within the safety of our embrace. Yet there are times when we must let them struggle. Children can't grow without taking risks. Toddlers can't walk initially without falling down. Students can't learn without facing some hardships. And ultimately, an adolescent can't enter young adulthood until we release him from our protective custody.[6]

**Why is it so difficult for mothers, especially, to grant this independence and freedom to their kids?**

There are several reasons for the reluctance to let go. I've observed that the most common motivation reflects the unconscious emotional needs of the mother. Perhaps the romance has gone out of her marriage, leaving the child as the only real source of affection. Maybe she has trouble making lasting friendships. For whatever reason, she wants to be the "heavy" in the life of her child. Thus, she becomes his servant. She refuses to obtain her freedom from him for the specific purpose of denying him his. I know one mother-daughter team which maintained this interlocutory relationship until the mother's death at ninety-four years of age. The daughter, then seventy-two, found herself unmarried, alone, and on her own for the first time in her life. It's a frightening thing to endure in old age what other people experienced in adolescence.

I recently counselled another mother whose husband had died when their only son, Davie, was a baby. She had been left with the terrifying task of raising this lad by herself, and Davie was the only person left in the world whom she really loved. Her reaction was to smother him totally. The boy was seven years of age when she came to me. He was afraid to sleep in a room by himself. He refused to stay with a baby-sitter, and he even resisted going to school. He did not dress himself and his behavior was infantile in every regard. In fact, instead of waiting in the reception room while I talked to his mother, he found my office and stood with his hand on the doorknob for an hour, whimpering and begging to be admitted. His mother interpreted all of this as evidence of his fear that she would die, as his father had done. In response, she bound him even more tightly to her, sacrificing all her own needs and desires: she could neither go on dates nor bring any men into their home; she could not get involved in any activities of her own or have any adult experiences without her cling-along son. You see, she had never gained her freedom from Davie, and in turn, Davie had not gained his freedom from his lovin' momma.[7]

**I sense that this task of letting go is one of the most important responsibilities parents face.**

You are right. If I were to list the five most critical objectives of parenting, this one would rest near the top: "Hold them close and let them go." Parents should be deeply involved in the lives of their young children, providing love and protection and authority. But when those children reach their late teens and early twenties, the cage door must be opened to the world outside. That is the most frightening time of parenthood, particularly for Christian mothers and fathers who care so deeply about the spiritual welfare of their families. How difficult it is to await an answer to the question, "Did I train them properly?" The tendency is to retain control in order to avoid hearing the wrong reply to that all-important question. Nevertheless, our sons and daughters are more likely to make proper choices when they do not have to rebel against our meddling interference.

Let me emphasize the point by offering another phrase which could easily have been one of King Solomon's Proverbs, although it does not appear in the Bible. It states, "If you love something, set it free. If it comes back to you, then it's yours. If it doesn't return, then it never was yours in the first place." This little statement contains great wisdom. It reminds me of a day last year when a wild coyote pup trotted in front of my house. He had strayed into our residential area from the nearby mountains. I managed to chase him into our backyard where I trapped him in a corner. After fifteen or twenty minutes of effort, I succeeded in placing a collar and leash around his neck. He fought the noose with all his strength, jumping, diving, gnawing, and straining at the tether.

Finally, in exhaustion, he submitted to his servitude. He was my captive, to the delight of the neighborhood children. I kept the little rascal for an entire day and considered trying to make a pet of him. However, I contacted an authority on coyotes, who told me the chances were very slim that I could tame his wild streak. Obviously, I could have kept him chained or caged, but he would never really have belonged to me. Thus, I asked a game warden to return the lop-eared creature to his native territory in the canyons above Los Angeles. You see, his "friendship" meant nothing to me unless I could set him free and he would remain with me by his own choice.

My point is that love demands freedom. It is true not only of relationships between animals and man, but also in all human interactions. For example, the quickest way to destroy a romantic love between a husband and wife is for one partner to clamp a steel cage around the other. I've seen hundreds of women trying unsuccessfully to demand love and fidelity from their husbands. It won't work. Think back to your dating experiences before marriage. Do you recall that romantic relationships were doomed the moment one partner began to worry about losing the other, phoning six or eight times a day and hiding behind trees to see who was competing for the lover's attention? That hand wringing performance will devastate a perfectly good love affair in a matter of days. To repeat, *love demands freedom.*

Why else did God give us the choice of either serving Him or rejecting His companionship? Why did He give Adam and Eve the option of eating forbidden fruit in the Garden of Eden, instead of forcing their obedience? Why didn't He just make men and women His slaves who were programmed to worship at His feet? The answers are found in the meaning of love. God gave us a free choice because there is no significance to love that knows no alternative. It is only when we come to Him because we hungrily seek His fellowship and communion that the relationship has any validity. Isn't this the meaning of Proverbs 8:17, whereby He says, "I love them that love me; and those that seek me early shall find me" (KJV)? That is the love that only freedom can produce. It cannot be demanded or coerced or required or programmed against our will. It can only be the product of a free choice which is honored even by the Almighty.

The application of this perspective to older adolescents (especially those in their early twenties) should be obvious. There comes a point where our record as parents is in the books, our training has been completed, and the moment of release has arrived. As I did with the young coyote, we must unsnap the leash and remove the collar. If our "child" runs, he runs. If he marries the wrong person, he marries the wrong person. If he takes drugs, he takes drugs. If he goes to the wrong school, or rejects his faith, or refuses to work, or squanders his inheritance on liquor and prostitutes, then he must be permitted to make these destructive choices and take the consequences of those decisions.

In summary, let me say that adolescence is not an easy time of life for either generation; in fact, it can be downright terrifying. But the key to surviving this emotional experience is to lay the proper foundation and then face it with courage. Even the inevitable rebellion of the teen years can be a healthy factor. This conflict contributes to the process by which an individual changes from a dependent child to a mature adult, taking his place as a co-equal with his parents. Without that friction, the relationship could continue to be an unhealthy "mommie-daddy-child" triad, late into adult life, with serious implications for future marital harmony. If the strain between generations were not part of the divine plan of human development, it would not be so universally prevalent, even in homes where love and authority have been maintained in proper balance.[8]

**The following question was posed by *Family Life Today,* a Christian magazine devoted to family issues and interests:**

> **What do you do when your child, at age eighteen or twenty, makes choices quite different from what you had hoped? Parents feel frustrated and embarrassed—at a loss to influence the child they thought had been "trained up in the way he should go" but who is now "departing from it." Parenting begins when a child is born. But does it ever end? Should it? If so, when? And how?**

My answer reprinted below is used by permission of *Family Life Today* magazine (Copyright © 1982), and was originally published in the March 1982 issue.

"The process of letting go of our offspring should begin shortly after birth and conclude some twenty years later with the final release and emancipation," said Dobson, who readily admits this is the most difficult assignment parents face. "The release is not a sudden event. In fact, from infancy onward, the parent should do nothing for the child that the child can profit from doing for himself. Refusal to grant appropriate independence and freedom results in rebellion and immaturity—whether during the terrible twos or later in adolescence."

A strong advocate of loving discipline during the early years, Dobson contends that there comes a time when the relationship between generations must change. "By the time a child is eighteen or twenty," he noted, "the parent should begin to relate to his or her offspring more as a peer. This liberates the parent from the responsibility of leadership and the child from the obligation of dependency.

"It is especially difficult for us *Christian* parents to release our children into adulthood because we care so much about the outcome of our training. Fear of rebellion and rejection of our values and beliefs often leads us to retain our authority until it is torn from our grasp. By then, permanent damage may have been done to family relationship."

One of the most difficult times for parents to remain reserved is when their young adult offspring chooses a mate not to the parents' liking. "Though it is painful to permit what you think would be a marital mistake," Dobson warned, "it is unwise to become dictatorial and authoritarian in the matter. If you set yourself against the person your child has chosen to marry, you may struggle with in-law problems the rest of your life.

"If there are well-grounded reasons for opposing a potential marriage, a parent can be honest about those convictions at an opportune moment and in an appropriate manner. But that does not entitle the older generation to badger and nag and criticize those who are trying to make this vitally important decision."

For example, he suggested that in such a situation a parent might say: "I have great concern about what you're doing and I'm going to express my views to you. Then I'll step aside and allow you to make up your own mind. Here are the areas of incompatibility that I foresee (etc.) . . . I'm going to be praying for you as you seek the Lord's will in this important matter." The most critical ingredient, Dobson concluded, is to make it clear that the decision is "owned" by the offspring—not the parent.

What are the consequences of not handling these crises properly? "Unresolved conflicts during late adolescence have a way of continuing into the adult years," replied Dobson. A recent mail-in survey he conducted revealed that 89 percent of the 2,600 people responding felt that they suffered from long-term strained relationships with their own parents. Forty-four percent complained specifically that their parents had never set them free or granted them adult status.

And, added Dobson, the letters that accompanied the survey responses told incredible stories—of a twenty-three-year-old girl who was regularly spanked for misbehavior and others in mid-life who still did not feel accepted and respected by their parents. "Clearly," he said, "the process of letting go is a very difficult process for *most* parents."

What can a mother or father do if the offspring has gone into openly sinful behavior that violates everything the parent has stood for? And how should they react, for example, when their grown kids forsake family ties and join a "New Age" religious group?

"I have not recommended that parents keep their concerns and opinions to themselves," said Dobson, "especially when eternal issues hang in the balance. There is a time to speak up. But the manner in which the message is conveyed must make it clear that the parents' role is advisory . . . not authoritarian. The ultimate goal is for parents to assure the young person of their continued love and commitment, while speaking directly about the dangers that are perceived. And I repeat, it must be obvious that the responsibility for decision-making ultimately rests with the offspring."

Dobson, whose books on family interaction have dominated the "top ten" Christian best-seller lists for many months, mused that his next book will probably be about guilt in parenthood. Referring to Proverbs 22:6, he said he agrees with Dr. John White that the Proverbs are presented as *probabilities,* not *promises:* "Even if we train up a child in the way he should go, he *sometimes* goes his own way! That's why we parents tend to experience tremendous guilt that is often unjustified. Our kids live in a sinful world and they often emulate their peers; despite our teaching to the contrary, God gives each child a free will and He will not take it from them—nor can we."

Citing several enviornmental and inborn factors that parents do not control—including individual temperament, peer-group pressures and the innate will of the child—Dobson noted that these combined forces are probably more influential than parental leadership itself. "It is simply unfair to attribute everything young adults do . . . good or bad . . . to parental skill or ignorance.

"A hundred years ago when a child went wrong, he was written off as a 'bad kid.' Now, any failure or rebellion in the younger generation is blamed on the parents—supposedly reflecting their mistakes and shortcomings. Such a notion is often unjust and fails to acknowledge a young adult's freedom to run his own life."

What attitude, then, should a parent have toward a twenty-one-year-old offspring who insists on living with someone of the opposite sex? "It is difficult to force anything on a person that age, and in fact, a parent shouldn't try," Dobson warned. "But Mom and Dad certainly do not have to pay for the folly."

He noted that the father of the Prodigal Son, symbolizing God's patient love, permitted his son to enter a life of sin. But he didn't send his servants to "bail out" his erring youngest when times got difficult.

"It was the son's choice to go into a sinful life-style, and the father permitted both the behavior and the consequences," Dobson observed. "An over-protective parent who continually sends money to an irresponsible offspring, often breaks this necessary connection between sinful behavior and painful consequences.

"A parent's goal should be to build a friendship with his or her child from the cradle onward," Dobson concluded. "When his task is done properly, both generations can enjoy a lifetime of fellowship after the child has left home and established a family of his own."

After talking with this noted Christian psychologist, one

leaves with the impression that parents who once looked with awe and wonder at their bundle of new life may find the delivery of that same child into adulthood two decades later no less a marvel. And just as they could not keep their newborn child in the safety and protection of the womb, they must ultimately permit his or her passage into the grown-up world at the end of childhood. Along the way, wise Christian parents will prayerfully try to influence—but not prolong control over—their maturing child. The rest they leave in the hands of the Creator.

# SECTION 13

# SIBLING RIVALRY

**Nothing irritates me as much as the fighting and bickering that occurs between my two boys. Do all parents struggle with sibling conflict or does it result from failure on my part?**

If American women were asked to indicate *the* most irritating feature of child rearing, I'm convinced that sibling rivalry would get their unanimous vote. Little children (and older ones, too) are not content just to hate each other in private. They attack one another like miniature warriors, mobilizing their troops and probing for a weakness in the defensive line. They argue, hit, kick, scream, grab toys, taunt, tattle, and sabotage the opposing forces. I knew one child who deeply resented being sick with a cold while his older sibling was healthy, so he secretly blew his nose on the mouthpiece of his brother's musical instrument! The big loser from such combat, of course, is the harassed mother who must listen to the noise of the battlefield and then try to patch up the wounded. If her emotional nature requires peace and tranquility (and most women do), she may stagger under the barrage of cannonfire.

Columnist Ann Landers recently asked her readers to respond to the question, "If you had known then what you know now, would you have had children?" Among ten thousand women who answered, 70 percent said No! A subsequent survey by *Good Housekeeping* posed the same question and 95 percent of the respondents answered Yes. It is impossible to explain the contradictory results from these two inquiries, although the accompanying comments were enlightening. One unidentified woman wrote, "Would I have children again? A thousand times, No! My children have completely destroyed my life, my marriage, and my identity as a person. There are no joys. Prayers don't help—nothing stops a 'screaming kid.' "

It is my contention that something *will* stop a screaming kid, or even a dozen of them. It is not necessary or healthy to allow children to destroy each other and make life miserable for the adults around them. Sibling rivalry is difficult to "cure" but it can certainly be treated.[1]

**What causes sibling rivalry?**

Sibling rivalry is not new, of course. It was responsible for the first murder on record (when Cain killed Abel), and has been represented in virtually every two-child family from that time to this. The underlying source of this conflict is old-fashioned jealousy and competition between children. Marguerite and Willard Beecher, writing in their book *Parents on the Run*,[2] expressed the inevitability of this struggle as follows:

> It was once believed that if parents would explain to a child that he was having a little brother or sister, he would not resent it. He was told that his parents had enjoyed him so much that they wanted to increase their happiness. This was supposed to avoid jealous competition and rivalry. It did not work. Why should it? Needless to say, if a man tells his wife he has loved her so much that he now plans to bring another wife into the home to "increase his happiness," she would not be immune to jealousy. On the contrary, the fight would just begin—in exactly the same fashion as it does with children.[3]

**If jealousy between kids is so common, then how can parents minimize the natural antagonism which children feel for their siblings?**

The first step is to avoid circumstances which compare them unfavorably with each other. Lecturer Bill Gothard has stated that the root of all feelings of inferiority is comparison. I agree. The question is not "How am I doing?" it is "How am I doing compared with John or Steven or Marion?" The issue is not how fast can I run, but who crosses the finish line first. A boy does not care how tall he is; he is vitally interested in "who is tallest."

Each child systematically measures himself against his peers, and is tremendously sensitive to failure within his own family.

Accordingly, parents should guard against comparative statements which routinely favor one child over another. This is particularly true in three areas.

First, children are extremely sensitive about the matter of physical attractiveness and body characteristics. It is highly inflammatory to commend one child at the expense of the other. Suppose, for example, that Sharon is permitted to hear the casual remark about her sister, "Betty is sure going to be a gorgeous girl." The very fact that Sharon was not mentioned will probably establish the two girls as rivals. If there is a significant difference in beauty between the two, you can be assured that Sharon has already concluded, "Yeah, I'm the ugly one." When her fears are then confirmed by her parents, resentment and jealousy are generated.

Beauty is *the* most significant factor in the self-esteem of Western children, as I attempted to express in *Hide or Seek*. Anything that a parent utters on this subject within the hearing of children should be screened carefully. It has the power to make brothers and sisters hate one another.

Second, the matter of intelligence is another sensitive nerve to be handled with care. It is not uncommon to hear parents say in front of their children, "I think the younger boy is actually brighter than his brother." Adults find it difficult to comprehend how powerful that kind of assessment can be in a child's mind. Even when the comments are unplanned and are spoken routinely, they convey how a child is "seen" within his family. We are all vulnerable to that bit of evidence.

Third, children (and especially boys) are extremely competitive with regard to athletic abilities. Those who are slower, weaker, and less coordinated than their brothers are rarely able to accept "second best" with grace and dignity. Consider, for example, the following note given to me by the mother of two boys. It was written by her nine-year-old son to his eight-year-old brother, the evening after the younger child had beaten him in a race.

> Dear Jim:
>
> I am the greatest and your the badest. And I can beat everybody in a race and you can't beat anybody in a race. I'm the smartest and your the dumbest. I'm the best sport player and your the badest sport player. And your also a

hog. I can beat anybody up. And that's the truth. And that's the end of this story.

Yours truly,
Richard

This note is humorous to me, because Richard's motive was so poorly disguised. He had been badly stung by his humiliation on the field of honor, so he came home and raised the battle flags. He will probably spend the next eight weeks looking for opportunities to fire torpedoes into Jim's soft underbelly. Such is the nature of mankind.[4]

**Are you suggesting that parents eliminate all aspects of individuality within family life or that healthy competition should be discouraged in order to minimize the jealousy factor between children?**
Definitely not. I am saying that in matters relative to beauty, brains, and athletic ability, each child should know that in his parents' eyes, he is respected and has equal worth with his siblings.

Praise and criticism *at home* should be distributed as evenly as possible, although some children will inevitably be more successful in the outside world. And finally, we should remember that children do not build fortresses around strengths—they construct them to protect weakness. Thus, when a child like Richard begins to brag and boast and attack his siblings, he is revealing the threats he feels at that point. Our sensitivity to those signals will help minimize the potential for jealousy within our children.[5]

**Sometimes I feel as though my children fight and argue as a method of attracting my attention. If this is the case, how should I respond?**
You are probably correct in making that assumption. Sibling rivalry often represents a form of manipulation of parents. Quarreling and fighting provide an opportunity for both children to "capture" adult attention. It has been written, "Some children had rather be wanted for murder than not wanted at all." Toward this end, a pair of obnoxious kids can tacitly agree to bug their parents until they get a response—even if it is an angry reaction.

One father told me recently that his son and his nephew began to argue and then beat each other with their fists. Both fathers were nearby and decided to let the fight run its natural course. During the first lull in the action one of the boys glanced sideways toward the passive men and said, "Isn't anybody going to stop us before we get hurt?!" The fight, you see, was something neither boy wanted. Their violent combat was directly related to the presence of the two adults and would have taken a different form if the boys had been alone. Children will often "hook" their parents' attention and intervention in this way.

Believe it or not, this form of sibling rivalry is easiest to control. The parent must simply render the behavior unprofitable to each participant. I would recommend that you review the problem (for example, a morning full of bickering) with the children, and then say, "Now listen carefully. If the two of you want to pick on each other and make yourselves miserable, then be my guest [assuming there is a fairly equal balance of power between them]. Go outside and fight until you're exhausted. But it's not going to occur under my feet anymore. It's over! And you know that I mean business when I make that kind of statement. Do we understand each other?"

Having made the boundaries clear, I would act decisively the *instant* either boy returned to his bickering. If I had separate bedrooms, I would confine one child to each room for at least thirty minutes of complete boredom—without radio or television. Or I would assign one to clean the garage and the other to mow the lawn. Or I would make them take a nap. My avowed purpose would be to make them believe me the next time I submitted a request for peace and tranquility.

What is most surprising is that children are happiest when their parents enforce these reasonable limits with love and dignity. Instead of wringing their hands and crying and begging and screaming (which actually reinforces the disruptive behavior and makes it worse), a mother or father should approach the conflict with dignity and self-control.[6]

**I've been very careful to be fair with my children and give them no reason to resent one another. Nevertheless, they continue to fight. What can I do?**

The problem may rest in your lack of disciplinary control at home. Sibling rivalry is at its worst when there is an inadequate system of justice among children—where the "lawbreakers" do not get caught, or if apprehended are set free without standing trial. It is important to understand that laws in a society are established and enforced for the purpose of protecting people from each other. Likewise, a family is a mini-society with the same requirement for protection of human rights.

For purposes of illustration, suppose that I live in a community where there is no established law. Policemen do not exist and there are no courts to whom disagreements can be appealed. Under those circumstances, my neighbor and I can abuse each other with impunity. He can take my lawnmower and throw rocks through my windows, while I steal the peaches from his favorite tree and dump my leaves over his fence. This kind of mutual antagonism has a way of escalating day by day, becoming ever more violent with the passage of time. When permitted to run its natural course, as in early American history, the end result can be feudal hatred and murder.

As indicated, individual families are similar to societies in their need for law and order. In the absence of justice, "neighboring" siblings begin to assault one another. The older child is bigger and tougher, which allows him to oppress his younger brothers and sister. But the junior member of the family is not without weapons of his own. He strikes back by breaking the toys and prized possessions of the older sibling and interferes when friends are visiting. Mutual hatred then erupts like an angry volcano, spewing its destructive contents on everyone in its path.

Nevertheless, when the children appeal to their parents for intervention, they are often left to fight it out among themselves. In many homes, the parents do not have sufficient disciplinary control to enforce their judgments. In others, they are so exasperated with constant bickering among siblings that they refuse to get involved. In still others, parents require an older child to live with an admitted injustice "because your brother is smaller than you." Thus, they tie his hands and render him utterly defenseless against the mischief of his bratty little brother or sister. Even more commonly today, mothers and fathers are both working while their children are home busily disassembling each other.

I will say it again to parents: one of your most important responsibilities is to establish an equitable system of justice and a balance of power at home. There should be reasonable "laws" which are enforced fairly for each member of the family. For purposes of illustration, let me list the boundaries and rules which have evolved through the years in my own home.

1. Neither child is ever allowed to make fun of the other in a destructive way. Period! This is an inflexible rule with no exceptions.
2. Each child's room is his private territory. There are locks on both doors, and permission to enter is a revokable privilege. (Families with more than one child in each bedroom can allocate available living space for each youngster.)
3. The older child is not permitted to tease the younger child.
4. The younger child is forbidden to harass the older child.
5. The children are not required to play with each other when they prefer to be alone or with other friends.
6. We mediate any genuine conflict as quickly as possible, being careful to show impartiality and extreme fairness.

As with any plan of justice, this plan requires (1) children's respect for leadership of the parent, (2) willingness by the parent to mediate, (3) occasional enforcement or punishment. When this approach is accomplished with love, the emotional tone of the home can be changed from one of hatred to (at least) tolerance.[7]

**My older child is a great student and earns straight A's year after year. Her younger sister, now in the sixth grade, is completely bored in school and won't even try. The frustrating thing is that the younger girl is probably brighter than her older sister. Why would she refuse to apply her ability like this?**

There could be many reasons for her academic disinterest, but let me suggest the most probable explanation. Children will often refuse to compete when they think they are likely to place second instead of first. Therefore, a younger child may diligently avoid challenging an older sibling in his area of greatest strength. If Son Number One is a great athlete, then Son Number Two may be more interested in collecting butterflies. If Daughter Number One is a disciplined pianist, then Daughter Number Two may be a boy-crazy goof-off.

This rule does not always hold, of course, depending on the child's fear of failure and the way he estimates his chances of successful competition. If his confidence is high, he may blatantly wade into the territory owned by big brother, determined to do even better. However, the more typical response is to seek new areas of compensation which are not yet dominated by a family superstar.

If this explanation fits the behavior of your younger daughter, then it would be wise to accept something less than perfection from her school performance. Every child need not fit the same mold—nor can we force them to do so.[8]

**(The following excerpt was taken from an actual letter sent to me by a creative mother.)**

**You recommended in *Dare to Discipline* and *Hide or Seek* that we use a monetary reward system to encourage our children to accept new responsibilities. This approach has helped a great deal and our family is functioning much smoother. However, I had an idea for improving the system which has worked beautifully with my two boys, ages six and eight. In order for them to earn a reward for brushing their teeth, making their beds, putting away their clothes, etc., they both must complete the jobs as assigned. In other words, I tax them both for one child's failure and reward them both for mutual successes. They got in the spirit of working together to achieve the goal. It has made them business partners, in a sense. I thought you would be interested in this approach.**

This mother has done what I hope other parents will do: use my writings as a springboard to creative approaches of their own. My illustrations merely show that the most successful parents are those who find unique solutions to the routine problems of living. The writer of this letter has done that beautifully.[9]

**We are planning our family very carefully, and want to space the children properly. Is there an ideal age span that will bring greater harmony between them?**

Children who are two years apart and of the same sex are more likely to be competitive with one another. On the other hand, they are also more likely to enjoy mutual companionship. If you produce your babies four or more years apart there will be less camaraderie between them but at least you'll have only one child in college at a time. My evasive reply to your question reflects my personal bias: There are many more important reasons for planning a baby at a particular time than the age of those already born. Of greater significance is the health of the mother, the desire for another child, financial considerations, and the stability of the marriage. The relative ages of siblings is not one of the major determiners, in my opinion.[10]

**Before our new baby was born last month, our three-year-old son was thrilled at the prospect of a baby brother or sister. Now, however, he shows signs of jealousy, sucking his thumb sullenly when I nurse the baby, and getting very loud and silly when friends drop in to bring a gift to the new arrival. Please suggest some ways I can ease him through this period of adjustment.**
Your son is revealing a "textbook" reaction to the invasion that has occurred in his private kingdom. We saw a similar response when our second child was born. Our son arrived on the scene when his sister was five years of age. She had been the only granddaughter on either side of the family and had received all the adult attention that can be heaped upon a child. Then suddenly, her secure palace was invaded by a cute little fellow who captured and held center stage. All of the relatives cuddled, cooed, rocked, bounced, and hugged baby Ryan, while Danae watched suspiciously from the wings. As we drove home from Grandmother's house on a Sunday afternoon, about a week after Ryan's arrival, our daughter suddenly said, "Daddy, you know I'm just talking. You know, I don't mean to be bad or anything, but sometimes I wish little Ryan wasn't here!"

She had given us a valuable clue to her feelings in that brief sentence, and we immediately seized the opportunity she had provided. We moved her into the front seat of the car so we could discuss what she had said. We told her we understood how she felt and assured her of our love. We also explained that a baby is completely helpless and will die if people don't take care of him—feed, clothe, change, and love him. We reminded her that she was taken care of that way when she was a baby, and explained that Ryan would soon grow up, too. We were also careful in the months that followed to minimize the threat to her place in our hearts. By giving careful attention to her feelings and security, the relationship with her brother developed into a lasting friendship and love.

Danae's admission was not a typical response among children. Much more commonly, a child will be unable or unwilling to express the insecurity brought by a newborn rival, requiring his parents to read more subtle signs and cues. The most reliable symptoms of the I've-been-replaced syndrome is a sudden return to infantile behavior. Obviously, "If babyhood is where it's at, then I'll be a baby again." Therefore, the child throws temper tantrums, wets the bed, sucks his thumb, holds tightly to Momma, baby talks, etc. In this situation, the child has observed a clear and present danger and is solving it in the best way he knows.

If your firstborn child seems to feel like a has-been, I would suggest the following procedures be implemented:

1. Bring his feelings out in the open and help him verbalize them. When a child is acting silly in front of adults, trying to make them laugh or notice him, it is good to take him in your arms and say, "What's the matter, Joey? Do you need some attention today?" Gradually, a child can be taught to use similar words when he feels excluded or rejected. "I need some attention, Dad. Will you play with me?" By verbalizing his feelings, you also help him understand himself better.

2. Don't let antisocial behavior succeed. If the child cries when the baby-sitter arrives, leave him anyway. A temper tantrum can be greeted with a firm swat, etc. However, reveal little anger and displeasure, remembering that the entire episode is motivated by a threat to your love.

3. Meet his needs in ways that grant status to him for being older. Take him to the park, making it clear that the baby is too little to go; talk "up" to him about the things he can do that the baby can't—he can use the bathroom instead of his pants, for example. Let him help take care of the baby so he will feel he is part of the family process.

Beyond these corrective steps, give your son some time to adjust to his new situation. Even though it stresses him somewhat today, he should profit from the realization that he does not sit at the center of the universe.[11]

SECTION 14

# TEACHING CHILDREN TO BE RESPONSIBLE

**You have indicated that a child's willful defiance should be handled differently than mere childish irresponsibility. I'm not sure I understand the distinction between these two categories of behavior. Can you explain them further?**

Willful defiance, as the name implies, is a deliberate act of disobedience. It occurs only when the child knows what his parents expect and then is determined to do the opposite. In short, it is a refusal to accept parental leadership, such as running away when called, screaming insults, acts of outright disobedience, etc. By contrast, childish irresponsibility results from forgetting, accidents, mistakes, a short attention span, a low frustration tolerance, and immaturity. In the first instance, the child knows he was wrong and is waiting to see what his parent can do about it; in the second, he has simply blundered into a consequence he did not plan. It is wrong, in my view, to resort to corporal punishment for the purpose of instilling responsibility (unless, of course, the child has defiantly refused to accept it).

Ultimately, the appropriate disciplinary reaction by a mother or father should be determined entirely by the matter of *intention*. Suppose my three-year-old son is standing in the doorway and I say, "Ryan, please shut the door." But in his linguistic immaturity he misunderstands my request and opens the door even further. Will I punish him for disobeying me? Of course not, even though he did the opposite of what I asked. He may never even know that he failed the assignment. My tolerance is dictated by his intention. He honestly tried to obey me.

However, if when I ask Ryan to pick up his toys, he stamps his little foot and screams, "No!" before throwing a Tonka truck in my direction—then I am obligated to accept his challenge. In short, my child is never so likely to be punished as when I'm sure *he knows* he deserves it.

The Bible teaches quite clearly that human beings have a universal tendency toward rebellion and that must be dealt with during childhood when it is focused primarily upon the parents. If that defiance is not suppressed in the tender years, it may develop into general rebellion against all authority, including that of God Himself. Our Creator has warned of the consequences of this rebellion, stating in Proverbs 29:1, "He, that being often reproved hardeneth his neck, shall suddenly be destroyed, and that without remedy" (KJV). Thus, we should teach our children to submit to our loving leadership as preparation for their later life of obedience to God.[1]

**How should parents deal with childish irresponsibility when it involves neither defiance nor passive aggression?** Kids love games of all sorts, especially if adults will get involved with them. It is often possible to turn a teaching situation into a fun activity which "sensitizes" the entire family to the issue you're trying to teach. Let me tell you how we taught our children to put their napkins in their laps before eating. We tried reminding them for two or three years, but simply weren't getting through. Then we turned it into a family game.

Now, if one of the Dobsons takes a single bite of food before putting his napkin in his lap, he is required to go to his bedroom and count to twenty-five in a loud voice. This game is highly effective, although it has some definite disadvantages. You can't imagine how foolish Shirley and I feel when we're standing in an empty section of the house, counting to twenty-five while our children giggle. Ryan, particularly, *never* forgets his napkin and he loves to catch the rest of us in a moment of preoccupation. He will sit perfectly still, looking straight ahead until the first bite of food goes in. Then he wheels toward the offender, points his finger, and says, "Gotcha!"

For all of those many parenting objectives that involve teaching responsibility (rather than conquering willful defiance), game-playing should be considered as the method of choice.[2]

**Do you think a child should be required to say "thank you" and "please" around the house?**
I sure do. Requiring these phrases is one method of reminding the child that this is not a "gimmie-gimmie" world. Even though his mother is cooking for him and buying for him and giving to him, he must assume a few attitudinal responsibilities in return. Appreciation must be taught and this instructional process begins with fundamental politeness at home.[3]

**My ten-year-old can be the most irresponsible kid I've ever known. He hates to work and he has lost or broken everything of value he's ever been given. I've read many books about teaching children to be mature and responsible, and we're working on these objectives. My problem is that I lose my patience with him too often. I yell at him and accuse him of being stupid and lazy. Then I feel terrible about my lack of control. Am I damaging his self-esteem by these outbursts?**
Children are usually very resilient and most of them can absorb occasional parental outbursts without sustaining permanent harm. In fact, your displeasure is part of the teaching process whereby a parent nudges his child in the direction of maturity. However, if you realize you are over-reacting frequently or habitually, especially if it involves labeling him unfairly, you would do well to remember what someone has said about the way people perceive themselves:

We are not what we think we are . . .
We are not even what *others* think we are . . .
We are what we *think* others think we are.

There is great truth in this statement. Each of us evaluates what we believe our associates are thinking about us, and then we often play that prescribed role. This explains why we wear a very different "face" with different groups. A doctor may be an unsmiling professional with his patients, being reserved and wise in their presence. They "see" him that way and he complies. That evening, however, he is reunited with his former college friends who remember him as a postadolescent screwball. His personality may oscillate 180 degrees between afternoon and night, being totally unrecognizable if seen by an amazed patient. Similarly, most of us *are* what we think others think we are.

That being true, your child will conform to the image he

thinks you hold of him. If you call him lazy and stupid, his behavior will prove that assessment to be correct. Fortunately, the opposite is also true. So whenever possible, control your impulsive reactions and give him a high image to shoot for. Otherwise, he will stoop to match the one you are now communicating.

I know! I know! It sounds easy on paper, but it is tough to implement. I have trouble following this advice, too. But we can at least *try* to provide what our imperfect kids need from us imperfect parents.

**Must I brag on my child all day for every little thing he does? Isn't it possible to create a spoiled brat by telling him his every move is wonderful?**

Yes, inflationary praise is unnecessary. Junior quickly catches on to your verbal game, and your words then lose their meaning. It is helpful to distinguish between the concepts of *flattery* versus *praise*. Flattery is unearned. It is what Grandma says when she comes for a visit: "Oh, look at my beautiful little girl! You're getting prettier each day. I'll bet you'll have to beat the boys off with a club when you get to be a teenager!" Or, "My, what a smart boy you are." Flattery occurs when you heap compliments upon the child for something he did not achieve.

Praise, on the other hand, is used to reinforce positive, constructive behavior. It should be highly specific rather than general. "You've been a good boy . . . " is unsatisfactory. "I like the way you kept your room straight today," is better. Parents should always watch for opportunities to offer genuine, well-deserved praise to their children, while avoiding empty flattery.[4]

**How can I acquaint my junior higher with the need for responsible behavior throughout his life? He is desperately in need of this understanding.**

The overall objective during the preadolescent period is to teach the child that his actions have inevitable consequences. One of the most serious casualties in a permissive society is the failure to connect those two factors, behavior and consequences. Too often, a three-year-old child screams insults at his mother, but Mom stands blinking her eyes in confusion. A first grader launches an attack on his teacher, but the school makes allowances for his age and takes no action. A ten-year-old is caught stealing candy in a store, but is released to the recognizance of his parents. A fifteen-year-old sneaks the keys to the family car, but his father pays the fine when is he arrested. A seventeen-year-old drives his Chevy like a maniac and his parents pay for the repairs when he wraps it around a telephone pole. You see, all through childhood, loving parents seem determined to intervene between behavior and consequences, breaking the connection and preventing the valuable learning that could have occurred.

Thus, it is possible for a young man or woman to enter adult life, not really knowing that life bites—that every move we make directly affects our future—that irresponsible behavior eventually produces sorrow and pain. Such a person applies for his first job and arrives late for work three times during the first week; then, when he is fired in a flurry of hot words, he becomes bitter and frustrated. It was the first time in his life that Mom and Dad couldn't come running to rescue him from the unpleasant consequences. (Unfortunately, many American parents still try to "bail out" the grown children even when they are in their twenties and live away from home.) What is the result? This overprotection produces emotional cripples who often develop lasting characteristics of dependency and a kind of perpetual adolescence.

How does one connect behavior with consequences? By being willing to let the child experience a reasonable amount of pain or inconvenience when he behaves irresponsibly. When Jack misses the school bus through his own dawdling, let him walk a mile or two and enter school in midmorning (unless safety factors prevent this). If Janie carelessly loses her lunch money, let her skip a meal. Obviously, it is possible to carry this principle too far, being harsh and inflexible with an immature child. But the best approach is to expect boys and girls to carry the responsibility that is appropriate for their age, and occasionally to taste the bitter fruit that irresponsibility bears.[5]

**I have a horrible time getting my ten-year-old daughter ready to catch the school bus each morning. She will get up when I insist, but she dawdles and plays as soon as I leave the room. I have to goad and push and warn her every few minutes or else she will be late. So I get more and more angry, and usually end up by screaming insults at her. I know this is not the best way to handle the little**

**brat, but I declare, she makes me want to clobber her. Tell me how I can get her moving without this emotion every day.**

You are playing right into your daughter's hands by assuming the responsibility for getting her ready each morning. A ten-year-old should definitely be able to handle that task on her own steam, but your anger is not likely to bring it about. We had a very similar problem with our own daughter when she was ten. Perhaps the solution we worked out will be helpful to you.

Danae's morning time problem related primarily to her compulsivity about her room. She will not leave for school each day unless her bed is made perfectly and every trinket is in its proper place. This was not something we taught her; she has always been very meticulous about her possessions. (I should add that her brother, Ryan, does not have that problem.) Danae could easily finish these tasks on time if she were motivated to do so, but she was never in a particular hurry. Therefore, my wife began to fall into the same habit you described, warning, threatening, pushing, shoving, and ultimately becoming angry as the clock moved toward the deadline.

Shirley and I discussed the problem and agreed that there had to be a better method of getting through the morning. I subsequently created a system which we called "Checkpoints." It worked like this. Danae was instructed to be out of bed and standing erect before 6:30 each morning. It was her responsibility to set her own clock-radio and get herself out of bed. If she succeeded in getting up on time (even one minute later was considered a missed item) she immediately went to the kitchen where a chart was taped to the refrigerator door. She then circled "yes" or "no," with regard to the first checkpoint for that date. It couldn't be more simple. She either did or did not get up by 6:30.

The second checkpoint occurred forty minutes later at 7:10. By that time, she was required to have her room straightened to her own satisfaction, be dressed and have her teeth brushed, hair combed, etc., and be ready to begin practicing the piano. Forty minutes was ample time for these tasks, which could actually be done in ten or fifteen minutes if she wanted to hurry. Thus, the only way she could miss the second checkpoint was to ignore it deliberately.

Now, what meaning did the checkpoints have? Did failure to meet them bring anger and wrath and gnashing of teeth? Of course not. The consequences were straightforward and fair. If Danae missed one checkpoint, she was required to go to bed thirty minutes earlier than usual that evening. If she missed two, she hit the "lily whites" an hour before her assigned hour. She was permitted to read during that time in bed, but she could not watch television or talk on the telephone. This procedure took all the morning pressure off Shirley and placed it on our daughter's shoulders, where it belonged. There were occasions when my wife got up just in time to fix breakfast, only to find Danae sitting soberly at the piano, clothed and in her right mind.

This system of discipline can serve as a model for parents who have similar behavioral problems with their children. It was not oppressive; in fact, Danae seemed to enjoy having a target to shoot at. The limits of acceptable performance were defined beyond question. The responsibility was clearly placed on the child. And it required no adult anger or foot stamping.

There is an adaptation of this concept available to resolve other thorny conflicts in your home, too. The only limit lies in the creativity and imagination that you bring to the situation.[6]

**My eight-year-old often puts his milk glass too close to his elbow when eating, and has knocked it over at least six times. I keep telling him to be careful but it just isn't within him to slow down. When he spilt the milk again yesterday, I jerked him up and gave him a spanking with a belt. Today I don't feel good about the incident. Should I have reacted more patiently?**

Yes, it appears that you overreacted. Spanking should only be applied in circumstances when the *intent* of the child is to disobey or defy your authority. A table accident, even if it occurs often, does not fall in that category of rebellious behavior. Therefore, the spanking was inappropriate in the instance you described (even though I understand the frustration that caused it). It would have been better to create a method of capturing his attention and helping him remember to return his glass to a safe area. For example, you could have cut an "off limits" zone from red construction paper, and taped it to the side of his plate. If Junior placed his glass on the paper, he would have to help wash the dishes after the evening meal. I guarantee you that he would seldom "forget" again. In fact, this procedure would probably sensitize him to the location of the glass, even after the paper was removed. Again, it's important to remember that irresponsible behavior is quite different in motive than defiance and rebellion, and should be handled more creatively.[7]

**My two adopted daughters are sisters. They were six- and eight-years-old when we got them last month. They have adjusted pretty well to our home, and they respond eagerly to our love. However, they have many sloppy habits: they hadn't been taught to use a fork, so they grab food with their hands. They leave water running, won't hang up wet towels, and would never brush their teeth if I didn't stand over them. How can I teach them to take responsibility for themselves like other children their ages?**

One of the most effective tools available for teaching responsibility to children involves the use of specific rewards for proper behavior. The system by which they are motivated is expressed in the "Law of Reinforcement," described by the first educational psychologist, E. L. Thorndike. It states, "Behavior which achieves desirable consequences will recur." In other words, if an individual likes what happens as a result of his behavior, he will be inclined to repeat that act. If Sally gets favorable attention from the boys on the day she wears a new dress, she will want to wear the dress again and again. If Pancho wins with one tennis racket and loses with another, he will prefer the racket with which he has found success. This principle is disarmingly simple, but it has profound implications for human learning.

My point is that a correct use of rewards (reinforcements) can make your children *want* to brush their teeth and eat with a fork and hang up wet towels. Unfortunately, it is not sufficient to dole out gifts and prizes in an unplanned manner. There are specific principles which must be followed if the Law of Reinforcement is to achieve its full potential.

Among the most important of those particulars is the need for *immediate* reinforcement. Parents often make the mistake of offering long-range rewards to children, but their successes are few. It is usually unfruitful to offer nine-year-old Joey a car when he is sixteen if he'll work hard in school during the next seven years. Second- and third-grade elementary school children are often promised a trip to Grandma's house next summer in exchange for good behavior throughout the year. Their obedience is typically unaffected by this lure. Likewise, it is unsatisfactory to offer Mary Lou a new doll for Christmas if she'll keep her room straight in July. Most children have neither the mental capacity nor the maturity to hold a long-range goal in mind day after day. Time moves slowly for them; consequently, the reinforcement seems impossible to reach and uninteresting to contemplate. For animals, a reward should be offered approximately two seconds after the behavior has occurred. A mouse will learn the turns in a maze much faster if the cheese is waiting at the end than if a five-second delay is imposed. Although children can tolerate longer delays than animals, the power of a reward is weakened with time.

Returning to the question, it is important for you to understand that the irresponsible behavior of your adopted girls has been learned. Children learn to laugh, play, run, and jump; they also learn to whine, bully, pout, fight, throw temper tantrums, or be tomboys. The universal teacher is reinforcement. The child repeats a behavior which he considers to be successful. A youngster may be cooperative and helpful because he enjoys the effect that behavior has on his parents; another will sulk and pout for the same reason. When parents recognize characteristics which they dislike in their children, they should set about *teaching* more admirable traits by allowing good behavior to succeed and bad behavior to fail.[8]

**You have referred to children who manipulate their mothers and fathers. On the other hand, isn't the parent manipulating the child by the use of rewards and punishment?**

No more than a factory supervisor is manipulating his employees by insisting that they arrive at work by 9:00 A.M. No more than a policeman manipulates the speeding driver by giving him a traffic ticket. No more than an insurance company manipulates that same driver by increasing his premium. The word "manipulation" implies a sinister or selfish motive. I prefer the term "leadership," which is in the best interest of everyone—even when it involves unpleasant consequences.[9]

**I am uncomfortable using rewards to influence my kids. It seems too much like bribery to me. I'd like to hear your views on the subject.**

Many parents feel as you do, and in response I say, don't use them if you are philosophically opposed to the concept. It is unfortunate, however, that our most workable teaching device is often rejected because of what I would consider to be a misunderstanding of terms. Our entire society is established on a system of reinforcement, yet we don't want to apply it where it is needed most: with young children. As adults, we go to work each day and receive a pay check on Friday. Getting out of bed each morning is thereby rewarded. Medals are given to brave soldiers; plaques are awarded to successful businessmen and watches are presented to retiring employees. Rewards make responsible effort worthwhile. The main reason for the overwhelming success of capitalism is that hard work and personal discipline are rewarded materially. The great weakness of socialism is the absence of reinforcement; why should a man struggle to achieve if there is nothing special to be gained? The most distasteful aspect of my brief military experience was the absence of reinforcement; I could not get a higher rank until a certain period of time had passed, no matter how hard I worked. The size of my pay check was determined by Congress, not by my competence or output. This system is a destroyer of motivation, yet some parents seem to feel it is the only way to approach children. They expect little Marvin to carry responsibility simply because it is noble for him to do so. They want him to work and learn and sweat for the sheer joy of personal discipline. He isn't going to buy it!

Consider the alternative approach to the "bribery" I've recommended. How are *you* going to get your five-year-old son to behave more responsibly? The most frequently used substitutes are nagging, complaining, begging, screaming, threatening, and punishing. The mother who objects to the use of rewards may also go to bed each evening with a headache, vowing to have no more children. She doesn't like to accentuate materialism in this manner, yet later she will be giving money to her child. Since her youngster never earns his own cash, he doesn't learn how to save it or spend it wisely or pay tithe on it. The toys she buys him are purchased with her money, and he values them less. But most important, he is not learning self-discipline and personal responsibility that is possible through the careful reinforcement of that behavior.[10]

**If you don't consider the judicious use of rewards with children to be a form of bribery, then what *does* constitute an inappropriate gift?**

Rewards become bribes when they serve as a "pay-off" for disobedient or irresponsible behavior. For example, it is not recommended that rewards be utilized when the child has challenged the authority of the parent. Mom may say, "Come here, Lucy," and Lucy shouts "No!" It is a mistake for Mom to then offer a piece of candy if Lucy will comply with her request. She would actually be rewarding her for defiance. Nor should rewards be used as a substitute for authority; both reward and punishment have a place in child management, and reversals bring undesirable results.[11]

**I worry about putting undue emphasis on materialism with my kids. Do rewards *have* to be in the form of money or toys?**

Certainly not. When my daughter was three years of age, I began to teach her some pre-reading skills, including the alphabet. By planning the training sessions to occur after dinner each evening, bits of chocolate candy provided the chief source of motivation. (In those days I was less concerned about the effect of excess sugar consumption than I am now.) Late one afternoon I was sitting on the floor drilling her on several new letters when a tremendous crash shook the neighborhood. The whole family rushed outside immediately to see what had happened, and observed that a teenager had wrecked his car on our quiet residential street. The boy was not badly hurt, but his automobile was a mess. We sprayed the smoldering car with water and made the necessary phone call to the police. It was not until the excitement began to lessen that we realized our daughter had not followed us out of the house. I returned to the den where I found her elbow deep in the two-pound bag of candy I had left behind. She had put at least a pound of chocolate into her mouth, and most of the remainder was distributed around her chin, nose, and forehead. When she saw me coming, she managed to jam another mouthful into her chipmunk cheeks. From this experience, I learned one of the limitations of using material, or at least edible, reinforcement.

Anything that is considered desirable to an individual can serve as reinforcement for behavior. The most obvious rewards for animals are those which satisfy physical needs, although humans are further motivated to resolve their overwhelming psychological needs. Some children, for example, would rather receive a sincere word of praise than a ten dollar bill, particularly if the adult approval is expressed in front of other children. Children and adults of all ages seek constant satisfaction of their emotional needs, including the desire for love, social acceptance, and self-respect. Additionally, they hope to find excitement, intellectual stimulation, entertainment, and pleasure.

Verbal reinforcement should permeate the entire parent-child relationship. Too often our parental instruction consists of a million "don'ts" which are jammed down the child's throat. We should spend more time rewarding him for the behavior we do admire, even if our "reward" is nothing more than a sincere compliment. Remembering the child's need for self-esteem and acceptance, the wise parent can satisfy those important longings while using them to teach valued concepts and behavior. A few examples may be helpful:

> *Mother to daughter:* You certainly colored nicely within the lines on that picture, Rene. I like to see that kind of neat art work. I'm going to put this on the bulletin board in the hall.
>
> *Mother to husband in son's presence:* Jack, did you notice how Don put his bicycle in the garage tonight? He used to leave it out until we told him to put it away; he is becoming much more responsible, don't you think?
>
> *Father to son:* I appreciate your being quiet while I was figuring the income tax, son. You were very thoughtful. Now that I have that job done, I'll have more time. Why don't we plan to go to the zoo next Saturday?
>
> *Teacher to high school student:* You've made a good point, Juan. I hadn't thought of that aspect of the matter. I enjoy your original way of looking at things.
>
> *Mother to small son:* Kevin, you haven't sucked your thumb all morning. I'm very proud of you. Let's see how long you can go this afternoon.

It is unwise for a parent to compliment the child for behavior she does not admire. If everything the child does earns him a big hug and a pat on the back, Mom's approval gradually becomes meaningless. Inflation can destroy the value of her reinforcement. Specific behavior warranting genuine compliments can be found if it is sought, even in the most immature youngster.[12]

**I think I used a reward properly last Saturday night when my husband and I went out to dinner. As we were leaving, our four- and five-year-old sons set up a howl. They screamed and threw temper tantrums until I remembered how effective rewards can be. I went to the cupboard and got a sucker for each of them. Their crying stopped and we left in peace. Is this an example of using the Law of Reinforcement properly?**

Unfortunately, it is not. Instead of reinforcing maturity and responsibility as you were leaving, you have inadvertently rewarded the opposite response. You see, you have made it to your children's advantage to cry the next time you plan to leave. The candy actually reinforced the tears, in this instance.

It is vitally important for parents to understand these principles, if for no other reason than to avoid rewarding unacceptable behavior. In fact, it is remarkably easy and common to propagate undesirable behavior in young children by allowing it to succeed. Suppose, for example, that Mr. and Mrs. Weakknee are having guests in for dinner tonight, and they put three-year-old Ricky to bed at 7:00 P.M. They know Ricky will cry, as he always does, but what else can they do? Indeed, Ricky cries. He begins at a low pitch (which does not succeed) and gradually builds to a high intensity scream. Finally, Mrs. Weakknee becomes so embarrassed by the display that she lets Ricky get up. What has the child learned? That he must cry loudly if he wants to get up. Mr. and Mrs. Weakknee had better be prepared for a tearful battle tomorrow night, too, because the method was successful to Ricky the night before.

Let's look at another example. Betty Sue is an argumentative teenager. She never takes "no" for an answer. She is very cantankerous; in fact, her father says the only time she is ever homesick is when she is at home. Whenever her mother is not sure about whether she wants to let Betty go to a party or ball game, she will first tell her she *can't* go. By saying an initial "no," Betty's mom doesn't commit herself to a "yes" before she's had a chance to think it over. She can always change her mind from negative to positive, but it is difficult to go the other way. However, what does this system tell Betty? She can see that "no" really means "maybe." The harder she argues and complains, the more likely she is to obtain the desired "yes." Many parents make the same mistake as Betty Sue's mother. They allow arguing, sulking, pouting, door-slamming, and bargaining to succeed. A parent should not take a definitive position on an issue until he has thought it over thoroughly. Then he should stick tenaciously to his stand. If the teenager learns that "no" means "absolutely no," he is less likely to waste his effort appealing his case to higher courts.

Perhaps a final example will be helpful: seven-year-old Abe wants the attention of his family, and he knows of no constructive way to get it. At the dinner table one evening his mother says, "Eat your beans, Abe," to which he replies defiantly, "No! I won't eat those rotten beans!" He has the eyes and ears of the whole family—something he wanted in the first place. Abe's mother can solidify the success of his defiance (and guarantee its return) by saying, "If you'll eat your beans I'll give you a treat."

Obviously, a parent must be careful in the behavior he allows to succeed. He must exercise self-discipline and patience to insure that the reinforcement which takes place is positive, not negative in its results.[13]

**My four-year-old daughter, Karen, is a *whiner.* She rarely speaks in a normal voice anymore. How can I break her of this habit?**

It is a well-established fact that unreinforced behavior will eventually disappear. This process, called *extinction* by psychologists, can be very useful to parents and teachers who want to alter the characteristics of children. The animal world provides many interesting examples of extinction. Consider the process by which circus elephants are taught not to throw their mighty power against the restraining chain each evening. When an elephant is young, his foot is chained to a cement block that is totally immovable. He will pull repeatedly against the barrier without success, thereby extinguishing his escape behavior. Later, a small rope and fragile stake will be sufficient to restrain the powerful elephant.

In order to eliminate an undesirable behavior, one must identify and then withhold the critical reinforcement. Let's apply this principle to the matter of whining, which you mentioned. Why does your child whine instead of speaking in a normal voice? Because you have inadvertently reinforced her whining! As long as Karen is speaking in her usual voice you are too busy to listen to her. I'm sure she babbles all day long, anyway, so you have often tuned out most of her verbiage. But when Karen speaks in a grating, irritating, obnoxious tone, you turn to see what is wrong. Karen's whining brings results; her normal voice does not: she becomes a whiner. In order to extinguish the whining, you must merely reverse the reinforcement. You should begin by saying, "I can't hear you because you're whining, Karen. I have funny ears; they just can't hear whining." After this message has been passed along for a day or two, you should show no indication of having heard a moan-tone. You should then offer immediate attention to a request made in a normal voice. If this control of reinforcement is applied properly, I guarantee it to achieve the desired results. All learning is based on this principle, and the consequences are certain and definite. Of course, Grandma and Uncle Albert may continue to reinforce the behavior you are trying to extinguish, and they can keep it alive.[14]

**Isn't this system of extinction applied by the businesses that help people conquer a smoking habit or the tendency to overeat?**
That's right. The objective is to eliminate the pleasantness (reinforcement) usually produced by inhaling cigarette smoke. A tube is aimed at the face of the smoker from which will come very stale, concentrated tobacco smoke. Whenever the individual takes a puff from his own cigarette, he is shot in the face with the putrid smoke from the tube. The smoker begins to associate cigarettes with the stinking, foul blast in the face, and a high percentage of cases have reported to develop a strong dislike for smoking.[15]

**My child is afraid of the dark. Can the principle of extinction be helpful in overcoming this fear?**
Extinction is one of the most effective tools in helping children overcome irrational fears. I consulted with a mother who was also worried about her three-year-old daughter's fear of the dark. Despite the use of a night light and leaving the bedroom door open, Marla was afraid to stay in her room alone. She insisted that her mother sit with her until she went to sleep each evening, which became very time-consuming and inconvenient. If Marla happened to awaken in the night, she would call for help. It was apparent that the child was not bluffing; she was genuinely frightened. Fears such as this are not innate characteristics in the child; they have been learned. Parents must be

very careful in expressing their fears, because their youngsters are amazingly perceptive in adopting those same concerns. For that matter, good-natured teasing can also produce problems for a child. If a youngster walks into a dark room and is pounced upon from behind the door, he has learned something from the joke: the dark is not always empty! In Marla's case, it is unclear where she learned to fear the dark, but I believe her mother inadvertently magnified the problem. In her concern for Marla, she conveyed her anxiety, and Marla began to think that her fears must be justified. "Even mother is worried about it." The fright became so great that Marla could not walk through a dimly lit room without an escort. It was at this point that the child was referred to me.

I suggested that the mother tell Marla she was going to help her see that there was nothing to be afraid of. (It is usually unfruitful to try to *talk* a child out of his fears but it helps to show him you are confident and unthreatened.) She bought a package of stars and created a chart that showed how a new phonograph player could be "earned." Then she placed her chair just outside Marla's bedroom door. Marla was offered a star if she could spend a short time (ten seconds) in her bedroom with the light on and the door open. This first step was not very threatening, and Marla enjoyed the game. It was repeated several times; then she was asked to walk a few feet into the darkened room with the door still open while Mother (clearly visible in the hall) counted to ten. Marla accomplished this task several times and was given the stars on each occasion. On subsequent trips, the door was half shut and finally closed except for the narrowest of opening. Eventually, Marla had the courage to enter the dark room, shut the door and sit on the bed while her mother counted to ten. She knew she could come out immediately if she wished. Mother talked confidently and quietly. The length of time in the dark was gradually lengthened, and instead of producing fear, it produced stars and eventually a record player; a good source of pleasure for a small child. Courage was being reinforced; fear was being extinguished. The cycle of fright was thereby broken, being replaced by a more healthy attitude.

The uses of extinction are limited only by the imagination and creativity of the parent or teacher. The best method of changing a behavior is to withhold its reinforcement while rewarding its replacement.[16]

# SECTION 15

# HYPER-ACTIVITY IN CHILDREN

**What is hyperactivity and what causes it?**
Hyperactivity (also called hyperkinesis, minimal brain dysfunction, impulse disorder, and at least thirty other terms) is defined as excessive and *uncontrollable* movement. It usually involves distractability, restlessness, and a short attention span. I italicized the word uncontrollable because the severely affected child is absolutely incapable of sitting quietly in a chair or slowing down his level of activity. He is propelled from within by forces he can neither explain or ameliorate.

One such youngster was a seven-year-old boy named Kurt who was afflicted with Downs Syndrome (a form of mental retardation which was originally called mongolism). This little fellow was frantically active, and literally "attacked" my furniture when he entered the room. He scrambled over the top of my desk, knocking over pictures and files and paper weights. Then this lad grabbed for the telephone and held it in the direction of my ear. I humored him by faking a conversation with a mythical caller, but Kurt had other purposes in mind. He jumped from my desk and scurried into the office of a psychologist next door, insisting that my colleague play the same game. As it happened, our two phones were on the same extension, and this little seven-year-old had succeeded in outsmarting the two child development "experts." There we were, talking to each other on the phone without anything relevant to say. It was a humbling experience.

A truly hyperactive child can humble any adult, particularly if the disorder is not understood by his parent. The condition often appears related to damage to the central nervous system, although it can also be caused by emotional stress and fatigue.

Some authorities believe that virtually all children born through the birth canal (that is, not by caesarean section) are likely to sustain damage to brain tissue during the birth process. The difference between patients who are severely affected (and are called cerebral palsied) and those who have no obvious symptoms may reflect three variables: (1) Where the damage is located; (2) How massive the lesion is; and (3) How quickly it occurred. Thus, it is possible that some hyperactive children were very early afflicted by an unidentified brain interference which caused no other symptoms or problems. I must emphasize, however, that this explanation is merely speculative and that the medical understanding of this disorder is far from complete.[1]

**How can damage to brain tissue cause frantic activity in a child?**

Relatively little is known about the human brain and its malfunctions. I knew one neurologically impaired child, for example, who could read the words, "Go shut the door," with no understanding of the written command. However, if a tape recording was made while he read, "Go shut the door," this child could hear the replay of his own voice and understand the words perfectly. Another patient in a mental hospital could completely disassemble and repair complex television sets, yet did not have the common sense to handle the routine responsibilities of living outside a hospital setting. Another man, wounded in combat, had the sad characteristic of being unable to keep any thought to himself. He mumbled his innermost ideas, to the embarrassment and shock of everyone nearby.

Brain disorders are expressed in many strange ways, including the frenzy of hyperactivity. No one can explain exactly why it happens, other than the obvious fact that the electrochemical mechanisms which control body movement have been altered, resulting in excessive stimulation to the muscles.[2]

**How can anxiety or emotional problems cause hyperactivity?**

When adults are under severe stress or anxiety, their inner tension is typically expressed in the form of physical activity. An expectant father "paces the floor," or smokes one cigarette after another, or his hands may tremble. A basketball coach will race up and down the sidelines while the outcome of the game is in doubt. Another anxious person may sit quietly in a chair, but his fingernails will be chewed to the quick or he will move his lower jaw slowly from side to side. My point is that tension increases the amount of bodily movement observed in adults.

How much more true that is of an immature child. He doesn't merely drum his fingers on a table when he is anxious; he tries to climb the curtains and walk on the ceiling.[3]

**How early can the problem be identified?**
The severely hyperactive child can be recognized during early toddlerhood. In fact, he can't be ignored. By the time he is thirty months of age he may have exhausted his mother, irritated his siblings, and caused the grandparents to retire from baby-sitting duties. No family member is "uninvolved" with his problem. Instead of growing out of it, as the physician may promise, he continues to attack his world with the objective of disassembling it (at least until puberty).[4]

**Is there a "normal" hyperactivity?**
Certainly. Not every child who squirms, churns, and bounces is technically "hyperactive." Most toddlers are "on the move" from dawn to dark (as are their mothers).[5]

**Then how can I tell whether my child is just normally active or genuinely hyperactive? And how can I decipher whether his problem is the result of emotional or a physical impairment?**
These questions are difficult to answer, and few parents have the training to resolve them. Your best resource in evaluating your child's problem is your pediatrician or family physician. Even he may have to guess at a diagnosis and its cause. He can, however, make a complete medical evaluation and then refer you, if necessary, to other professionals for specific assistance. Your child may require the services of a remedial reading teacher or a speech and hearing therapist or a psychologist who can assess intellectual and perceptual abilities and offer management advice. You should not try alone to cope with an excessively active child if this additional support and consultation is available.[6]

**What role does nutrition play?**
The role of nutrition in hyperactivity is a very controversial issue which I am not qualified to resolve; I can only offer my opinion on the subject. American people have been told that hyperactivity is a product of red food coloring, too much sugar intake, inadequate vitamins, and many related causes resulting from poor nutrition. I don't doubt for a moment that improper eating habits have the capacity to destroy us physically and could easily be related to the phenomenon of hyperactivity. However, I am of the opinion that the writers of many faddish books on this subject are trying to make their guesses sound like proven facts. Many of the answers are not yet available, which explains why so many "authorities" disagree violently among themselves.

The nutritionists whom I respect most highly are those who take a cautious, scientific approach to these complex questions. I am suspicious of the self-appointed experts who bypass their own professional publications and come directly to the lay public with unsupported conclusions which even their colleagues reject.

The above paragraph may irritate some parents who are following the advice of a lone-wolf nutritional writer. To those readers I can only say, "Do what succeeds." If your child is more calm and sedate when avoiding certain foods, then use your judgment as you continue the successful dietary regimen. Your opinion is probably as valid as mine.[7]

**How common is hyperactivity?**
Authorities disagree on the incidence of hyperactivity, but this disorder apparently afflicts between 6 and 10 percent of all children under ten years of age. Males outnumber females four to one.[8]

**There are times when I strongly resent my hyperactive child. Do other mothers share this frustration?**
Your response is typical. Every mother of a hyperactive child occasionally experiences a distressing tug-of-war in her mind. On the one side, she understands her child's problem and feels a deep empathy and love for her little fellow. There is nothing that she wouldn't do to help him. But on the other side, she resents the chaos he has brought into her life. Speedy Gonzales spills

his milk and breaks vases and teeters on the brink of disaster throughout the day. He embarrasses his mother in public and shows little appreciation for the sacrifices she is making on his behalf. By the time bedtime arrives, she often feels as if she has spent the entire day in a foxhole.

What happens, then, when genuine love and strong resentment collide in the mind of a mother or father? The inevitable result is parental guilt in sizeable proportions—guilt that is terribly destructive to a woman's peace of mind and even to her health.[9]

**What other problems does the hyperactive child face?**
The child with exaggerated activity usually experiences three specific difficulties in addition to his frantic motion. First, he is likely to develop psychological problems resulting from rejection by his peers. His nervous energy is not only irritating to adults, but tends to drive away friends as well. He may be branded as a troublemaker and goof-off in the classroom. Furthermore, his emotional response is often unstable, swinging unpredictably from laughter to tears in a matter of moments, and causing his peers to think him strange. In short, the hyperactive child can easily fall victim to feelings of inferiority and the emotional upheaval which is inevitably generated by rejection and low self-esteem.

Second, the active child frequently experiences severe learning problems during the school years. He finds it difficult, if not impossible, to remain in his seat and concentrate on his lessons. His attention span is miniscule throughout elementary school, which leads to mischievousness and distractability while his teachers are speaking. He never seems to know what the educational program is all about, and his frustrated teachers often describe him as being "in a fog."

But there is another academic difficulty which is also extremely common among hyperactive children: visual-perceptual problems. A child may have perfectly normal vision, yet not "perceive" symbols and printed material accurately. In other words, his eyes may be perfect but his brain does not process the signal properly. Such a child may "see" letters and numbers reversed or distorted. It is particularly difficult for him to learn to read or write.

Reading is a highly complex neurological skill. It requires the recognition of symbols and their transmittal to the brain, where they must be interpreted, remembered, and (perhaps) spoken as a language. Any break in this functional chain will inhibit the final product. Furthermore, this process must occur rapidly enough to permit a steady flow of ideas from the written materials. Many hyperactive children simply do not have the neurological apparatus to develop these skills and are destined to experience failure during the primary grades in school.[10]

**What are the solutions?**

There are dozens of medications which have been shown to be effective in calming the hyperactive child. Since every child's chemistry is unique, it may be necessary for a physician to "fish" for the right substance and dosage. Let me stress that I am opposed to the administration of such drugs to children who do not require them. In some instances these substances have been given indiscriminately to children simply because their parents or teachers preferred them sedated, which is inexcusable. Every medication has an undesirable side effect (even aspirin) and should be administered only after careful evaluation and study. However, if your child displays extreme symptoms of hyperactivity and has been evaluated by a neurologist or other knowledgeable physician, you should not hesitate to accept his prescription of an appropriate medication. Some dramatic behavioral changes can occur when the proper substance is identified for a particular child.[11]

**But won't the long-term use of medication increase the possibility of my child becoming a drug user during adolescence?**

Most authorities feel that the use of medication in childhood does not necessarily lead to drug abuse in later life. In fact, a federal task force was appointed in 1971 to consider that possibility. The conclusion from their investigation emphasized the appropriateness of medications in treatment of hyperactive children. Some children need, and should get, the proper calming agent.[12]

**Do medications solve all the problems?**

Usually not. Let's consider the three primary symptoms as related to medications:

1. Hyperactivity. The proper prescription can be very effective in "normalizing" a child's motor activity. Treatment is most successful in controlling this symptom.

2. Psychological difficulties. Medication is less effective in eliminating emotional problems. Once a child has been "slowed down," the process of building his self-image and social acceptance must begin in earnest. The administration of drugs may make the objective possible, but it does not, in itself, eradicate the problem.

3. Visual-perceptual problems. Drug usage is of no value in resolving neurological malfunctions which interfere with perception. There are training materials available which have been shown to be helpful, including those provided by the Marianne Frostig Center for Educational Therapy. Dr. Frostig is a pioneer in the field of learning disabilities, and has provided books, films, and evaluative tests for use by teachers and trained professionals. Your local school district can obtain a list of available resources by contacting this organization at 5981 Venice Boulevard, Los Angeles, California 90034. Many school districts also provide special classes for children with unique learning disabilities, which can be of inestimable value to a handicapped student.

It is obvious that drug therapy cannot provide the total remedy. A pharmaceutical approach must be combined with parental adaptations and educational alternatives, among others.[13]

**How does the parent "discipline" a hyperactive child?**
It is often assumed that an excessively active child should be indulged, simply because he has a physical problem. I couldn't disagree more. Every youngster needs the security of defined limits, and the hyperactive boy or girl is no exception. Such a child should be held responsible for his behavior, like the rest of the family. Of course, your level of expectation must be adjusted to fit his limitations. For example, most children can be required to sit in a chair for disciplinary reasons, whereas the hyperactive child would not be able to remain there. Similarly, spankings are sometimes ineffective with a highly excitable little bundle of electricity. As with every aspect of parenthood, disciplinary measures for the hyperactive child must be suited to his unique characteristics and needs.

How, then, is the child to be controlled? What advice is available for the parents of a child with this problem? Listed below are eighteen helpful suggestions quoted from a very helpful book entitled *The Hyperactive Child*, by Dr. Domeena Renshaw.[14]

1. Be carefully consistent in rules and disciplines.
2. Keep your own voice quiet and slow. Anger is normal. Anger can be controlled. Anger does not mean you do not love a child.
3. Try hard to keep your emotions cool by bracing for expectable turmoil. Recognize and respond to any positive behavior, however small. If you search for good things, you will find a few.
4. Avoid a ceaselessly negative approach: "Stop"—"Don't"—"No"—
5. Separate behavior which you may not like, from the child's person, which you like, e.g., "I like you. I don't like your tracking mud through the house."
6. Have a very clear routine for this child. Construct a timetable for waking, eating, play, TV, study, chores, and bedtime. Follow it flexibly although he disrupts it. Slowly your structure will reassure him until he develops his own.
7. Demonstrate new or difficult tasks, using action accompanied by short, clear, quiet explanations. Repeat the demonstration until learned. This uses audio-visual-sensory perceptions to reinforce the learning. The memory traces of a hyperkinetic child take longer to form. Be patient and repeat.
8. Try a separate room or a part of a room which is his own special area. Avoid brilliant colors or complex patterns in decor. Simplicity, solid colors, minimal clutter, and a worktable facing a blank wall away from distractions assist concentration. A hyperkinetic child cannot "filter" out overstimulation himself yet.
9. Do one thing at a time: give him one toy from a closed box; clear the table of everything else when coloring; turn off the radio/TV when he is doing homework. Multiple stimuli prevent his concentration from focusing on his primary task.
10. Give him responsibility, which is essential for growth. The task should be within his capacity, although the assignment may need much supervision. Acceptance

and recognition of his efforts (even when imperfect) should not be forgotten.

11. Read his preexplosive warning signals. Quietly intervene to avoid explosions by distracting him or discussing the conflict calmly. Removal from the battle zone to the sanctuary of his room for a few minutes is useful.
12. Restrict playmates to one or at most two at one time, because he is so excitable. Your home is more suitable, so you can provide structure and supervision. Explain your rules to the playmate and briefly tell the other parent your reasons.
13. Do not pity, tease, be frightened by, or overindulge this child. He has a special condition of the nervous system which is manageable.
14. Know the name and dose of his medication. Give these regularly. Watch and remember the effects to report back to your physician.
15. Openly discuss any fears you have about the use of medications with your physician.
16. Lock up all medications, including these, to avoid accidental misuse.
17. Always supervise the taking of medication, even if it is routine over a long period of years. Responsibility remains with the parents! One day's supply at a time can be put in a regular place and checked routinely as he becomes older and more self-reliant.
18. Share your successful "helps" with his teacher. The outlined ways to help your hyperkinetic child are as important to him as diet and insulin are to a diabetic child.[15]

**What does the future hold?**

In case you haven't heard, help is on the way. The maturation and glandular changes associated with puberty often calm the hyperactive youngster between twelve and eighteen years of age. This explains why we seldom see adults jumping from the backs of chairs and rolling on the floor. But for harassed parents who spend their days chasing a nonstop toddler around the house, there may be little consolation in knowing that the crisis will last only nine more years.

*Note:* For parents who want to learn more about children with hyperactivity, I would refer them to Dr. Renshaw's excellent book. While the writing style is somewhat technical, it is certainly readable and contains helpful insights. See footnote 14 for publication details.[16]

# SECTION 16

# COPING WITH ADOLESCENCE

**I know it is my responsibility to teach Ricky, my preteenager, the essentials of reproduction and sex education before he reaches adolescence. But what else should I tell him?**

He must be told, among other things, about the dramatic physical changes that are about to occur within his body. I have found that uninformed teenagers fall into two broad categories: The first group doesn't know these changes are coming and are worried sick by what they see happening. The second group is aware that certain features are supposed to appear and are anxious because the changes are late in arriving. That's why doubts and fears are so common during the adolescent years. Yet, they can be avoided by healthy, confident parental instruction before the fears develop.[1]

**Please be more specific. What are the major physical changes which I should tell Ricky about?**

There are four topics that are "musts" for a conversation of this nature. Let me present them briefly.

1. Rapid growth will occur, sapping energy and strength for a while. The teenager will actually need more sleep and better nutrition than when he was younger.

2. Tell your child that his body will quickly change to that of an adult. His sex organs will become more mature and will be surrounded by pubic hair. (For males, stress this point: the size of the penis is of no physical importance. Many boys worry about having a smaller organ, but that has *nothing* to do with fathering a child or sexual satisfaction as an adult. For your

daughter, breast development should also be discussed in the same manner.)

3. The full details of the menstrual cycle must be made clear to your girl before her first period. It is a terrifying thing for a girl to experience this aspect of maturity without forewarning. Many books and films are available to help explain this developmental milestone, and should be used. The most important parental responsibility at this point is to convey confidence, optimism, and excitement regarding menstruation, rather than saying sadly, "This is the cross you must bear as a woman."

4. It is most important that the timing of puberty be discussed with your children, for herein lies *much* grief and distress. This period of heightened sexual development may occur as early as twelve or as late as nineteen years of age in boys and from ten to seventeen in girls. Thus, it may arrive seven years earlier in some children than in others! And the youngsters who develop very early or very late usually face some upsetting psychological problems. There are four extremes which should be considered:

*The Late-Maturing Boy.* This little fellow knows perfectly well that he is still a baby while his friends have grown up. He picks up the telephone and the operator calls him "Ma'am"! What an insult! He's very interested in athletics at this age, but he can't compete with the larger, stronger boys. He gets teased in the locker room about his sexual immaturity, and his self-esteem nosedives. And adding insult to injury, he is actually shorter than most of the girls for a couple of years! (They have had their growth spurt and he has not.) He fears that there is something drastically wrong in his case, but he dares not mention his thoughts to anyone. It's too embarrassing. The prepubertal child can often be the worst troublemaker in the school, for he has many things to prove about his doubtful manhood.

*The Late Maturing Girl.* Life is no easier for the girl whose internal clock is on the slow side. She looks down at her flat chest and then glances at her busty friends. For two or three years, her girl friends have been sharing confidences about menstruation, but she can't participate in the discussions. She has been nicknamed "baby face" by the gang, and in fact, she does look about eight years old. Remembering the role physical attractiveness plays in self-esteem, the reader can see that inferiority can overwhelm the late developer, even if he or she *is* attractively arranged. And unless someone tells them otherwise, they are likely to conclude that they will never grow up.

*The Early Maturing Girl.* If it is disadvantageous to be late in maturing, one would think that the opposite would be emotionally healthy. Not so. Since girls tend to develop sexually one or two years before boys, on an average, the girl who enters puberty before other girls is miles ahead of everybody else her age. Physical strength offers her no real advantages in our society, and it is simply not acceptable to be boy-crazy at ten years of age. For two or three uncomfortable years, the early maturing girl is out of step with all her age mates.

*The Early Maturing Boy.* By contrast, the early maturing boy is blessed with a great social advantage. He is strong at a time when power is worshiped by his peers, and his confidence soars as his athletic successes are publicized. His early development places him on a par with the girls in his class, who are also awakening sexually. Thus, he has the field all to himself for a year or two. Research confirms that the early maturing boy is more frequently emotionally stable, confident, and socially accepted than other boys. It also shows that he is more likely to be more successful in later adult life, as well.

In the discussion of these extremes with your preteenager, assure him that it is "normal" for some youngsters to be early or late in developing. It does not mean that anything is wrong with his body. If indeed your child is a late bloomer, he will need additional reassurance and encouragement at the time of this conversation to open the door of communication regarding the fears and anxieties associated with physical growth and development.[2]

**My thirteen-year-old son has become increasingly lazy in the past couple of years. He lies around the house and will sleep half a day on Saturday. He complains about being tired a lot. Is this typical of early adolescence? How should I deal with it?**

It is not uncommon for boys and girls to experience fatigue during the pubertal years. Their physical resources are being invested in a rapid growth process during that time, leaving less energy for other activities. This period doesn't last very long and is usually followed by the most energetic time of life.

I would suggest, first, that you take your son for a routine physical examination to rule out the possibility of a more serious explanation for his fatigue. If it does turn out to be a phenomenon of puberty, as I suspect, you should "go with the flow." See that he gets plenty of rest and sleep. This need is often not met, however, because teenagers feel that they should not have to go to bed as early as they did when they were children. Therefore, they stay up too late and then drag through the next day in a state of exhaustion. Surprisingly, a twelve- or thirteen-year-old person actually needs more rest than when he was nine or ten, simply because of the acceleration in growth.

What I'm saying is that you should let your son sleep on Saturday morning, if possible. It is often difficult for mothers and fathers to permit their overgrown son or daughter to lie in bed until 9:30 A.M., when the grass needs mowing. However, they should know that he is lying in bed because he needs more sleep, and they would be wise to let him get it. *Then* ask him to mow the lawn when he awakens.

Second, the foods your son eats are also very important during this time. His body needs the raw materials with which to construct new muscle cells, bones, and fibers that are in the plans. Hot dogs, donuts, and milkshakes just won't do the job. Again, it is even more important to eat a *balanced* diet during this time.

In summary, your son is turning overnight from a boy to a man. Some of the physical characteristics you are observing are part of that transformation. Do everything you can to facilitate it.[3]

**My thirteen-year-old daughter is still built like a boy, but she is insisting that her mother buy her a bra. Believe me, she has no need for it, and the only reason she wants one is because most of her friends do. Should I give in?**
Your straight and narrow daughter needs a bra to be like her friends, to compete, to avoid ridicule, and to feel like a woman. Those are excellent reasons. Your wife should meet this request by tomorrow morning, if not sooner.[4]

**Our teenage daughter has become extremely modest in recent months, demanding that even her sisters leave her room when she's dressing. I think this is silly, don't you?**

No, I would suggest that you honor her requests for privacy. Her sensitivity is probably caused by an awareness that her body is changing, and she is embarrassed by recent developments (or the lack of them). This is likely to be a temporary phase and you should not oppose her in it.[5]

**Children seem to be growing up at a younger age today than in the past. Is this true, and if so, what accounts for their faster development?**

Yes, it *is* true. Statistical records indicate that our children are growing taller today than in the past, probably resulting from better nutrition, medicine, exercise, rest and recreation. And this more ideal physical environment has apparently caused sexual maturity to occur at younger and younger ages. It is thought that puberty in a particular child is "turned on" when he reaches a certain level of growth; therefore, when environmental circumstances propel him upward at a faster rate, he becomes sexually mature much earlier. For example, in 1850, the average age of menarche (first menstruation) in Norwegian girls was 17.0 years of age; in 1950, it was 13.0. The average age of puberty had dropped four years in that one century. In the United States the average age of the menarche dropped from 14.2 in 1900 to 12.9 in 1950. More recent figures indicate the average has now dropped closer to 12.6 years of age! Thus, the trend toward younger dating and sexual awareness is a result, at least in part, of this physiological mechanism. I suppose we could slow it down by taking poorer care of our children . . . but I doubt if that idea will gain much support.[6]

**I am hurt because my teenager seems to be ashamed to be seen with me. I gave birth to him and have nourished and devoted my entire life to him. Now he's suddenly embarrassed to be seen with me, especially when his friends are around. Is this normal? Should I resist or accept it?**

You should understand that teenagers are engulfed by a tremendous desire to be adults, and they resent anything which implies that they are still children. When they are seen with "Mommie and Daddy" on a Friday night, for example, their humiliation is almost unbearable. They are not really ashamed of their parents; they are embarrassed by the adult-baby role that was more appropriate in prior years. Though it is difficult for you now, you would do well to accept this healthy aspect of growing up without becoming defensive about it. Your love relationship with your child will be reestablished in a few years, although it will never be a parent-child phenomenon again. And that's the way God designed the process to work.[7]

**Must I act like a teenager myself in dress, language, tastes, and manner in order to show my adolescent that I understand him?**
No. There is something disgusting about a thirty-five-year-old "adolescent has-been." It wasn't necessary for you to crawl on the floor and throw temper tantrums in order to understand your two-year-old; likewise, you can reveal an empathy and acceptance of the teen years without becoming an anachronistic teenybopper yourself. In fact, the very reason for your adolescent's unique manner and style is to display an identity separate from yours. You'll turn him off quickly by invading his territory, leading him to conclude, "Mom tries so hard, but I wish she'd grow up!" Besides, he will still need an authority figure on occasion, and you've got the job![8]

**How can I teach my fourteen-year-old the value of money?**
One good technique is to give him enough cash to meet a particular need, and then let him manage it. You can begin by offering a weekly food allowance to be spent in school. If he squanders the total on a weekend date, then it becomes his responsibility to either work for his lunches or go hungry. This is the cold reality he will face in later life, and it will not harm him to experience the lesson while still an adolescent.

I should indicate that this principle has been known to backfire, occasionally. A physician friend of mine has four daughters and he provides each one with an annual clothing allowance when they turn twelve years of age. It then becomes the girls' responsibility to budget their money for the garments that will be needed throughout the year. The last child to turn twelve, however, was not quite mature enough to handle the assignment. She celebrated her twelfth birthday by buying an expensive coat, which cut deeply into her available capital. The following spring, she exhausted her funds totally and wore shredded stockings, holey panties, and frayed dresses for the last three months of the year. It was difficult for her parents not to intervene, but they had the courage to let her learn this valuable lesson about money management.

Perhaps your son has never learned the value of money because it comes too easily. Anything in abundant supply becomes rather valueless. I would suggest that you restrict the pipeline and maximize the responsibility required in all expenditures.[9]

**What is the most difficult period of adolescence, and what is behind the distress?**

The thirteenth and fourteenth years commonly are the most difficult twenty-four months in life. It is during this time that self-doubt and feelings of inferiority reach an all-time high, amidst the greatest social pressures yet experienced. An adolescent's worth as a human being hangs precariously on peer group acceptance, which can be tough to garner. Thus, relatively minor evidences of rejection or ridicule are of major significance to those who already see themselves as fools and failures. It is difficult to overestimate the impact of having no one to sit with on the school-sponsored bus trip, or of not being invited to an important event, or of being laughed at by the "In" group, or of waking up in the morning to find seven shiny new pimples on your bumpy forehead, or of being slapped by the girl you thought had liked you as much as you liked her. Some boys and girls consistently face this kind of social catastrophe throughout their teen years. They will never forget the experience.

Dr. Urie Bronfenbrenner, eminent authority on child development at Cornell University, told a Senate committee that the junior high years are probably the most critical to the development of a child's mental health. It is during this period of self-doubt that the personality is often assaulted and damaged beyond repair. Consequently, said Bronfenbrenner, it is not unusual for healthy, happy children to enter junior high school, but then emerge two years later as broken, discouraged teenagers.

I couldn't agree more emphatically with Bronfenbrenner's opinion at this point. Junior high school students are typically brutal to one another, attacking and slashing a weak victim in much the same way a pack of northern wolves kill and devour a deformed carabao. Few events stir my righteous indignation more that seeing a vulnerable child—fresh from the hand of the Creator in the morning of his life—being taught to hate himself and despise his physical body and wish he had never been born.[10]

**Nothing is so distressing to me as when I see my son suffering from low self-esteem. He is in junior high now, and I know he's going through a tough time. Can you assure me that he'll come out of this difficult phase? Or is it going to mess up his life for years to come?**

Despite all that I have written about the heartache of low self-esteem, there is a positive side of the matter which will encourage you. Remember that the human personality grows through mild adversity, *provided it is not crushed in the process.* Contrary to what you might believe, the ideal environment for your child is not one devoid of problems and trials. I would not, even if I could, sweep aside every hurdle from the paths of my children, leaving them to glide along in mirth. They deserve the right to face problems and profit from the confrontation.

I have verified the value of minor stress from my own experience. My childhood was remarkably happy and carefree. I was loved beyond any doubt, and my academic performance was never a cause for discomfort. In fact, I have enjoyed happiness and fulfillment thus far my entire lifetime, with the exception of two painful years. Those stressful years occurred during my seventh- and eighth-grade days, lasting through ages thirteen and fourteen.

During this period of time, I found myself in a social crossfire, giving rise to the same intense feelings of inferiority and self-doubt I have described herein. As strange as it seems, however, these two years have contributed more positive features to my adult personality than any other span of which I am aware. My empathy for others, my desire to succeed in life, my motivation in graduate school, my understanding of inferiority, and my communication with teenagers are primarily the products of an agitated adolescence. Who would have thought anything useful could have come from those twenty-four months? Yet the discomfort proved to be a valuable instructor in this instance.

Though it is hard to accept at the time, your child also needs the minor setbacks and disappointments which come his way. How can he learn to cope with problems and frustration if his early experiences are totally without trial? A tree which is planted in a rain forest is never forced to extend its roots downward in search of water; consequently it remains poorly anchored and can be toppled by a moderate wind storm. But a mesquite tree planted in a dry desert is threatened by its hostile environment. It can only survive by sending its roots more than thirty feet deep into the earth, seeking cool water. Through its adaptation to the arid land, something else happens. The well-rooted tree becomes strong and steady against all assailants.

This illustration applies to our children, as well: those who have learned to conquer their problems are more secure than those who have never faced them. Our task as parents, then, is not to eliminate every challenge for our children; it is to serve as a confident ally on their behalf, encouraging when they are distressed, intervening when the threats are overwhelming, and above all, giving them the tools with which to overcome the obstacles.[11]

**Our fifteen-year-old son literally seethes with hostility at home—at his mother and me—at his sisters—at the world. Believe me, we have done nothing to provoke this anger and I don't understand what has caused it. But other parents of teens report the same problem. Why are so many adolescents angry at their parents and family? Sometimes they seem to hate the people who love them the most!**

At least part of the answer to that question can be explained by the "in-between" status of teenagers. They live in an era when they enjoy neither the privileges of adulthood nor the advantages of childhood. Consider the plight of the average fifteen-year-old. All of the highly advertised adult privileges and vices are forbidden to him because he is "too young." He can't drive or marry or enlist or drink or smoke or work or leave home. And his sexual desires are denied gratification at a time when they scream for release. The only thing he is permitted to do, it seems, is stay in school and read his dreary textbooks. This is an overstatement, of course, but it is expressed from the viewpoint of the young man or woman who feels disenfranchised and insulted by society. Much of the anger of today's youth is generated by their perception of this injustice.

There is another side to this issue of adolescent volatility. I'm now convinced that the hormonal changes occurring in a developing body may be more important to feelings than we thought earlier. Just as emotions are set on edge by premenstrual tension, menopause, and extreme fatigue, it is entirely possible that the adolescent experience is largely hormonal as well. How else can we explain the *universality* of emotional instability during these years? Having watched thousands of children sail from childhood to early adolescence, it still amazes me to witness textbook characteristics suddenly appearing on schedule as though responding to a preprogrammed computer. In fact, they probably are. I can't prove this hypothesis to be valid, but it is making more sense to me year by year.

**All right, so my kid feels disrespected and hostile. I still have to impose some limits and discipline on him, don't I?**
Yes, but it is possible to lead teenagers without insulting and antagonizing them unnecessarily. I learned this lesson when I was a junior high school teacher. It became clear to me very early that I could impose all manner of discipline and strict behavioral requirements on my students, *provided* I treated each young person with genuine dignity and respect. I earned their friendship before and after school, during lunch, and through classroom encounters. I was tough, especially when challenged, but never discourteous, mean, or insulting. I defended the underdog and tenaciously tried to build each child's confidence and self-respect. However, I never compromised my standards of deportment. Students entered my classroom without talking each day. They did not chew gum, behave disrespectfully, curse, or stab one another with ball point pens. I was clearly the captain of the ship and I directed it with military zeal.

The result of this combination of kindness and firm discipline stands as one of the most pleasant memories of my professional life. I *loved* my students and had every reason to believe that I was loved in return. I actually missed them on weekends (a fact my wife never quite understood). At the end of the final year when I was packing my books and saying good-bye, there were twenty-five or thirty teary-eyed kids who hung around my gloomy room for several hours and finally stood sobbing in the parking lot as I drove away. And yes, I shed a few tears of my own that day. (Please forgive this self-congratulatory paragraph. I haven't bothered to tell you about my failures, which are far less interesting.)[12]

**My teenage son rarely mixes with his peers and is involved in very few activities. He just wants to stay in his room most of the time, and rarely even talks on the telephone. What do you think causes him to isolate himself in this way?**

He may have adopted one of the most common ways of dealing with deep feelings of inadequacy and inferiority, which is to surrender and withdraw. The individual who chooses this approach has concluded in his own mind that he *is* inferior. He measures his worth by the reaction of his peers, which can be devastating during the competitive adolescent years. Thus, he concludes, "Yes, it's true! I am a failure, just as I feared. Even now people are laughing at me. Where can I hide?"

Having accepted his own unworthiness, which was his first mistake, he is forced to guard his wounded ego from further damage. "Caution" becomes his watchword. He withdraws into a shell of silence and loneliness, choosing to take no chances nor assume any unnecessary emotional risks.

Especially during the elementary school years, I believe we have much greater reason to be concerned about the emotional health of the withdrawing child than we do the more aggressive troublemaker. Children at both extremes often need adult intervention, but the surrenderer is much less likely to get it. He doesn't bug anybody. He cooperates with his teacher and tries to avoid conflict with his peers. But his quiet manner is dangerously misleading. The adults in his life may fail to notice that his destructive self-image is rapidly solidifying and will never be pliable again. Considering all the alternative ways to cope with inferiority, withdrawal is probably the least effective and most painful.

Knowing what your son is feeling, you should have a greater understanding of what he needs from you in the way of love and support.[13]

**My son, Brian, is now fourteen years old and he has suddenly entered a period of rebellion like nothing I've ever seen. He is breaking rules right and left and he seems to hate the entire family. He becomes angry when his mother and I try to discipline him, of course, but even during more tranquil times he seems to resent us for merely being there. Last Friday night he arrived home an hour beyond his deadline, but refused to explain why he was late or make apologetic noises. We are in the midst of a nightmare I *never* anticipated when he was younger.**

**This is my question. I would like you to tell me exactly how to approach this situation, even roleplaying my task of confronting him. I need to know what to say when that moment arrives.**

Certainly. I would recommend that you invite Brian out to breakfast on a Saturday morning, leaving the rest of the family at home. It would be best if this event could occur during a relatively tranquil time, certainly not in the midst of a hassle or intergenerational battle. Admit that you have some important matters to discuss with him which can't be communicated adequately at home, but don't "tip your hand" before Saturday morning. Then at the appropriate moment during breakfast convey the following messages (or an adaptation thereof):

A. Brian, I wanted to talk to you this morning because of the changes that are taking place in you and in our home. We both know that the past few weeks have not been very pleasant. You have been angry most of the time and have become disobedient and rude. And your mother and I haven't done so well either. We've become irritable and we've said things that we've regretted later. This is not what God wants of us as parents, or of you as our son. There has to be a more creative way of solving our problems. That's why we're all here.

B. As a place to begin, Brian, I want you to understand what is happening. You have gone into a new period of life known as adolescence. This is the final phase of childhood, and it is often a very stormy and difficult few years. Nearly everyone on earth goes through these rough years during their early teens, and you are right on schedule at this moment. Many of the problems you face today were predictable from the day you were born, simply because growing up has never been an easy thing to do. There are even greater pressures on kids today than when we were young. I've said that to tell you this: we understand you and love you as much as we ever did, even though the past few months have been difficult in our home.

C. What is actually taking place, you see, is that you have had a taste of freedom. You are tired of being a little boy who was told what to wear and when to go to bed and what to eat. That is a healthy attitude which will help you grow up. However, now you want to be your own boss and make your own decisions without interference from anyone. Brian, you will get what you want in a very short time. You are fourteen now, and you'll soon be fifteen and seventeen and nineteen. You will be grown in a twinkling of an eye, and we will no longer have any responsibility for you. The day is coming when you will marry whomever you wish, go to whatever school you choose, select the profession or job that suits you. Your mother and I will not try to make those decisions for you. We will respect your adulthood. Furthermore, Brian, the closer you get to those days, the more freedom we plan to give you. You have more privileges now than you had last year, and that trend will continue. We will soon set you free, and you will be accountable only to God and yourself.

D. But, Brian, you must understand this message: you are not grown yet. During the past few weeks, you have wanted your mother and me to leave you alone—to let you stay out half the night if you chose—to fail in school—to carry no responsibility at home. And you have "blown up" whenever we have denied even your most extreme demands. The truth of the matter is, you have wanted us to grant you twenty-year-old freedom during the fourteenth year, although you still expect to have your shirts ironed and your meals fixed and your bills paid. You have wanted the best of both worlds with none of the responsibilities. So what are we to do? The easiest thing would be for us to let you have your way. There would be no hassles and no conflict and no more frustration. Many parents of fourteen-year-old sons and daughters have done just that. But we must not yield to this temptation. You are not ready for that complete independence, and we would be showing hatred for you (instead of love) if we surrendered at this time. We would regret our mistake for the rest of our lives, and you would soon blame us, too. And as you know, you have two younger sisters who are watching you very closely, and must be protected from the things you are teaching them.

E. Besides, Brian, God has given us a responsibility as parents to do what is right for you, and He is holding us accountable for the way we do that job. I want to read you an important passage from the Bible which describes a father named Eli who did not discipline and correct his two unruly teenage sons. (Read the dramatic story from *The Living Bible,* 1 Samuel 2:12-17, 22-25, 27-34; 3:11-14; 4:1-3 and 10-22.) It is very clear that God was angry at Eli for permitting his sons to be disrespectful and disobedient. Not only did He allow the sons to be killed in battle, but He also punished their father for not accepting his parental responsibilities. This assignment to parents can be found throughout the Bible: mothers and fathers are expected to train their children and discipline them when required. What I'm saying is that God will not hold us blameless if we let you behave in ways that are harmful to yourself and others.

F. That brings us to the question of where we go from this moment. I want to make a pledge to you, here and now: your mother and I intend to be more sensitive to your needs and feelings than we've been in the past. We're not perfect, as you well know, and it is possible that you will feel we have been unfair at one time or another. If that occurs, you can express your views and we will listen to you. We want to keep the door of communication standing wide open between us. When you seek a new privilege, I'm going to ask myself this question, "Is there any way I can grant this request without harming Brian or other people?" If I can permit what you want in good conscience, I will do so. I will compromise and bend as far as my best judgment will let me.

G. But hear this, Brian. There will be a few matters that cannot be compromised. There will be occasions when I will have to say "no." And when those times come, you can expect me to stand like the Rock of Gibraltar. No amount of violence and temper tantrums and door slamming will change a thing. In fact, if you choose to fight me in those remaining rules, then I promise that you will lose dramatically. Admittedly you're too big and grown up to spank, but I can still make you uncomfortable. And that will be my goal. Believe me, Brian, I'll lie awake nights figuring how to make you miserable. I have the courage and the determination to do my job during these last few years you are at home, and I intend to use all of my resources for this purpose, if necessary. So it's up to you. We can have a peaceful time of cooperation at home, or we can spend this last part of your childhood in unpleasantness and struggle. Either way, you *will* arrive home when you are told, and you *will* carry your share of responsibility in the family and you *will* continue to respect your mother and me.

H. Finally, Brian, let me emphasize the message I gave you in the beginning. We love you more than you can imagine, and we're going to remain friends during this difficult time. There is so much pain in the world today. Life involves disappointment and loss and rejection and aging and sickness and ultimately death. You haven't felt much of that discomfort yet, but you'll taste it soon enough. So with all that heartache outside our door, let's not bring more of it on ourselves. We need each other. We need you, and believe it or not, you still need us occasionally. And that, I suppose, is what we wanted to convey to you this morning. Let's make it better from now on.

I. Do you have things that need to be said to us?

The content of this message should be modified to fit individual circumstances and the needs of particular adolescents. Furthermore, the responses of children will vary tremendously from person to person. An "open" boy or girl may reveal his deepest feelings at such a moment of communication, permitting a priceless time of catharsis and ventilation. On the other hand, a stubborn, defiant, proud adolescent may sit immobile with head downward. But even if your teenager remains stoic or hostile, at least the cards have been laid on the table and parental intentions explained.[14]

**You stated earlier that you do not favor spanking a teenager. What would you do to encourage the cooperation of my fifteen-year-old who deliberately makes a nuisance of himself? He throws his clothes around, refuses to help out with any routine tasks in the house, and pesters his little brother perpetually.**

I would seek to find a way to link his behavior to something important to the fourteen-year-old, such as privileges or even money. If he receives an allowance, for example, this money could provide an excellent tool with which you can generate a little motivation. Suppose he is given two dollars a week. That maximum can be taxed regularly for violation of predetermined rules. For example, each article of clothing left on the floor might cost him a dime. A deliberate provocation of his brother would subtract a quarter from his total. Each Saturday, he would receive the money remaining from the taxation of the last week. This system conforms to the principle behind all adolescent discipline: give the individual reason for obeying other than the simple fact that he was told to do so.[15]

**I have a fourteen-year-old daughter, Margretta, who wants to date a seventeen-year-old boy. I don't feel good about letting her go, but I'm not sure just how to respond. What should I say to her?**

Rather than stamping your foot and screaming, "No! And that's semi-final!" I would work out a reasonable plan for the years ahead and a rationale to support it. You might say, "Margretta, you are fourteen years old and I understand your new interest in boys. That's the way it's supposed to be. However, you are not ready to handle the pressures that an older boy can put on a girl your age." (Explain what you mean if she asks.)

"Your dad and I want to help you get ready for dating in the future, but there are some in-between steps you need to take. You have to learn how to be 'friends' with boys before you become a 'lover' with one. To do this, you should get acquainted in groups of boys or girls your age. We'll invite them to our house or you can go to the homes of others. Then when you are between fifteen and sixteen, you can begin double-dating to places that are chaperoned by adults. And finally, you can go on single dates sometime during your sixteenth year.

"Your dad and I want you to date and have fun with boys, and we intend to be reasonable about this. But you're not ready to plunge into single dating with a high school senior, and we'll just have to find other ways to satisfy your social needs."[16]

**My unmarried daughter recently told me that she is three months pregnant. What should be my attitude toward her now?**

You cannot reverse the circumstances by being harsh or unloving at this point. Your daughter needs more understanding now than ever before, and you should give it to her if possible. Help her grope through this difficulty and avoid "I told you so" comments. She will face many important decisions in the next few months and she will need a calm, rational mother and father to assist in determining the best path to take. Remember that lasting love and affection often develop between people who have survived a crisis together.[17]

**My fifteen-year-old is a nature-lover through and through. His room is filled with caged snakes, wasp nests, plants, and insects. Even the garage is occupied by various animals he has caught and tamed. I hate all this stinky stuff and want him to get interested in something else. What should I do?**
If he keeps his zoo clean and well managed, then you should let him follow his interests. Just remember that at fifteen, "bugs" beat "drugs" as a hobby![18]

**Most teenagers know that drug use is harmful to their bodies and can even kill them. Why, then, do they do it? Are they usually the victims of unscrupulous "pushers" who get them hooked on narcotics?**
Not usually. The introduction to drug usage is usually made from friend to friend in a social atmosphere. Marijuana and pills are frequently distributed at parties where a nonuser cannot refuse to participate without appearing square and unsophisticated. Many teenagers would literally risk their lives if they thought their peer group demanded them to do so, and this need for social approval is instrumental in the initiation of most drug habits.[19]

**What should parents look for as symptoms of drug abuse?**
Listed below are eight physical and emotional symptoms that may indicate substance abuse by your child.

1. Inflammation of the eyelids and nose is common. The pupils of the eyes are either very wide or very small, depending on the kind of drugs internalized.
2. Extremes of energy may be represented. Either the individual is sluggish, gloomy, and withdrawn, or he may be loud, hysterical, and jumpy.
3. The appetite is extreme—either very great or very poor. Weight loss may occur.
4. The personality suddenly changes; the individual may become irritable, inattentive, and confused, or aggressive, suspicious, and explosive.
5. Body and breath odor is often bad. Cleanliness is generally ignored.
6. The digestive system may be upset—diarrhea, nausea, and vomiting may occur. Headaches and double vision are also

common. Other signs of physical deterioration may include change in skin tone and body stance.

7. Needle marks on the body, usually appearing on the arms, are an important symptom. These punctures sometimes get infected and appear as sores and boils.

8. Moral values often crumble and are replaced by new, way-out ideas and values.[20]

**Do you think better education is the answer to the drug abuse problem among teenagers?**

Unfortunately, narcotics usage among teenagers will not be conquered by instructional programs that explain its hazards. The kids already know the consequences of drug use—probably better than their parents do. They are not deaf, and their abuse of substances is usually done *in spite of* the obvious price tag. Though we have to support our educational efforts with the young (it is our only hope for change), the drug problem will continue until it is no longer fashionable to "trip out." When it becomes disgraceful to use drugs, the epidemic will be over—but not a minute sooner.[21]

**How can I help my child withstand the adolescent pressure to conform on important matters such as drug use and sexual immorality?**

It is important for your preteenager to know about group pressure before it reaches its peak. Someday he may be sitting in a car with four friends who decide to take some little red pills, and he needs to know *in advance* how he will handle that moment. Roleplay that moment with him, teaching him what to say and do. Your preparation is no guarantee that he will have the courage to stand alone at that crucial time, but his knowledge of peer influence could provide the independence to do what is right. I would, therefore, recommend that this matter of conformity be thoroughly discussed and rehearsed with your ten- or eleven-year-old.[22]

**You have described adolescent conformity in graphic detail, and we recognize it in our teenage daughter. But what about adults in the Western culture? Are we also vulnerable to group pressure and conformity?**

One of the great American myths is that we are a nation of rugged individualists. We really have ourselves fooled at this point. We like to think of ourselves as Abraham Lincolns, Patrick Henrys, and cowboys, standing tall and courageous in the face of social rejection. But that image is palpably uncharacteristic of most Americans. In truth, we are a nation of social cowards. It seems to me that a major proportion of our energy is expended in trying to be like everyone else, cringing in fear of true individuality.

There are numerous exceptions to this generalization, of course, but social independence and confidence do not appear to be predominant characteristics in the American psyche.

**How do you feel about the dangers of marijuana usage today? I've heard that it isn't addictive and therefore isn't harmful; I've also heard that it is very dangerous. What are the facts?**

Let me permit Harold Voth, M.D., to speak to that question. Dr. Voth has served as senior psychiatrist and psychoanalyst for the Menninger Foundation in Topeka, Kansas, and is also associate chief of psychiatry for education at Topeka Veterans Administration Medical Center, Topeka, Kansas. These are his words:

> My own family has provided a major stimulus for me to become involved in the problem of drug abuse. Seeing our three sons grow into wholesome manhood provides such a vivid contrast to those youngsters I have observed over the years whose lives have been damaged or destroyed by marijuana.
>
> Witnessing a young person harm himself is a tragic sight; it is heartbreaking. I think of what might have been for all of them, of their parents' broken dreams and of the sadness that has beclouded the lives of their families.
>
> Therefore, to prevent others from walking down the path of deception offered the potential drug user, I refer you to the following facts.
>
> - All parties agree, even those dedicated to the legalization and open distribution of marijuana, that children, teenagers, and young adults whose minds and bodies have not yet matured, as well as pregnant women, should never smoke marijuana.

- 90% of those using hard drugs such as heroin started with marijuana.
- Five marijuana cigarettes have the same cancer causing capacity as 112 conventional cigarettes.
- Marijuana stays in the body, lodged in the fat cells, for three to five weeks. Mental and physical performance is negatively affected during this entire period of time.
- A person smoking marijuana on a regular basis suffers from a cumulative build-up and storage of THC, a toxic chemical, in the fat cells of the body, particularly in the brain. It takes three to five months to detoxify effectively a regular user.
- The part of the brain that allows a person to focus, concentrate, create, learn and conceptualize at an advanced level is still growing during the teenage years. Continuous use of marijuana over a period of time will retard the normal growth of these brain cells.
- A study at Columbia University revealed that female marijuana smokers suffer a sharp increase in cells with damaged DNA (the chemical that carries the genetic code). It was also found that the female reproductive eggs are especially vulnerable to damage by marijuana.
- A second Columbia University study found that a control group smoking a single marijuana cigarette every other day for a year, had a white blood cell count that was 39% lower than normal, thus damaging the immune system and making the user far more susceptible to infection and sickness.
- One marijuana cigarette causes a 41% decrease in driving skills. Two cigarettes cause a 63% decrease.

**How can I recognize the symptoms of marijuana use in my sixteen-year-old son?**

According to Drug Abuse Central in San Antonio, Texas, the symptoms of marijuana use are as follows:

1. Diminished drive, reduced ambition.
2. Significant drop in the quality of school work.
3. Reduced attention span.
4. Impaired communication skills.
5. Distinct lessening in social warmth; less care for the feelings of others.

6. Pale face, imprecise eye movements, red eyes.
7. Neglect of personal appearance.
8. Inappropriate overreaction to mild criticism.
9. A change from active competitive interests to a more passive, withdrawn personality.
10. Association with friends who refuse to identify themselves or simply hang up if parents answer the phone.
11. An increased secretiveness about money or the disappearance of money or valuables from the house.

**You've expressed strong opinions about the need for mothers to be at home when their children are small. How do you feel about the mothers of elementary and high school students being employed outside the home?**

If you had asked me this question five years ago, I would have said that mothers are needed at home primarily during the preschool years. After kindergarten, the critical factor is to be there when the kids get home from school. That would have been my reply when our children were five years younger. But now that Danae is sixteen and Ryan is eleven, I feel even more strongly about the need for mothers to be at home during the adolescent years. This will not be a popular view, but I can only report honestly what I feel and have observed.

The frantic activities of teenagers create great stresses on families which require adult attention. Who will be there to taxi the kids back and forth and get ready for the slumber party and sew the new dress and attend the first football game and keep up with all the "must dos" of those years? Not only is Mom needed to hold things together at home during these pressurized days, but she must brace herself for the conflict so typical of these years. It is not a good time for her to come home exhausted each evening from a job that has required her total commitment. That sets the stage for emotional explosions between generations.

# SECTION 17

# QUESTIONS FROM ADOLESCENTS

**I am a teenager and I want to look and dress just like all my friends. My parents tell me I should be an individual and be willing to be different, but I just can't do it. Do *you* understand?**

Sure I do. Let me explain why you feel such pressure to be like everyone else. The answer involves feelings of inferiority, which are usually very strong during adolescence. You see, when you feel worthless and foolish—when you don't like yourself—then you are more frightened by the threat of ridicule or rejection by your friends. You become more sensitive about being laughed at. You lack the confidence to be different. Your problems seem bad enough without making them worse by defying the wishes of the majority. So you dress the way they tell you to dress, and you talk the way they tell you to talk, and all your ideas are the group's ideas. You become afraid to raise your hand in class or express your own ideas. Your great desire is to behave in the "safest" way possible. These behaviors all have one thing in common: they result from a lack of self-confidence.

Gradually, your self-respect will return as you become more mature and comfortable with the person God made you to be.[1]

**I am fourteen and I have crummy-looking pimples all over my face. What causes them and what can I do to clear up my skin?**

Practically every part of your body is affected in one way or another by the period of change you are now experiencing. Even your skin undergoes major changes, whether you are a boy or a girl. In fact, this is probably the most distressing aspect of all the physical events that take place in early adolescence. A study of two thousand teenagers asked the question, "What do you most dislike about yourself?" Skin problems outranked every other reply by a wide margin.

Skin eruptions occur primarily as a result of an oily substance which is secreted during adolescence. The pores of the skin tend to fill up with this oil and become blocked. Since the oil can't escape, it hardens there and causes pimples or blackheads. You might expect to have these imperfections on your skin for several years, although some cases are milder than others.

When you get numerous pimples and blackheads regularly, the condition is called acne. If this happens, it will be very important for you to keep your skin clean, minimizing the oil and dirt on your face. We used to think that certain greasy foods and chocolate contributed to the difficulty, but doctors now doubt this relationship. If the problem is severe, as you obviously feel it is, you should ask your parents to take you to a dermatologist, who is a doctor specializing in skin problems. Acne can now be treated effectively in most cases.[2]

**I am thirteen and I feel miserable about myself. Is there anything I can do?**

First, you need to understand that you are not alone. Begin observing the people around you and see if you detect hidden feelings of inferiority. When you go to school tomorrow, quietly watch the students who are coming and going. I assure you, many of them have the same concerns that trouble you. They reveal these doubts by being very shy and quiet, by being extremely angry and mean, by being silly, by being afraid to participate in a game or a contest, by blushing frequently, or by acting proud and "stuck-up." You'll soon learn to recognize the signs of inferiority, and then you'll know that it is a *very* common disorder! Once you fully comprehend that others feel as you do, then you *should never again* feel alone. It will give you more confidence to know that everyone is afraid of embarrassment and ridicule—that we're all sitting in the same leaky boat, trying to plug the watery holes. And would you believe, I nearly drowned in that same leaky boat when I was fourteen years old?

Second, I advise you to look squarely at the worries that keep gnawing at you from the back of your mind or from deep within your heart, causing a black cloud to hang over your head day and night. It would be a good idea to get alone, where there is no one to interfere with your thoughts. Then *list* all the things which you most dislike about yourself. Nobody is going to see this paper except the people to whom you choose to show it, so you can be completely honest. Write down everything that has been bothering you. Even admit the characteristics that you dislike, including the tendency to get mad and blow up (if that applies to you).

Identify your most serious problems as best as possible. Do you get frustrated and angry at people and then feel bad later? Or is it your shyness that makes you afraid when you're with other people? Is it your inability to express your ideas—to put your thoughts into words? Is it your laziness, your unkindness to other people, or the way you look? Whatever concerns you, write it down as best you can. Then when you're finished, go back through the list and put a mark by those items that worry you the most—the problems that you spend the most time thinking and fretting about.

Third, think about each item on the list. Give your greatest creative thought to what might be done to change the things you don't like. If you wish, you might share the paper with your pastor, counselor, parent, or someone in whom you have confidence: that person can then help you map out a plan for improvement. You'll feel better for having faced your problems, and you might even find genuine solutions to some of the troublesome matters.

Now, we come to an important step. The key to mental health is being able to accept what you cannot change. After you've done what you can to deal with your problems, I feel you should take the paper on which the most painful items are written, and burn it in a private ceremony before God. Commit your life to Him once more—strengths and weaknesses—good points and bad—asking Him to take what you have and bless it. After all, He created the entire universe from nothing, and He can make something beautiful out of your life.[3]

**I am also a teenager, and I have a very hard time making friends. Can you help me learn how to influence people and make them like me?**

"The best way to *have* a friend is to *be* a good friend to others." That's a very old proverb, but it's still true. Now let me give you a little clue that will help you deal with people of *any* age. Most people experience feelings of inferiority and self-doubt, as I have described. And if you understand and remember that fact, it will help you know the secret of social success. *Never* make fun of others or ridicule them. Let them know that you respect and accept them, and that they are important to you. Make a conscious effort to be sensitive to their feelings, and protect their reputations. I think you'll quickly find that many will do the same for you in return.[4]

**I'm twelve years old and my dad tells me my body will soon change a lot. It's already happened to some of the other guys I know. But I don't understand what's about to happen to me or why. Would you sort of fill me in?**
I'd be glad to. The growing up process is a wonderful and interesting event. It's all controlled by a tiny organ near the center of your brain called the *pituitary gland.* This little organ is only the size of a small bean, yet it's called the master gland because it tells the rest of your glands what to do. It's the "big boss upstairs," and when it screams, your glandular system jumps. Somewhere within your own pituitary gland is a plan for your body. At just the right time, it will send out chemical messengers, called hormones, which will tell the rest of the glands in your body, "Get moving, it's time to grow up." In fact, those hormones will have many implications for your body during the next few years of your life.

I'm glad your dad told you about the changes soon to occur. There are several reasons why you ought to understand this aspect of physical development. First, if you don't know what is about to happen to your body, it can be pretty terrifying when everything goes crazy all at one time. It's not unusual for a teenager to begin worrying about himself. He wonders, "What's going on here? Do I have a disease? Could this be cancer? Is there something wrong with my body? Dare I discuss it with anybody?" These are unnecessary fears that result from ignorance or misinformation about the body. When young people understand the process, they know that these changes represent normal, natural events which they should have been anticipating. So I'm going to tell you exactly what you can expect in the period of early adolescence. There's just no reason for you to be anxious over these rapid physical changes.

The most important change that you will notice is that your body will begin to prepare itself for parenthood. Now I didn't say that you are about to become a parent (that should be years away), but that your body is about to *equip itself* with the ability to produce a child. That's one of the major changes that occurs during this period. The correct name for this time of sexual awakening is *puberty*.

During puberty, you will begin to grow very rapidly, faster than ever before in your life. Your muscles will become much more like those of a man, and you'll get much stronger and better coordinated. That's why a junior high boy is usually a much better athlete than a fifth or sixth grader, and why a high school boy is a better athlete than a junior high boy. A dramatic increase occurs in his overall body size, strength, and coordination during this period.

Second, your hair will begin to look more like the hair of a man. You'll notice the beginnings of a beard on your face, and you'll have to start shaving it every now and then. Hair will also grow under your arms for the first time, and also on what is called the pubic region (or what you may have called the private area), around your sex organs. The sex organs themselves will become larger and more like those of an adult male. These are evidences that the little boy is disappearing forever, and in his place will come a man, capable of becoming a father and taking care of his wife and family. This fantastic transformation reminds me in some ways of a caterpillar, which spins a cocoon around itself and then after awhile comes out as a totally different creature—a butterfly. Of course the changes in a boy are not that complete, but you will never be the same after undergoing this process of *maturation* (the medical word for growing up).

These rapid changes are probably just around the corner for you. The frightening thing for some kids is that they occur very suddenly, almost overnight. The pituitary gland quickly begins kicking everything into action. It barks its orders right and left, and your entire body seems to race around inside, trying to carry out these commands.

Everything is affected—even your voice will be different. I'm sure you've noticed how much lower your dad's voice is than your own. Have you ever wondered how it got that way? Was it always deep and gruff? Did it always sound like a foghorn? Can you imagine your dad in his crib as a baby saying "Goo, goo" in a deep voice? Of course not. He wasn't born that way. His voice changed during puberty, and that's what will happen to yours, too. However an adolescent boy's voice is sometimes an embarrassment to him until this deepening process is finished, because it doesn't sound very solid. It squeaks and screeches and wobbles and cracks for a few months. But again, this is nothing to worry about, because the voice will soon be deep and steady. A little time is needed to complete this development of the vocal cords.

Another physical problem occurring with both boys and girls during puberty is fatigue, or lack of energy. Your body will be investing so many of its resources into the growing process that it will seem to lack energy for other activities for a period of time. This phase usually doesn't last very long. However, this tired feeling is something you ought to anticipate. In fact, it should influence your behavior in two ways.

First, you must get plenty of sleep and rest during the period of rapid growth. That need is often not met, however, because teenagers feel that they should not have to go to bed as early as they did when they were children. Therefore, they stay up too late and then drag through the next day in a state of exhaustion. Believe it or not, a twelve- or thirteen-year-old person actually needs more rest than when he was nine or ten, simply because of the acceleration in growth.

Second, the foods you eat will also be very important during adolescence. Your body has to have the raw materials with which to construct those new muscle cells and bones and fibers that are in the plans. It will be necessary for you to get a *balanced* diet during this time; it's even more important than when you were six or eight. If you don't eat right during this growth period, you will pay the price with sickness and various physical problems. Your body *must* have the vitamins and minerals and protein necessary to enlarge itself in so many ways.

These are some of the basic changes you can expect within a few years. And when they have occurred, you will be on your way to manhood.[5]

**My name is Kim. I am eleven and am a girl. What changes can I expect to take place? I'm especially interested in menstruation and how babies are made.**

A girl's body goes through even more complex changes than those of a boy, because it has to prepare itself for the very complicated task of motherhood. The way a woman's body functions to produce human life is one of the most beautiful mechanisms in all of God's universe. Let's look at that process for a moment.

All human life begins as one tiny cell, so small that you

couldn't see it without a microscope. This first cell of life is called a zygote, which begins to divide and grow inside the mother's uterus.

The uterus is a special place inside the mother's lower abdomen, or what you may have called the stomach. Actually, it's not in the stomach at all, but below it. The uterus is a special little pouch that serves as a perfect environment for a growing and developing embryo. (An *embryo* is the name for a baby in its earliest stages of development.)

All the baby's needs for warmth and oxygen and nourishment are met constantly by the mother's body during the nine months before his birth. Any little slip-up during those very early days (the first three months especially), and the growing child will die. The embryo is extremely delicate, and the mother's body has to be in good physical condition in order to meet the requirements of the growing child.

In order to meet these requirements, a girl's body undergoes many changes during puberty. One of those important developments is called menstruation, which I'm glad you asked about. This is a subject that girls will need to understand thoroughly in the days ahead. Most schools provide this information to girls in the fifth or sixth grade, so what I'll tell you now may just be a review of what you have seen and heard elsewhere. However, I feel it is important for boys to understand this process, too, although they are seldom informed properly.

When a woman becomes pregnant—that is, when the one-celled zygote is planted in her uterus after having a sexual relationship with a man—her body begins to protect this embryo and help it grow. It has to have oxygen and food and many chemicals which are necessary for life. The substances are delivered to the uterus automatically, through the mother's blood. But since the uterus has no way of knowing when a new life is going to be planted there, it must get ready to receive an embryo each month, just in case it happens. Therefore, blood accumulates on the walls of the uterus in order to nourish an embryo if the woman becomes pregnant. But if she *doesn't* become pregnant that month, then the uterine blood is not needed. It is released from the walls of the uterus and flows out through the vagina—that special opening through which babies are also born.

Every twenty-eight days (this number varies a bit from person to person), a woman's body will get rid of this unnecessary blood which would have been used to nourish a baby if she had become pregnant. It usually takes about three to five days for the flow to stop, and during this time she wears a kind of cloth pad to absorb the blood. This process is called *menstruation*.

There are some very important attitudes that I want you to understand through this discussion. First, menstruation is not something for girls to dread and fear. Since the subject of blood causes us to shudder, some girls get very tense over this process happening to them. They start worrying about it and dreading its arrival, and some do not want it to happen at all. But actually, menstruation makes possible the most fantastic and exciting event that can ever occur— the creation of a new human being. What a miracle it is for a single cell, the zygote, to quietly split into two, then four, eight, and sixteen cells, and continue to divide until trillions of new cells are formed! A little heart slowly emerges within the cluster of cells, and begins beating to the rhythm of life. Then come fingers and toes and eyes and ears and all the internal organs. A special liquid (called amniotic fluid) surrounds the baby to protect him from any bumps or bruises the mother might receive. And there he stays for nine months, until he is capable of surviving in the world outside. Then at just the right moment the mother's body begins pushing the baby down the birth canal (the vagina) and into the waiting hands of the physician.

The most beautiful aspect of this incredibly complicated system is that it all works *automatically* within a woman's body. It's almost as though the Master Designer, God Himself, were standing nearby, telling her what to do next. In fact, did you know that this is precisely what happens? We are told by King David, writing in the Psalms, that God is present during this creation of a new life. Let's read his description of that event:

> You made all the delicate, inner parts of my body, and knit them together in my mother's womb. Thank you for making me so wonderfully complex! It is amazing to think about. Your workmanship is marvelous—and how well I know it. You were there while I was being formed in utter seclusion! (Psa. 139:13-15 TLB).

Not only did God supervise David's development in his mother's womb (another word for uterus), but He did the same thing for you and me! He has also scheduled each day of our lives and recorded every day in His book. That is the most reassuring thought that I've ever known!

So you see, menstruation is not an awful event for girls to dread. It is a signal that the body is preparing itself to cooperate with God in creating a new life, if that proves to be His will for a particular woman. Menstruation is the body's way of telling a girl that she is growing up . . . that she is not a child anymore . . . and that something very exciting is happening inside.

Now, Kim, please don't worry about this aspect of your health. You will not bleed to death, I promise you. Menstruation is as natural as eating or sleeping or any other bodily process. If you feel you are abnormal in some way—if you're worried about some aspect of menstruation—if you think you're different or that maybe something has gone wrong—or if there's some pain associated with your menstruation or you have any question at all, then muster your courage and talk to your mother or your doctor or someone in whom you have confidence. In about 98 cases out of 100, the fears will prove to be unjustified. You will find that you are completely normal, and that the trouble was only in your lack of understanding of the mechanism.

Now, obviously, other things will begin to happen to your body at about the same time as menstruation. You will probably have a growth spurt just prior to your first menstruation. (Incidentally, the average age of first menstruation in American girls is now about twelve-and-a-half years of age, but it can occur as early as nine or ten years or as late as sixteen or seventeen. The age varies widely from girl to girl.)

During this time your body will become more rounded and curvy like your mother's. Your breasts will enlarge, and they may become sore occasionally (boys sometimes experience this soreness, too). This doesn't mean that you have cancer or some other disease, but simply that your breasts are changing, like everything else in your body. Hair will also grow under your arms, on your legs, and in the pubic region, as with boys. These are the most obvious physical changes which take place, and when you see them happening you can kiss good-bye to childhood—it's full speed ahead toward adulthood.[6]

**I am thirteen-and-a-half and I haven't started to change yet. I'm shorter and not as strong as most of my friends. And they have voices that are lower than mine. It's**

**embarrassing! I don't even have hair down below yet! Is there anything wrong with me?**
No. There is nothing wrong with you. You are just progressing on your own timetable. It's just as healthy to grow up later as earlier, and there's no reason to fear that you will never mature. Just hold steady for a year or two, and then the fireworks will all begin to pop for you, just as for everybody else! I can promise you that this is going to happen. If you don't believe me, take a look at all the adults around you. Do you see any of them that look like children? Of course not. *Everyone* grows up sooner or later.

Certainly it's never much fun to be laughed at by your friends, but if you know you'll be different for only a short time, maybe you can stand it. Most importantly, don't you be guilty of making another person feel bad about himself if you happen to grow before he does![7]

**Can I ask you a question about sex? I want to know more about making babies and all that stuff that my older brother talks about.**
That's a very important question and I'm glad you asked it. As your body starts to change, you'll notice that you're beginning to be more interested in people of the opposite sex. Suddenly girls begin to look great to boys and the boys start appealing to the girls. How do I know this will happen? How can I predict it so accurately? Because sex will soon become an "appetite" within you. If you missed your breakfast this morning, I can predict that you'll be plenty hungry by two o'clock in the afternoon. Your body will ask for food. It's made that way. There are chemicals in your body that will make you feel hungry when you haven't eaten.

In the same way, some new chemicals in your body will begin to develop a brand-new appetite when you're between twelve and fifteen years old. This will not be a craving for food, but it will involve the matter called sex, or the male or female aspects of your nature. Every year as you get older, this appetite will become more and more a part of you. You'll want to spend more of your time with someone of the opposite sex. Eventually this desire may lead you to marriage. Marriage is a wonderful union for those who find the right person. However, let me offer a word of caution on that subject.

One of the biggest mistakes you can make with your life is to get married *too soon*. That can be tragic. I want to stress that point in your mind. For two people to get married before they are ready can be a disaster. Unfortunately, this happens all too frequently. I will say more about this subject later in the book, but I strongly advise you not to get married until you're at least twenty years of age. *Half of all teenage marriages* blow up within five years, causing many tears and problems. I don't want yours to be one of those broken homes.

Now let me describe for you the feeling that sex will bring in the next few years. Boys will become very interested in the bodies of girls—in the way they're built, in their curves and softness, and in their pretty hair and eyes. Even their feminine feet may have an appeal to boys during this time. If you're a boy, it's very likely that you will think often about these fascinating creatures called girls, whom you used to hate so much! In fact, the sexual appetite is stronger in males between sixteen and eighteen years of age than at any other age in life.

Girls, on the other hand, will not be quite so excited over the shape and the look of a boy's body (although they will find them interesting). They will be more fascinated by the boy himself—the way he talks, the way he walks, the way he thinks. If you're a girl, you will probably get a "crush" on one boy after another. (A crush occurs when you begin to think that one particular person is absolutely fantastic, and you fantasize about the possibility of being married to that person. It is not uncommon to get a crush on a teacher or a pastor or older man. Usually crushes are constantly changing, lasting only a few weeks or months before another one takes its place.)

Now we need to talk very plainly about the subject of sexual intercourse, which is the name given to the act that takes place when a man and a woman remove all their clothing (usually done in bed) and the man's sex organ (his *penis*) becomes very hard and straight. He puts his penis into the vagina of the woman while lying between her legs. They move around, in and out, until they both have a kind of tingly feeling which lasts for a minute or two. It's a very satisfying experience, which husbands and wives do regularly. You probably already know about sexual intercourse as I described it. But did you know that a man and woman do not have intercourse just to have babies? They do it to express love for each other and because they enjoy doing it. In this way they satisfy each other. They may have sexual intercourse two or three times a week, or maybe only once a month; each couple is different. But this is a fun part of marriage, and something that makes a husband and wife very special to each other. This is an act which they save just for each other.

This appetite for sex is something that God created within you. I want to make this point very strongly. Sex is not dirty and it is not evil. Nothing that God ever created could be dirty. The desire for sex was God's idea—not ours. He placed this part of our nature in us; He created those chemicals (hormones) that make the opposite sex appealing to us. He did this so we would want to have a family of our own. Without this desire there would be no marriage and no children and no love between a man and a woman. So sex is not a dirty thing at all; it's a wonderful, beautiful mechanism, no matter what you may have heard about it.

However, I must also tell you that God intends for us to control that desire for sexual intercourse. He has stated repeatedly in the Bible that we are to save our body for the person we will eventually marry, and that it is wrong to satisfy our appetite for sex with a boy or girl before we get married. There is just no other way to interpret the biblical message. Some of your friends may tell you differently in the days ahead. You may hear Jack or Susie or Paul or Jane tell about how they explored each other's bodies. They'll tell you how exciting it was, and try to get you to do the same.

Let me state it more personally. It is very likely that *you* will have a chance to have sexual intercourse before you reach twenty years of age. Sooner or later that opportunity will come to you. You will be with a person of the opposite sex who will let you know that he or she will permit you to have this experience. You're going to have to decide between now and then what you'll do about that moment when it comes. You probably won't have time to think when it suddenly happens. My strongest advice is for you to decide *right now* to save your body for the one who will eventually be your marriage partner. If you don't control this desire you will later wish that you had.

God's commandment that we avoid sexual intercourse before marriage was not given in order to keep us from having pleasure. It was not His desire to take the fun out of life. To the contrary, it was actually His *love* that caused Him to forbid premarital intercourse, because so many harmful consequences occur when you refuse to obey Him.

You've probably heard about venereal disease, which is

caused from having intercourse with someone who has caught it from another carrier. Syphilis, gonorrhea, and other diseases are very widespread today. Our country is having an epidemic of these diseases, and they have a damaging effect on the body if they go untreated. But there are other consequences for those who have premarital sex. They run the risk of bringing an unwanted baby into the world by this act. When that occurs, they face the responsibility of raising a human being—a little life with all its needs for love and discipline and the stability of a home—but they have no way to take care of him or meet his needs. That is tragic.

But just as serious are the changes that take place within a person's *mind* when he has intercourse outside the bonds of marriage. First, and most important, his relationship with God is sacrificed. Premarital sex is a sin, and a person just can't be friends with God if he is going to continue to sin deliberately and willfully. First John 1:6 says, "If we say we are his friends but go on living in spiritual darkness and sin, we are lying" (TLB). It's as simple as that. Furthermore, nothing can be hidden from God, as you know, because He sees everything.

Sin always has a destructive effect on a young person. But I believe the sin of premarital sex is especially damaging to the young person who engages in it. He or she loses the innocence of youth, and sometimes becomes hard and cold as a person. It's also likely to affect his or her later marriage, because that special experience which should have been shared with just one person is not so special anymore. More than one person has had a sample of it.

So you see, there are many obvious reasons why God has told us to control our sexual desires. What I'm saying is that God has commanded us not to have sex before marriage in order to spare us these many other effects of this sin. In fact, the *worst* consequence is one I have not yet mentioned, relating to the judgment of God in the life to come. We are told very clearly in the Bible that our lives will be laid bare before Him, and He will know every secret. Our eternal destinies actually depend on our faith in God and our obedience to Him.

I hope this has answered your question. There is so much more I could say if time permitted. Why don't you make a list of additional questions to discuss with your father or youth leader at church?[8]

**What are wet dreams that I hear other boys talking about?**

Many boys have "wet dreams," or what doctors call *nocturnal emissions*. This refers to the fluid which comes out of a boy's penis occasionally at night. The fluid is called semen, and contains millions of cells so tiny that you can't even see them. One of these cells could become a child if it were injected into a female and combined with her egg cell. (That would compose the zygote which we discussed earlier.) This semen sometimes is released during a nighttime dream; then the boy finds the stain on his pajamas the next morning and begins to worry about what is going on. However, this event is perfectly normal. It happens to almost all boys, and is nothing to worry about. A nocturnal emission is just his body's way of getting rid of the extra fluid that has accumulated.[9]

**Is there anything else I need to know about growing up that I haven't thought to ask?**

Just that many young people worry about their bodies unnecessarily during this time. These kinds of questions plague them:

1. Are all these changes supposed to be happening?
2. Is there something wrong with me?
3. Do I have a disease or an abnormality?
4. Am I going to be different from other people?
5. Does this pain in my breast mean I have cancer? (Remember, I mentioned that the breasts sometimes get sore during adolescencc.)
6. Will I be able to have intercourse, or will there be something wrong with me?
7. Will the boys laugh at me? Will the girls reject me? (It's very common for people to feel they're not going to be attractive to the opposite sex and that nobody will want them because they are not as pretty or handsome as they wish they could be.)
8. Will God punish me for the sexual thoughts that I have? (I told you that you're likely to think about the opposite sex often during these years. When this happens you may feel guilty for the thoughts that occur.)
9. Wouldn't it be awful if I became a homosexual? (A homosexual is someone who is not attracted to the opposite sex, but who is attracted to the *same* sex. It's a boy's interest in boys or a girl's interest in girls. Homosexuality is an abnormal desire that

reflects deep problems, but it doesn't happen very often and it's not likely to happen to you.)

10. Could I get pregnant without having sexual relations? (This is another possibility that some young girls fear—that they could find themselves pregnant even if they haven't had sexual relations. I want you to know that this *never* happens; it's an impossibility. Only one time in all of history did this occur, and that's when the virgin Mary, Jesus' mother, became pregnant even though she had never had sexual intercourse. Jesus was conceived or planted in her uterus by God Himself. That's the only time in the world's history that a human being has ever been born without the father doing his part by providing half of the cell that becomes the zygote.)

11. Do some people fail to mature sexually? (Any system of the body can malfunction, but this one *rarely* fails.)

12. Will my modesty be sacrificed? (It's common during the early adolescent years for you to become extremely modest about your body. You know it's changing and you don't want anybody to see it. Therefore, you may worry about being in a doctor's office and having to take off your clothes in front of other people.)

Let me say it one more time: these kinds of fears are almost universal during the early years of adolescence. Nearly everyone growing up in our culture worries and frets over the subject of sex. I want to help you avoid those anxieties. Your sexual development is a normal event that is being controlled inside your body. It will work out all right, so you can just relax and let it happen. However, you will have to control your sexual desires in the years ahead, and that will require determination and willpower. But if you can learn to channel your sexual impulses the way God intended, this part of your nature can be one of the most fascinating and wonderful aspects of your life, perhaps contributing to a successful and happy marriage in the years ahead.[10]

SECTION 18

# SELF-ESTEEM IN ADULTHOOD

**If I understand your writings correctly, you believe a majority of Americans experience low self-esteem to one degree or another. Assuming that to be true, what are the *collective* implications of that poor self-concept?**

It has serious implications for the stability of the American culture because the health of an entire society depends on the ease with which its individual members can gain personal acceptance. Thus, whenever the keys to self-esteem are seemingly out of reach for a large percentage of the people, as in twentieth-century America, then widespread mental illness, neuroticism, hatred, alcoholism, drug abuse, violence, and social disorder will certainly occur. Personal worth is not something human beings are free to take or leave. We must have it, and when it is unattainable, everybody suffers.[1]

**Why do you think low self-esteem is so widespread among women today? Why is this problem more prevalent now than in the past?**

There appear to be three factors related to the epidemic of self-doubt among females at this time in our history. First, the traditional responsibilities of wives and mothers have become matters of disrespect and ridicule. Raising children and maintaining a home hold very little status in most areas of the country, and women who are cast into that role often look at themselves with unconcealed disenchantment.

The forces which have promulgated this viewpoint are everywhere at once—on television, in magazines, on radio, in newspapers, in written advertisements, in books and novels—

each one hacking steadily at the confidence and satisfaction of women at home. It is not surprising, then, that many American homemakers feel bypassed . . . disrespected by the society around them. They would have to be deaf and blind to have missed that message.

But the decline in self-respect among women has other causes, as well. Another highly significant factor has to do with the role of beauty in our society. Physical attractiveness (or the lack of it) has a profound impact on feminine self-esteem. It is very difficult to separate basic human worth from the quality of one's own body; therefore, a woman who feels ugly is almost certain to feel inferior to her peers. This pressure is greatly magnified in a highly eroticized society as ours. Isn't it reasonable that the more steamed up a culture becomes over sex (and ours is at the boiling point), the more likely it is to reward beauty and punish ugliness? When sex becomes super-significant as it is today, then those with the least sex appeal necessarily begin to worry about their inability to compete in that marketplace. They are bankrupt in the most valuable "currency" of the day. Millions have fallen into that trap.

A third source of low self-esteem among American women relates to basic intelligence. Simply stated, many feel dumb and stupid. Psychologists have known for decades that there is no fundamental difference in the overall level of intelligence between men and women, although there are areas of greater strength for each sex. Men tend to score higher on tests of mathematics and abstract reasoning, while women excel in language and all verbal skills. However, when the individual abilities are combined, neither sex has a clear advantage over the other. Despite this fact, women are much more inclined to doubt their own mental capacity than are men. Why? I don't know, but it is another very important factor in low self-esteem.[2]

**Then you are saying that low self-esteem among women is still greatly influenced by the same physical factors they worried about when they were younger?**

That's right. The importance of beauty does not end in adolescence. It continues to determine human worth to some degree until late in life. Let me give you an example of what I mean. I counseled a young woman who had been a beautiful airline stewardess a few years earlier. She was happily married to a man who was proud of her beauty. Then a most unfortunate thing happened. She was in a tragic automobile accident which scarred her face and twisted her body. Her back was broken and she was destined to walk with a cane for the rest of her life. She was no longer attractive and her husband quickly lost interest in her sexually. Their divorce followed shortly. As a cripple, she could no longer serve as a stewardess, of course, and she found it difficult to obtain a job of any type. In this instance, a girl with high personal worth plunged to a position of little social status in one brief moment. Her true value as a human being should not have been affected by her accident, but it certainly was in the eyes of her immature husband.

While there are many causes for low self-esteem among women today, that old nemesis called "the uglies" (which every woman experiences at least occasionally) keeps doing its dirty work throughout our society.[3]

**Are the influences of "beauty" and "brains" as important to adult males as females? How does the self-esteem of men differ from women in this regard?**

For men, physical attractiveness gradually submerges as a value during late adolescence and early adulthood, yielding first place to intelligence. For women, however, beauty retains its number-one position throughout life, even into middle age and beyond. *The reason the average woman would rather have beauty than brains is because she knows the average man can see better than he can think.* Her value system is based on his and will probably continue that way. A man's personal preferences are also rooted in the opinions of the opposite sex, since most women value intelligence over handsomeness in men.[4]

**My husband often makes fun of my body. He's just teasing, but his comments embarrass me and make me disinterested in sex. Why can't I just ignore his kidding, because I know he doesn't mean to hurt me?**

Sex for human beings is inseparately connected with our psychological nature, especially in women. A woman who feels ugly, for example, is often too ashamed of her imperfect body to participate in sex without embarrassment. She knows it is impossible to disguise forty-year-old thighs, and her flaws interfere with her sensuality. Likewise, the person who feels shy and timid and inferior will usually express his sexuality in similar terms, or on the other hand, a self-confident, emotionally healthy individual is more likely to have a spontaneous sex life.

You must teach this concept to your husband, if possible, helping him see that anything which reduces your self-esteem will probably be translated into bedroom problems. In fact, any disrespect which he reveals for you as a person is almost certain to crop up in your physical relationship. In this regard, our sexual behavior differs radically from the mechanistic responses of lower animals. The emotional concomitants simply cannot be denied or suppressed in human beings.[5]

**I have never felt beautiful or even attractive to the opposite sex. Does this explain why I am *extremely* modest, even being ashamed to be seen in a bathing suit?**

Modesty has three basic origins. First, it is built into our fallen human nature. After sinning in the Garden of Eden, Adam and Eve's eyes "were opened, and they knew that they were naked; and they sewed fig leaves together, and made themselves aprons" (Gen. 3:7 KJV). To a varying degree within the descendants of Adam, we have inherited this same sensitivity about our bodies.

Second, modesty is a product of early home life. Those who were taught to conceal themselves compulsively in front of other family members usually carry that excessive modesty even into their marital relationships. It can turn legitimate sexual experiences into a self-conscious obligation.

The third source of extreme modesty is the one you mentioned, and it is probably the most powerful. Those who are ashamed of their bodies are highly motivated to conceal them. One of the greatest fears among junior high students is that they will have to disrobe and shower in front of their peers. Boys and girls alike are terrified by the possibility of ridicule for their lack of development (or precociousness). This embarrassment is often retained in the adult years with feelings of inferiority stamped all over it.[6]

**What part does intelligence play in the self-esteem of *adults*? Do they tend to forget the trouble they had during the school years?**

It has been said that "a boy is the father of the man," meaning we grown-ups are direct products of our own childhood. Thus, everything I have written about self-esteem in children applies to adults as well. We are all graduates of the educational "fail factory," and few have escaped completely unscathed. Furthermore, our self-worth is *still* being evaluated on the basis of intelligence. Dr. Richard Herrnstein, a Harvard University psychologist, predicts that a caste system founded on IQ is coming to America. He believes people will soon be locked into rigid intellectual classes which will determine careers, earning power, and social status. Dr. Herrnstein's expectation is based on the disintegration of racial and sexual barriers to success, leaving only intelligence as the major remaining source of discrimination in America. I don't agree fully with Dr. Herrnstein, although I am certain we will see the continuing importance of mental ability to self-esteem in our technological world.[7]

**My sister struggles with feelings of low self-esteem much of the time. I have a hard time understanding what she is experiencing. Can you put into words what a person goes through when they feel inadequate and inferior?**
I will try to express the troubling thoughts and anxieties which reverberate through the backroads of an insecure mind. It is sitting alone in a house during the quiet afternoon hours, wondering why the phone doesn't ring . . . wondering why you have no "real" friends. It is longing for someone to talk to, soul to soul, but knowing there is no such person worthy of your trust. It is feeling that "they wouldn't like me if they knew the real me." It is becoming terrified when speaking to a group of your peers, and feeling like a fool when you get home. It is wondering why other people have so much more talent and ability than you do. It is feeling incredibly ugly and sexually unattractive. It is admitting that you have become a failure as a wife and mother. It is disliking everything about yourself and wishing, constantly wishing, you could be someone else. It is feeling unloved and unlovable and lonely and sad. It is lying in bed after the family is asleep, pondering the vast emptiness inside and longing for unconditional love. It is intense self-pity. And more than any other factor, it is the root cause of depression.[8]

**I have a friend who was married for nine years before her husband left her for another woman. I think she was a loving and devoted wife, yet she seemed to feel that the**

**break-up of her marriage was her own fault. As a result, her self-esteem disintegrated and has never recovered. Why would she blame herself when her husband lied and deceived her and ran off with a younger girl?**

It has always been surprising for me to observe how often the wounded marriage partner—the person who was clearly the victim of the other's irresponsibility—is the one who suffers the greatest pangs of guilt and feelings of inferiority. How strange that the one who tried to hold things together in the face of obvious rejection often finds herself wondering, "How did I fail him? . . . I just wasn't woman enough to hold my man . . . I am 'nothing' or he wouldn't have left . . . If only I had been more exciting as a sexual partner . . . I drove him to it . . . I wasn't pretty enough . . . I didn't deserve him in the first place."

The blame for marital disintegration is seldom the fault of the husband or the wife alone. It takes two to tangle, as they say, and there is always some measure of shared blame for a divorce. However, when one marriage partner makes up his mind to behave irresponsibly, to become involved extramaritally, or to run from his family commitments and obligations, he usually seeks to justify his behavior by magnifying the failures of his spouse. "You didn't meet my needs, so I had to satisfy them somewhere else," is a familiar accusation. By increasing the guilt of his partner in this way, he reduces his own culpability. For a husband or wife with low self-esteem, these charges and recriminations are accepted as fact when hurled his way. "Yes, it was my fault. I drove you to it!" Thus, the victim assumes the full responsibility for his partner's irresponsibility, and self-worth shatters.

I would not recommend that your friend sit around hating the memory of her husband. Bitterness and resentment are emotional cancers that rot us from within. However, if I were counseling her I would encourage her to examine the facts carefully. Answers to these questions should be sought: "Despite my human frailties, did I value my marriage and try to preserve it? Did my husband decide to destroy it and then seek justification for his actions? Was I given a fair chance to resolve the areas of greatest irritation? Could I have held him even if I had made all the changes he wanted? Is it reasonable that I should hate myself for this thing that has happened?"

Your friend should know that social rejection breeds feelings of inferiority and self-pity in enormous proportions. And rejection by the one you love, particularly, is *the* most powerful destroyer of self-esteem in the entire realm of human experience. She might be helped to see herself as a victim of this process, rather than a worthless failure at the game of love.[9]

**I am acquainted with a woman who needs people so badly, but she unintentionally drives them away. She talks too much and constantly complains and makes everyone want to run from her. I know she has a terrible inferiority complex, but I could help her if she would let me. How can I tell her about these irritating faults without making her feel even worse about herself?**

You do it the way porcupines make love: *very*, very carefully. Let me offer a general principle that has thousands of applications in dealing with people, including the situation you have posed. *The right to criticize must be earned, even if the advice is constructive in nature.* Before you are entitled to tinker with another person's self-esteem, you are obligated *first* to demonstrate your own respect for him as a person. This is accomplished through an atmosphere of love and kindness and human warmth. Then when a relationship of confidence has been carefully constructed, you will have earned the right to discuss a potentially threatening topic. Your motives have thereby been clarified.

In response to your specific question, I would suggest that you invest some effort in building a healthy relationship with your verbose friend, and then feed her your suggestions in very small doses. And remember all the while that someone, somewhere, would like to straighten out a few of your flaws, too. We all have them.[10]

**I have suffered from low self-esteem for years, and sought help from a psychiatrist during a particularly depressed period of my life. Rather than building my self-worth, however, he was cold and aloof with me. I had the feeling he was merely doing a job and never really cared about me. I wonder how *you* would approach a patient with my kind of problem.**

It has been discouraging for me to see how often my professional colleagues (psychiatrists, psychologists, and counselors) have overlooked the feelings you described as a most obvious root cause for emotional distress. Lack of self-esteem produces more symptoms of psychiatric disorders than any other factor yet identified.

Time and time again in my casework as a psychologist, I sit talking to a person with deep longings to be respected and accepted. How badly he needs human affection and kindness, as well as emotional support and suggestions for change. Yet if that same needy patient had gone to Dr. Sigmund Freud in his day, the immortal grandfather of psychoanalysis would have sat back in detached professionalism, analyzing the patient's sexual repressions. If the patient had sought treatment from Dr. Arthur Janov, originator of Primal Scream therapy, he would have been encouraged to roll on the floor and bawl like a baby. (How foolish that form of "therapy" appears from my perspective!) Other modern therapists would have required the same patient to assault and be assaulted by other members of an "encounter group," or remove his clothing in a group, or beat his mother and father with a belt. Believe it or not, one of the major areas of controversy at psychiatric conferences a few years ago involved the wisdom of female patients having sexual intercourse with their male therapists! Have we gone completely mad? Whenever men abandon their ethics, they cease to make sense, regardless of their professional degrees and licenses. Perhaps this is why psychiatry is called "the study of the id by the odd." (No disparagement is intended to the more orthodox profession of psychiatry itself.)

The most successful approach to therapy for a broken patient, I firmly believe, is to convey the following message with conviction (though perhaps not with words): "Life has been tough and you have become acquainted with pain. To this point, you've faced your problems without much human support, and there have been times when your despair has been overwhelming. Let me, now, share that burden. From this moment forward, I am interested in you as a person; you deserve and shall have my respect. As best as possible, I want you to quit worrying about your troubles. Instead, confide them to me. Our concentration will be on the present and the future; together we will seek appropriate solutions."

Suddenly, the beleaguered patient no longer feels alone—the most depressing of human experiences. "Someone cares! Someone understands! Someone assures me with professional confidence that he is certain I will survive. I'm not going to drown in this sea of despondence, as I feared. I have been thrown a life preserver by a friend who promises not to abandon me in the storm." This is real therapy, and it exemplifies the essence of the Christian commandment that we "bear one another's burdens."[11]

**I am *not* coping so well with the problems of self-doubt. I feel ugly and disrespected and unworthy. What encouragement can you offer?**

Isn't it about time that you made friends with yourself? Aren't there enough headaches in life without beating your skull against that old brick wall of inadequacy, year after year? If I were to draw a caricature that would symbolize the millions of adults like you with low self-esteem, I would depict a bowed, weary traveler. Over his shoulder I would place the end of a mile-long chain to which is attached tons of scrap iron, old tires, and garbage of all types. Each piece of junk is inscribed with the details of some humiliation—a failure—an embarrassment—a rejection from the past. He could let go of the chain and free himself from that heavy load which immobilizes and exhausts him, but he is somehow convinced that it must be dragged throughout life. So he plods onward, digging a furrow in the good earth as he goes.

You can free yourself from the weight of the chain if you will but turn it loose. Your inferiority is based on a distortion of reality seen through childish eyes. The standards by which you have assessed yourself are themselves changing and fickle. Dr. Maxwell Maltz, the plastic surgeon who authored *Psycho-Cybernetics*, said women came to him in the 1920s requesting that their breasts be reduced in size. Today they are asking that he pump them up with silicone. False values! In King Solomon's biblical love song, he asked his bride to overlook his dark skin that had occurred from exposure to the sun. In his day, right meant white. But now the brown brother Solomon would be the pride of the beach. False values! Modern women are ashamed to admit that they carry an extra ten pounds of weight, yet Rembrandt would have loved to paint their plump, rotund bodies. False values! Don't you see that your personal worth is not really dependent on the opinions of others and the temporal, fluctuating values they represent? The sooner you can accept the transcending worth of your humanness, the sooner you can come to terms with yourself. I must agree with the writer who said: "While in the race to save our face, why not conquer inner space?" It's not a bad idea.[12]

**I am dealing with my own inadequacies pretty well, and now feel I am ready to take additional steps in the direction of self-confidence. What do you recommend?**
I could take a week to answer this question, but let me just offer the first suggestion that comes to mind. I have repeatedly observed that a person's own needs and problems seem less threatening when he is busy helping someone else handle theirs! It is difficult to concentrate on your own troubles when you are actively shouldering another person's load and seeking solutions to his problems. Therefore, I would recommend that you consciously make a practice of giving to others. Visit the sick. Bake something for your neighbors. Use your car for those without transportation. And perhaps most important, learn to be a good listener. The world is filled with lonely, disheartened people like you were, and you are in an excellent position to empathize with them. And while you're doing it, I guarantee that your own sense of uselessness will begin to fade.[13]

You might also enjoy reading the book by Dr. W. Peter Blitchington, *The Christian Woman's Search for Self-Esteem* (Thomas Nelson, Inc., 1982), which provides many helpful suggestions.

**You are strongly in favor of building self-esteem in children, but I have some theological problems with that objective. The Bible condemns "pride" from Genesis to Revelation, and speaks of humans as no better than worms. How do you defend your position in the light of Scripture?**
It is my opinion that great confusion has prevailed among followers of Christ on the distinction between pride and self-esteem. You are apparently among the people who actually believe that Christians should maintain an attitude of inferiority in order to avoid the pitfalls of self-sufficiency and haughtiness. I don't believe it.

After speaking to a sizable audience in Boston a few years ago, I was approached by an elderly lady who questioned my views. I had discussed the importance of self-confidence in children, and my comments had contradicted her theology. In fact, she even made reference to the same Scripture in Psalm 22:6.

She said, "God wants me to think of myself as being no better than a worm."

"I would like to respect myself," she continued, "but God

could not approve of that kind of pride, could He?"

I was touched as this sincere little lady spoke. She told me she had been a missionary for forty years, even refusing to marry in order to serve God more completely. While on a foreign field, she had become ill with an exotic disease which now reduced her frail body to ninety-five pounds. As she spoke, I could sense the great love of the Heavenly Father for this faithful servant. She had literally given her life in His work, yet she did not even feel entitled to reflect on a job well done during her closing years on earth.

Unfortunately, this fragile missionary (and thousands of other Christians) had been taught that she was worthless. But that teaching did not come from the Scriptures. Jesus did not leave His throne in heaven to die for the "worms" of the world. His sacrifice was intended for that little woman, and for me and all of His followers, whom He is not embarrassed to call brothers. What a concept! If Jesus is now my brother, then that puts me in the family of God, and guarantees that I will outlive the universe itself. And that, friends, is what I call genuine self-esteem!

It's true that the Bible clearly condemns the concept of human pride. In fact, God apparently holds a special hatred for this particular sin. I have counted 112 references in Scripture which specifically warn against an attitude of pride. Proverbs 6:16-19 makes it unmistakably clear:

> These six things doth the Lord hate: yea, seven are an abomination unto him: A proud look, a lying tongue, and hands that shed innocent blood, an heart that deviseth wicked imaginations, feet that be swift in running to mischief, a false witness that speaketh lies, and he that soweth discord among brethren (KJV).

Isn't it interesting that a *proud look* (or *haughtiness*, as paraphrased in *The Living Bible*) is listed *first* among God's seven most despised sins, apparently outranking adultery, profanity, and other acts of disobedience? Anything given that prominence in the Word had better be avoided scrupulously by those wishing to please the Lord. But first we must interpret the meaning of the word *pride*.

Language is dynamic and the meaning of words changes with the passage of time. In this instance, the word *pride* has many connotations today which are different from the biblical usage of the word. For example, a parent feels "pride" when his son or daughter succeeds in school or wins a race. But I can't believe the Lord would be displeased by a father glowing with affection when he thinks of the boy or girl entrusted to his care.

We speak, also, about the "Pride of the Yankees," or a person taking pride in his work, or the pride of a southern cook. These are very positive emotions that mean the individual is dedicated to his craft, that he has self-confidence, and that he will deliver what he promises. Certainly those attitudes could not represent the pinnacle of the seven deadliest sins.

I'm equally convinced that the Bible does not condemn an attitude of quiet self-respect and dignity. Jesus commanded us to love our neighbors *as* ourselves, implying not only that we are permitted a reasonable expression of self-love, but that love for others is impossible—until we experience a measure of self-respect.

Then what *is* the biblical meaning of pride? I believe sinful pride occurs when our arrogant self-sufficiency leads us to violate the two most basic commandments of Jesus: first, to love God with all our heart, mind, and strength; and second, to love our neighbor as ourselves. A proud person is too pompous and haughty to bow humbly before his Maker, confessing his sins and submitting himself to a life of service to God; or he is hateful to his fellowman, disregarding the feelings and needs of others. And as such, most of the ills of the world, including war and crime, can be laid at its door. That's why the writer of Proverbs put "a proud look" above all other evils, for that is where it belongs.

May I stress, further, that the quest for self-esteem *can* take us in the direction of unacceptable pride. During the past decade, for example, we've seen the rise of the "Me" generation, nurtured carefully by humanistic psychologists, who accept no scriptural dictates. One of the best-selling books of this era was entitled *Looking Out for #1*, which instructed its readers to grab the best for themselves. Widely quoted mottos reflect the same selfish orientation, including IF IT FEELS GOOD, DO IT! and DO YOUR OWN THING. This philosophy of "me first" has the power to blow our world to pieces, whether applied to marriage, business, or international politics.

In summary, I have not recommended a philosophy of Me-ism. I have not suggested that children be taught arrogance and self-sufficiency or that they be lured into selfishness. (That will occur without any encouragement from parents.) My purpose has been to help mothers and fathers preserve an inner physical, mental, and spiritual health. And I believe that objective is in harmony with biblical perspectives.[14]

# SECTION 19

# A CHRISTIAN PERSPECTIVE ON ANGER

**The Bible condemns the emotion of anger, and yet Christians and non-Christians experience it. How can we be expected to remove this most common human response from our personalities?**

Before we conclude that we cannot do what the Scriptures require, we must be sure we understand the context. Remember that words change their meaning with the passage of time. Just as the word "pride" has many meanings, so too has "anger" become a sort of "catch-all" phrase. Many of the behaviors which have been included under the definition of anger may have nothing to do with scriptural condemnation. Consider these examples:

1. Extreme fatigue produces a response which has the earmarks of anger. A mother who is exhausted from the day's activities can become very "angry" when her four-year-old spills his third glass of milk. This mother might give her life for her child if required, and she would not harm a hair on his fuzzy little head. Nevertheless, her exhausted state of distress is given the same generalized label as the urge which caused Cain to kill Abel. There is no relationship between the two distinct emotions represented.

2. Extreme embarrassment typically produces a reaction which is categorized under the same overworked heading.

3. Extreme frustration gives rise to an emotional response which we also call anger. I have seen this reaction from a high school basketball player, for example, who had an "off night" when everything went wrong. Perhaps he fumbled the ball away and double-dribbled and missed all his shots at the basket. The more he tried, the worse he played and the more foolish

he felt. Such frustration can trigger a volcanic emotional discharge at the coach or anyone in his way. Such are the irritations which cause golf clubs to be wrapped around trees and tennis rackets to be impaled on net-posts.

4. Rejection is another occurrence which often generates a kind of angry response. A girl who is jilted by the boy she loves, for example, may retaliate with a flurry of harsh words. Far from hating him, however, her response is motivated by the deep hurt associated with being thrown over—discarded—disrespected.

You see, anger has come to represent many strong, negative feelings in a human being. Accordingly, I doubt if all the Scriptures which address themselves to the subject of anger are referring equally to the entire range of emotions under that broad category.[1]

**Is all anger sinful?**

Obviously, not everything that can be identified under the heading of anger is a violation of God's law, for Ephesians 4:26 instructs us to be "be angry, and sin not." That verse says to me that there is a difference between *strong feeling,* and the seething hostility which is consistently condemned in Scripture. Our first task, it would appear, is to clarify that distinction.[2]

**Is it possible to prevent all feelings of anger?**

No. It's important to remember that anger is not only emotional—it is biochemical, as well. The human body is equipped with an automatic defensive system, called the "flight or fight" mechanism, which prepares the entire organism for action. Adrenalin is pumped into the bloodstream which sets off a series of physiological responses within the body. Blood pressure is increased in accordance with an acceleration in heartbeat; the eyes are dilated for better peripheral vision; the hands get sweaty and the mouth becomes dry; and the muscles are supplied with a sudden burst of energy. In a matter of seconds, the individual is transformed from a quiet condition to an "alarm reaction state." *Most important, this is an involuntary response which occurs whether or not we will it.*

Once the flight or fight hormones are released, it is impossible to ignore the intense feelings they precipitate. It would be like denying the existence of a toothache or any other tumultuous physical occurrence. And since God created this system as a means by which the body can protect itself against danger, I do not believe He condemns us for its proper functioning.

On the other hand, our *reaction* to the feeling of anger is more deliberate and responsive to voluntary control. When we sullenly "replay" the agitating event over and over in our minds, grinding our teeth in hostility and seeking opportunities for revenge, or lash out in some overt act of violence, then it is logical to assume that we cross over the line into sinfulness. If this interpretation of the Scripture is accurate, then the exercise of the *will* stands in the gap between the two halves of the verse "be angry," . . . "and sin not."[3]

**But doesn't the Bible take an absolute position on the subject of anger? Where does it allow for the individual differences you described?**

Didn't the Apostle Paul write in Romans 12:18, "As much as lieth in you, live peaceably with all men"? In other words, we are all expected to exercise self-control and restraint, but some will be more successful than others by the nature of the individual temperaments. While we are at different levels of maturity and responsibility, the Holy Spirit gently leads each of us in the direction He requires, until a moment of truth arrives when He demands our obedience.[4]

**All right, you have made it clear that some reactions which are called "anger" are involuntary and appear not to be condemned by God. Now flip that coin over. Under what circumstances is anger sinful, in your opinion?**

I see unacceptable anger as that which motivates us to hurt our fellowman—when we want to slash and cut and inflict pain on another person. Remember the experience of the Apostle Peter when Jesus was being crucified? His emotions were obviously in a state of turmoil, seeing his beloved Master being subjected to an unthinkable horror. However, Jesus rebuked him when he severed the Roman soldier's ear with a sword. If there ever was a person with an "excuse" to lash out in anger, Peter seemed to be justified; nevertheless, Jesus did not accept his behavior and He compassionately healed the wounded soldier.

There is a vitally important message for all of us in this recorded event. *Nothing* justifies an attitude of hatred or a desire to harm another person, and we are treading on dangerous ground when our thoughts and actions begin leading us in that direction. Not even the defense of Jesus Christ would justify that kind of aggression.[5]

**Are you saying that being "right" on an issue does not purify a wrong attitude or behavior?**
Yes. In fact, having been in the church all my life, I've observed that Christians are often in greater danger when they are "right" in a conflict than when they are clearly wrong. In other words, a person is more likely to become bitter and deeply hostile when someone has cheated him or taken advantage of him than is the offender himself. E. Stanley Jones agreed, stating that a Christian is more likely to sin by his reactions than his actions. Perhaps this is one reason why Jesus told us to "turn the other cheek" and "go the second mile," knowing that Satan can make devastating use of anger in an innocent victim.[6]

**If anger is unquestionably sinful when it leads us to hurt another person, then is the evil only involved in the aggressive act itself? What if we become greatly hostile but hold it inside where it is never revealed?**
Jesus told us that hatred for a brother is equivalent to murder (Matt. 5:22). Thus, sinful anger can occur in the mind, even if it is never translated into overt behavior.[7]

**Many psychologists seem to feel that all anger should be ventilated or verbalized. They say it is emotionally and physically harmful to repress or withhold any intense feeling. Can you harmonize this scientific understanding with the scriptural commandment that "every man [should] be swift to hear, slow to speak, slow to wrath: For the wrath of man worketh not the righteousness of God" (Jas. 1:19, 20).**
Let me state the one thing of which I am absolutely certain: *Truth is unity.* In other words, when complete understanding is known about a given topic, then there will be no disagreement between science and the Bible. Therefore, when these two sources of knowledge appear to be in direct contradiction—as in the matter of anger—then there is either something wrong with

our interpretation of Scripture or else the scientific premise is false. Under no circumstance, however, will the Bible be found to err. It was inspired by the Creator of the universe, and He does not make mistakes!

In regard to the psychological issues involved in your question, there is undoubtedly some validity to the current view that feelings of anger should not be encapsulated and internalized. When *any* powerful, negative emotion is forced from conscious thought while it is raging full strength, it has the potential of ripping and tearing us from within. The process by which we cram a strong feeling into the unconscious mind is called "repression," and it is psychologically hazardous. The pressure that it generates will usually appear elsewhere in the form of depression, anxiety, tension, or in an entire range of physical disorders.

We must harmonize the psychological finding that anger should be ventilated with the biblical commandment that we be "slow to wrath." Personally, I do not find these objectives to be in contradiction. God does not want us to "repress" our anger—sending it unresolved into the memory bank. Why else did the Apostle Paul tell us to settle our irritations before sundown each day (Eph. 4:26), effectively preventing an accumulation of seething hostility with the passage of time?

But how can intense negative feelings be resolved or ventilated without blasting away at the offender—an act which is specifically prohibited by Scripture? Are there other ways of releasing pent-up emotions? Yes, including those that follow:

By making the irritation a matter of prayer.

By explaining our negative feelings to a mature and understanding "third party" who can advise and lead.

By going to an offender and showing a spirit of love and forgiveness.

By understanding that God often permits the most frustrating and agitating events to occur, so as to teach us patience and help us grow.

By realizing that *no* offense by another person could possibly equal our guilt before God, yet He has forgiven us; are we not obligated to show the same mercy to others?

These are just a few of the mechanisms and attitudes which act to neutralize a spirit of resentment.[8]

**I have a very unhappy and miserable neighbor who can't get along with anybody. She has fought with everyone she knows at one time or another. I decided that I was going to make friends with her if it was humanly possible, so I went out of my way to be kind and compassionate. I thought I had made progress toward this goal until she knocked on the front door one day and attacked me verbally. She had misunderstood something I said to another neighbor, and she came to my house to "tell me off." This woman said all the mean things she could think of, including some very insulting comments about my children, husband, and our home.**

**I was agitated by her attempt to hurt me when I had tried to treat her kindly, and I reacted with irritation. We stood arguing with each other at the front door and then she left in a huff. I feel bad about the conflict now, but I don't know if I could handle it better today. What should have been my reaction?**

Perhaps you realize that you missed the greatest opportunity you will probably ever have to accomplish your original objective of winning her friendship. It is difficult to convince someone of your love and respect during a period of shallow amicability. By contrast, your response to a vicious assault can instantly reveal the Christian values by which you live.

What if you had said, for example, "Mary, I don't know what you heard about me, but I think there's been a misunderstanding of what I said. Why don't you come in and we'll talk about it over a cup of coffee." Everything that you had attempted to accomplish through the previous months might have been achieved on that morning. I admit that it takes great courage and maturity to return kindness for hostility, but we are commanded by Jesus to do just that. He said in Matthew 5:43, 44:

> Ye have heard that it hath been said, Thou shalt love thy neighbor, and hate thine enemy. But I say unto you, Love your enemies, bless them that curse you, do good to them that hate you, and pray for them which despitefully use you, and persecute you (KJV).[9]

**What do you have to say to the many people who sincerely try to control their anger, but who get irritated and frustrated and still lose their temper time and time again?**

**How can they bring this area under control? Or is it possible?**

It has been my observation that the Lord often leads his children, including those with rampaging tempers, in a patient and progressively insistent manner. It begins with a mild sense of condemnation in the area where God wants us to grow and improve. Then as time goes by, a failure to respond is followed by a sense of guilt and awareness of divine disapproval. We are subsequently led to a time of intense awareness of God's requirements. We hear His message revealed (perhaps unwittingly) by the pastor on Sunday morning and in the books we read and even in secular programs on radio and television. It seems as though the whole world is organized to convey the same decree from the Lord. And finally, we come to a crisis point where God says, "You understand what I want. *Now do it!*"

Growth in the Christian life depends on obedience in those times of crisis. The believer who refuses to accept the new obligation despite unmistakable commandments from God is destined to deteriorate spiritually. From that moment forward, he begins to drift away from his Master. But for the Christian who accepts the challenge, regardless of how difficult it may be, his growth and enlightenment are assured.

John Henry Jowett said, "The will of God will never lead you where the grace of God cannot keep you." This means that the Lord won't demand something of you which He doesn't intend to help you implement.[10]

**There are times when it is obvious that my kid is *trying* to provoke my anger, just for the fun of it. Why would he want to upset me when he knows I love him?**

It may be the result of a power play between him and you. Indeed, there are times when I think children understand this struggle for control even better than their parents who are bogged down with adult responsibilities and worries. That is why so many kids are able to win the contest of wills; they devote their *primary* effort to the game, while we grown-ups play only when we must. One father overheard his five-year-old daughter, Laura, say to her little sister who was doing something wrong, "Mmmm, I'm going to tell Mommie on you. No! I'll tell Daddy. He's worse!" Laura had evaluated the disciplinary measures of her two parents, and concluded that one was more effective than the other.

This same child was observed by her father to have become especially disobedient and defiant. She was irritating other family members and looking for ways to avoid minding her parents. Her dad decided not to confront her directly about this change in behavior, but to punish her consistently for every offense until she settled down. Thus, for three or four days, he let Laura get away with nothing. She was spanked, stood in the corner, and sent to her bedroom. At the conclusion of the fourth day, she was sitting on the bed with her father and younger sister. Without provocation, Laura pulled the hair of the toddler who was looking at a book. Her dad promptly thumped her on the head with his large hand. Laura did not cry, but sat in silence for a moment or two, and then said, "Hurrummph! All my tricks are not working!"

If the reader will recall his own childhood years, he will probably remember similar events in which the disciplinary techniques of adults were analyzed consciously and their weaknesses probed. When I was a child, I once spent the night with a rambunctious friend who seemed to know every move his parents were going to make. Earl was like a military general who had deciphered the enemy code, permitting him to outmaneuver his opponents at every turn. After we were tucked into our own twin beds that night, he gave me an astounding description of his father's temper.

Earl said, "When my dad gets very angry, he uses some really bad words that will amaze you." (He listed three or four startling examples from past experience.)

I replied, "I don't believe it!"

Mr. Walker was a very tall, reserved man who seemed to have it all together. I just couldn't conceive of his saying the words Earl had quoted.

"Want me to prove it to you?" said Earl mischievously. "All we have to do is keep on laughing and talking instead of going to sleep. My dad will come and tell us to be quiet over and over, and he'll get madder and madder every time he has to settle us down. Then you'll hear his cuss words. Just wait and see."

I was a bit dubious about this plan, but I did want to see the dignified Mr. Walker at his profane best. So Earl and I kept his poor father running back and forth like a Yo-Yo for over an hour. And as predicted, he became more intense and hostile each time he returned to our bedroom. I was getting very nervous and would have called off the demonstration, but Earl had been through it all before. He kept telling me, "It won't be long now."

Finally, about midnight, it happened. Mr. Walker's patience expired. He came thundering down the hall toward our room, shaking the entire house as his feet pounded the floor. He burst through the bedroom door and leaped on Earl's bed, flailing at the boy who was safely buried beneath three or four layers of blankets. Then from his lips came a stream of words that had seldom reached my tender ears. I was shocked, but Earl was delighted.

Even while his father was whacking the covers with his hand and screaming his profanity, Earl raised up and shouted to me, "Did ya hear 'em? Huh? Didn't I tell ya? I told ya he would say it!" It's a wonder that Mr. Walker didn't kill his son at that moment!

I lay awake that night thinking about the episode and made up my mind *never* to let a child manipulate me like that when I grew up. Don't you see how important disciplinary techniques are to a child's respect for his parents? When a forty-five-pound bundle of trouble can deliberately reduce his powerful mother or father to a trembling, snarling mass of frustrations, then something changes in their relationship. Something precious is lost. The child develops an attitude of contempt which is certain to erupt during the stormy adolescent years to come. I sincerely wish every adult understood that simple characteristic of human nature.[11]

# SECTION 20

# ROMANTIC LOVE

**Do you believe love at first sight occurs between some people?**

Though some readers will disagree with me, love at first sight is a physical and emotional impossibility. Why? Because love is not simply a feeling of romantic excitement; it is more than a desire to marry a potential partner; it goes beyond intense sexual attraction; it exceeds the thrill at having "captured" a highly desirable social prize. These are emotions that are unleashed at first sight, but they *do not constitute love.*

Real love, in contrast to popular notions, is an expression of the deepest appreciation for another human being; it is an intense awareness of his or her needs and longings—past, present, and future. It is unselfish and giving and caring. And believe me, these are not attitudes one "falls" into at first sight, as though we were tumbling into a ditch.

I have developed a lifelong love for my wife, but it was not something I fell into. I *grew* into it, and that process took time. I had to know her before I could appreciate the depth and stability of her character—to become acquainted with the nuances of her personality, which I now cherish. The familiarity from which love has blossomed simply could not be generated on "Some enchanted evening, across a crowded room." One cannot love an unknown object, regardless of how attractive or sexy or nubile it is![1]

**Do you believe real love can easily be distinguished from infatuation?**

No, I do not. I must stress this fact with the greatest emphasis:

The exhilaration of infatuation feels like love at its best, but it is *never* a permanent condition. Period! If you expect to live on the top of that mountain, year after year, you can forget it! Emotions swing from high to low to high in cyclical rhythm, and since romantic excitement is an emotion, it too will certainly oscillate.

How, then, can real love be distinguished from temporary infatuation? If the feeling is unreliable, how can one assess the commitment of his will? There is only one answer to those questions: It takes time. The best advice I can give a couple contemplating marriage (or any other important decision) is this: make *no* important, life-shaping decisions quickly or impulsively, and when in doubt, stall for time. That's not a bad suggestion for all of us to apply.[2]

**Do you believe that God selects one particular person for each Christian to marry and He relentlessly brings them together?**

No, and that is a dangerous supposition to rely on. A young man whom I was counseling once told me that he awoke in the middle of the night with the strong impression that God wanted him to marry a young lady whom he had only dated casually a few times. They were not even going together at that time and hardly knew each other. The next morning he called her and relayed the message which God had supposedly sent him during the night. The girl figured she shouldn't argue with God, and she accepted the proposal. They have now been married for seven years and have struggled for survival since their wedding day!

Anyone who believes that God preempts free choice and thereby guarantees a successful marriage to every Christian is in for a shock. This is not to say the He is disinterested in the choice of a mate, or that He will not answer a specific request for guidance on this all-important decision. Certainly, His will should be sought in such a critical matter, and I consulted Him repeatedly before proposing to my wife. However, I do not believe that God performs a routine match-making service for everyone who worships Him. He has given us judgment, common sense, and discretionary powers, and He expects us to exercise these abilities in matters matrimonial. Those who believe otherwise are likely to enter marriage glibly, thinking, "God would have stopped us if He didn't approve." That is a dangerous posture to assume on so important a decision.[3]

**Do you believe that genuine love between a husband and wife is permanent, lasting a lifetime?**
It can be, and indeed, should be. However, even genuine love is a fragile flower. It must be maintained and protected if it is to survive. Love can perish when a husband works seven days a week . . . when there is no time for romantic activity . . . when he and his wife forget how to talk to each other. The keen edge on a loving relationship may be dulled through the routine pressures of living. Where does your marriage rank on your hierarchy of values? Does it get the leftovers and scraps from your busy schedule, or is it something of great worth to be preserved and supported? It can die if left untended.[4]

**I am a nineteen-year-old girl and I'm still single. I'm aware of some pretty awful circumstances that can occur in marriage. If that's the way it is, why should I bother to get married at all?**
Coping with a bad marriage can be a terrible experience, I'll grant you, but a good marriage is a lifelong treasure. I can tell you from a personal point of view that my marriage to Shirley is the best thing that ever happened to me, and there are millions who can offer a similar testimony. You see, life involves problems no matter what your choices are; if you remain single, your frustrations will be of a different nature but they will occur, nevertheless. As to whether you should get married or not, I would offer you the same advice given me when I was an eight-year-old child, by a Sunday school teacher whose name I don't even remember: He said, "Don't marry the person you think you can live with; marry the person you think you can't live without . . . if such an individual ever comes along." Either way, I think you're ahead by knowing in advance that married life offers no panacea—that if it is going to reach its potential, it will require an all-out investment by both husband and wife.[5]

**Do you think happily married husbands and wives should be able to live together without fighting with one another?**
No. The healthiest marriages are those where the couple has learned *how* to fight—how to ventilate anger without tearing one another apart. I'm saying that there is a difference between healthy and unhealthy combat, depending on the way the

disagreement is handled. In an unstable marriage, the hostility is usually hurled directly at the personhood of the partner: "You never do anything right; why did I ever marry you? You are incredibly dumb and you're getting more like your mother every day." These personal comments strike at the heart of one's self-worth and produce an internal upheaval. Obviously, such vicious combat is extremely damaging to a marital relationship. Healthy conflict, on the other hand, remains focused on the issue around which the disagreement began: "You are spending money faster than I can earn it!" "It upsets me when you don't tell me you'll be late for dinner." "I was embarrassed when you made me look foolish at the party last night." These areas of struggle, though admittedly emotional and tense, are much less damaging to the egos of the opposing forces. A healthy couple can work through them by compromise and negotiations with few imbedded barbs to pluck out the following morning.

The ability to fight *properly* may be the most important concept to be learned by newlyweds. Those who never comprehend the technique are usually left with two alternatives: (1) turn the anger and resentment inward in silence, where it will fester and accumulate through the years, or (2) blast away at the personhood of one's mate. The divorce courts are well represented by couples in both categories.[6]

# SECTION 21

# CONFLICT IN MARRIAGE

**What is *the* most common marital problem you hear about in your office?**

Let's suppose I have a counseling appointment at four o'clock tomorrow afternoon with a person whom I've never met. Who is that person and what will be the complaint that brings them to me? First, the patient will probably be Mrs. Jones, not her husband. A man is seldom the first to seek marriage counseling, and when he does, it is for a different motive than his wife seeks it. She comes because her marriage is driving her crazy. He comes because his *wife* is driving him crazy.

Mrs. Jones will be, perhaps, between twenty-eight and forty-two years of age, and her problem will be *extremely* familiar to me. Though the details will vary, the frustration she communicates on that afternoon will conform to a well-worn pattern. It will sound something like this:

> John and I were deeply in love when we got married. We struggled during the first two or three years, especially with financial problems, but I knew he loved me and he knew I loved him. But then something began to change. I'm not sure how to describe it. He received a promotion about five years ago, and that required him to work longer hours. We needed the money, so we didn't mind the extra time he was putting in. But it never stopped. Now he comes home late every evening. He's so tired I can actually hear his feet dragging as he approaches the porch. I look forward to his coming home all day 'cause I have so much to tell him, but he doesn't feel much like talking. So I fix his dinner and he eats it alone. (I usually eat with the kids earlier in the evening.) After dinner, John makes a few phone

> calls and works at his desk. Frankly, I like for him to talk on the telephone just so I can hear his voice. Then he watches television for a couple of hours and goes to bed. Except on Tuesday night he plays basketball and sometimes he has a meeting at the office. Every Saturday morning he plays golf with three of his friends. Then on Sunday we are in church most of the day. Believe me, there are times when we go for a month or two without having a real, in-depth conversation. You know what I mean? And I get so lonely in the house with three kids climbing all over me. There aren't even any women in our neigborhood I can talk to, because most of them have gone back to work. But there are other irritations about John. He rarely takes me out to dinner and he forgot our anniversary last month, and I honestly don't believe he's ever had a romantic thought. He wouldn't know a rose from a carnation, and his Christmas cards are signed, just "John." There's no closeness or warmth between us, yet he wants to have sex with me at the end of the day. There we are, lying in bed, having had no communication between us in weeks. He hasn't tried to be sweet or understanding or tender, yet he expects me to becomc passionate and responsive to him. I'll tell you, I can't do it. Sure, I go along with my duties as a wife, but I sure don't get anything out of it. And after the two-minute trip is over and John is asleep, I lie there resenting him and feeling like a cheap prostitute. Can you believe that? I feel used for having sex with my own husband! Boy, does that depress me! In fact, I've been awfully depressed lately. My self-esteem is rock bottom right now. I feel like nobody loves me . . . I'm a lousy mother and a terrible wife. Sometimes I think that God probably doesn't love me, either. Well, now I'd better tell you what's been going on between John and me more recently. We've been arguing a lot. I mean really fighting. It's the only way I can get his attention, I guess. We had an incredible battle last week in front of the kids. It was awful. Tears. Screaming. Insults. Everything. I spent two nights at my mother's house. Now, all I can think about is getting a divorce so I can escape. John doesn't love me anyway, so what difference would it make? I guess that's why I came to see you. I want to know if I'll be doing the right thing to call it quits.

Mrs. Jones speaks as though she were the only woman in the world who has ever experienced this pattern of needs. But she is not alone. It is my guess that 90 percent of the divorces that occur each year involve at least some of the elements she described—an extremely busy husband who is in love with his work and who tends to be somewhat insensitive, unromantic, and noncommunicative, married to a lonely, vulnerable, romantic woman who has severe doubts about her worth as a human being. They become a matched team: he works like a horse and she nags.[1]

**My husband is somewhat insensitive to my needs, but I believe he is willing to do better if I can teach him how I am different from him. Can you help me communicate my needs to him effectively?**

First, let me tell you how *not* to handle this assignment. Do not resort to what I have called the "bludgeoning technique," which includes an endless barrage of nagging, pleading, scolding, complaining, and accusing. This is how that approach sounds to an exhausted man who has come home from work moments before: "Won't you just put down that newspaper, George, and give me five minutes of your time? Five minutes—is that too much to ask? You never seem to care about my feelings, anyway. How long has it been since we went out for dinner? Even if we did, you'd probably take the newspaper along with you. I'll tell you, George, sometimes I think you don't care about me and the kids anymore. If just once . . . just once . . . you would show a little love and understanding, I would drop dead from sheer shock," etc., etc., etc.

Obviously, that is not the way to get George's attention. It's like pounding him behind the ear with a two-by-four, and it rarely achieves more than a snarl when he gets up from the floor. Instead, you should look for opportunities to teach your husband during moments of closeness and understanding. That instruction requires the proper timing, setting, and manner to be effective.

1. *Timing.* Select a moment when your husband is typically more responsive and pleasant; perhaps that opportunity will occur immediately after the evening meal, or when the light goes out at night, or in the freshness of the morning. The worst time of the day is during the first sixty minutes after he arrives home from work, yet this is the usual combat hour. Don't lumber into such a heavy debate without giving it proper planning and forethought, taking advantage of every opportunity for the success of the effort.

2. *Setting.* The ideal situation is to ask your husband to take you on an overnight or weekend trip to a pleasant area. If financial considerations will cause him to decline, save the money out of household funds or other resources. If it is impossible to get away, the next best alternative is to obtain a baby-sitter and go out to breakfast or dinner alone. If that too is out of the question, then select a time at home when the children are occupied and the phone can be taken off the hook. Generally speaking, however, the farther you can get him from home, with its cares and problems and stresses, the better will be your chance to achieve genuine communication.

3. *Manner.* It is extremely important that your husband does not view your conversation as a personal attack. We are all equipped with emotional defenses which rise to our aid when we are being vilified. Don't trigger those defensive mechanisms. Instead, your manner should be as warm, loving, and supportive as possible under the circumstances. Let it be known that you are attempting to interpret *your* needs and desires, not *his* inadequacies and shortcomings. Furthermore, you must take his emotional state into consideration, as well. Postpone the conversation if he is under unusual stress from his work, or if he isn't feeling well, or if he has recently been stung by circumstances and events. Then when the timing, setting, and manner converge to produce a moment of opportunity, express your deep feelings as effectively as possible. And like every good boy scout: be *prepared.*[2]

**Are you suggesting that a woman should crawl on her belly like a subservient puppy, begging her master for a pat on the head?**

Certainly not! It is of the highest priority to maintain a distinct element of dignity and self-respect *throughout* the husband-wife relationship. This takes us into an area that requires the greatest emphasis. I have observed that many (if not most) marriages suffer from a failure to recognize a universal characteristic of human nature. *We value that which we are fortunate to get; we discredit that with which we are stuck! We lust for the very thing which is beyond our grasp; we disdain that same item when it becomes a permanent possession.* No toy is ever as much fun to play with as it appeared to a wide-eyed child in a store. Seldom does an expensive automobile provide the satisfaction anticipated by the man who dreamed of its ownership. This principle is even more dramatically accurate in romantic affairs, particularly with reference to men.

Let's look at the extreme case of a Don Juan, the perpetual lover who romps from one feminine flower to another. His heart throbs and pants after the elusive princess who drops her glass slipper as she flees. Every ounce of energy is focused on her capture. However, the intensity of his desire is dependent on her unavailability. The moment his passionate dreams materialize, he begins to ask himself, "Is this what I really want?" Farther down the line, as the relationship progresses toward the routine circumstances of everyday life, he is attracted by new princesses and begins to wonder how he can escape the older model.

Now, I would not imply that all men, or even the majority of them, are as exploitative and impermanent as the gadabout I described. But to a lesser degree, most men *and* women are impelled by the same urges. How many times have I seen a bored, tired relationship become a torrent of desire and longing the moment one partner rejects the other and walks out. After years of apathy, the "dumpee" suddenly burns with romantic desire and desperate hope.

This principle hits even closer to home for me at this moment. Right now, as I am writing these words, I am sitting in the waiting room of a large hospital while my wife is undergoing major abdominal surgery. I am writing to ease my tension and anxiety. While I have always been close to Shirley, my appreciation and tender love for her are maximal this morning. Less than five minutes ago, a surgeon emerged from the operating room with a grim face, informing the man near me that his wife is consumed with cancer. He spoke in unguarded terms of the unfavorable pathological report and the malignant infestation. I will be speaking to Shirley's surgeon within the hour and my vulnerability is keenly felt. While my love for my wife has *never* flagged through our fourteen years together, it has rarely been as intense as in this moment of threat. You see, not only are our emotions affected by the challenge of pursuit, but also by the possibility of irrevocable loss. (The surgeon arrived as I was writing the sentence above, saying my wife came through the operation with no complications, and the pathologist recognized no abnormal tissue. I am indeed a grateful man! My deepest sympathy is with the less fortunate family whose tragedy I witnessed today.)

Forgive the redundancy, but I must restate the principle: *we crave that which we can't attain, but we disrespect that which we can't escape.* This axiom is particularly relevant in romantic matters, and has probably influenced *your* love life, too. Now, the forgotten part of this characteristic is that marriage does not erase or change it. Whenever one marriage partner grovels in his own disrespect . . . when he reveals his fear of rejection by his mate . . . when he begs and pleads for a handout . . . he often faces a bewildering attitude of disdain from the one he needs and loves. Just as in the premarital relationship, nothing douses more water on a romantic flame than for one partner to fling himself emotionally on the other, accepting disrespect in stride. He says in effect, "No matter how badly you treat me, I'll still be here at your feet, because I can't survive without you." That is the best way I know to kill a beautiful friendship.

So what am I recommending . . . that husbands and wives scratch and claw each other to show their independence? No! That they play a sneaky cat and mouse game to recreate a "challenge"? Not at all! I am merely suggesting that self-respect and dignity be maintained in the relationship.[3]

**I'm certain that I'm losing my husband. He shows signs of boredom and total disinterest in me. He treats me rudely in public and is virtually silent at home. And of course, our sex life is non-existent. I have begged and pleaded with him to love me, but I'm losing ground every day. What can I do to save my marriage?**

These are symptoms of a condition which I call "the trapped syndrome." More often than not, the man is thinking these kinds of thoughts: "I'm thirty-five years old" (or whatever age) "and I'm not getting any younger. Do I really want to spend the rest of my life with this one woman? I'm bored with her and there are others who interest me more. But there's no way out 'cause I'm stuck." These are the feelings which usually precede esoteric infidelity, and they certainly can be felt in the strain between a husband and wife.

How should a woman respond when she reads the cues and realizes that her husband feels trapped? Obviously, the worst thing she could do is reinforce the cage around him, yet that is likely to be her initial reaction. As she thinks about how important he is to her, and what-on-earth she would do without him, and whether he's involved with another woman, her anxiety may compel her to grab and hold him. Her begging and pleading only continue to drive him to disrespect her more, and the relationship continues to splinter. There is a better way which I have found productive in counseling experience. The most successful approach to bringing a partner back toward the center of a relationship is not to follow when he moves away from it. Instead of saying, "Why do you do me this way?"and "Why won't you talk to me?" and "Why don't you care anymore?" a wife should pull back a few inches herself. When she passes her husband in the hall and would ordinarily touch him or seek his attention, she should move by him without notice. Silence by him is greeted by silence in return. She should not be hostile or aggressive, ready to explode when he finally asks her to say what is on her mind. Rather, she responds in kind . . . being quietly confident, independent, and mysterious. The effect of this behavior is to open the door on his trap. Instead of clamping herself to his neck like a blood-sucking leech, she releases her grip and introduces a certain challenge in his mind, as well. He may begin to wonder if he has gone too far and may be losing something precious to him. If that will not turn him around, then the relationship is stone, cold dead.

What I am recommending to you is extremely difficult to express in written form, and I am certain to be misinterpreted by some of my readers on this issue. I haven't suggested that you rise up in anger—that you stamp your feet and demand your domestic rights, or that you sulk and pout in silence. Please do not associate me with those contemporary voices which are mobilizing feminine troops for all-out sexual combat. Nothing is less attractive to me than an angry woman who is determined to grab her share, one way or the other. No, the answer is not found in hostile aggression, but in quiet self-respect!

In short, personal dignity in a marriage is maintained the same way it was produced during the dating days. The attitude should be, "I love you and am totally committed to you, but I only control my half of the relationship. I can't demand your love in return. You came to me of your free will when we agreed to marry. No one forced us together. That same free will is necessary to keep our love alive. If you choose to walk away from me, I will be crushed and hurt beyond description, because I have withheld nothing of myself. Nevertheless, I will let you go and ultimately I will survive. I couldn't demand your affection in the beginning, and I can only request it now."

Somehow, that releasing of the door on the trap often results in revolutionary changes in a relationship.[4]

**As much as I love my wife (and I'm convinced she loves me), our relationship has become stagnant in recent years. It seems like all we do is work—clean house, take care of the kids, fix the leaking roof, have the car repaired, etc.—you know, trying to keep up with the routine responsibilities of living. How can we escape this deadening lifestyle? How can we liven up our marriage?**
You have described a situation which I call the "straight life," referring to the never-ending responsibilities of adult living that become oppressive and deadening to a marriage. To let it continue unchanged is to sacrifice something precious in your relationship. I suggest you make a conscious effort to put four new ingredients back into your lives, beginning with pleasure. You and your wife should go on a date at least once a week, leaving children at home. Likewise, some form of sports or recreational activity should be enjoyed as a family, whether it be tennis, golf, swimming, skiing, or another option.

Second, you should seek to keep the romantic fires aglow in your relationship, by the use of love notes and surprises and candlelight dinners and unexpected weekend trips, among other possibilities.

Third, you *must* reserve some of your time and energy for meaningful sexual activity. Tired bodies make for tired sex. The physical aspect of the relationship can be approached creatively, and indeed, must be.

Fourth, the most successful marriages are those where both husband and wife seek to build the self-esteem of the other. Ego needs *can* be met within the bonds of marriage, and nothing contributes more to closeness and stability than to convey respect for the personhood of the spouse.

Every responsible adult must cope with the concerns of the straight life, but those obligations need not assault mental and physical health and marital harmony.[5]

**I've concluded that my husband *cannot* comprehend my emotional needs. He will not read books that I give him, nor will he attend seminars, listen to tapes, or even talk to me about my frustrations. Nevertheless, he is a good man who is faithful to me and has been an effective father. What do you suggest I do with this dilemma?**
The answer I'm about to give you will *not* satisfy you. But I know it is consistent with the will of God. My advice is that you

change that which can be altered, explain that which can be understood, teach that which can be learned, revise that which can be improved, resolve that which can be settled, and negotiate that which is open to compromise. Create the best marriage possible from the raw materials brought by two imperfect human beings with two distinctly unique personalities. *But for all the rough edges which can never be smoothed and the faults which can never be eradicated, try to develop the best possible perspective on the difficulty and determine in your mind to accept reality exactly as it is.* The first principle of mental health is to accept that which cannot be changed. You could easily go to pieces over the adverse circumstances beyond your control, but you can also resolve to withstand them. You can *will* to remain stable, or you can yield to cowardice.

Someone wrote:

> Life can't give me joy and peace;
> it's up to me to *will* it.
> Life just gives me time and space;
> it's up to me to fill it.

Can you accept the fact that your husband will *never* be able to meet all your needs and aspirations? Seldom does one human being satisfy every longing and hope in the breast of another. Obviously, this coin has two sides: You can't be his perfect woman, either. He is no more equipped to resolve your entire package of emotional needs than you are to become his sexual dream machine every twenty-four hours. Both partners have to settle for human foibles and faults and irritability and fatigue and occasional nighttime "headaches." A good marriage is not one where perfection reigns; it is a relationship where a healthy perspective overlooks a multitude of "unresolvables." Thank goodness my wife, Shirley, has adopted that attitude toward me![6]

**You mentioned the term "perspective" twice in the previous answer. Explain what you mean by it.**

Let me say it another way. A slight revision in your perception of your husband can make him appear much more noble. The gifted author (and my friend) Joyce Landorf has explained this perspective better than anyone I've heard. During the early years of her marriage, she found herself angry at her husband for dozens of reasons. Dick inadvertently conveyed insults to her by his manner and personality. For example, just before retiring each evening, he would say, "Joyce, did you lock the back door?" She always answered affirmatively, whereupon Dick walked to the door to verify that it was bolted. There were only two ways for Joyce to interpret his behavior. Either he thought she was lying about the door, or else he didn't think she had the brains to remember locking it. Both alternatives made her furious. This scenario symbolized many other sources of conflict between them.

Then one night as Dick proceeded to check the lock, the Lord spoke to Joyce.

"Take a good look at him, Joyce," He said.

"What do you mean, Lord?" she replied.

"I have made your husband a door checker. He's a detail man. That's why he's such a good banker. He can examine a list of figures and instantly locate an error that others have overlooked. I gave him that ability to handle banking responsibilities. Yes, Joyce, I made Dick a 'door checker,' and I want you to accept him that way."

What a fantastic insight. Many times a man's most irritating characteristic is a by-product of the quality his wife most respects. Perhaps his frugality and stinginess, which she hates, have made him successful in business, which she greatly admires. Or perhaps his attentiveness to his mother's needs, which his wife resents, is another dimension of his devotion to his own family. Or, maybe his cool stability in the face of crisis, which drew his wife to him, is related to his lack of spontaneity and exuberance during their tranquil days. The point is, *God gave your husband the temperament he wears, and you must accept those characteristics that he cannot change. After all, he must do the same for you.* This is what I meant when I said I *knew* it is God's will for us to persevere. He wants us to be tough—to see this life as temporary and not all that important: The Apostle Paul expressed this mental toughness best as he sat in jail, writing to his Christian friends. He said,

> For I have learned, in whatsoever state I am, therewith to be content. I know both how to be abased, and I know how to abound: every where and in all things I am instructed both to be full and to be hungry, both to abound and to suffer need. I can do all things through Christ which strengtheneth me (Phil. 4:11-13 KJV).[7]

**I must admit that my husband is also unable to meet my needs. He's an unromantic, noncommunicative man who will *always* be like that. The impasse is set in concrete. Rather than persevere, as you suggested, I've been thinking about getting a divorce. But I'm reluctant to do it and am continually "arguing" with myself over whether to bail out or not. Tell me, is divorce the answer for people like me?**

How often I have seen women go through the agitation you describe. Such a person contemplates this alternative of divorce day and night, weighing the many disadvantages against the one major attraction: *escape*. She worries about the effect of separation on the kids and wonders how she'll be able to support them and wishes she didn't have to tell her parents. Round and round go the positives and negatives. Should I or shouldn't I? She is both attracted and repelled by the idea of a dissolution.

This contemplative stage reminds me of a classic documentary film which was shot during the earliest days of motion pictures. The cameraman captured a dramatic event that took place on the Eiffel Tower. There, near the top, was a naive "inventor" who had constructed a set of bird-like wings. He had strapped them to his arms for the purpose of using them to fly, but he wasn't totally convinced that they would work. The film shows him going to the rail and looking downward, then pacing back and forth. Next he stood on the rail trying to get enough courage to jump, then returned to the platform. Even with the primitive camera of those days, the film has captured the internal struggle of that would-be-flier. "Should I or shouldn't I? If the wings work, I'll be famous. If they fail, I'll fall to my death." What a gamble!

The man finally climbed on the rail, turned loose of the nearby beam, and wobbled back and forth for a breathless moment of destiny. Then he jumped. The last scene was shot with the camera pointed straight downward, as the man fell like a rock. He didn't even bother to flap his wings on his way to the ground.

In some respects, the depressed homemaker is like the man on the ledge. She knows that divorce is a dangerous and unpredictable leap, but perhaps she will soar with the freedom of a bird. Does she have the courage to jump? No, she'd better stay on the safety of the platform. On the other hand, this could be the long-sought escape. After all, everyone else is doing it. She wavers momentarily in confusion . . . and often takes the plunge.

But what happens to her then? It's been my observation that her "wings" do not deliver the promised support. After the wrenching legal maneuvers and custody fight and property settlement, life returns to a monotonous routine. And what a routine. She has to get a job to maintain a home, but her marketable skills are few. She can be a waitress or a receptionist or a sales lady. But by the time she pays a baby-sitter (*if* she can find one) there is little money left for luxuries. Her energy level is in even shorter supply. She comes home exhausted to face the pressing needs of her kids, who irritate her. It's a rugged experience.

Then she looks at her ex-husband who is coping much better. He earns more money than she and the absence of kids provides him more freedom. Furthermore (and this is an important point), in our society there is infinitely more status in being a divorced man than a divorced woman. He often finds another lover who is younger and more attractive than his first wife. Jealousy burns within the mind of the divorcee, who is lonely and, not surprisingly, depressed again.

This is no trumped-up story just to discourage divorce. It is a characteristic pattern. I've observed that many women who seek divorce for the same reasons indicated (as opposed to infidelity) will live to regret their decision. Their husbands whose good qualities eventually come into view, begin to look somewhat attractive again. But these women have stepped off the ledge . . . and they must yield to the forces of nature.

Divorce is not the answer to the problem of busy husbands and lonely wives. Just because the secular world has liberalized its attitudes toward the impermanence of marriage, no such revision has occurred in the biblical standard. Would you like to know *precisely* what God thinks of divorce? He has made His view abundantly clear in Malachi 2:13-17, especially with reference to husbands who seek a new sexual plaything:

> Yet you cover the altar with your tears because the Lord doesn't pay attention to your offerings anymore, and you receive no blessing from him. "Why has God abandoned us?" you cry. I'll tell you why; it is because the Lord has seen your treachery in divorcing your wives who have been faithful to you through the years, the companions you promised to care for and keep. You were united to your wife

> by the Lord. In God's wise plan, when you married, the two of you became one person in his sight. And what does he want? Godly children from your union. Therefore guard your passions! Keep faith with the wife of your youth.
>
> For the Lord, the God of Israel, says he hates divorce and cruel men. Therefore control your passions—let there be no divorcing of your wives.
>
> You have wearied the Lord with your words.
>
> "Wearied him?" you ask in fake surprise. "How have we wearied him?"
>
> By saying that evil is good, that it pleases the Lord! Or by saying that God won't punish us—he doesn't care (TLB).[8]

**Why are men so insensitive to women's needs today? They seem oblivious to the longings of their wives, even when every effort is made to communicate and educate.**

I question whether men have really changed all that much over the years. Rather, I doubt if men have *ever* responded as women preferred. Did the farmer of a century ago come in from the fields and say, "Tell me how it went with the kids today"? No, he was as oblivious to his wife's nature as husbands are today. What has changed is the *relationship between women!*

A century ago women cooked together, canned together, washed clothes at the creek together, prayed together, went through menopause together, and grew old together. And when a baby was born, aunts and grandmothers and neighbors were there to show the new mother how to diaper and feed and discipline. Great emotional support was provided in this feminine contact. A woman was never really alone.

Alas, the situation is very different today. The extended family has disappeared, depriving the wife of that source of security and fellowship. Her mother lives in New Jersey and her sister is in Texas. Furthermore, American families move every three or four years, preventing any long-term friendships from developing among neighbors. And there's another factor that is seldom admitted: American women tend to be economically competitive and suspicious of one another. Many would not even consider inviting a group of friends to the house until it was repainted, refurnished, or redecorated. As someone said, "We're working so hard to have beautiful homes and there's nobody in them!" The result is isolation—or should I say insulation—and its first cousin: loneliness.[9]

**I'm beginning to recognize a "blind spot" in my attitude toward my wife. I have always felt that I had done my job as a husband if I provided adequately for my family's financial needs and if I was faithful to Anita. But are you saying that I am also responsible to help meet her emotional needs, too?**

That's right, especially today when homemakers are under such attack. Everything they have been taught from earliest childhood is being subjected to ridicule and scorn. Hardly a day passes when the traditional values of the Judeo-Christian heritage are not blatantly mocked and undermined.

- The notion that motherhood is a worthwhile investment of a woman's time suffers unrelenting bombardment.
- The concept that a man and woman should become one flesh, finding their identity in each other rather than as separate and competing individuals, is said to be intolerably insulting to women.
- The belief that divorce is an unacceptable alternative has been abandoned by practically everybody. (Have you heard about Sue and Bob?)
- The description of the ideal wife and mother, as offered in Proverbs 31:10-31 is now unthinkable for the modern woman. (She's come a long way, baby.)
- The role of the female as help-mate, bread-baker, wound-patcher, love giver, home builder, and child-bearer is nothing short of disgusting.

All of these deeply ingrained values, which many of today's homemakers are trying desperately to sustain, are continually exposed to the wrath of hell itself. The Western media—radio, television and the press—are working relentlessly to shred the last vestiges of Christian tradition. And the women who believe in that spiritual heritage are virtually hanging by their thumbs! They are made to feel stupid and old-fashioned and unfulfilled, and in many cases, their self-esteem is suffering irreparable damage. They are fighting a sweeping social movement with very little support from anyone.

Let me say it more directly. For the man who appreciates the willingness of his wife to stand against the tide of public opinion—staying at home in her empty neighborhood in the exclusive company of jelly-faced toddlers and strong-willed adolescents—it is about time her husband gave her some help. I'm not merely suggesting that he wash the dishes or sweep the floor. I'm referring to the provision of emotional support . . . of conversation . . . of making her feel like a lady . . . of building her ego . . . of giving her one day of recreation each week . . . of taking her out to dinner . . . of telling her that he loves her. Without these armaments, she is left defenseless against the foes of the family—the foes of *his* family![10]

**What effect does this breakdown in the relationship between women have on marriages?**

It can be devastating. Depriving a woman of all meaningful emotional support from outside the home puts enormous pressure on the husband-wife relationship. The man then becomes her primary source of conversation, ventilation, fellowship, and love. But she's not his only responsibility. He is faced with great pressure, both internal and external, in his job. His self-esteem hangs on the way he handles his business, and the status of the entire family depends on his success. By the time he gets home at night, he has little left with which to prop up his lonely wife . . . even if he understands her.

Let me speak plainly to the homemaker with a busy but noncommunicative husband: *you cannot depend on this man to satisfy all your needs.* You will be continually frustrated by his failure to deliver. Instead, you must achieve a network of women friends with whom you can talk, laugh, gripe, dream, and recreate. There are thousands of wives and mothers around you who have the same needs and experience. They'll be looking for you as you begin your search for them. Get into exercise classes, group hobbies, church activities, Bible studies, bicycle clubs—whatever. But at all costs, resist the temptation to pull into the four walls of a house, sitting on the pity pot and waiting for your man to come home on his white horse.[11]

# SECTION 22

# THE HOMEMAKER

**As a homemaker, I resent the fact that my role as a wife and mother is no longer respected as it was in my mother's time. What forces have brought about this change in attitudes in the Western world?**

Female sex-role identity has become a major target for change by those who wish to revolutionize the relationship between men and women. The women's movement and the media have been remarkably successful in altering the way females "see" themselves at home and in society. In the process, every element of the traditional concept of femininity has been discredited and scorned, especially those responsibilities associated with homemaking and motherhood. Thus, in a period of a single decade, the term *housewife* has become a pathetic symbol of exploitation, oppression, and—pardon the insult—stupidity, at least as viewed from the perspective of radical feminists. We can make no greater mistake as a nation than to continue this pervasive disrespect shown to women who have devoted their lives to the welfare of their families.[1]

**You mentioned the role of the media in this changing concept of femininity. Are you implying that network television and movie producers have *deliberately* attempted to destroy or change the traditional role played by American women?**

There is no doubt in my mind about that fact. The entertainment industry has worked tirelessly to create a totally new woman with remarkable capacities. We saw her during the seventies as Wonder Woman and the Bionic Woman and Spider

Woman and Charlie's Angels and a host of other powerful (but sexy) females. In my book, *What Wives Wish Their Husbands Knew About Women,** I described this new socially prescribed role as follows:

> This image of women now being depicted is a ridiculous combination of wide-eyed fantasy and feminist propaganda. Today's woman is always shown as gorgeous, of course, but she is more—much more. She roars around the countryside in a racy sports car, while her male companion sits on the other side of the front seat anxiously biting his nails. She exudes self-confidence from the very tips of her fingers, and for good reason: she could dismantle any man alive with her karate chops and flying kicks to the teeth. She is deadly accurate with a pistol and she plays tennis (or football) like a pro. She speaks in perfectly organized sentences, as though her spontaneous remarks were being planned and written by a team of tiny English professors sitting in the back of her pretty head. She is a sexual gourmet, to be sure, but she wouldn't be caught dead in a wedding ceremony. She has the grand good fortune of being perpetually young and she never becomes ill, nor does she ever make a mistake or appear foolish. In short, she is virtually omniscient, except for a curious inability to do anything traditionally feminine, such as cook, sew, or raise children. Truly, today's screen heroine is a remarkable specimen, standing proud and uncompromising, with wide stance and hands on her hips.[2]

But she is unreal—just as phony as the masculine superheroes played by Burt Reynolds and Roger Moore. It is sheer fantasy on either side of the line of gender.[3]

**What has been the result of this revolution in feminine sex-role identity and where is it likely to lead us from here?**

It has produced a decade of depression and self-doubt among women. God created us as sexual beings, and any confusion in that understanding is devastating to the self-concept. Those most affected are the women who are inextricably identified with the traditional role, those who perceive themselves to be "stranded" in a homemaking responsibility. Thus, wives and

*Published in the UK as *Man to Man about Women.*

mothers have found themselves wondering, "Who am I?" and then nervously asking, "Who *should* I be?" It appears that we tore down the old value system before the new one was ready for occupancy, bringing widespread confusion and agitation.

Now a new and surprising phenomenon is taking place. The self-doubt has spread to the masculine gender. I suppose it was inevitable. Any social movement creating chaos in half the population was certain to afflict the other half, sooner or later. As a result, men are now entering the winter of their discontent.

*Psychology Today* published an article by James Levine in which he reviewed three new books on the subject of manhood in transition. His opening paragraph is indicative of their content:

> After countless books about the condition of women that have been published in the last decade, we are now getting a spate of studies about men. *One theme comes through loud and clear: the male is in crisis.* Buffeted by the women's movement, constrained by a traditional and internalized definition of "masculinity," men literally don't know who they are, what women want from them, or even what they want from themselves (November 1979).

It's true. Men *are* in a state of confusion over the meaning of sex-role identity. We know it is unacceptable to be "macho" (whatever in the world that is), but we're a little uncertain about how a real man behaves. Is he a breadwinner and a protector of his family? Well, not exactly. Should he assume a position of leadership and authority at home? Not if he's married to a woman who's had her "consciousness raised." Should he open doors for his wife or give a lady his seat on the train or rise when she enters the room? Who knows? Will he march off to defend his homeland in times of war, or will his wife be the one to fight on foreign soil? Should he wear jewelry and satin shoes or carry a purse? Alas, is there anything that marks him as different from his female counterpart? Not to hear the media tell it!

Again, I must make the point that this confused sex-role identity is not the result of random social evolution. It is a product of deliberate efforts to discredit the traditional role of manliness by those who seek *revolution* within the family. Notice that James Levine referred to traditional masculinity as *constraining.* That is precisely how the liberal media and humanistic behavioral scientists perceive the biblical concept of maleness.[4]

**Are you saying that we should all be locked into traditional male and female sex roles, whether we choose them or not? Are you telling every woman that she must bear children even if she doesn't want them?**

Of course not. It is a woman's prerogative not to have a baby, so I would not be so foolish as to try to force that decision on anyone. However, there's something ambiguous about insisting on a "right" which would mean the end of the human race if universally applied! If women wearied of childbearing for a mere thirty-five years on earth, the last generation of mortals would grow old and die, leaving no offspring to reproduce. What godlike power is possessed by the female of the species! She can take the bit in her mouth and gallop down the road to oblivion with a wagonload of humanity bumping along behind. No hydrogen bomb could destroy us more effectively, without bloodshed or pollution.

But this is not merely a bad dream with no basis in reality. For several years, it has been almost impossible to find anything positive written about human babies in liberal and leftist publications. Kids have been perceived as an imposition, a nuisance, and a drain on the world's natural resources. They're seen as part of the "population bomb" that supposedly plagues the earth. I'm convinced that this negative bias plays a role in the epidemic of child abuse that rages throughout this country. It is certainly related to the shameful abortion phenomenon occurring during the past decade. More than a million American babies are now aborted annually (55 million worldwide), infants who will never take their place in the fabric of our society. What remains is an aging population with fewer children to step into our shoes.

What I'm saying is that sex-role attitudes are closely related to the survival of a society. What will happen, for example, if the present generation reaches retirement age and still outnumbers the younger workers? Who would support the social security system when today's adults become too old to earn a living? Who would populate the military when America is threatened from abroad? What would happen to an economy that is based on decreasing returns rather than growth from productivity? Yes, the liberated woman will have had her way—her "right" to abortion and childlessness. She will have proved that no one could tell her what to do with her body. But what a victory![5]

**What answer do you have for those who say being a mother and a housewife is boring and monotonous?**
They are right—but we should recognize that practically every other occupation is boring, too. How exciting is the work of a telephone operator who plugs and unplugs switchboard connections all day long—or a medical pathologist who examines microscopic slides and bacterial cultures from morning to night—or a dentist who spends his lifetime drilling and filling, drilling and filling—or an attorney who reads dusty books in a secluded library—or an author who writes page after page after page? Few of us enjoy heart-thumping excitement each moment of our professional lives. On a trip to Washington, D.C., a few years ago, my hotel room was located next to the room of a famous cellist who was in the city to give a classical concert that evening. I could hear him through the walls as he practiced hour after hour. He did not play beautiful symphonic renditions; he repeated scales and runs and exercises, over and over and over. This practice began early in the morning (believe me!) and continued until the time of his concert. As he strolled on stage that evening, I'm sure many individuals in the audience thought to themselves, "What a glamorous life!" Some glamor! I happen to know that he had spent the entire day in his lonely hotel room in the company of his cello. Musical instruments, as you know, are terrible conversationalists. No, I doubt if the job of a housewife and mother is much more boring than most other jobs, particularly if the woman refuses to be isolated from adult contact. But as far as importance of the assignment is concerned, *no* job can compete with the responsibility of shaping and molding a new human being.

May I remind mothers of one more important consideration: you will not always be saddled with the responsibility you now hold. Your children will be with you for a few brief years and the obligations you now shoulder will be nothing more than dim memories. Enjoy every moment of these days—even the difficult times—and indulge yourself in the satisfaction of having done an essential job right!

**How do you feel about mothers being employed outside the home, especially in situations where it is not financially necessary for her to work?**
*Editor's note:* This question is of such significance and controversy in the Western world today, that it cannot be answered

with a brief reply. Therefore, the decision was made to reprint an article written by Dr. Dobson in which he addressed the matter of full-time employment for women.

WORKING MOTHERS AND THEIR FAMILIES

America is currently witnessing an unprecedented movement of women into the work force. More than half the 84 million adult females in this country are now formally employed; one in every three mothers of children under six is working outside the home, and the numbers are steadily rising. Whether or not this trend is healthy or pathological is one of the most volatile issues of our time, and one which generates heated debates and considerable conflict. Alas, everyone seems to have an opinion on the subject. You're about to read mine.

It would be presumptuous for any family specialist, particularly a man, to tell the women of America how to live their lives. The decision to have a career or be a homemaker is an intensely personal choice that can only be made by a woman and her husband. Indeed, the search for employment is often required by the inflationary pressures of today's economy. And there are marital disruptions where the husband either cannot work or is removed from the home. These and related problems obviously demand the financial contribution of the women involved. Thus, when a Christian wife and mother concludes that she must enter the labor force, the response from her friends and associates should be one of tolerance and understanding.

I must honestly report my observation, however, that working wives and their families often face some special frustrations and problems. Getting a job, especially for the mother of small children, can produce a whole catalog of new challenges which she may not comprehend in the beginning. In fact, I am concerned about the untruthful messages often given to the mother who can choose whether to work or stay home. Specifically, there are three false concepts being energetically conveyed to her through various forms of feminist propaganda. Let me consider them individually.

1. Every female in America who isn't "working" is being cheated and exploited by the male-dominated society in which she lives. If she has any gumption or intelligence, she'll seek fulfillment in a career.

Since the beginning of human existence, women in most cultures have identified themselves with child rearing and nest building. It was an honorable occupation that required no apology. How has it happened, then, that homemaking has fallen on such lean times in the Western world? Why do women who remain at home in the company of little children feel such disrespect from the society in which they live? A partial answer to these questions can be found in the incessant bombardment by the media on all traditional Judeo-Christian values.

Accordingly, it would appear that many women have accepted employment as a means of coping with the disrespect that they experienced as full-time mothers. To understand this process, let's look at a contrived example.

Suppose it suddenly became very unpopular to be a dentist. Suppose every magazine carried an article or two about the stupidity of the tooth-and-gum boys, making them look foolish and gauche. Suppose television commercials and dramas and comedy programs all poked fun at the same battered target. Suppose the humor associated with dentistry then died, leaving contempt and general disrespect in its place. Suppose the men in white were ignored at social gatherings and their wives were excluded from "in" group activities. Suppose dentists had difficulty hiring assistants and associates because no one wanted his friends to know he was working for a "tooth fairy." What would happen if all social status were suddenly drained from the profession of dentistry? I suspect that it would soon become very difficult to get a cavity drilled and filled.

The illustration is extreme, admittedly, but the analogy to women can hardly be missed. Housewives have been teased and ridiculed and disrespected. They have been the butt of jokes and sordid humor until the subject is no longer funny. As I have spoken to family groups across the country, great frustration has been expressed by women who have been made to feel dumb and foolish for wanting to stay at home. Those who are dedicated to their responsibilities are currently being mocked in women's magazines as "Supermoms." They have heard the prevailing opinion: "There must be something wrong with those strange creatures who seem to like domestic duties and responsibilities."

Closely related to the myth that "homemakers are losers" is a similar distortion related to child rearing.

2. Children, even those under five years of age, don't really need the extensive nurturing and involvement of their mothers, anyway. They will become more independent and assertive if raised in various child-care settings.

If the above statement were accurate, it would conveniently expunge all guilt from the consciences of overcommitted parents. But it simply won't square with scientific knowledge. I attended a national conference on child development held in Miami, Florida, a few years ago. Virtually every report of research presented during that three-day meeting ended with the same conclusion: the mother-child relationship is absolutely vital to healthy development of children. The final speaker of the conference was Dr. Urie Bronfenbrenner, the foremost authority on child development today. He concluded his remarks by saying that feminine responsibilities are so vital to the next generation that the future of our nation actually depends on how we "see" our women. I agree.

Nevertheless, modern women are struggling to convince themselves that state-sponsored child-care centers offer a convenient substitute for the traditional family concept. It will not work! It hasn't succeeded in the countries where it has been tried. As Dr. Bronfenbrenner wrote:

> . . . with the withdrawal of the social supports for the family to which I alluded . . . the position of women and mothers has become more and more isolated. With the breakdown of the community, the neighborhood, and the extended family, an increasing responsibility for the care and upbringing of children has fallen on the young mother. Under these circumstances, it is not surprising that many young women in America are in revolt. I understand and share their sense of rage, but I fear the consequences of some of the solutions they advocate, which will have the effect of isolating children still further from the kind of care and attention they need.[7]

Children *cannot* raise themselves properly. This fact was illustrated again in a recent conversation with a research psychologist who visited my office. He had been studying the early childhoods of inmates at a state prison in Arizona. He and his associates were seeking to discover the common characteristics which the prisoners shared, hoping to unlock the causes for their antisocial behavior. It was initially assumed that poverty would be the common thread, but their findings contradicted these expectations. The inmates came from all socioeconomic levels of society, though most of them attempted to excuse their crimes by professing to have been poor. Instead, the researchers discovered one fundamental characteristic shared by the men:

an absence of adult contact in their early home lives. As children, they spent most of their time in the company of their peers . . . or altogether alone. Such was the childhood of Lee Harvey Oswald, Charles Manson, and many other perpetrators of violent crimes later in life. The conclusion is inescapable: there is no substitute for loving parental leadership in the early development of children.

But my intense personal opinions on this matter of "preschool mothering" are not only based on scientific evidence and professional experience. My views have also been greatly influenced within my own home. Let me share a statement I wrote several years ago in my book *What Wives Wish Their Husbands Knew About Women.**

> Our two children are infinitely complex, as are all children, and my wife and I want to guide the formative years ourselves. Danae is nine years old. She will be an adolescent in four more seasons, and I am admittedly jealous of anything robbing me of these remaining days of her childhood. Every moment is precious to me. Ryan is now four. Not only is he in constant motion, but he is also in a state of rapid physical and emotional change. At times it is almost frightening to see how dynamic is the development of my little toddler. When I leave home for a four- or five-day speaking trip, Ryan is a noticeably different child upon my return. The building blocks for his future emotional and physical stability are clearly being laid moment by moment, stone upon stone, precept upon precept. Now I ask you who disagree with what I have written, to whom am I going to submit the task of guiding that unfolding process of development? Who will care enough to make the necessary investment if my wife and I are too busy for the job? What baby-sitter will take our place? What group-oriented facility can possibly provide the individual love and guidance which Ryan and Danae need and deserve? Who will represent my value and beliefs to my son and daughter and be ready to answer their questions during the peak of interest? To whom will I surrender the prime-time experiences of their day? The rest of the world can make its own choice, but as for me and my house, we welcome the opportunity to shape the two little lives which have been loaned to us. And I worry about a nation which calls that task "unrewarding and unfulfilling and boring."

---

*Published in the UK as *Man to Man about Women.*

This brings us to the third and final myth to be considered.

3. *Most* mothers of small children can work all day and still have the energy to meet their family obligation . . . perhaps even better than if they remained at home.

There is only so much energy within the human body for expenditure during each twenty-four hours, and when it is invested in one place it is not available for use in another. It is highly improbable that the average woman can arise early in the morning and get her family fed and located for the day, then work from 9:00 to 5:00, drive home from 5:01 to 5:30, and still have the energy to assault her "homework" from 5:31 until midnight. Oh, she may cook dinner and handle major household chores, but few women alive are equipped with the superstrength necessary at the end of a workday to meet the emotional needs of their children, to train and guide and discipline, to build self-esteem, to teach the true values of life, and beyond all that, to maintain a healthy marital relationship as well. Perhaps the task can be accomplished for a week or a month, or even a season. But for years on end? I simply don't believe it. To the contrary, I have observed that exhausted wives and mothers often become irritable, grouchy, and frustrated, setting the stage for conflict within the home. As such, I believe more divorces are caused by mutual overcommitment by husbands and wives than all other factors combined. It is the number one marriage killer!

In summary, circumstances may require that wives and mothers seek full-time employment outside the home. In those instances, Christian onlookers should express tolerant understanding of the person's unspoken needs and obligations. However, the decision for Mom to work has profound implications for her family and especially for her small children. That decision must be made in the full light of reality . . . being unedited by the biases of current social fads. And most importantly, we dare not strip the dignity from the most noble occupation in the universe . . . that of molding little lives during their period of greatest vulnerability.

Let me conclude by sharing a note written to me recently by a ten-year-old boy. He said: "Dear Dr. Dobson, I have a working mom and a working dad and I would like to know what us kids can do. Brian."

I will permit America's parents to respond to Brian's question. They are, after all, the only ones who *can* provide a satisfactory answer to it.[8]

Dear Dr. Dobson:

Enclosed is an article that appeared recently in the *Washington Post* newspaper, which I know you will find interesting. The writer, Mary Fay Bourgoin, is a mother who is employed full time, and expresses her opinions from a secular point of view. Years ago, the Lord taught me the same things she is now learning the hard way. Hope you enjoy the article.

A radio listener

WORKING MOTHERS—SUPERMOMS OR DRONES?

These days it seems that my home, Washington, D.C., is a city of weary women, or, more accurately, exhausted working mothers. For several months, I have been among those who rise at dawn to shower, blow dry their hair, pack lunches, do a load of wash, plug in the crock pot, and glance at the morning paper to make sure the world is not ending before 9 A.M.

Provided there is no last-minute scramble for missing shoes, homework, or show-and-tell items, my three daughters are at school by 8:40 and I am on my way to "the real world."

My job is interesting, working on Capitol Hill as a journalist, investigating the legislative process, interviewing members of Congress—all described in my alumnae magazine as "glamorous." But most of the time I feel that I have one foot on a banana peel and the other on ice.

Balancing marriage, motherhood, and career has become the classic women's problem of the '80s. For those who can pull it all together, life is a first-class act. But judging from my own experience and from talking with other women, life is often a constant round of heartburn, ulcers, and anxiety attacks.

In the '50s, my generation had a different set of pressures. Eighteen years ago I was a college senior. Romanticizing marriage and family life, we talked about weddings, not resumes. Shortly after graduation, the rush began. One by one my classmates, star-struck lovers in wedding satin, stood at flower-decked altars and uttered vows—promises of eternal bliss. We were the color-coordinated generation, never thinking beyond silver patterns, Bermuda honeymoons, and four-bedroom colonials.

In 1964, my views shifted when I experienced my first feminist stirrings on a Greyhound bus from Philadelphia to Washington, D.C. I became engrossed in Betty Friedan's book, *The Feminine Mystique*. It was a page turner. The happy housewife heroine was a myth. Millions of college-educated women, despite career opportunities in a modern society, had been "brainwashed" to believe that their only purpose in life was to find a husband and bear children. Countless women, unable to live up to the feminine ideal, suffered depression, popping bonbons, booze, or pills to ease their troubled psyches.

As the bus neared Washington, it passed suburban developments, clusters of ranch and split-level houses on treeless lots. I believed that behind all that aluminum siding dwelled miserable women wearing chenille bathrobes and muttering, "Is this all?"

Times have changed and so have I. Now I ride the subway into the city. Surrounded by grim-faced women wearing somber dress-for-success suits, aware of my growing uneasiness about some aspects of the feminist movement, I mumble, "Is this liberation?"

During the past decade, more and more women entered the labor force—a million a year. According to studies, the number of working mothers has grown more than tenfold since the end of World War II. Although much discussion about career opportunities for women focuses on personal growth and fulfillment, the fact is that the majority of women work because they need the money.

Yet it seems that my generation has now romanticized careers as the cure-all for identity crisis, the supermom syndrome, the housewife blues, and the empty-nest heartache.

Replacing the happy housewife heroine is the successful business woman who climbs up the corporate ladder without chipping her nail polish, who breezes through the day wearing immaculately tailored clothes, and who returns home, hairdo intact, to an adoring husband and two well-adjusted children.

The sad and obvious truth is that a great many women are now finding out what men have always known—dead-end jobs abound, most work eventually becomes boring, bosses, colleagues, and clients can be demanding, irritating, and nasty, and it is just as easy to feel trapped and unhappy sitting in a posh office amid the trappings of success as it is standing in the kitchen surrounded by whining preschoolers.

Career-oriented mothers confront still another reality—children. In some circles it is not fashionable to discuss the dark side of the women's movement and its impact on family life. After all, the experts assure us that it's only a myth that children of working mothers tend to be sullen, lonely, and neglected. And I, like many, adopted as gospel the feminist pronouncements that if women were free to pursue their professional interests we would be more independent and interesting, more loving wives and mothers.

But the breezy you-can-do-it-all articles leave out an important factor—energy. "Motherhood," as someone recently observed, "saps the energy." And so does a high-pressure career where upward job mobility is a way of life.

Marriage is also demanding, requiring inner strength and motivation to keep a relationship from growing stale. Simply put, when it comes to energy, physical or emotional, we have only so much.

So just as Friedan was tired of reading about the happy, energetic housewife, so I am weary of magazine articles about the successful, dynamic, mother-wife-career wonder woman. In both case histories, something is missing, the unglamorous parts are air-brushed out, the stories bear no relation to reality.

The tales I hear from women—conversations on the subway, concerns exchanged over coffee, instructions whispered over the phone to children, husbands, baby-sitters, teachers—describe the edited-out scenes: sick children sent to school or left home alone, baby-sitters who permit their charges to watch endless hours of television, no-show housekeepers, sleeping babies who are awakened at 6 A.M. and delivered to day care centers at 7 A.M., the growing number of latchkey children—eight- and nine-year-olds who are left on their own after school, unsupervised until a parent returns home—the endless makeshift arrangements for the dreaded school holidays, vacations, snow closings, and other realities that aren't cosmetically attractive for the women's movement.

I suspect these are some of the reasons why feminism has not attracted the poor, the struggling, the blue-collar woman like my mother, who was a seamstress in a shirt factory. For they know all too well the dark underside of the world of working mothers.

"Work," my mother often says, watching from the sidelines as I try successive variations of my marriage-children-career juggling act, "is terribly overrated."

One recent evening on my way home from work, bone-tired, worried about my equally busy husband, a melancholy daughter, and a cantankerous editor, I came across a newspaper article about several celebrity feminists. I read their musings with interest.

"It's nifty," said one, "that women are no longer bound by traditional role models and careers, that they are now swamped by options and that they are continuing to challenge sexual stereotyping." Yes, I agreed. Yet I had the feeling that she and the others were naively enthusiastic about the "new woman," viewing the world through the wrong end of the binoculars.

When I read how one panelist manages to do it all, my doubts turned to convictions. Describing the "joys of egalitarianism," she said, "My husband and I both work at home. We have a year-old child whose care is shared equally between the two of us and a nurse."

I was too tired to laugh.

SECTION 23

# DEPRESSION IN WOMEN

**Is depression more common among men or women?**
Depression occurs less frequently in men and is apparently more *crisis*-oriented. In other words, men get depressed over specific problems such as a business setback or an illness. However, they are less likely to experience the vague, generalized, almost indefinable feeling of discouragement which many women encounter on a regular basis. Even a cloudy day may be enough to bring on a physical and emotional slowdown, known as the blahs, for those who are particularly vulnerable to depression.[1]

**When women get depressed, what specific complaint or irritant is most commonly related to the condition?**
I have asked that question of more than 10,000 women who were given an opportunity to fill out a questionnaire entitled, "Sources of Depression in Women." At the top of the list was the problem of low self-esteem. More than 50 percent of an initial test group marked this item above every other alternative on the list, and 80 percent placed it in the top five. This finding is perfectly consistent with my own observations and expectations: even in seemingly healthy and happily married young women, self-doubt cuts the deepest and leaves the most wicked scars. This same old nemesis is usually revealed within the first five minutes of a counseling session; feelings of inadequacy and lack of confidence have become a way of life for millions of American women.[2]

**My wife has been severely depressed for nearly three months. What kind of treatment or therapy would you recommend for her?**
Get her to a physician, probably an internist, as soon as possible. This kind of prolonged depression can have serious medical and psychological consequences, yet it is usually very responsive to treatment. Antidepressant drugs are highly effective in controlling most cases of severe depression. Of course, the medication will not correct the circumstances which precipitated her original problem, and the possibility of low self-esteem and other causes must be faced and dealt with, perhaps with the help of a psychologist or psychiatrist.[3]

**I tend to feel depressed after every holiday, but I don't know why. These special days are very happy ones for my family. Why do I find myself "blue" after such enjoyable occasions?**
It will be helpful for you to understand the nature of emotional rhythm in human beings. Anything producing an extreme "high" will set the stage for a later "low," and vice versa. A few years ago, for example, my wife and I bought a newer home. We had waited several years to find the right house, and we became very excited when escrow closed and the property was finally ours. The elation lasted for several days, during which time I discussed the experience with Shirley. I mentioned that we had been very high and that our excitement could not continue indefinitely. Emotions don't operate at maximum velocity for very long. More important, it was likely that our mental set would drop below sea level within a short period of time. As expected, we both experienced a vague letdown into mild depression about three days later. The house didn't seem so wonderful and there wasn't anything worth much enthusiasm. However, having anticipated the "downer," we recognized and accepted its temporary fluctuation when it came.

Depression therefore should be understood as a relatively predictable occurrence. It is likely to appear, as in your case, following a busy holiday or after the birth of a baby, a job promotion, or even after a restful vacation. The cause for this phenomenon is partly physical in nature. Elation consumes greater quantities of body energy, since all systems are operating at an accelerated rate. The necessary consequence of this pace is fatigue and exhaustion, bringing with it a more depressed state. Thus, highs *must* be followed by lows. The system is governed by a psychological law. You can depend on it. But in the healthy individual, fortunately, lows eventually give way to highs, too.[4]

**We live in what you have described as "routine panic" in our home. I have three children under six, and I never get caught up with my work. How can I slow down when it takes every minute of the day (and night) to care for my children?**

There may be a helpful answer in the way you spend your money. Most Americans maintain a "priority list" of things to purchase when enough money has been saved for that purpose. It is my conviction that domestic help for the mother of small children should appear on that priority list. Without it, she is sentenced to the same responsibility day in and day out, seven days a week. For several years, she is unable to escape the unending burden of dirty diapers, runny noses, and unwashed dishes. She will do a more efficient job in those tasks and be a better mother if she can share the load with someone else occasionally. This seems more important to the happiness of the home than buying new drapes or a power saw for Dad.

But how can middle class families afford housecleaning and baby-sitting services in these inflationary days? It might be accomplished by using competent high school students instead of older adults. I suggest that a call be placed to the counseling office of the nearest senior high school. Tell the counselor that you need a mature third- or fourth-year student to do some cleaning. Do not reveal that you're looking for a regular employee. When the referred girl arrives, try her out for a day and see how she handles responsibility. If she's very efficient, offer her a weekly job. If she is slow and flighty, thank her for coming and call for a another student the following week. There is a remarkable difference in maturity level between high school girls, and you'll eventually find one who works like an adult.

Here are some further suggestions to help you tolerate the pressures of your life:

1. Reserve some time for yourself. At least once a week, go bowling or shopping, or simply "waste" an occasional afternoon. In addition, a husband and wife should have a date every week or two, leaving the children at home, and even forgetting them for an evening.

2. Don't struggle with things you can't change. Concentrate on the good things in your life. Men and women should recognize that discontent can become nothing more than a bad habit—a costly attitude that can rob them of the pleasure of living.

3. Don't deal with any big problems late at night. All problems seem more unsolvable in the evenings, and the decisions that are reached then may be more emotional than rational.

4. Try making a list. The advantages of writing down one's responsibilities are threefold: (1) You know you aren't going to forget anything. (2) You can guarantee that the most important jobs will get done first. Thus, if you don't get finished by the end of the day, you will at least have done the items that were most critical. (3) The tasks are crossed off the list as they are completed, leaving a record of what has been accomplished.

5. Seek divine assistance. The concepts of marriage and parenthood were not human inventions. God, in His infinite wisdom, created and ordained the family as the basic unit of procreation and companionship. The solutions to the problems of modern parenthood can be found through the power of prayer and personal appeal to the Great Creator.[5]

**My wife is a full-time homemaker, and we have three children under six years of age. She often gets depressed, especially when she can't keep up with everything expected of her. But I have my hands full too and am required to put in so much overtime. What can I do to help Marge cope with these busy years?**

Let me make two suggestions to you:

1. For some reason, human beings (and particularly women) tolerate stresses and pressures much more easily if at least one other person knows they are enduring it. This principle is filed under the category of "human understanding," and it is highly relevant to homemakers. The frustrations of raising small children and handling domestic duties will be more manageable for your wife if you will let her know that you comprehend it all. Even if you can do nothing to change the situation, simply your awareness that Marge did an admirable job today will make it easier for her to repeat the assignment tomorrow. Instead, the opposite usually occurs. At least eight million husbands will stumble into the same unforgivable question tonight: "What did you do all day, dear?" The very nature of the question implies

that the little woman had been sitting on her back-side watching television and drinking coffee since arising at noon! The little woman could kill him for saying it.

*Everyone* needs to know that he is respected for the way he meets his responsibilities. Husbands get this emotional nurture through job promotions, raises in pay, annual evaluations, and incidental praise during the work day. Women at home get it from their husbands—if they get it at all. The most unhappy wives and mothers are often those who handle their fatigue and time pressure in solitude, and their men are never very sure why they always act so tired.

2. Husbands *and* wives should constantly guard against the scourge of overcommitment. Even worthwhile and enjoyable activities become damaging when they consume the last ounce of energy or the remaining free moments in the day. Though it is rarely possible for a busy family, everyone needs to waste some time every now and then—to walk along kicking rocks and thinking pleasant thoughts. Men need time to putter in the garage and women need to pluck their eyebrows and do the girlish things again. But as I have described, the whole world seems to conspire against such reconstructive activities. Even our vacations are hectic; "We have to reach St. Louis by sundown or we'll lose our reservations."

I can provide a simple prescription for a happier, healthier life, but it must be implemented by the individual family. *You* must resolve to slow your pace; you must learn to say "no" gracefully; you must resist the temptation to chase after more pleasures, more hobbies, more social entanglements; you must "hold the line" with the tenacity of a tackle for a professional football team. In essence, three questions should be asked about every new activity which presents itself: Is it worthy of our time? What will be eliminated if it is added? What will be its impact on our family life? My suspicion is that most of the items in our busy day would score rather poorly on this three-item test.[6]

**I notice that spiritual discouragement and defeat are much more common when I am tired than when I am rested. Is this characteristic of others?**

When a person is exhausted, he is attacked by ideas he thought he conquered long ago. The great football coach for the Green Bay Packers, Vince Lombardi, once told his team why he pushed them so hard toward proper physical conditioning. He said, "Fatigue makes cowards of us all." He was absolutely right. As the reserves of human energy are depleted, one's ability to reject distressing thoughts and wild impressions is greatly reduced.[7]

**I am depressed much of the time and worry about whether or not my kids will be affected by my moods. Are children typically vulnerable to parental discouragement and depression?**

According to Dr. Norman S. Brandes, child psychiatrist, children are *very* sensitive to depression in the adults around them. They often become depressed themselves, even though adults think they've hidden their despair from the children. Furthermore, you are being watched carefully by your children and they are "learning" how to deal with frustration. In short, you are effectively teaching them, through your own depression, to react similarly in the future.

If your depression continues to be chronic, as you indicated, I would suggest that you seek professional advice. Begin with your physician, who may recognize a physical cause for your constant discouragement. If not, he may refer you for psychological assistance. This does not mean you are mentally ill or neurotic. It may indicate nothing more than that you need to examine the things that are bothering you with the help of a competent counselor.[8]

**Can you explain why so many Americans express a dissatisfaction with life, despite the fact that we have more of the world's good things than any other country? It seems strange that the richest country on earth is inhabited by a high percentage of depressed and unhappy people.**

The human emotional apparatus is constructed so as to disregard that which is taken for granted. Good health, delicious food, pleasant entertainment, peaceful circumstances, and beautiful homes are of little consequence to those who have had them since birth. Can you recall seeing a healthy teenager get up in the morning and express appreciation because his joints didn't hurt, or his vision was excellent, or because he breathed with ease or he felt so good? Not likely. He has never known the meaning of prolonged pain or sickness, and he accepts his good health without even considering it. But when those greatest of life's blessings begin to vanish, our appreciation for them increases accordingly. For a man who faces continued physical deterioration and premature death, the whole world assumes new significance: the beauty of a tree, the privilege of watching a sunset, the company of loved ones—it all takes on meaning.

I think this concept explains many of the emotional problems and psychiatric symptoms which beset us. We have been taught to anticipate the finest and best from our existence on this earth. We feel almost entitled, by divine decree, to at least seventy-two years of bliss, and anything less than that is a cause for great agitation. In other words, our *level of expectations* is incredibly high. But life rarely delivers on that promise. It deals us disappointment and frustration and disease and pain and loneliness, even in the best of circumstances. Thus, there is an inevitable gap between life as it *is* and life as it ought to be.

The result is a high incidence of depression, especially among women, an unacceptable rate of suicide, especially among the young, and a general anxiety among the rest of us. I have watched men develop ulcers over relatively insignificant business reverses. I have seen women suffer daily agitation over the most minor inconveniences, such as having a ragged couch or a cranky neighbor, when every other dimension of their lives was without blemish.

Compare the instability of such individuals with the attitudes of German families near the close of World War II. Every day, a thousand British bombers unloaded their destructive cargo over Hamburg and Berlin and Munich. By night, the American planes did the same. Loved ones were dying on all sides. Neighborhoods were shattered and burned. Little children were maimed and killed. There was not enough food to eat and the water was polluted. The fabric of their lives was shredded. Yet historians tell us that their morale remained intact until the end of the war. They did not crack. They went about the business of reordering their homes and making the best of a horrible situation.

How can we account for this courage in the face of disaster, as compared with affluent Americans who, though they have everything, are wringing their hands in the offices of psychiatrists? The difference can be found in our level of expectations. The Germans expected to sacrifice and experience suffering. They were, therefore, prepared for the worst when it came. But we are vulnerable to the slightest frustration, because we have been taught that troubles can be avoided. We have permitted our emotions to rule us, and in so doing, we have become mere slaves to our feelings.[9]

# SECTION 24

# UNDER-STANDING PRE-MENSTRUAL TENSION

**Is the moodiness I feel before my menstrual periods something that all women suffer? I feel as if I am some kind of freak because I get so depressed and touchy each month.**

You are definitely not a freak! What you are experiencing is suffered by at least 30 percent of American women each month. There are many symptoms that characterize premenstrual tension, including sluggishness, irritability, lack of energy, hostility, low level of tolerance to noise, low self-esteem, depression, insecurity, low libido (sex drive), and a vague apprehension about the future.[1]

**Describe in greater detail the mood fluctuations that are associated with the menstrual cycle each month. Is it true that this chemical influence is evident not only during or before a period, but at other times also?**

It has been said, quite accurately, that the four weeks of the menstrual cycle can be characterized by the four seasons of the year. The first week after a period can be termed the springtime of the physiological calendar. New estrogens (female hormones) are released each day and a woman's body begins to rebound from the recent winter.

The second week represents the summertime of the cycle, when the living is easy. A woman during this phase has more self-confidence than during any other phase of the month. It is a time of maximum energy, enthusiasm, amiability, and self-esteem. Estrogen levels account for much of this optimism, reaching a peak during mid-cycle when ovulation occurs. The relationship between husband and wife is typically at its best during these days of summer, when sexual drive (and the potential for pregnancy) are paramount.

But alas, fall must surely follow summer. Estrogen levels steadily dwindle as the woman's body prepares itself for another period of menstruation. A second hormone called progesterone is released, which reduces the effect of estrogen and initiates the symptoms of premenstrual tension. It is a bleak phase of the month. Self-esteem deteriorates day by day, bringing depression and pessimism with it. A bloated and sluggish feeling often produces not only discomfort but also the belief that "I am ugly." Irritability and aggression become increasingly evident as the week progresses, reaching a climax immediately prior to menstruation. Then come the winter and the period of the menstrual flow.

Women differ remarkably in intensity of these symptoms, but most experience some discomfort. Those most vulnerable even find it necessary to spend a day or two in bed during the "winter" season, suffering from cramping and generalized misery. Gradually, the siege passes and the refreshing newness of springtime returns.[2]

**I've noticed that I experience the greatest feeling of inadequacy and inferiority during the "premenstrual" phase, a few days before my period. Can you explain why this would be true?**

Few women know that there is direct relationship between estrogen levels (the primary female sex hormones) and self-esteem. Thus, self-worth typically fluctuates predictably through the twenty-eight-day cycle. The graph which appears below depicts this relationship.

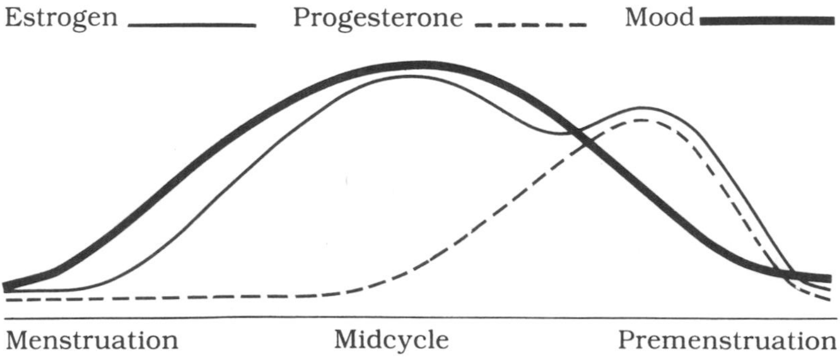

*Normal Hormone Levels and Mood.* In the normal menstrual cycle, estrogen peaks at midcycle (ovulation). Both estrogen and progesterone circulate during the second half of the cycle, falling off rapidly just prior to menstruation. Moods change with the fluctuating hormone levels: women feel the greatest self-esteem, and the least anxiety and hostility, at midcycle.

Notice that estrogen levels are at their lowest point during menstruation (at the left of the graph), as is the general "mood." The production of estrogen increases day by day until it peaks near the time of ovulation at midcycle. That midpoint also happens to be the time of greatest emotional optimism and self-confidence. Then another hormone, progesterone, is produced during the second half of the cycle, bringing with it increasing tension, anxiety, and aggressiveness. Finally, the two hormones decrease during the premenstrual period, reducing the mood to its lowest point again.[3]

**How do we know that the symptoms of premenstrual tension are not merely psychological; perhaps women feel bad each month because they expect (or have been conditioned) to be miserable.**

In the first place menstrual difficulties are seen in women around the world in vastly different cultures. Furthermore, the effect of premenstrual tension is not only observable clinically, but it can be documented statistically.

The incidences of suicides, homicides, and infanticides perpetrated by women are significantly higher during the period of premenstrual tension than any other phase of the month. Consider also the findings of Alec Coppen and Neil Kessel, who studied 465 women and observed that they were more irritable and depressed during the premenstrual phase than during midcycle.

> This was true for neurotic, psychotic, and normal women alike. Similarly, Natalie Sharness found the premenstrual phase associated with feelings of helplessness, anxiety, hostility, and yearning for love. At menstruation, this tension and irritability eased, but depression often accompanied the relief, and lingered until estrogen increased.[4]

Thousands of studies have validated this same conclusion. If you doubt their findings, ask a woman.[5]

**Even though I know my depression is the result of physiological conditions each month, I still forget that fact and find myself suffering from low self-esteem and general anxiety. How can I prepare myself to do a better job of coping with the menstrual cycle?**

It is impossible to prepare yourself for premenstrual tension unless you know what to expect, so you need to begin by conducting some research on your own body. I suggest that you keep a diary on which you describe at least three elements of functioning: (1) your energy level, (2) your general mood, and (3) your achievements and accomplishments. Chart these three indicators *every day* for at least four months. Most women report that a surprisingly consistent pattern exists from month to month. Once it is identified and understood, further steps can be taken to brace yourself for the predictable valleys and tunnels.

Once the period of premenstrual tension arrives, you should interpret your feelings with caution and skepticism. If you can remember that the despair and sense of worthlessness are hormonally induced and have nothing to do with reality, you can withstand the psychological nosedive more easily. You should have a little talk with yourself each month, saying: "Even though I feel inadequate and inferior, I refuse to believe it. I know I'll feel differently in a few days and it is ridiculous to let this get me down. Though the sky looks dark, my perception is distorted. My real problem is physical, not emotional, and it will soon improve!"[6]

**I don't think my husband understands the problems I experience during the menstrual cycle. Will you offer some advice to him about these physiological factors?**

Having never had a period, it is difficult for a man to comprehend the bloated, sluggish feeling which motivates his wife's snappy remarks and irritability during the premenstrual period.

I am reminded of an incident related to me by my late friend Dr. David Hernandez, who was an obstetrician and gynecologist in private practice. The true story involves Latin men whose wives were given birth control pills by a pharmaceutical company. The Federal Drug Administration in America would not permit hormonal research to be conducted, so the company selected a small fishing village in South America which agreed to cooperate. All the women in the town were given the pill on the same date, and after three weeks the prescription was terminated to permit menstruation. That meant, of course, that every adult female in the community was experiencing premenstrual tension at the same time. The men couldn't take it. They all headed for their boats each month and remained at sea until the crisis passed at home.

Going fishing is not the answer to monthly physiological stresses, of course. It is extremely important for a man to learn to anticipate his wife's menstrual period, recognizing the emotional changes which will probably accompany it. Of particular importance is the need for affection and tenderness during this time, even though she may be rather unlovable for three or four days. He should also avoid discussions of financial problems or other threatening topics until the internal storm has passed, and keep the home atmosphere as tranquil as possible. He might even give his wife the speech described in the previous answer.

Let me conclude by addressing a final comment directly to husbands, expanding on the advice offered above. Because stress is such an influential factor in this problem of premenstrual tension, anything you can do to reduce environmental pressure is sure to help her feel better. If you are aware of the times when she is going to be feeling the strain, you should lighten the family commitments. Eating out can reduce the obligation to plan and cook meals. Do what you can to keep the kids out of her hair, especially the noisy younger ones. Take them to the park for an afternoon. Read to them or engage them in a quiet game, leaving their mother free to relax as much as possible.

Because your wife's sexual desire is at a low ebb that week, make fewer physical demands on her—but continue to be affectionate, reassuring, and loving toward her. Remember that women often feel "ugly" when they are experiencing premenstrual tension, so let her know that you find her as attractive as ever.

In some ways, the husband's role during his wife's menstrual period should be that of an understanding, loving, gentle parent. Just as parents do more giving than receiving, this is a man's time to support his wife in every way possible.[7]

**Why are some women more prone than others to have unpleasant symptoms at the crucial time of the month?**
Some good answers to this question are supplied in an excellent booklet entitled *Premenstrual Blues*, written by a California physician, Dr. Guy Abraham. He has kindly given me permission to refer to information in that booklet, although the following items are not direct quotations.

Dr. Abraham pinpoints six factors which may make some women particularly prone to premenstrual tension:

1. Marriage. Married women are more susceptible than single women. In fact, premenstrual tension has been identified as a major cause of divorce.
2. Childbirth. The more pregnancies a woman has had, the more likely she is to experience the distressing symptoms associated with the days preceding menstruation.
3. Age. The premenstrual syndrome appears to become more and more acute during the childbearing years, up to the late thirties.
4. Stress. Time pressure and psychological tension contribute significantly to the problem.
5. Diet. Poor nutrition is a culprit here, including the excessive use of refined sugars and salt in the diet.
6. Exercise. Women who suffer from premenstrual tension are usually those who do not engage in regular outdoor exercise such as walking, bicycling, swimming, tennis, and other such activities.[8]

**You mentioned the role of nutrition in the severity of premenstrual tension. Can I really help relieve the symptoms by eating right? If so, what should my diet consist of?**
I am firmly convinced of the importance of good nutrition . . . this is true for everyone, of course, but especially for women during the childbearing years. And yes, a proper diet *is* related to the symptoms of premenstrual stress. One of the most uncomfortable symptoms of PMT (premenstrual tension), for example, is the bloated feeling a woman gets from having excess fluid in her body. This can be relieved by ingesting a low-salt diet, thus avoiding the retention of fluids. Of further help is restricting carbohydrates, especially sugar, and eating more protein. This may require considerable discipline, because there seems to be an unusual craving for sweets at this

time—especially for chocolate. You should also increase the intake of vitamin C and the B complex vitamins, either in pill form or by eating more of the foods which contain these vitamins.

Regular exercise will also prove to be an asset to your health and well-being. Be sure to include some walking, bicycling, jogging, swimming, golfing, or other activity in your schedule every day.[9]

**Is PMT similar to menopause in emotional characteristics?**

In the sense that estrogen levels are reduced during both phases, yes. Since self-esteem is apparently related to estrogen, for example, a woman's feelings of low self-esteem are evident both premenstrually and during menopause. It has also been hypothesized that women who experience severe emotional fluctuations during their periods are more likely to experience some degree of menopausal distress in years to come. In other words, the vulnerability to estrogen is demonstrated early in life and confirmed during the middle-age years.[10]

**When my wife is suffering from PMT, she not only becomes irritable and short-tempered, but she seems to become even more angry when I try to tell her everything will be all right and that it isn't as bad as it seems. How do you explain that?**

You are observing the same lesson that I had to learn in my earlier counseling experience. I remember one patient in particular who used to call me or visit my office every twenty-eight days without exception. She was always tremendously depressed and agitated, but she never seemed to realize that her despair was related to her hormonal calendar. I would explain to her that she wasn't really so bad off, and things would be much better in a few days. To my surprise, however, these attempts to console her only caused greater frustration and made her try to prove to me how terrible things were in her life. After thinking about her plight for a while, I realized that she had not come to me for answers, but for the assurance that one other human being on earth understood what she was going through.

After that, when this woman came to see me, I offered her

empathy and understanding, helping her express the frustrations bottled up within. She would weep for forty or fifty minutes, telling me that there was no hope at all, and then blow her nose and sniff and say, "Thank you for your help. I feel so much better and I don't know what I would have done without you to talk to today." All I had done was let her know I understood. That was enough.

I suspect that your wife wants the same reassurance. There are times when we could *all* use a dose of that medicine.[11]

**Since "the pill" is actually composed of estrogen, do women who take it fluctuate emotionally as you have described?**

It depends on the kind of pill prescribed. If estrogen and progestin (synthetic progesterone) are given *simultaneously* for twenty days and then ceased, the mood remains at a moderately low level and is characterized by mild anxiety throughout the month. However, if estrogen is given for fifteen days and estrogen-progestin for five, the mood fluctuation is very similar to the normal non-pill cycle. Your physician can provide more information as to your particular pill and its emotional reverberations.[12]

# SECTION 25

# COPING WITH MENOPAUSE

**Our children are all on their own now and my husband and I are free to do some of the traveling we have always planned to do when we got them through college. But lately I feel too tired even to keep the house clean, and too depressed to care about planning anything extra. Some days I can hardly get out of bed in the morning. I just want to put my head under the pillow and cry—for no reason at all. So why do I feel so terrible? My husband is trying to be patient, but this morning he growled, "You have everything a woman could want . . . what do *you* have to be blue about?" Do you think I could be losing my mind?**
I think it is quite unlikely that you have anything wrong with your mind. The symptoms you describe sound as if you may be entering a physiological phase called menopause, and your discomfort may be caused by the hormonal imbalance that accompanies glandular upheaval. I suggest that you make an appointment to see a gynecologist in the next few days.

**Can you give me a simple definition of menopause?**
It is a period of transition in a woman's life when the reproductive capacity is phasing out and her body is undergoing the many chemical and psychological changes associated with that cessation. Menstruation, which has occurred monthly since perhaps eleven or twelve years of age, now gradually stops, and hormonal readjustments occur. Specifically, the ovaries produce only about one-eighth the estrogen that they once did. This affects not only the reproductive system, but the body's entire physical and psychological apparatus.[1]

**Do all women feel as miserable as I do when menopause occurs?**

It is estimated that approximately 85 percent of women go through menopause without major disruption in their daily lives. They may experience distressing symptoms for a time, but they are able to function and cope with the responsibilities of living. The remaining 15 percent, however, experience much more serious difficulties. Some are completely immobilized by the chemical changes occurring within.[2]

**What are the primary symptoms of hormone imbalance during menopause?**

I will list them, although I must caution you to understand that other physical and emotional problems can also produce the same or similar difficulties. Furthermore, this list is not complete. Menopausal physiology can be expressed in a wide variety of symptoms, varying in intensity.

*Emotional Symptoms*

1. Extreme depression, perhaps lasting for months without relief.
2. Extremely low self-esteem, bringing feelings of utter worthlessness and disinterest in living.
3. Extremely low frustration tolerance, giving rise to outbursts of temper and emotional ventilation.
4. Inappropriate emotional responses, producing tears when things are not sad and depression during relatively good times.
5. Low tolerance to noise. Even the sound of a radio or the normal responses of children can be extremely irritating. Ringing in the ears is also common.
6. Great needs for proof of love are demanded, and in their absence, suspicion of a rival may be hurled at the husband.
7. Interferences with sleep patterns.
8. Inability to concentrate and difficulty in remembering.

*Physical Symptoms*

1. Gastrointestinal disorders, interfering with digestion and appetite.
2. "Hot flashes" which burn in various parts of the body for a few seconds.
3. Vertigo (dizziness).

4. Constipation.
5. Trembling.
6. Hands and feet tingle and "go to sleep."
7. Dryness of the skin, especially in specific patches in various places, and loss of elasticity.
8. Dryness of the mucous membranes, especially in the vagina, making intercourse painful or impossible.
9. Greatly reduced libido (sexual desire).
10. Pain in various joints of the body, shifting from place to place (neuralgias, myalgias and arthralgias).
11. Tachycardia (accelerated or racing heartbeat) and palpitation.
12. Headaches.
13. Dark, gloomy circles around the eyes. (This is the symptom which I have found most useful in preliminary diagnosis.)
14. Loss of weight.

For the besieged woman who staggers into her physician's office with most of these symptoms, her condition has facetiously been called "The falling hand syndrome." She points to her left eyebrow and says, "Oh! My head has been splitting, and my ears have this funny ringing, and my breasts hurt and oh! My stomach is killing me; and I've got this pain in my lower back, and my buttocks hurt and my knee is quivering." Truly, her hand tumbles inch by inch from the top of her crown to the bottom of her aching feet. A physician told me recently that his nurse was attempting to obtain a medical history from such a woman who answered affirmatively to every possible disorder. Whatever disease or problem she mentioned, the patient professed to have had it. Finally in exasperation, the nurse asked if her teeth itched, just to see what the patient would say. The women frowned for a moment, then ran her tongue over her front teeth and said, "Come to think of it, they sure do!" A menopausal woman such as this is likely to think *everything* has gone wrong.[3]

**When I was young, my mother told me that menopause happens when a woman is about forty-five. I'm having some of the symptoms you have described, but I'm only thirty-seven. Surely I'm too young for menopause, don't you think?**

The age of onset of menopause varies widely. It can occur at *any* adult age—as early as the twenties or as late as the fifties. As your mother indicated, the early forties represent the mid-range, but individuals differ significantly.[4]

**I am going through menopause now. The things you have said about the causes of my uncomfortable symptoms are very helpful, and I really understand myself better now. But what I want to know is, "Will this ever end? Will I feel like my old self again someday?"**

There is definitely a silver lining to the dark cloud that hangs over you now! The experience is not a permanent state, but a stage of a journey through which some women must go. But "this too shall pass." It may last for several years, but *it will pass.* Just as with men in mid-life crisis, the period after menopause can be brighter, happier, more stable and more healthy than any other period of life. Often, a more balanced personality develops after menopause and greater energy is experienced. A better day *is* coming!

Incidentally, the human female is the only member of the animal kingdom who outlives its reproductive capacity by a significant period of time. (Does that help your self-esteem?)[5]

**Why do some women make it through menopause without the need for estrogen replacement therapy?**

I don't think anyone can answer that question, because no one knows for sure what estrogen does to the feminine neurological apparatus. Perhaps the ovaries or the adrenal glands emit enough estrogen to satisfy the needs of a less vulnerable individual. At this point, little is known about the chemistry of the brain and the substances which are necessary for its proper functioning. The guide in treatment then, is the clinical signs and symptoms which the physician observes.[6]

**Is there a "male menopause" comparable to what is experienced by women?**

This is a question with strong cultural overtones which have clouded the truth. Some women apparently fear that female menopause will be used as an excuse to withhold positions of leadership from middle-aged women. Therefore, they stress the existence of a comparable "male menopause." While men do experience a climacteric which can be called menopausal, it is very different in origin and impact from that experienced by women. For men, the changes are not so related to hormonal alterations but are more psychological in nature. It is difficult for a man to face the fact that he will never reach the occupational goals that he set for himself . . . that his youth is rapidly vanishing . . . that he will soon be unattractive to the opposite sex . . . that his earlier dreams of glory and power will never be realized. Some men who have achieved less than they hoped are devastated by the realization that life is slipping away from them. This, primarily, is the male menopause. Some individuals respond to it by seeking an affair with a young girl to prove their continued virility; others become alcoholics; still others enter into dramatic periods of depression. But even when the emotional impact is extreme, it is usually motivated by the man's evaluation of his outside world. These same influences agitate a woman, but she has an additional hormonal turmoil undermining her security from within. Other things being equal, the feminine variety is more difficult to endure, particularly if it remains untreated.[7]

*Dr. Dobson's note: In January 1982 the Focus on the Family radio broadcast featured a series of interviews between myself and Southern California physician, Dr. Paul Chapman, on the subject of hormone imbalance—its symptoms and treatments.*

*As a companion to that series, Focus on the Family offered the following article which was brought to our attention by our guest-physician. Although it was originally published in 1963, Dr. Chapman feels the content of this article continues to represent the most concise and accurate explanation available on the subject of hormone imbalance in mid-life.*

*Notably missing from the article, of course, is any reference to the more recent controversy that has arisen over the use of estrogen replacement therapy (ERT). Several medical articles published during the mid-seventies served to validate the suspicion that prolonged and indiscriminate use of ERT seemed to be related to cancer of the uterus in some women. However, physicians remain divided on the risks involved in the careful, monitored use of the hormone. There are those, including Dr. Chapman, who believe that the consequences of not providing ERT to a woman who desperately needs it are more threatening than are the known risks of its use. Other physicians are philosophically opposed to estrogen replacement therapy in any instance.*

*Further gynecological investigations are currently underway in medical centers around the country. In the absence of definitive conclusions at this time, it is recommended that women with menopausal symptoms seek and accept the counsel of their physicians.*

HORMONE IMBALANCE IN MID-LIFE
*by Lawrence Galton*

A profound change now taking place in medical thinking could affect the life of millions of women—in fact, of virtually every woman.

"In my practice the menopause is a disease process, requiring active intervention." In these emphatic words Dr. Allan C. Barnes, chairman of the department of obstetrics and gynecology at Johns Hopkins University School of Medicine, has stated a revolutionary new concept now held by a growing number of leading gynecologists. It is a concept of importance to all women—and especially to younger women.

The concept is based on mounting evidence that—whether it comes as early as age thirty-five (as it does for some women) or as late as age fifty-five (as it does for some others)—the decline of the ovaries that brings on "change of life" can have more than a temporary impact. There can be serious, previously unappreciated consequences for the rest of a woman's life:

- This decline in ovarian function can take away from a woman many of her prized feminine attributes, changing the appearance of her body and even to some extent masculinizing it.
- The decline can produce many degenerative or irritative changes within her body.
- After menopause a woman may become prone, as she was not earlier, to heart disease and painful bone disease.
- The menopause can lead to a rapid decline in a woman's mental functioning—to an acceleration of her intellectual and psychological aging as well as her physical aging.

But this gloomy picture fortunately has a brighter side. There is evidence that these consequences need not be inevitable—that, if women are alert to them and seek help for them, they can often be overcome. And if young women are alert to them and seek help early enough, the consequences can often be prevented.

Indeed, the promise is that for young women a whole new era

of preventive medicine is at hand; for them, a diminishing return from life is not something to be listlessly expected but something to be actively avoided.

The new concept says, in effect, that menopause can be a deficiency disease—just as diabetes is a deficiency disease and hypothyroidism is a deficiency disease—and deficiency can be made up for the menopause just as it can be made up for other disorders.

*The Case of the Frantic Pituitary.* This concept developed because doctors have in recent years been devoting a great deal of study to the obvious symptoms of the menopause and also to other effects that have been not so obvious at all.

The obvious symptoms are the acute ones about which every woman has heard *ad nauseam.* The classic ill-famed one is the hot flash, a sudden sensation of heat that sweeps over the body to the head, producing an intense flushing of the face that is often followed by profuse sweating and cold shivering. Others include headache, weakness, palpitation, insomnia, and dizziness.

Often there are emotional difficulties. "It is as if the color of the lenses through which a woman sees the world were changed from rose to blue," one physician has said. "She becomes anxious, apprehensive, depressed, melancholic, irritable, and emotionally unstable."

What causes such disturbances?

Even as recently as two generations ago there was no basic understanding. Until the 1920s no one knew that the ovaries produce estrogen. Since that time it has become clear that it is this hormone that shapes a girl into a woman and permits her to bear children. The decline of the ovaries and of their estrogen production brings on menopause and, in doing so, grinds menstruation to a halt. But the ovarian decline can also produce upsets for other glands. The picture is this:

All through their active years the ovaries secrete estrogen under the command of the pituitary. The pituitary, master gland of the body at the base of the brain, also commands other important endocrine glands, including the thyroid and the adrenals. When at menopause the ovaries no longer are able to respond adequately to its order, the pituitary becomes disturbed. Its control over other glands is affected, and the result may be hormonal imbalance that affects the whole nervous system.

*More Than a "Brief Transition."* Not all women have great difficulty with acute menopausal symptoms. Actually, the decline in ovarian production during the aging process has extreme variation—and this is the reason there is such wide variation in the age at which menopause arrives.

When it does arrive, the ovaries may not shut down completely but may continue to secrete some estrogen; the adrenal glands atop the kidneys also produce some. The total varies from one woman to another. And so do the symptoms.

Thus, in one study covering 1,000 women, 50.8 percent were found to have no acute discomfort. Of those who experienced difficulties, 89.7 percent could work as usual without interruption; only 10.3 percent were truly incapacitated at intervals.

Treatment has in the past been largely conservative. The principle has been that "change of life" is simply a period of adjustment that may last from a few months to a year or two—till the body has a chance to become attuned to the new situation in which the ovaries no longer play their once-active role in the physical economy.

Reassurance has been a major part of therapy. The thought has been that women can, by understanding that menopause is a passing phase and any discomforts will before long disappear, go through the adjustment period much more easily. And the fact is that many have been relieved to a considerable extent of nervous and emotional disturbances and even of hot flashes by simple reassurance from a doctor in whom they have faith and who has been willing to take the time to provide reassurance.

In more severe cases estrogen has been used. The objective has been to employ it briefly, to use just enough to quiet the excited pituitary, and gradually to taper off the doses to help the body reach a new balance in easy stages—in short, to smooth the transition.

But of late there has been increasing evidence that there is much more to be considered than a short transition—that the ovaries, through their secretion of estrogen, have many roles beyond that of making reproduction possible and that their decline can have wide repercussions for the rest of a woman's life.

*A Key to Broken Hips and Heart Attacks.* One of the most striking—and potentially serious—consequences of estrogen decline is loss of protection against heart trouble.

Recent studies have been showing that hardening and narrowing of the arteries that feed the heart, a major cause of heart attacks, is as much as ten times more prevalent in men under age forty than in women of similar age. But after menopause the picture changes, and women as a group become equally prone to develop coronary disease. Estrogen, it seems, is a major factor in keeping down the blood levels of cholesterol and other fats that in excess are associated with *athero-sclerosis,* the hardening and narrowing of the coronary arteries. With the decline of ovarian-estrogen production a woman loses her favored status.

Another common aftermath of that decline is *osteoporosis,* a thinning of the bone structure. Estrogen has an influence on protein balance. With lower levels of the hormone, protein may be lost from bone, and calcium depletion may follow.

One frequent symptom of osteoporosis is chronic back pain. Osteoporosis may also weaken the bones enough so that they tend to break or to collapse more easily. "The eighty-year-old woman who suffers a fractured hip," says Dr. Barnes, "can blame it to some extent on the fact that her ovaries ceased functioning thirty years earlier." And fractures of other bones—in the wrists and ribs—often occur after mild injury.

Often, too, bones in the spinal column become compressed so that height is lost. And the spine may also develop an abnormal curvature that leads to the unattractive bent appearance that has come to be called "dowager's hump."

*A Loss of Femininity?* Estrogen has a great influence also on the *skin*—on its blood supply, elasticity, and other qualities. As ovarian-estrogen output wanes, the skin tends to lose its softness and to become tough, dry, inelastic, and scaly. Some women develop an annoying itch; others are bothered by sensations similar to those produced by insects crawling over the skin.

And there may be masculinization as well. In both men and women both male and female sex hormones are produced. It's the balance that counts. In women the adrenal glands secrete androgen, the male hormone. At menopause they continue to do so, and, with the ovaries producing less estrogen, the balance may be upset enough to cause an increase in facial hair and sometimes a tendency to baldness.

Nor do the effects of estrogen deprivation stop there. It is the increasing supply of estrogen at puberty that brings about breast development, leads to other changes in body contour, and causes the uterus to grow and the vagina to mature. And it is the declining supply at the menopause that leads to reverse changes in all these areas.

Deprived of high levels of the hormone, breasts lose their firmness and tend to become flabby. There is a tendency for fat to be deposited on the hips and upper thighs. The uterus begins to revert to its smaller preadolescent size. The vagina becomes shorter, loses its expandability, and—also because of estrogen deprivation—the lining of the vagina thins and tends to lose its normal acidity.

The loss of acidity may encourage the growth of infectious organisms, and the thinning of the vaginal lining also invites infection. The result is the common problem known as *senile vaginitis*, with its itching, burning, discharge, and sometimes the inability to have marital relations without pain.

Because there is a lymphatic connection between the vagina and the bladder through which infection may spread, vaginitis may lead to *cystitis*, a bladder inflammation that produces urinary urgency and frequency.

For some women there are distressing *arthralgias*, or joint pains. Estrogen deprivation does not, however, foment rheumatoid arthritis (peak incidence occurs before menopause) or osteoarthritis (this tends to increase in severity from late childhood).

*Emotional Woes May Develop.* As for *emotional upsets*, some physicians now feel that the physical changes occasioned by estrogen deprivation play a more important role than they have been credited with in the past.

True, there can be many other significant factors in bringing about anxiety and depression. Usually, when a woman reaches "the change," her children are grown up and leading their own lives and are no longer in need of her close attention. Her husband may be at the height of his career and preoccupied with it. She may feel less useful—especially if her life has been totally concentrated on her family and if she has no other interests.

Yet, as one physician puts it, "While these factors are disturbing, a mental adjustment for most women would not be too difficult were if not for the physical changes. A woman becomes acutely aware of her loss of physical attractiveness . . . sees the marked skin changes, disfiguring fat deposits, atrophy of her breasts. An irritated or inadequate vagina may bring more unhappiness. All of this has a profound effect upon her psyche."

*One Third of a Lifetime* . . . All told, the list of possible consequences stemming from the decline of the ovaries is a formidable one, and these consequences have grown in importance as the average life span of women has increased from only forty-eight years at the turn of the century to seventy-five years today. The average woman can expect to live one third of her life (and many women will live half their life) after what in effect amounts to the "death" of the ovaries.

Dr. William H. Masters of Washington University School of Medicine has termed this inability of the ovaries to keep functioning along with other organs "the Achilles' heel of a woman's body." And more and more physicians share his conviction that the medical profession, responsible for adding many years to life, must now face up to doing something about the ovarian-decline problem—"must accept the responsibility of developing effective physiological support."

In 1961 a special report on the status of therapy for the menopause authorized by the American Medical Association's Council on Drugs declared that not just the one to two years of menopause but management of the remaining years of a woman's life "has become the major problem."

*How Estrogen Therapy Can Help.* There now is evidence from many studies—some carried out over extended periods of time—that the problem can be solved. Estrogen for therapeutic use has been available for more than twenty-five years.

Dr. Stanley Wallach and Dr. Philip H. Hennemann of the Harvard Medical School recently reviewed their records of more than 200 women for whom they prescribed estrogen during the past quarter century:

- Of these women 94 were treated primarily for severe hot flashes that had in many cases been present for three or more years and that had in some cases failed to yield to sedatives and other measures. Estrogen quickly brought relief for 93 of the 94.
- There were 119 other women with severe osteoporosis. Complete relief or great reduction of pain occurred in 90 percent treated with estrogen. Usually pain diminished markedly within two months after start of treatment. A progressive further decrease in discomfort and increase in ability to move freely followed.

• In some of the women osteoporosis had led to losses of height—as much as five inches. Height loss ceased after estrogen was employed.

• And, significantly, in still another group of women, Dr. Wallach and Dr. Hennemann found that when estrogen was started early enough, before osteoporosis could develop, the hormone had a preventive effect. The bone disorder never did develop.

*Protection Against Heart Trouble.* Estrogen's value for coronary-artery disease—both for treatment and prevention—is being demonstrated increasingly. Physicians have been giving the hormone to women (and to men, as well) who had already experienced a first heart attack. The treatment has markedly reduced the incidence of subsequent attacks and has extended life.

In long-term studies covering more than 200 women, Dr. M. Edward Davis and his associates at the University of Chicago have been investigating estrogen's preventive value. They have reported that, in comparison with other women, those receiving the hormone after menopause have lowered levels of cholesterol and other fats in the blood and also show a lower incidence of the abnormal electrocardiograms that indicate heart trouble. And another gratifying finding has been that women under treatment with estrogen for ten or more years have a lowered incidence of high blood pressure.

*Can Other Problems Be Avoided?* Doctors have been finding estrogen valuable—sometimes dramatically so—in combating many of the other problems of women during and after menopause.

The hormone is no panacea for the skin and will not restore the bloom of sixteen, but estrogen treatment does greatly improve elasticity and can help to overcome dryness.

In vaginitis, estrogen is remarkably effective, often restoring the vaginal lining to normal within a month and reestablishing vaginal acidity as well. Itching and discharge disappear. Cystitis may also improve.

Many women with joint pains have had gratifying relief with estrogen treatment. And, Dr. Masters has reported, except for the ovaries themselves, all pelvic organs and the breasts are capable of reversing their decline and returning to normal size and function under the influence of estrogen therapy.

Investigators at the Washington University department of

neuropsychiatry have reported studies indicating that estrogen treatment is of some value for intellectual function—that such basic mental processes as memory for recent events, power of definitive thinking, and the ability to absorb new material show some degree of improvement. The amount varies among individuals, but appears to be directly related to the time when treatment is begun—and the earlier treatment is started, the better.

In April, 1963, a medical report, "A Plea for the Maintenance of Adequate Estrogen from Puberty to the Grave," in *The Journal of the American Geriatrics Society* summed up by noting that women in the past *had* to become "stiff, frail, bent, wrinkled, and apathetic . . . they stumbled through their remaining years. The amount and variety of suffering was great. There was little or nothing to do for their skin problems . . . osteoporosis, irritating leucorrheas [vaginal discharge], cracked and bleeding vulvas. It was part of being old. If left to nature, it still is, but most of this suffering can now be prevented and effectively treated."

*What Risk of Cancer?* Is there any risk in hormone treatment? In the past there has been fear that estrogen might provoke breast or genital cancer. But the 1961 report authorized by the A.M.A.'s Council on Drugs declared that such fear "does not seem justified on the basis of available evidence."

Evidence *against* any such hazard has been coming increasingly from many sources.

For one thing, incidence of cancer at all sites in women increases steadily with age, even as production of estrogen decreases.

For another, investigators have been pointing out that if estrogen provoked cancer, breast cancer should then be encountered frequently in pregnancy because estrogen levels increase greatly, especially in the late months. But breast cancer has been found to be rare in pregnancy.

Studies with animals given large doses of estrogen have revealed no cancer-producing effect—and neither have a number of long-term studies of estrogen treatment in women.

In one study 206 women were treated over a five-and-a-half-year period; no case of cancer developed. In another study covering 120 post-menopausal women treated over an extended period, no cancer was observed, though five to six malignancies were to be expected in that time.

In reporting their twenty-five-year experience with the use of estrogen, Dr. Wallach and Dr. Hennemann of Harvard noted that cancer of the breast was not detected in any patient during prolonged treatment, and only one genital cancer developed. They concluded that "prolonged, cyclic, oral estrogen therapy combined with periodic pelvic and vaginal examinations is a safe and effective therapy."

In 1962 in the *Journal of the American Medical Association* Dr. Robert A. Wilson of the Methodist Hospital of Brooklyn reported on a group of 304 women whose ages ranged from forty to seventy years and who had been treated with estrogens for periods up to twenty-seven years. An estimated eighteen cases of cancer, either breast or genital, he pointed out, would normally have been expected to occur in this number of women. Instead, no cases of cancer were seen.

Far from inducing cancer, Dr. Wilson noted, estrogen may very well have a *preventive* action. "It would seem advisable," he reported, "to keep women endocrine-rich and consequently cancer-poor throughout their lives."

*There Are Side Effects.* Use of estrogen, however, has not been without problems in the past, and there are some today.

The first compounds were useless when taken by mouth; they had to be injected. Now there are numerous preparations that are effective if taken orally, but they must be used under close medical supervision with careful attention to proper individual dosage.

Some women benefit from very tiny amounts; others require ten times as much. Especially in large amounts, the hormone may provoke irregular bleeding in some women.

Such bleeding is of no importance in itself; it will stop when the drug is withdrawn for a time. But such bleeding clouds the problem of early diagnosis of uterine cancer. Irregular bleeding in the later years can come from not-serious causes, such as polyps, but may also indicate malignancy. And because such malignancy can be cured in its early stages, doctors have learned for safety's sake to consider irregular bleeding as an indication of cancer till definitely proved otherwise.

Trying to avoid the problem of irregular bleeding—and the possible need for curettage to rule out cancer—some doctors use cyclic administration of estrogen and find it effective. They have women take the drug for twenty-five days, stop it for five days, and then resume again—or use another similar schedule of on-and-off treatment.

Some physicians employ a combination of estrogen and androgen, the male sex hormone. And androgen often has another happy effect: It increases the general sense of well-being.

But the estrogen-androgen ratio can be critical. While a ration of twenty units of androgen to one of estrogen has proved valuable for the majority of women, it produces hirsutism, especially growth of facial hair, in about 20 percent. Some physicians have recently been finding that a ten-to-one ratio is effective and greatly reduces the incidence of hirsutism.

It is hoped that pharmaceutical research—now intensive in the hormone field—will before long be able to produce new synthetic compounds that will not have undesirable properties.

*A Matter of "Medical Management."* Today the big question among gynecologists is just how many women need hormone supplementation.

Some physicians are convinced that every woman should have estrogen treatment not just at menopause but for the rest of life. They feel that other forms of medical management should not be abandoned. Explanation, reassurance, nutritional-and-weight guidance, the use of tranquilizers and other drugs all have their place in individual cases. But these physicians see menopause marking the beginning of a state of estrogen deficiency that demands prolonged estrogen treatment just as diabetes or any other deficiency state demands continued treatment.

Some start treatment after a woman has been free of menses for six months—though estrogen may be employed as early as two months after the last period if a woman complains of hot flashes or other uncomfortable symptoms. And these physicians believe in the need for treatment regardless of whether symptoms are present.

Many other physicians, because there can be great variations in natural estrogen production during and after menopause, are not convinced that treatment should be routine for every woman.

"They do feel, however," says Dr. Edmund Overstreet, professor of obstetrics and gynecology at the University of California, "that approximately 25 percent of post-menopausal women have a true estrogen-deficiency disease that should be supplemented with estrogen therapy for the rest of these women's lives in order to protect them."

All authorities unite in emphasizing one thing—the need for

recognizing that estrogen does not "fix everything." Although it can be valuable in many ways, estrogen is certainly no cure-all. Problems can arise during or after menopause, just as at any other time of life, that have nothing to do with the menopause and for which estrogen is of no value. Careful and regular medical checkups remain vital.

*A Test for Estrogen Deficiency.* It will take years of experience before the question of whether every woman needs treatment is settled. Better tests could help. Currently the *vaginal smear*—the same test used for cancer detection—can be used to estimate the degree of estrogen deprivation. The smear shows changes in the vaginal lining caused by lack of the hormone and, because the smear also shows beneficial changes when estrogen is given, helps determine the proper dosage. But many physicians feel that more refined and exact tests are needed and will soon be coming.

As of now, most doctors undoubtedly will prefer not to use hormone supplementation routinely but on an individual basis—nor would it be wise for any woman to demand it willy-nilly.

The really important point is this: Every woman can now count on her doctor to take a vigorous interest, more vigorous than ever before, in her progress through and beyond menopause; to be alert to her needs and—with the mounting evidence of its effectiveness and safety—to use hormone treatment, if it seems called for, to make the "change of life" and all the rest of her life healthier and happier. [End of article.]

# SECTION 26

# MALE AND FEMALE UNIQUENESS

**How do men and women differ emotionally?**
Female emotions are influenced by three exclusively feminine reproductive functions: menstruation, lactation, and pregnancy. Furthermore, the hypothalamus, which is located at the base of the brain and has been called the "seat of the emotions," is apparently wired very differently for males than for females. For example, a severe emotional shock or trauma can be interpreted by the hypothalamus, which then sends messages to the pituitary by way of neurons and hormones. The pituitary often responds by changing the biochemistry of the woman, perhaps interrupting the normal menstrual cycle for six months or longer. Female physiology is a finely tuned instrument, being more complex and vulnerable than the masculine counterpart. Why some women find that fact insulting is still a mystery to me.[1]

**You've mentioned some of the ways the sexes differ physiologically and concomitantly in emotional responses. Could you now describe some of the more *subtle* ways males and females are unique?**
Medical science has not begun to identify all the ramifications of sexual uniqueness. The implications are extremely subtle. For example, when researchers quietly walked on high school and college campuses to study behavior of the sexes, they observed that males and females even transported their books in different ways. The young men tended to carry them at their sides with their arms looped over the top. Women and girls, by contrast, usually cradled their books at their breasts, in much the same

way they would a baby. Who can estimate how many other sex-related influences lie below the level of consciousness?

Admittedly, some of the observed differences between the sexes are culturally produced. I don't know how to sort out those which are exclusively genetic from those which represent learned responses. Frankly, it doesn't seem to matter a great deal. The differences exist, for whatever reason, and the current cultural revolution will not alter most of them significantly. At the risk of being called a sexist, or a propagator of sexual stereotypes, or a male chauvinist pig (or worse), let me delineate a few of the emotional patterns typical of women as compared with men.

The reproductive capacity of women results in a greater appreciation for stability, security, and enduring human relationships. In other words, females are more *future*-oriented because of their procreative physiology and its motivating concern for children.

Related to the first item is a women's emotional investment in her home, which usually exceeds that of her husband. She typically cares more than he about the minor details of the house, family functioning, and such concerns. To cite a personal example, my wife and I decided to install a new gas barbecue unit in our backyard. When the plumber completed the assignment and departed, Shirley and I both recognized that he had placed the appliance approximately six inches too high. I looked at the device and said, "Hmmm, yes sir, he sure made a mistake. That post is a bit too high. By the way, what are we having for dinner tonight?" Shirley's reaction was dramatically different. She said, "The plumber has that thing sticking up in the air and I don't think I can stand it!" Our contrasting views represented a classic difference of emotional intensity relating to the home.

But the sexes are also different in competitive drive. Anyone who doubts that fact should observe how males and females approach a game of Ping-Pong, Monopoly, dominoes, horseshoes, volleyball, or tennis. Women may use the event as an excuse for fellowship and pleasant conversation. For men, the name of the game is *conquest*. Even if the setting is a friendly social gathering in the host's backyard, the beads of sweat on each man's forehead reveal his passion to win. This aggressive competitiveness has been attributed to cultural influences. I don't believe it. As Dr. Richard Restak said in his book, *The Brain! The Lost Frontier:* "At a birthday party for five-year-olds, it's not usually the girls who pull hair, throw punches, or smear each other with food."

Furthermore, a maternal inclination apparently operates in most women, although its force is stronger in some than others. The desire to procreate is certainly evident in those who are unable to conceive. I receive a steady influx of letters from women who express great frustration from their inability to become mothers. Although culture plays a major role in these longings, I believe they are rooted in female anatomy and physiology.

These items are illustrative and are not intended to represent a scientific delineation of male and female differences. Thus, the examples I've listed merely scratch the surface, and you are invited to add your own observations and make your own interpretations.[2]

**You have stated in your books that men and women develop self-esteem in a different way. Would you explain that uniqueness?**

Men and women have the same needs for self-worth and belonging, but they typically approach those needs from a different angle . . . especially if the woman is a full-time homemaker. A man derives his sense of worth primarily from the reputation he earns in his job or profession. He draws emotional satisfaction from achieving in business, becoming financially independent, developing a highly respected craft or skill, supervising others, becoming "boss," or by being loved and appreciated by his patients, clients, or fellow businessmen. The man who is successful in these areas does not depend on his wife as his *primary* shield against feelings of inferiority. Of course, she plays an important role as his companion and lover, but she isn't essential to his self-respect day by day.

By contrast, a homemaker approaches her marriage from a totally different perspective. She does not have access to "other" sources of self-esteem commonly available to her husband. She can cook a good dinner, but once it is eaten, her family may not even remember to thank her for it. Her household duties do not bring her respect in the community, and she is not likely to be praised for the quality of her dusting techniques. Therefore, the more isolated she becomes, the more vital her man will be to her sense of fulfillment, confidence, and well-being. Let's reduce it to a useful oversimplification: men derive self-esteem by being respected; women feel worthy when they are *loved.* This may be the most important personality distinction between the sexes.[3]

**Is the felt need for sex the same in both males and females?**

Men and women differ significantly in their manifestations of sexual desire. Recent research seems to indicate that the intensity of pleasure and excitation at the time of orgasm in women and ejaculation in men is about the same for both sexes, although the pathway to that climax takes a different route. Most men can become excited more quickly than women. They may reach a point of finality before their mates get their minds off the evening meal and what the kids will wear tomorrow morning. It is a wise man who recognizes this feminine inertia, and brings his wife along at her own pace.

This coin has two sides, however. Women should also understand how their husbands' needs differ from their own. When sexual response is blocked in males, they experience an accumulating physiological pressure which demands release. Two seminal vesicles (small sacs containing semen) gradually fill to capacity; as maximum level is reached, hormonal influences sensitize the man to all sexual stimuli. Whereas a particular woman would be of little interest to him when he is satisfied, he may be eroticized just to be in her presence when he is in a state of deprivation. A wife may find it difficult to comprehend this accumulating aspect of her husband's sexual appetite, since her needs are typically less urgent and pressing. Thus, she should recognize that his desire is dictated by definite biochemical forces within his body, and if she loves him, she will seek to satisfy those needs as meaningfully and as regularly as possible. I'm not denying that women have definite sexual needs which seek gratification; rather, I am merely explaining that abstinence is usually more difficult for men to tolerate.[4]

**Can you be more specific regarding the differences in sexual desire and preferences between males and females? Since I'm getting married next July, I would like to know how my future husband's need will differ from my own. Could you summarize the major distinctions that will occur between us?**

You are wise to ask this question, because the failures to understand male and female preferences often produces a continual source of marital frustration and guilt.

First, men are primarily aroused by *visual* stimulation. They are turned on by feminine nudity or peek-a-boo glimpses of semi-nudity. Women, on the other hand, are much less visually oriented than men. Sure,they are interested in attractive masculine bodies, but the physiological mechanism of sex is not triggered, typically, by what they see; women are stimulated primarily by the sense of touch. Thus, we encounter the first source of disagreement in the bedroom; he wants her to appear unclothed in a lighted room, and she wants him to caress her in the dark.

Second, and much more important, men are not very discriminating in regard to the person living within an interesting body. A man can walk down a street and be stimulated by a scantily clad female who shimmies past him, even though he knows nothing about her personality or values or mental capabilities. He is attracted by her body itself. Likewise, he can become almost as excited over a photograph of an unknown nude model as he can in a face-to-face encounter with someone he loves. In essence, the sheer biological power of sexual desire in a male is largely focused on the physical body of an attractive female. Hence, there is some validity to the complaint by women that they have been used as "sex objects" by men. This explains why female prostitutes outnumber males by a wide margin and why few women try to "rape" men. It explains why a roomful of toothless old men can get a large charge from watching a burlesque dancer "take it all off." It reflects the fact that masculine self-esteem is more motivated by a desire to "conquer" a woman than in becoming the object of her romantic love. These are not very flattering characteristics of male sexuality, but they are well documented in the professional literature.

Women, on the other hand, are much more discriminating in their sexual interests. They less commonly become excited by observing a good-looking charmer, or by the photograph of a hairy model; rather, their desire is usually focused on a particular individual whom they respect or admire. A woman is stimulated by the romantic aura which surrounds her man, and by his character and personality. She yields to the man who appeals to her emotionally as well as physically. Obviously, there are exceptions to these characteristic desires, but the fact remains: sex for men is a more physical phenomenon; sex for women is a deeply emotional experience.[5]

**You've discussed physical differences between the sexes as related to reproduction. Could you list the other *physical* characteristics of males and females?**

Dr. Paul Popenoe, the late founder of the American Institute of

Family Relations in Los Angeles, wrote a brief article on the subject you have raised. I will let him respond to the question, *Are Women Really Different?*[6]

1. Men and women differ in every cell of their bodies. This difference in the chromosome combination is the basic cause of development into maleness or femaleness as the case may be.

2. Woman has greater constitutional vitality, perhaps because of this chromosome difference. Normally, she outlives man by three or four years in the U.S.

3. The sexes differ in their basal metabolism—that of woman being normally lower than that of man.

4. They differ in skeletal structure, woman having a shorter head, broader face, chin less protruding, shorter legs, and longer trunk. The first finger of a woman's hand is usually longer than the third; with men the reverse is true. Boys' teeth last longer than do those of girls.

5. Woman has a larger stomach, kidneys, liver, and appendix, and smaller lungs.

6. In function, woman has several very important ones totally lacking in man—menstruation, pregnancy, lactation. All of these influence behavior and feelings. She has more different hormones than does man. The same gland behaves differently in the two sexes—thus woman's thyroid is larger and more active; it enlarges during pregnancy but also during menstruation; it makes her more prone to goiter, provides resistance to cold, is associated with the smooth skin, relatively hairless body, and thin layer of subcutaneous fat which are important elements in the concept of personal beauty. It also contributes to emotional instability—she laughs and cries more easily.

7. Woman's blood contains more water (20 percent fewer red cells). Since these supply oxygen to the body cells, she tires more easily, is more prone to faint. Her constitutional viability is therefore strictly a long-range matter. When the working day in British factories, under wartime conditions, was increased from ten to twelve hours, accidents of women increased 150 percent, of men not at all.

8. In brute strength, men are 50 percent above women.

9. Woman's heart beats more rapidly (80, versus 72 for men); blood pressure (ten points lower than man) varies from minute to minute; but she has much less tendency to

high blood pressure—at least until after the menopause.

10. Her vital capacity or breathing power is lower in the 7:10 ratio.

11. She stands high temperature better than does man; metabolism slows down less.[7]

SECTION 27

# THE MEANING OF MASCULINITY

**It is apparent from reading your book, *Straight Talk to Men and Their Wives*, that you are a strong advocate of masculine leadership at home. What response do you offer to activist women who would consider this view to be chauvinistic and archaic?**

It is important to understand what I mean by masculine leadership. I don't attempt to justify men who oppress their children or show disregard for the needs and wishes of their wives. That kind of nineteenth century authoritarianism is dead, and may it rest in peace. However, I do believe that the Scriptures (which are the standard by which I measure *everything*) make it clear that men have been assigned the primary responsibility for the provision of authority in the home. At least, this is the way I understand the biblical prescription. Ephesians 5:22-28 states:

> Wives, be subject to your husbands, as to the Lord. For the husband is the head of the wife as Christ is the head of the church, his body, and is himself its Savior. As the church is subject to Christ, so let wives also be subject in everything to their husbands. Husbands, love your wives, as Christ loved the church and gave himself up for her, that he might sanctify her, having cleansed her by the washing of water with the word, that he might present the church to himself in splendor, without spot or wrinkle or any such thing, that she might be holy and without blemish. Even so husbands should love their wives as their own bodies. He who loves his wife loves himself (RSV).

This Scripture, combined with the many others relating to wives' submission to husbands' authority (1 Peter 3:1 KJV, for example: "Likewise, ye wives, be in subjection to your own husbands; that, if any obey not the word, they also may without the word be won by the conversation of the wives.") makes it clear to me that a Christian man is obligated to lead his family to the best of his ability. God apparently expects a man to be the ultimate decision-maker in his family. Likewise, he bears heavier responsibility for the outcome of those decisions. If his family has purchased too many items on credit, then the financial crunch is ultimately his fault. If the family never reads the Bible or seldom goes to church on Sunday, God holds the man to blame. If the children are disrespectful and disobedient, the primary responsibility lies with the father . . . not his wife. (I don't remember Eli's wife being criticized for raising two evil sons; it was her husband who came under God's wrath. See 1 Samuel 3:13.)

From this perspective, what happens to a family when the designated leader doesn't do his job? Similar consequences can be seen in a corporation whose president only pretends to direct the company. The organization disintegrates very quickly. The parallel to leaderless families is too striking to be missed. In my view, America's greatest need is for husbands to begin guiding their families, rather than pouring every physical and emotional resource into the mere acquisition of money.[1]

**Would you be more specific about the relationship between the sexes? Am I to assume you do not favor a fifty-fifty arrangement in the husband-wife interaction?**
That is correct. However, let me offer two opinions about the ideal relationship between husbands and wives that may clarify my viewpoint. First, because of the fragile nature of the male ego and a man's enormous need to be respected, combined with female vulnerability and a woman's need to be loved, I feel it is a mistake to tamper with the time-honored relationship of husband as loving protector and wife as recipient of that protection.

Second, because two captains sink the ship and two cooks spoil the broth, I feel that a family must have a leader whose decisions prevail in times of differing opinions. If I understand the Scriptures, that role has been assigned to the man of the house. However, he must not incite his crew to mutiny by heavy-handed disregard for their feelings and needs. He should, in fact, put the best interests of his family above his own, even to the point of death, if necessary. Nowhere in Scripture is he authorized to become a dictator or slave-owner.

Other combinations of husband-wife teamwork have been successful in individual families, but I've seen many complications occurring in marriages where the man was passive, weak, and lacking in qualities of leadership. None of the modern alternatives has improved on the traditional masculine role as prescribed in the Good Book. It was, after all, inspired by the Creator of mankind.[2]

**Much has been written and said recently about the "macho" man who is unable to reveal his true emotions and feelings. Do you agree that American men have too tight a rein on their emotions and should learn to loosen them up?**

Perhaps so. It is important for men to be willing (and able) to cry and love and hope. My father, who symbolized masculinity for me, was a very tender man who was not ashamed to weep. On the other hand, there are dangers in permitting emotions to rule our minds. Feelings must not dominate rational judgment, especially in times of crisis, nor should we allow the minor frustrations of living to produce depression and despair. Both men and women must learn to ventilate their feelings and be "real" people, without yielding to the tyranny of fluctuating emotions.[3]

**What do you feel is a father's number one priority?**

His most important responsibility, I believe, is to communicate the real meaning of Christianity to his children. This mission can be likened to a three-man relay race. First, your father runs his lap around the track, carrying the baton, which represents the gospel of Jesus Christ. At the appropriate moment, he hands the baton to you, and you begin your journey around the track. Then finally, the time will come when you must get the baton safely in the hands of your children. But as any track coach will testify, *relay races are won or lost in the transfer of the baton.* There is a critical moment when all can be lost by a fumble or miscalculation. The baton is rarely dropped on the back side of the track when the runner has it firmly in his grasp. If failure is to occur, it will probably happen in the exchange between generations.

According to the Christian values which govern my life, my most important reason for living is to get the baton, the gospel, safely in the hands of my children. Of course, I want to place it in as many other hands as possible; *nevertheless, my number one responsibility is to evangelize my own children.* I hope millions of other fathers agree with that ultimate priority.[4]

**I agree with your belief that the father should be the spiritual leader in the family, but it just doesn't happen that way at our house. If the kids go to church on Sunday, it's because I wake them up and see that they get ready. If we have family devotions, it's done at my insistence, and I'm the one who prays with the children at bedtime. If I didn't do these things, our kids would have no spiritual training. Nevertheless, people keep saying that I should wait for my husband to accept spiritual leadership in our family. What do you advise in my situation?**

That's an extremely important question, and a subject of some controversy right now. As you indicated, some Christian leaders instruct women to wait passively for their husbands to assume spiritual responsibility. Until that leadership is accepted, they recommend that wives stay out of the way and let God put pressure on the husband to assume the role that He's given to men. I strongly disagree with that view when small children are involved. If the issue focused only on the spiritual welfare of a husband and wife, then a woman could afford to bide her time. However, the presence of boys and girls changes the picture dramatically. Every day that goes by without spiritual training for them is a day that can never be recaptured.

Therefore, if your husband is not going to accept the role of spiritual leadership that God has given him, then I believe you must do it. You have no time to lose. You should continue taking the family to church on Sunday. You should pray with the children and teach them to read the Bible. Furthermore, you must continue your private devotions and maintain your own relationship with God. In short, I feel that the spiritual life of children (and adults) is simply too important for a woman to postpone for two or four or six years, hoping her husband will eventually awaken. Jesus made it clear that members of our own family can erect the greatest barriers to our faith, but must not be permitted to do so. He says, "Do not think that I have come to bring peace on earth; I have not come to bring peace, but a sword. For I have come to set a man against his father, and a daughter against her mother, and a daughter-in-law against her mother-in-law; and a man's foes will be those of his own household. He who loves father or mother more than me is not worthy of me; and he who loves son or daughter more than me is not worthy of me" (Matt. 10:34-37 RSV).

This conflict has been experienced with our own family. My grandfather, R. L. Dobson, was a moral man who saw no need for the Christian faith. His spiritual disinterest placed my grandmother, Juanita Dobson, under great pressure, for she was a devout Christian who felt she must put God first. Therefore, she accepted the responsibility of introducing her six children to Jesus Christ. There were times when my grandfather exerted tremendous pressure on her, not to give up the faith, but to leave him out of it.

He said, "I am a good father and provider, I pay my bills, and I am honest in dealing with my fellow man. That is enough."

His wife replied, "You are a good man, but that is *not* enough. You should give your heart to God." This he could not comprehend.

My 97-pound grandmother made no attempt to force her faith on her husband, nor did she treat him disrespectfully. But she quietly continued to pray and fast for the man she loved. For more than forty years she brought this same petition before God on her knees.

Then at sixty-nine years of age, my grandfather suffered a stroke, and for the first time in his life he was desperately ill. One day his young daughter came into his room to clean and straighten. As she walked by his bed, she saw tears in his eyes. No one had ever seen him cry before.

"Daddy, what's wrong?" she asked.

He responded, "Honey, go to the head of the stairs and call your mother."

My grandmother ran to her husband's side and heard him say, "I know I'm going to die and I'm not afraid of death, but it's so dark. There's no way out. I've lived my whole life through and missed the one thing that really matters. Will you pray for me?"

"Will I pray?" exclaimed my grandmother. She had been hoping for that request throughout her adult life. She fell to her knees and the intercessions of forty years seemed to pour out through that bedside prayer. R. L. Dobson gave his heart to God that day in a wonderful way.

During the next two weeks, he asked to see some of the

church people whom he had offended and requested their forgiveness. He concluded his personal affairs and then died with a testimony on his lips. Before descending into a coma from which he would never awaken, my grandfather said, ". . . Now there is a way through the darkness."

The unrelenting prayers of my little grandmother had been answered.

Returning to the question, I would like to caution women not to become "self-righteous" and critical of their husbands. Let everything be done in a spirit of love. However, there may be some lonely years when the burden of spiritual leadership with children must be carried alone. If that is the case, the Lord has promised to walk with you through these difficult days.[5]

**I keep hearing that it is unwise to get too carried away with the successes of your kids, but I can't help it. Is it wrong for me to feel a sense of fatherly pride when my son succeeds in basketball? How can I not *care* about the quality of his performance?**

There's nothing wrong about feeling good about the successes of our children. The problem occurs when parents care *too much* about those triumphs and failures . . . when their own egos are riding on the kids' performances . . . when winning is necessary to maintain their parents' respect and love. Boys and girls should know they are accepted simply because they are God's own creation. That is enough!

I'm reminded of John McKay, the former football coach from the University of Southern California. I saw him interviewed on television at a time when his son, John, Junior, was a successful football player on the USC team. The interviewer referred to John's athletic talent and asked Coach McKay to comment on the pride he must feel over his son's accomplishments on the field. His answer was most impressive:

"Yes, I'm pleased that John had a good season last year. He does a fine job and I am proud of him. But I would be just as proud if he had never played the game at all."

Coach McKay was saying, in effect, that John's football talent is recognized and appreciated, but his human worth does not depend on his ability to play football. Thus, his son would not lose respect if the next season brought failure and disappointment. John's place in his dad's heart was secure, being independent of his performance. I wish every child could say the same.

**Traditionally, fathers have been relatively uninvolved in the discipline of preschool children. How do you feel about the importance of paternal involvement?**
It is extremely important for fathers to help discipline and participate in the parenting process when possible. Children need their fathers and respond to their masculine manner, of course, but wives need the involvement of their husbands, too. This is especially true of homemakers who have done combat duty through the long day and find themselves in a state of battle fatigue by nightfall. Husbands get tired too, of course, but if they can hold together long enough to help get the little tigers in bed, nothing could contribute more to the stability of their homes. I am especially sympathetic with the mother who is raising a toddler or two and an infant at the same time. There is no more difficult assignment on the face of the earth. Husbands who recognize this fact can help their wives feel understood, loved, and supported in the vital jobs they are doing.[6]

**Our two children will obey my husband with just a word from him, even responding to a slight frown when we are in a group setting. But I have to scream and threaten to make them mind. Why do you suppose this is true?**
That difference in response usually results from the factors: (1) The father is more likely to back up his commands with *action* if the children don't obey, and the kids know it; (2) The mother spends more time with the children, and as they say, "familiarity breeds contempt"—her authority gradually erodes under constant pressure.

There is another phenomenon at work, however, which I would like to consider in greater detail. I'm referring to the fact that children naturally look to their father for authority. When our son Ryan was four years old, he overheard a reference to my childhood.

"Daddy, were you ever a little boy?" he asked.

"Yes, Ryan, I was smaller than you," I replied.

"Were you ever a baby?" he inquired with disbelief.

"Yes. Everyone is a tiny baby when he is born."

Ryan looked puzzled. He simply could not comprehend his 6-foot 2-inch, 190-pound father as an infant. He thought for a minute and then said, "Were you a daddy-baby?"

It was impossible for Ryan to imagine me without the mantle of authority, even if I were a tiny newborn. His nine-year-old sister reacted similarly the first time she was shown home movies of me when I was only four. There on the screen was a baby-faced, innocent lad on a horse. Danae had to be assured that the picture was of me, whereupon she exclaimed, "That kid spanks me?"

Danae and Ryan both revealed their perception of me . . . not as a man who had been given authority . . . but as a man who *was* authority. Such is the nature of childhood. Boys and girls typically look to their fathers, whose size and power and deeper voices bespeak leadership. That's why, despite numerous exceptions, men teachers are likely to handle classroom discipline more easily that soft ladies with feminine voices. (A woman teacher once told me that the struggle to control her class was like trying to keep thirty-two Ping-Pong balls under water at the same time.)

That is also why mothers need the disciplinary involvement of their husbands. Not that a man must handle every act of disobedience, but he should serve as the frame on which parental authority is constructed. Furthermore, it must be clear to the kids that Dad is in agreement with Mother's policies and he will defend her in instances of insurrection. Referring to 1 Timothy 3:4, this is what is meant by a father having the "proper authority in his own household."[7]

**What is the "mid-life" crisis that many men experience?**
It is a time of intense personal evaluation when frightening and disturbing thoughts surge through a man's mind, posing questions about who he is and why he's here and what it all matters. It is a period of self-doubt and disenchantment with everything familiar and stable. It represents terrifying thoughts that can't be admitted or revealed even to those closest to him. These anxieties often produce an uncomfortable separation between loved ones at a time when support and understanding are desperately needed.[8]

**When does the mid-life crisis typically occur and how universal is it among men?**
This time of self-doubt usually occurs during the third or fourth decades of life, but can transpire during the fifth. Concerning the incidence, Lee Stockford reported the findings of three studies involving more than 2100 persons and concluded that 80 percent of the executives between thirty-four and forty-two

years of age experience a mid-life trauma of some variety. This estimate is consistent with my own observations, especially among highly motivated, successful business and professional men.[9]

**What does a man experience during a full-fledged mid-life crisis?**

Dr. Jim Conway has written a book called *Men in Mid-Life Crisis* (David C. Cook, 1978) which I recommend highly. In it, he identifies four major "enemies" which plague a man entering this stressful period. The first is his own body. There is no doubt about it; that guy they called "Joe College" just a few years ago is now growing older. His hair is falling out, despite desperate attempts to coddle and protect every remaining strand. "Me, bald?" he shudders. Then he notices he doesn't have the stamina he once had. He begins getting winded on escalators. Before long, words assume new meanings for Ol' Joe. "The rolling stones" are in his gall bladder and "speed" (which once referred to amphetamines or fast driving) is his word for prune juice. He takes a business trip and the stewardess offers him "coffee, tea, or milk of magnesia." The cells in his face then pack up and run south for the winter, leaving a shocked and depressed Joseph standing two inches from the mirror in disbelief.

To summarize this first great concern of the mid-life years, a man approaching forty is forced to admit: (1) he is getting older; (2) the changes produced by aging are neither attractive nor convenient; (3) in a world that equates human worth with youth and beauty, he is about to suffer a personal devaluation; and (4) old age is less than two decades away, bringing eventual sickness and death. When a man confronts this package for the first time, he is certain to experience an emotional reverberation from its impact.

The second enemy facing a man in his mid-life years is his work. He typically resents his job and feels trapped in the field he has chosen. Many blue- and white-collar workers wish they'd had the opportunity to study medicine or law or dentistry. Little do they realize that physicians and attorneys and orthodontists often wish they had selected less demanding occupations . . . jobs that could be forgotten on evenings and weekends . . . jobs that didn't impose the constant threat of malpractice suits . . . jobs that left time for recreation and hobbies. This occupational unrest at all socioeconomic levels reaches a peak of intensity in the middle years, when the new awareness of life's brevity makes men reluctant to squander a single day that remains. But, on the other hand, they have little choice. The financial needs of their families demand that they keep pressing . . . so the kids can go to college . . . so the house payment can be met . . . so the lives they have known can continue. Thus, their emotions are caught in an ever-tightening vise.

The third enemy that rises to confront a middle-aged man is, believe it or not, his own family. These stormy years of self-doubt and introspection can be devastating to marriage. Such a man often becomes angry and depressed and rebellious toward those closest to him. He resents the fact that his wife and kids need him. No matter how hard he works, they always require more money than he can earn, and that agitates him further. At a time when he is in a selfish mood, wanting to meet his own needs, it seems that every member of the family is pulling on him. Even his parents have now become his financial and emotional responsibility. Again, he is seized by the urge to run.

The fourth and final enemy of a man in mid-life crisis appears to be God Himself. Through a strange manipulation of logic, man blames the Creator for all his troubles, approaching Him with rebellion and anger. In return, he feels condemned and abandoned and unloved by God. The consequence is a weakened faith and a crumbling system of beliefs. This explains, more than any other factor, the radical changes in behavior that often accompany the struggles of middle life.

Let me give this latter point the strongest possible emphasis. One of the most common observations made by relatives and friends of a man in mid-life crisis reflects this sudden reversal of personality and behavior.

"I don't understand what happened to Loren," a wife will say. "He seemed to change overnight from a stable, loving husband and father to an irresponsible rogue. He quit going to church. He began openly flirting with other women. He lost interest in our sons. Even his clothing became more modish and flamboyant. He started combing his hair forward to hide his baldness and he bought a new sports car that we couldn't afford. I just can't figure out what suddenly came over my dependable husband."

This man has obviously experienced the changes we have described, but his *basic* problem is spiritual in nature. As his system of beliefs disintegrated, then his commitment to related biblical concepts was weakened accordingly. Monogamy, fidelity, responsibility, life after death, self-denial, Christian witnessing, basic honesty, and dozens of other components of his former faith suddenly became invalid or suspect. The result was a rapid and catastrophic change in lifestyle which left his family and friends in a state of confusion and shock. This pattern has occurred for thousands of families in recent years.[10]

**I am twenty-nine years old and want to avoid a mid-life crisis, if possible. What causes this period of trauma, and how can I head it off?**

It is my firm conviction that mid-life crisis results from what the Bible refers to as "building your house upon sand." It is possible to be a follower of Jesus Christ and accept His forgiveness from sin, yet still be deeply influenced by the values and attitudes of one's surrounding culture. Thus, a young Christian husband and father may become a workaholic, a hoarder of money, a status-seeker, a worshiper of youth, and a lover of pleasure. These tendencies may not reflect his conscious choices and desires; they merely represent the stamp of society's godless values on his life and times.

Despite his unchristian attitudes, the man may appear to "have it all together" in his first fifteen years as an adult, especially if he is successful in early business pursuits. But he is in considerable danger. Whenever we build our lives on values and principles that contradict the time-honored wisdom of God's Word, we are laying a foundation on the sand. Sooner or later, the storms will howl and the structure we have laboriously constructed will collapse with a mighty crash.

Stated succinctly, a mid-life crisis is more likely to be severe for those whose values reflect the temporal perspectives of this world. A man does not mourn the loss of his youth, for example, if he honestly believes that his life is merely a preparation for a better one to follow. And God does not become the enemy of a man who has walked and talked with Him in daily communion and love. And the relationship between a man and wife is less strained in the mid-life years if they have protected and maintained their friendship since they were newlyweds. In short, the mid-life crisis represents a day of reckoning for a lifetime of wrong values, unworthy goals, and ungodly attitudes.

Perhaps this explains my observation that most men in the throes of a mid-life crisis are long-term workaholics. They have built their mighty castles on the sandy beach of materialism, depending on money and status and advancement and success to meet all their needs. They reserved no time for wife, children, friends, and God. Drive! Push! Hustle! Scheme! Invest! Prepare! Anticipate! Work! Fourteen-hour days were followed by week-ends at the office and forfeited vacations and midnight oil. Then after twenty years of this distorted existence, they suddenly have cause to question the value of it all. "Is this really what I want to do with my life?" they ask. They realize too late that they have frantically climbed the ladder of success, only to discover that it was leaning against the wrong wall.[11]

**You are describing me, virtually word for word. Will I always be this depressed and miserable?**

No. A mid-life crisis has a predictable beginning and end. An analogy to adolescence is helpful at this point: both periods are relatively short-term, age-related times of transition which produce intense anxiety, self-doubt, introspection, and agitation. Fortunately, however, neither adolescence nor the mid-life years represent permanent traps which hold victims captive. Rather, they can be thought of as doors through which we must all pass and from which we will all emerge. What I'm saying is that *normality will return* (unless you make some disruptive mistakes in a desperate attempt to cope).[12]

A final comment to the confirmed workaholic: I have examined America's breathless lifestyle and find it to be *unacceptable*. At forty-three years of age (I would be forty-four but I was sick a year), I have been thinking about the stages of my earthly existence and what they will represent at its conclusion. There was a time when all of my friends were graduating from high school. Then I recall so many who entered colleges around the country. And alas, I lived through a phase when everyone seemed to be getting married. Then a few years later, we were besieged by baby shower announcements. You see, my generation is slowly but relentlessly moving through the decades, as have 2400 generations that preceded it. Now, it occurs to me that a time will soon come when my friends will be dying. ("Wasn't it tragic what happened to Charles Painter yesterday?")

My aunt, Naomi Dobson, wrote me shortly before her death in 1978. She said, "It seems like every day another of my close friends either passes away or is afflicted with a terrible disease." Obviously, she was in that final phase of her generation. Now she is also gone.

What does this have to do with my life today? How does it relate to yours? I'm suggesting that we stop and consider the brevity of our years on earth, perhaps finding new motivation to preserve the values that will endure. Why should we work ourselves into an early grave, missing those precious moments with loved ones who crave our affection and attention? It is a question that every man and woman should consider.

Let me offer this final word of encouragement for those who are determined to slow the pace: once you get out from under constant pressure, you'll wonder why you drove yourself so hard for all those years. *There is a better way!*[13]

SECTION 28

# ADULT SEXUALITY

**Why are some men and women less sensual than others?** Adult attitudes toward sexual relations are largely conditioned during childhood and adolescence. It is surprising to observe how many otherwise well-adjusted people still think of married sex as dirty, animalistic, or evil. Such a person who has been taught a one-sided, negative approach to sex during the formative years may find it impossible to release these carefully constructed inhibitions on the wedding night. The marriage ceremony is simply insufficient to reorient one's attitude from "Thou shalt not" to "Thou shalt—regularly and with great passion!" That mental turnabout is not easily achieved.

But I should emphasize another factor: Not all differences in intensity of the sex drive can be traced to errors in childhood instruction. Human beings differ in practically every characteristic. Our feet come in different sizes; our teeth are shaped differently; some folks eat more than others, and some are taller than their peers. We are unequal creatures. Accordingly, we differ in sexual appetites. Our intellectual "computers" are clearly programmed differently through the process of genetic inheritance. Some of us "hunger and thirst" after our sexuality, while others take it much more casually. Given this variability, we should learn to accept ourselves sexually, as well as physically and emotionally. This does not mean that we shouldn't try to improve the quality of our sex lives, but it does mean that we should stop struggling to achieve the impossible—trying to set off an atomic bomb with a matchstick!

As long as husband and wife are satisfied with each other, it doesn't matter what *Cosmopolitan* magazine says their inadequacies happen to be. Sex has become a statistical monster. "The average couple has intercourse three times a week! Oh no! What's wrong with us? Are we undersexed?" A husband worries if his genitalia are of "average" size, while his wife contemplates her insufficient bust line. We are tyrannized by the great, new "sexual freedom" which has beset us. I hereby make a proposal: let's keep sex in its proper place; sure it is important, but it should serve us and not the other way around![1]

**My wife has very little sexual desire, despite the fact that we love each other and take a lot of time to be together. She reports that this lack of sex drive is extremely depressing to her, and she is in therapy now to help her deal with it. I want to understand better what she is feeling. Can you help me?**

It is certain that she is keenly aware of the erotic explosion which burns throughout her society. While her grandmother could have hidden her private inhibitions behind the protection of verbal taboo, today's unresponsive woman is reminded of her inadequacy almost hourly. Radio, television, books, magazines, and movies make her think that the entire human race plunges into orgies of sexual ecstasy every night of the year. An inhibited wife can easily get the notion that the rest of America lives on Libido Lane in beautiful downtown Passion Park while she resides on the lonely side of Blizzard Boulevard. This unparalleled emphasis on genital gymnastics creates emotional pressure in enormous proportions. How frightening to feel sexless in a day of universal sensuality!

Sexual misfires—those icy bedroom encounters which leave both partners unsatisfied and frustrated—tend to be self-perpetuating. Unless each orgasm is accompanied by roman candles, skyrockets, and "The Stars and Stripes Forever," the fear of failure begins to gnaw on body and soul. Every disappointing experience is likely to interfere with the ability to relax and enjoy the next episode, which puts double stress on all those which follow. It is easy to see how this chain reaction of anxieties can assassinate whatever minimal desire was there in the first place. Then when sex finally loses its appeal, great emotions sweep down on the unresponsive lover. A woman who finds no pleasure in intercourse usually feels like a failure as a wife; she fears she may not be able to "hold" her husband who faces flirtatious alternatives at the office. She experiences incredible guilt for her inability to respond, and inevitably her self-esteem gets clobbered in the process.

With this understanding, it should be obvious what you as her husband can do to reduce the anxieties and restore her confidence.[2]

**You said that failure to understand sexual uniqueness can produce a continual state of marital frustration and guilt. Will you explain that concern further?**

Even where genuine love is evident, feminine emotions are critical to sexual response. Unless a woman feels a certain closeness to her husband at a particular time—unless she believes he respects her as a person—she may be unable to enjoy a sexual encounter with him. To the contrary, a man can come home from work in a bad mood, spend the evening slaving over his desk or in his garage, watch the eleven o'clock news in silence, and finally hop into bed for a brief nighttime romp. The fact that he and his wife have had no tender moments in the entire evening does not inhibit his sexual desire significantly. He sees her on her way to bed in her clingy nightgown and that is enough to throw his switch. But his wife is not so easily moved. She waited for him all day, and when he came home and hardly even greeted her, she felt disappointment and rejection. His continuing coolness and self-preoccupation put a padlock on her desires: therefore, she may find it impossible to respond to him later in the evening.

Let me go one step further: when a woman makes love in the absence of romantic closeness, she feels like a prostitute. Instead of participating in a mutually exciting interchange between lovers, she feels used. In a sense, her husband has exploited her body to gratify himself. Thus, she may either refuse to submit to his request, or else she will yield with reluctance and resentment. The inability to explain this frustration is, I believe, a continual source of agitation to women.

If I had the power to communicate only one message to every family in America, I would specify the importance of romantic love to every aspect of feminine existence. It provides for a woman's self-esteem, her joy in living, and her sexual responsiveness. Therefore, the vast number of men who are involved in bored, tired marriages—and find themselves locked out of the bedroom—should know where the trouble possibly lies. Real love can melt an iceberg.[3]

**I find that I am easily distracted during intimate moments, especially by the fear of being overheard by the kids. This doesn't seem to bother my husband at all. Am I being foolish to worry about such things?**
Your problem is very common among women, who are typically more easily distracted than men; they are also more aware of the "geography" of sex, the techniques of lovemaking, and the noises and smells than are their husbands. Privacy is often more important to women, too.

Another rather common inhibitor to women, according to the concerns verbalized in counseling sessions, is the lack of cleanliness by their husbands. A service station operator or a construction worker may become sexually aroused by something he has seen or read during the day, causing him to desire intercourse with his wife as soon as he arrives home from his job. He may be sweaty and grimy from the day's work, smelling of body odor and needing to use some Crest on his teeth. Not only are his fingernails dirty, but his rough, calloused hands are irritating to his wife's delicate skin. An interference such as this can paralyze a woman sexually, and make her husband feel rejected and angry.

Spontaneity has its place in the marital bed, but "sudden sex" often results in "sudden failure" for a less passionate woman. In general, I believe sex should be planned for, prepared for, and anticipated. For the man who has been dissatisfied with his recent sex life, I suggest that he call a local hotel or motel and make reservations for a given night, but tell no one about his plans. He might arrange secretly for the children to be cared for until morning, and then ask his wife to go out to dinner with him. After they have eaten a good meal, he should drive to the hotel without going home or announcing his intentions. The element of surprise and excitement should be preserved to the very last moment. Once inside the hotel room (where flowers may be waiting), their hormones will dictate the remainder of the instructions. My point is that sexual excitation requires a little creativity, particularly in cases of a "tired" relationship. For example, the widespread notion that males are inherently active and females are inherently passive in a sexual sense is nonsense; the freedom to express passion spontaneously is vital to enjoyment. When one makes love in the same old bedroom, from the same position and surrounded by the same four walls, it *has* to become rather routine after so many years. And routine sex is usually bored sex.[4]

**My husband and I don't get in bed until nearly midnight every evening, and then I'm too tired to really get into love making. Is there something unusual or wrong with me for being unable to respond when the opportunity presents itself?**

There is nothing unusual about your situation. Physical exhaustion plays a significant part in many women's inability to respond sexually, and you are one of them. By the time a mother has struggled through an eighteen-hour day—especially if she has been chasing an ambitious toddler or two—her internal pilot light may have flickered and gone out. When she finally falls into bed, sex represents an obligation rather than a pleasure. It is the last item on her "to do" list for that day. Meaningful sexual relations utilize great quantities of body energy and are seriously hampered when those resources have already been expended. Nevertheless, intercourse is usually scheduled as the final event in the evening.

If sex is important in a marriage, and we all know that it is, then some prime time should be reserved for its expression. The day's working activities should end early in the evening, permitting a husband and wife to retire before exhausting themselves on endless chores and responsibilities. Remember this: *whatever* is put at the bottom of your priority list will probably be done inadequately. For too many families, sex languishes in last place.

You may have read Dr. David Reuben's best-selling book entitled, *What You've Always Wanted to Know about Sex but Were Afraid to Ask.* (I bought Dr. Reuben's book because I've always liked his sandwich so well.) But after considering the frequent inhibitions caused by utter exhaustion, I think Dr. Reuben should have called his book, *What You've Always Wanted to Know about Sex but Were Too Tired to Ask!*[5]

**My husband and I never talk about the subject of sex, and this is frustrating to me. Is this a common problem in marriage?**

It is, especially for those who are having sexual difficulties. It is even more important that the doors of communication be kept open in marriage where sex is a problem. When intercourse has been unenthusiastic, and when anxiety has been steadily accumulating, the tendency is to eliminate all reference to the topic in everyday conversation. Neither partner knows what to do about the problem, and they tacitly agree to ignore it. Even during sexual relations, they do not talk to one another.

One woman wrote me recently to say that her sex life with her husband resembled a "silent movie." Not a word was ever spoken.

How incredible it seems that an inhibited husband and wife can make love several times a week for a period of years without ever verbalizing their feelings or frustrations on this important aspect of their lives. When this happens, the effect is like taking a hot Coke bottle and shaking it until the contents are ready to explode. Remember this psychological law: any anxiety-producing thought or condition which cannot be expressed is almost certain to generate inner pressure and stress. The more unspeakable the subject, the greater the pressurization. And as I have described, anxious silence leads to the destruction of sexual desire.

Furthermore, when conversation is prohibited on the subject of sex, the act of intercourse takes on the atmosphere of a "performance"—each partner feeling that he is being critically evaluated by the other. To remove these communication barriers, the husband should take the lead in helping his wife to verbalize her feelings, her fears, her aspirations. They should talk about the manners and techniques which stimulate—and those which don't. They should face their problems as mature adults . . . calmly and confidently. There is something magical to be found is such soothing conversation; tensions and anxieties are reduced when they find verbal expression. To the men of the world, I can only say, "Try it."[6]

**Would you say that *most* martial problems are caused by sexual difficulties?**

No, the opposite is more accurate. Most sexual problems are caused by marital difficulties. Or stated another way, marital conflicts occurring *in bed* are usually caused by marital conflicts occurring *out of bed.*[7]

**My wife rarely experiences orgasms, and yet she says she enjoys our sexual relationship. Is this possible?**
Many wives, like yours, can participate fully in sexual relations and feel satisfied at the conclusion even though there is no convulsing, ecstatic climax to the episode. (Other, more sensual women feel tremendous frustration if the tension and the vascular engorgement are not discharged.) The important thing is that a husband not *demand* that his wife experience orgasms, and he should certainly not insist that they occur simultaneously with his. To do this is to ask for the impossible, and it puts a woman in an unresolvable conflict. When the husband insists that his wife's orgasms be part of *his* enjoyment, she has but three choices: (1) She can lose interest in sex altogether, as happens with constant failure in any activity; (2) She can try and try and try—and cry; or (3) She can "fake it." Once a woman begins to bluff in bed, there is no place to stop. Forever after, she must make her husband think she's on a prolonged pleasure trip, when in fact her car is still in the garage.

An important key to a satisfactory sex life is to take it as you find it, and enjoy it the way it is. Attempting to meet some arbitrary standard or conform to the testimonials of others is a certain road to frustration.[8]

**You stated on one of your television programs that the sexual revolution has resulted in a higher incidence of certain physical problems. Explain what you mean.**
I was discussing that observation with my guest, the late Dr. David Hernandez, an obstetrician and gynecologist from the University of Southern California School of Medicine. He had noted an increase in the presence of the disorders which are known to be "soft spots" for emotional pressures—gastrointestinal (digestive) disorders, migraine headaches, high blood pressure, colonitis and general fatigue. Dr. Hernandez believed, and I agree, that these medical problems are more prevalent among those who struggle to overcome sexual mediocrity—those who are now under such intense pressure to "perform" in bed. The stress and anxiety that they feel over their orgasmic inadequacies actually affects their physical health adversely.

Incidentally, Dr. Hernandez commented further that many

men and women engage in sexual intercourse for reasons which God never intended. He listed a few of those illicit motives:

1. Sex is often permitted as a marital duty.
2. It is offered to repay or secure a favor.
3. It represents conquest or victory.
4. It stands as a substitute for verbal communication.
5. It is used to overcome feelings of inferiority (especially in men who seek proof of their masculinity).
6. It is an enticement for emotional love (especially by women who use their bodies to obtain masculine attention).
7. It is a defense against anxiety and tension.
8. It is provided or withheld in order to manipulate the partner.
9. It is engaged in for the purpose of bragging to others.

These "non-loving" reasons for participating in the sex act rob it of meaning and reduce it to an empty and frustrating social game. Sexual intercourse in marriage should bring pleasure, of course, but it should also provide a method of communicating a very deep spiritual commitment. Women are typically more sensitive to this need.[9]

**You have said that the sexual revolution has the power to destroy us as a people. On what evidence do you base that supposition?**

Mankind has known intuitively for at least fifty centuries that indiscriminate sexual activity represented both an individual and a corporate threat to survival. The wisdom of those years has now been documented. Anthropologist J. D. Unwin conducted an exhaustive study of the eighty-eight civilizations which have existed in the history of the world. Each culture has reflected a similar life cycle, beginning with a strict code of sexual conduct and ending with the demand for complete "freedom" to express individual passion. Unwin reports that *every* society which extended sexual permissiveness to its people was soon to perish. There have been no exceptions.[10]

***Why* do you think the sexual behavior of a people is related to the strength and stability of their nation? I don't see how those factors are connected.**

Sex and survival are linked because the energy which holds a people together is sexual in nature! The physical attraction between men and women causes them to establish a family and invest themselves in its development. It is this force which encourages them to work and save and toil to insure the survival of their families. This sexual energy provides the impetus for the raising of healthy children and for the transfer of values from one generation to the next. It urges a man to work when he would rather play. It causes a woman to save when she would rather spend. In short, the sexual aspect of our nature—when released exclusively within the family—produces stability and responsibility that would not otherwise occur. When a nation is composed of millions of devoted, responsible family units, the entire society is stable and responsible and resilient.

Conversely, the indiscriminate release of sexual energy outside the boundaries of the family is potentially catastrophic. The very force which binds a people together then becomes the agent for its own destruction. Perhaps this point can be illustrated by an analogy between sexual energy in the nuclear family and physical energy in the nucleus of a tiny atom. Electrons, neutrons, and protons are held in delicate balance by an electrical force within each atom. But when that atom and its neighbors are split in nuclear fission (as in an atomic bomb), the energy which had provided the internal stability is then released with unbelievable power and destruction. There is ample reason to believe that this comparison between the nucleus of an atom and the nuclear family is more than incidental.

Who can deny that a society is seriously weakened when the intense sexual urge between men and women becomes an instrument for suspicion and intrigue within millions of individual families . . . when a woman never knows what her husband is doing when away from home . . . when a husband can't trust his wife in his absence . . . when half of the brides are pregnant at the altar . . . when each newlywed has slept with numerous partners, losing the exclusive wonder of the marital bed . . . when everyone is doing his own thing, particularly that which brings him immediate sensual gratification? Unfortunately, the most devastated victim of an immoral society of this nature is the vulnerable little child who hears his parents scream and argue; their tension and frustrations spill over into his world, and the instability of his home leaves its ugly scars on his young mind. Then he watches his parents separate in anger, and he says, "good-bye" to the father he needs and loves. Or perhaps we should speak of the thousands of babies born to unmarried teenage mothers each year, many of whom will never know the meaning of a warm, nurturing home. Or maybe we should discuss the rampant scourge of venereal disease which has reached epidemic proportions among America's youth. This is the true vomitus of the sexual revolution, and I am tired of hearing it romanticized and glorified. God has clearly forbidden irresponsible sexual behavior, not to deprive us of fun and pleasure, but to spare us the disastrous consequences of this festering way of life. Those individuals, and those nations, which choose to defy His commandments on this issue will pay a dear price for their folly.[11]

**How common is the *desire* for extramarital sexual encounters in men, even among those who would never be unfaithful to their wives?**

Dr. Robert Whitehurst, from the Department of Sociology at the University of Windsor, Ontario, was once asked this question: "Do most men, at some point, have extramarital desires?" His reply, published in the journal, *Sexual Behavior*, included these comments: ". . . *All* men from the first day of marriage onward *think* about this possibility . . . *Although* these tendencies toward extramarital sexual activity diminish in later middle age and beyond, they never entirely vanish or disappear in normal men."

These strong statements leave little room for exceptions, but I'm inclined to agree with their conclusions. The lure of infidelity has incredible power to influence human behavior. Even Christian men, who are committed to God and their wives, must deal with the same sexual temptations. Nevertheless, the Apostle Peter wrote in unmistakable terms about people who yield to these pressures: "With eyes full of adultery, they never stop sinning; they seduce the unstable; they are experts in greed—an accursed brood! *They have left the straight way* and wandered off to follow the way of Balaam son of Beor, who loved the wages of wickedness" (2 Pet. 2:14, 15 NIV, emphasis added).[12]

**If we are to believe the statistics we read today, infidelity has become extremely common in the Western culture. Why do people do it? What is the *primary* motivator that would cause a husband or wife to "cheat"—to even risk destroying their homes and families for an illicit affair?** Every situation is different, of course, but I have observed the most powerful influence to emanate from *ego needs.* Both men and women appear equally vulnerable to this consuming desire to be admired and respected by members of the opposite sex. Therefore, those who become entangled in an affair often do so because they want to prove that they are still attractive to women (or men). The thrill comes from knowing "someone finds me sexy, or intelligent, or pretty or handsome. That person enjoys hearing me talk . . . likes the way I think . . . finds me exciting." These feelings flow from the core of the personality—the ego—and they can make a sane man or woman behave in foolish and dishonorable ways.

I'm reminded of the seventh chapter of Proverbs, wherein King Solomon is warning young men not to patronize prostitutes. These are the words of Israel's wisest king:

> I was looking out the window of my house one day, and saw a simple-minded lad, a young man lacking common sense, walking at twilight down the street to the house of this wayward girl, a prostitute. She approached him, saucy and pert, and dressed seductively. She was the brash, coarse type, seen often in the streets and markets, soliciting at every corner for men to be her lovers.
>
> She put her arms around him and kissed him, and with a saucy look she said, "I've decided to forget our quarrel! I was just coming to look for you and here you are! My bed is spread with lovely, colored sheets of finest linen imported from Egypt, perfumed with myrrh, aloes and cinnamon. Come on, let's take our fill of love until morning, for my husband is away on a long trip. He has taken a wallet full of money with him, and won't return for several days."
>
> So she seduced him with her pretty speech, her coaxing and her wheedling, until he yielded to her. *He couldn't resist her flattery.* He followed her as an ox going to the butcher, or as a stag that is trapped, waiting to be killed with an arrow through its heart. He was as a bird flying into a snare, not knowing the fate awaiting it there.

> Listen to me, young men, and not only listen but obey; don't let your desires get out of hand; don't let yourself think about her. Don't go near her; stay away from where she walks, lest she tempt you and seduce you. For she has been the ruin of multitudes—a vast host of men have been her victims. If you want to find the road to hell, look for her house (Prov. 7:6-27 TLB, emphasis added).

The key phrase in Solomon's description is found in the italicized words above: "He couldn't resist her flattery." While the sexual motive was evident, he finally fell victim to his own ego needs. Millions have done likewise![13]

**How about the desire for sex, itself. Does it play an equally influential role in motivating infidelity among men and women?**
It is risky to generalize, because human beings reveal such wide diversity in sexuality from person to person. I believe, however, that unfaithful men are typically more interested in the excitation of sexual intercourse, and women are more motivated by emotional involvement. This is why a woman often gets hurt in such an encounter, because the man loses interest in their relationship when his mistress ceases to stimulate him as before. Someone wrote, "Men love women in proportion to their strangeness to them." Although the word "love" is used inappropriately in that proverb, there is a grain of truth in its message.[14]

**You have been in a position to observe those who get involved in affairs in order to deal with their unmet needs. What happens to them? If we checked in on them two or three years later, what would be found?**
I have carefully watched such people who have left the world of responsibility—the "straight life"—and have observed a virtual inevitability. These individuals eventually establish another "straight life." The grass is greener on the other side of the fence, but it still has to be mowed. Sooner or later, the pleasure of an illicit affair has to come to an end. Folks have to get back to work. Nor can the fantastic romantic feeling last forever. In fact, the new lover soon becomes rather commonplace, just like the former husband or wife. His or her flaws come into focus, and

the couple has their first fight. That takes the edge off the thrill. And the sexual relationship gradually loses its breathtaking quality because it's no longer new. There are times when it doesn't appeal at all. But most significantly, the man and woman eventually turn their thoughts to earning a living and cooking and cleaning and paying taxes again, permitting ego needs to accumulate as before. Alas, after the emotions have been on a moon-shot, they are destined to come back down to earth once more.

Then what does our amorous couple do when they conclude for the second time that the straight life has become intolerably heavy? I am acquainted with men and women, and so are you, who have ripped from one straight life to another in vain search of prolonged pleasure and sex- and ego-gratification. In so doing, they leave in their wake former husbands or wives who feel rejected and bitter and unloved. They produce little children who crave the affection of a father or mother . . . but never find it. All that is left on the march toward old age is a series of broken relationships and shattered lives and hostile children. A scriptural principle foretells the inevitable outcome: "Then when lust hath conceived, it bringeth forth sin: and sin, when it is finished, bringeth forth death" (Jas. 1:15 KJV).[15]

**Have you found in your counseling practice that even professing Christians are being caught in the trap of marital infidelity?**

It's extremely naive, I think, to believe that those who call themselves Christians are not affected by the moral depravity of our times. Outside of hunger, the most powerful of all human urges and drives is the sexual appetite. Christians are also influenced by the same biochemical forces within their bodies as are non-Christians. I find that Satan can sometimes use this as a tool against us when other temptations do not work, because the sexual desire becomes intertwined with our natural need for love, acceptance, belonging, caring, and tenderness. The trap is laid, and many Christians are falling into it, just like those outside the Christian community.[16]

**It is my understanding that some women fail to enjoy sex because of weakness of the muscular structure in the pelvic region. Is this true? What can be done about it?**

The late Dr. Arnold Kegel, professor of obstetrics and gynecology at USC School of Medicine, accumulated considerable evidence to show that sexual response is inhibited in women whose pubococcygeal muscle was flaccid. He offered simple exercises to tone up the muscle, and reported remarkable results from women who had previously been inorgasmic. There are other causes for sexual dysfunction, obviously, but for women who are interested in learning more about this physical explanation, I suggest they read *The Act of Marriage* by Tim LaHaye (Zondervan).[17]

**Would you express your opinion on the matter of abortion on demand? How do you see the moral issues involved, especially from a Christian perspective?**
I have considered the abortion issue from every vantage point and now I find myself absolutely and unequivocably opposed to "abortion on demand." There were many considerations which led to this position, including the impact of abortions on our perception of human life. It is interesting to note, for example, that a woman who plans to terminate her pregnancy usually refers to the life within her as "the fetus." But if she intends to deliver and love and care for the little child, she affectionately calls him "my baby." The need for this distinction is obvious: If we are going to kill a human being without experiencing guilt, we must first strip it of worth and dignity. We must give it a clinical name that denies its personhood. That has been so effectively accomplished in our society that an unborn child during his first six months in gestation can now be sacrificed with no sense of loss on anyone's part. There would be a far greater public outcry if we were destroying puppies or kittens than there is for the million abortions that occur in America each year. Psychiatrist Thomas Szasz reflects the casualness with which we have accepted these deaths by writing, "[abortions] should be available in the same way as, say, an operation for beautification of the nose."

I agree with Francis Schaeffer that the changing legal attitudes toward abortions carry major implications for human life at all levels. If the rights of an unborn child can be sacrificed by reinterpretation by the Supreme Court, why could not other unnecessary people be legislated out of existence? For example, the expense and inconvenience of caring for the severely retarded could easily lead to the same social justification that has encouraged us to kill the unborn (i.e., they will be an expensive nuisance if permitted to live). And how about getting rid of the very old members of our population who contribute nothing to society? And why should we allow deformed infants to live, etc? Perhaps the reader feels those chilling possibilities would never materialize, but I'm not so sure. We already live in a society where some patients will kill an unborn child if they determine through amniocentesis that its sex is not the one they desired.

There are many other aspects of the abortion issue that underscore its inherent evil, but the most important evidence for me came from the Scripture. Of course, the Bible does not address itself directly to the practice of abortions. However, I was amazed to observe how many references are made in both the Old and New Testaments to God's personal acquaintance with children prior to birth. Not only is He aware of their gestations but He is specifically knowledgeable of them as unique individuals and personalities.

Consider the following examples:

1. The angel Gabriel said of John the Baptist, "and he shall be filled with the Holy Ghost, *even from his mother's womb*" (Luke 1:15 KJV, emphasis added).
2. The prophet Jeremiah wrote about himself, "The Lord said to me, I knew you *before* you were formed within your mother's womb; *before you were born* I sanctified you and appointed you as my spokesman to the world' " (Jer. 1:4, 5 TLB, emphasis added).

These two individuals were hardly inhuman embryos before their birth. They were already known to the Creator, who had assigned them a life's work by divine decree.

3. In the book of Genesis we are told that

> Isaac pleaded with Jehovah to give Rebekah a child, for even after many years of marriage she had no children. Then at last she became pregnant. And it seemed as though children were fighting each other inside her!
>
> "I can't endure this," she exclaimed. So she asked the Lord about it.
>
> And he told her, "The sons in your womb shall become two rival nations. One will be stronger than the other; and the older shall be the servant of the younger!" (Gen. 25:21-23 TLB).

Again, God was aware of the developing personalities in these unborn twins and foretold their future conflicts. The mutual hatred of their descendants is still evident in the Middle East today.

4. Jesus Himself was conceived by the Holy Spirit, which fixes God's involvement with Christ from the time He was a single cell inside Mary's uterus. (See Matt. 1:18.)

5. The most dramatic example, however, is found in the 139th Psalm. King David describes his own prenatal relationship with God, which is stunning in its impact.

> You made all the delicate, inner parts of my body, and knit them together in my mother's womb. Thank you for making me so wonderfully complex! It is amazing to think about. Your workmanship is marvelous—and how well I know it. You were there while I was being formed in utter seclusion! You saw me before I was born and scheduled each day of my life before I began to breathe. Every day was recorded in your Book! (Psa. 139:13-16 TLB).

That passage is thrilling to me, because it implies that God not only scheduled each day of David's life, but He did the same for *me*. He was there when *I* was being formed in utter seclusion, and He personally made all the delicate inner parts of *my* body. Imagine that! The Great Creator of the universe lovingly supervised my development during those preconscious days *in utero*, as He did for every human being on earth. Surely, anyone who can grasp that concept without sensing an exhilaration is stone-cold dead!

From my point of view, these scriptural references absolutely refute the notion that unborn children do not have a soul or personhood until they are born at full term. I can't believe it! No rationalization can justify detaching a healthy little human being from his place of safety and leaving him to suffocate on a porcelain table. No social or financial considerations can counter-balance our collective guilt for destroying those lives which were being fashioned in the image of God Himself. Throughout the Gospels, Jesus revealed a tenderness toward boys and girls ("Suffer little children to come unto me"), and some of His most frightening warnings were addressed to those who would hurt them. It is my deepest conviction that He will not hold us blameless for our wanton infanticide. As He said to Cain, who killed Abel, "Your brother's blood calls to me from the ground!"

Surely, other Christians have drawn the same conclusion. I must ask, where are those moral leaders who agree with me? Why have pastors and ministers been so timid and mute on this vital matter? It is time that the Christian church found its tongue and spoke in defense of the unborn children who are unable to plead for their own lives.[18]

# SECTION 29

# HOMO-SEXUALITY

**What causes homosexuality?**
Homosexuality has many causes, in the same way that a fever may occur from different sources. However, as a generalization, it can be said that homosexuality often seems to result from an unhappy home life, usually involving confusion in sexual identity.[1]

**What is the most common home environment of a future homosexual?**
Again, conditions vary tremendously, and any generalization offered can be contradicted by numerous exceptions. If there is a common thread, it seems to be a home where the mother is dominating, overprotective, and possessive, while the father is rejecting and ridiculing of the child. The opposite situation occurs, too, where the mother rejects her son because he is a male. There are other cases where homosexuality occurs in a seemingly happy home where no obvious distortion in parent roles can be observed. I must stress that there are many hypotheses (guesses) about the origins of this perversion, but absolute conclusions are still not available.[2]

**What can parents do to prevent homosexuality in their children?**
The best prevention is to strengthen their home life. Homosexuality can occur in a loving home, as indicated, although it is less likely where parents are reasonably well adjusted to one another. I don't think it is necessary to fear this

unfortunate occurrence as a force beyond our control. If parents will provide a healthy, stable home environment, and not interfere with the child's appropriate sex role, then homosexuality is highly unlikely to occur in the younger set.[3]

**What should be the Christian's attitude toward homosexuality?**

I believe our obligation is to despise the sin but love the sinner. Man men and women who experience homosexual passions have not sought their way of life; it occurred for reasons which they can neither recall nor explain. Some were victims of early traumatic sexual encounters by adults who exploited them. I remember one homosexual teenager whose drunken father forced him to sleep with his mother after a wild New Year's Eve party. His disgust for heterosexual sex was easy to trace. Such individuals need acceptance and love from the Christian community, as they seek to redirect their sexual impulses.

On the other hand, I cannot justify the revisionist view of Scripture which would interpret homosexuality as just another lifestyle available to the Christian. The divinely inspired biblical writers would not have referred to homosexuality with such abhorrence if it were not an evil practice in the eyes of God. Whenever this perversion is mentioned in the New Testament, it is listed with the most heinous of sins and misbehaviors. For example, Paul wrote in 1 Corinthians 6:9, 10:

> Don't you know that the wicked will not inherit the kingdom of God? Do not be deceived: Neither the sexually immoral nor idolaters nor adulterers nor male prostitutes nor homosexual offenders nor thieves nor the greedy nor drunkards nor slanderers nor swindlers will inherit the kingdom of God. (NIV).

Romans 1:26, 27 describes God's attitude toward homosexuality in equally unmistakable terms:

> Because of this, God gave them over to shameful lusts. Even their women exchanged natural relations for unnatural ones. In the same way the men also abandoned natural relations with women and were inflamed with lust for one another. Men committed indecent acts with other men, and received in themselves the due penalty for their perversion (NIV).

**What is the responsibility, then, of the person who wants to be a Christian but struggles with a deeply ingrained attraction to members of his or her own sex?**
If I interpret Scripture properly, that person is obligated to subject his sexual desires to the same measure of self-control that heterosexual single adults must exercise. In other words, he must refrain from the expression of his lusts. I know that it is easier to write about this self-discipline than to implement it, but we are promised in Scripture, "God is faithful, and he will not let you be tempted beyond your strength, but with the temptation will also provide the way of escape, that you may be able to endure it" (1 Cor. 10:13 RSV).

Second, I would recommend that the homosexual enter into a therapeutic relationship with a *Christian* psychologist or psychiatrist who is equally committed to Christian virtues. This condition *can* be treated successfully when the individual wants to be helped, and when a knowledgeable professional is dedicated to the same goal. Some of my colleagues report better than a 70 percent "cure" rate when these conditions exist ("cure" being defined as the individual becoming comfortable in a heterosexual relationship and making at least a moderately successful adjustment to a non-homosexual lifestyle).

**What is bisexuality and why are we hearing so much about it now?**
A bisexual is someone who participates in both heterosexual and homosexual acts of passion. Since the mid-seventies, bisexuality has been a fad among swingers and has received enormous amounts of publicity in the American press. The cover of a *Cosmopolitan* magazine posed the question, "Is Bisexuality Thinkable (or Even Do-able) for Non-nut Cases?" Inside, the caption read, "Could *you* be ready for a lesbian encounter? Well, a surprising number of perfectly 'normal' man-loving females are—." The article concluded with this statement: "Whether or not we're all predestined to be bisexual remains in question. Still, whatever happens in the future, I've concluded that, right now, for the many who've tried it, bisexuality offers a satisfying—and often loving—way of life."[4]

*Vogue* magazine carried a similar feature story with the same message. Alex Comfort, writing in *More Joy,* predicted that bisexuality will be the standard, middle-class morality within ten years.

These immoral "prophets" remind me of the eternal words of another prophet named Isaiah, writing in the Old Testament. He said, "Woe unto them that call evil good, and good evil; that put darkness for light, and light for darkness; that put bitter for sweet, and sweet for bitter! . . . Therefore, as the fire devoureth the stubble, and as the flame consumeth the chaff, so their root shall be as rottenness, and their blossom shall go up as dust: because they have cast away the law of the Lord of hosts, and despised the word of the Holy One of Israel" (Isa. 5:20, 24).

Morality and immorality are not defined by man's changing attitudes and social customs. They are determined by the God of the universe, whose timeless standards cannot be ignored with impunity![5]

# SECTION 30

# TELEVISION AND VIOLENCE

**What is your view of TV, generally? Should parents attempt to regulate what their children watch?**
Most television programming is awful! According to Dr. Gerald Looney, University of Arizona, by the time the average preschool child reaches fourteen years of age, he will have witnessed 18,000 murders on TV, and countless hours of related violence, nonsense, and unadulterated drivel! Dr. Saul Kapel states, furthermore, that the most time-consuming activity in the life of a child is neither school nor family interaction. It is television, absorbing 14,000 valuable hours during the course of childhood! That is equivalent to sitting before the tube eight hours a day, continuously for 4.9 years!

There are other aspects of television which demand its regulation and controls. For one thing, it is an enemy of communication within the family. How can we talk to each other when a million-dollar production in living color is always beckoning our attention? I am also concerned about the current fashion whereby each program director is compelled to include all the avant-garde ideas—go a little farther—use a little more profanity—discuss the undiscussable—assault the public concept of good taste and decency. In so doing, they are hacking away at the foundations of the family and all that represents the Christian ethic. In recent seasons, for example, we were offered hilariously funny episodes involving abortion, divorce, extramarital relationships, rape, and the ever-popular theme, "Father is an idiot." If this is "social relevance," then I am sick unto death of the messages I have been fed.

Television, with its unparalleled capacity for teaching and edifying, has occasionally demonstrated the potential it carries.

"Little House on the Prairie" was for years the best program available for young children. I would not, therefore, recommend smashing the television set in despair. Rather, we must learn to control it instead of becoming its slave. When our children were young, they were permitted to watch one hour of cartoons on Saturday morning and a one-half hour program each afternoon, selected from an approved list. That still sounds like a reasonable schedule for elementary school children.[1]

**Since there are so many problems about the use of television in the home, wouldn't it be better just to get rid of our TV set until after our children are grown up?**
Some families have done just that, and I admire their courage in doing so. But I think it is *possible* to keep our television sets without being dominated by them. I would suggest that the entire family get together to talk specifically about television—what's wrong with it, how it can be managed, and how children can learn to be discerning and selective in their use of the TV set.

Furthermore, it is important for parents to watch television *with* their children, not only helping them understand what they are experiencing, but as a pleasant family activity. Watching TV together can be a wonderful springboard into various kinds of teaching and discussion if it is approached properly.

**I am also concerned about the impact of television in our home. How can we control it without resorting to dictatorial rules and regulations?**
It seems that we have three objectives as parents. First, we want to monitor the *quality* of the programs our children watch. Second, we want to regulate the *quantity* of television they see. Even good programs may have an undesirable influence on the rest of children's activities if they spend too much time in front of the tube. Third, we should include the entire family in establishing a TV policy, if possible.

I read about a system recently that is very effective in accomplishing all three of these purposes. First, it was suggested that parents sit down with the children and select a list of approved programs that are appropriate for each age level. Then type that list (or at least write it clearly) and enclose it in clear plastic so it can be referred to throughout the week.

Second, either buy or make a roll of tickets. Issue each child ten tickets per week, and let him use them to "buy" the privilege of watching the programs on the approved list. When his tickets are gone, then his television viewing is over for that week. This teaches him to choose carefully what he most wants to spend his time on. Ten hours a week is perhaps a good target to shoot at. I'm told that the average preschool child watches up to fifty-four hours of television per week. That's far too much, even for an elementary child.

This system can be modified to fit individual home situations or circumstances. If there's a special program that all the children want to see, such as a Charlie Brown feature or a holiday program during Christmas and Thanksgiving, you can issue more tickets. You might also give extra tickets as rewards for achievement or some other laudable behavior.

The real test will occur when parents reveal whether to not they have the courage to put themselves on that same limited system, too. We often need the same regulations in our viewing habits![2]

**What can we do about the violence and decadence of television?**

We have a lot more power to influence television than we think we do. I'm told that every letter that producers receive is estimated to represent 40,000 viewers who feel the same way but did not take time to sit down and write. But it's important to know whom we should write. I have sometimes written directors and producers and executives of television networks, and haven't felt that it made much difference. I've found it's more beneficial to write the sponsors—the people who are paying the bills. They are very responsive to our viewpoint because the reason they are supporting the program is to try to win our allegiance for their products. We can bring pressure to bear upon them by letting them know that we do not agree with what's going on. And indeed, we must![3]

**There must be a significant psychological factor in the Western culture that lends itself to violence, in addition to the influences of television and literature, etc. How do**

**you explain our predisposition to killing and acts of violence?**
You've asked a perceptive question. In addition to the influence of the entertainment industry, there is another factor which accounts for some of the violence around us. I'm referring to the hostility with which people commonly react to feelings of inferiority today. Everyone who perceives themselves to be short-changed or disrespected by society is expected to be angry, whether they be members of the women's liberation movement, or the gay liberation movement, or the Chicano movement (Brown Berets), or the Jewish Defense League, or the Black civil rights movement, or the handicapped. (Is there anyone left who doesn't belong to *some* oppressed minority?) Feelings of inferiority even account for the outbreak of wars and international hatred. What did Hitler tell the German people in 1939? He assured them that their loss in World War I was the fault of their incompetent leaders; they were really superior human beings. He was capitalizing on their self-doubt as a defeated, humiliated people. I suspect that their willingness to fight was more motivated by this new pride than any other factor. More recently, the 1973 Arab attack on Israel was primarily intended to avenge their disgraceful loss in the Six-Day War of 1967. The world scoffed at the Arab impotence, which was more intolerable than the loss of the land or the death and destruction they sustained. One Arab journalist was quoted in *Time* magazine (October 22, 1973) shortly after the 1973 war began: "It doesn't matter if the Israelis eventually counterattack and drive us back. What matters is that the world now no longer will laugh at us."

Recent evidence even suggests that inferiority is the major force behind the rampaging incidence of rape today. If sexual intercourse were the only objective of a rapist, then he could find satisfaction with a prostitute. But something else is involved. Most rapists apparently want to humiliate their victims. Having been unsuccessful with girls through adolescence and young adulthood, they seek sexual superiority by disgracing and exploiting defenseless women.

How about aggressive violence in American classrooms, which has been increasing steadily in recent years? Can it be attributed to the frustration of low self-esteem? I'm inclined to believe so. And what better explanation can there be for the vandalism which destroys millions of dollars worth of school property each year? Students feel foolish and disrespectful during the day and set about retaliating under the cover of night.

The examples are legion. That is why I have contended that social chaos in all its forms is increased when citizens feel inadequate and inferior. There are numerous other causes, of course, but none so powerful.[4]

**Would you comment on the violence in our society at large, and the forces which are propelling it? What do you think can and should be done about it?**

There are few subjects that cause me greater concern than the exposure being given to crime and violence in America today. Recently, a squadron of Los Angeles police cornered a desperate gunman in a residential area of the community. The fugitive had barricaded himself in a small house, and held three juvenile hostages inside. Television crews were on hand to photograph one of the children, a teenaged boy, as he was forced outside and then shot in the head by his abductor, who subsequently committed suicide. The pathetic young victim died on the sidewalk in a pool of his own blood. I sat stunned, literally sick to my stomach, while the drama was broadcast in full color last night.

A flood of emotions ran through my mind as I gazed into the immobile, unfocused eyes of the dying adolescent. Mixed with deep pity and remorse was a sudden outpouring of indignation—a revulsion which has been accumulating for years. I was angry at the profiteers who have nurtured violence in our society, and at those millions who seem to thrive on it; I was angry at movie producers like Sam Peckinpah, who have smeared blood and guts all over the silver screen; I was angry at theater patrons for demanding a dozen disembowelments per hour in their visual entertainment; I was angry at television networks for giving us continuous police stories, with their guns and silly automobile chases and karate chops and SWAT teams. I was angry at the Supreme Court for legalizing 1.5 million abortions by American women last year; I was angry at the Palestine Liberation Army for killing eight innocent athletes at the Olympic Games in Munich; I was angry at Truman Capote for writing *In Cold Blood*, and at his thrill-seeking readers for wanting to know how a peaceful family was mercilessly butchered on their farm; and I was particularly angry at the pathetic system of American justice which makes crime so profitable and punishment so improbable.

But my indignation will change nothing and the wave of violence and lawlessness will continue unabated. We have become so desensitized to human suffering and exploitation that even the most horrible events are accepted as part of our regular evening "entertainment" on the tube.

I think it is time that millions of decent, law-abiding citizens rise up with one voice to oppose the industries that are profiting from violence. A valiant campaign of this nature was waged in 1977 by the National Parent Teacher Association, directing their efforts at television networks and companies that support the most damaging programs. Of course, this pressure from the PTA brought an anguished cry of "foul play" from the greedy profiteers whose pockets were lined with blood-stained money. Nevertheless, Sears Roebuck, Union Oil, and other large companies pledged to sponsor no more violent programs on television. This form of economic sanction, more recently headed of Donald Wildmon and the National Federation for Decency, is the most powerful tool available to influence our free enterprise system, and we should use it incisively against those who would destroy us from within. We have sat on our hands long enough![5]

# SECTION 31

# UNDER-STANDING GUILT

**My wife and I are new Christians, and we now realize that we raised our kids by the wrong principles. They're grown now, but we continue to worry about the past, and we feel great regret for our failures as parents. Is there anything we can do at this late date?**

Let me deal, first, with the awful guilt you are obviously carrying. There's hardly a parent alive who does not have some regrets and painful memories of their failures as a mother or a father. Children are infinitely complex, and we cannot be perfect parents any more than we can be perfect human beings. The pressures of living are often enormous, and we get tired and irritated; we are influenced by our physical bodies and our emotions, which sometimes prevent us from saying the right things and being the model we should. We don't always handle our children as unemotionally as we wish we had, and it's very common to look back a year or two later and see how wrong we were in the way we approached a problem.

All of us experience these failures! *No one does the job perfectly!* That's why each of us should get alone with the Creator of parents and children, saying,

"Lord, You know my inadequacies. You know my weaknesses, not only in parenting, but in every area of my life. I did the best I could, but it wasn't good enough. As You broke the fishes and the loaves to feed the five thousand, now take my meager effort and use it to bless my family. Make up for the things I did wrong. Satisfy the needs that I have not satisfied. Wrap Your great arms around my children, and draw them close to You. And be there when they stand at the great crossroads between right and wrong. All I can give is my best, and I've done that. Therefore, I submit to You my children and myself and the job I did as a parent. The outcome now belongs to You."

I know God will honor that prayer, even for parents whose job is finished. The Lord does not want you to suffer from guilt over events you can no longer influence. The past is the past. Let it die, never to be resurrected. Give the situation to God, and let Him have it. I think you'll be surprised to learn that you're no longer alone![1]

**As a psychologist, would you explain what the conscience is and how it works in the mind?**
That question (what is the conscience?) was asked among children ages five through nine by the *National Enquirer* a few years ago. One six-year-old girl said a conscience is the spot inside that "burns if you're not good." A six-year-old boy said he didn't know, but thought it had something to do with feeling bad when you "kicked girls or little dogs." And a nine-year-old explained it as a voice inside that says "No" when you want to do something like beat up your little brother. Her conscience had "saved him a lot of times!"

Adults have also found the conscience difficult to define. Technically speaking, the conscience is a God-given mental faculty that permits us to recognize the difference between right and wrong. And guilt is the uncomfortable feeling that occurs when we violate this inner code of ethics. In other words, guilt is a message of disapproval from the conscience which says, in effect, "You should be ashamed of yourself!"[2]

**If guilt conveys a condemning message from our consciences, is it accurate to say that guilt feelings always contain a message of disapproval from God, too?**
No. Let me state with the strongest emphasis that God is *not* the author of all such discomfort. Some feelings of guilt are obviously inspired by the devil, and have nothing to do with the commandments, values, or judgments of our Creator. They can even be a powerful weapon Satan uses against us. By setting an ethical standard which is impossible to maintain, he can generate severe feelings of condemnation and spiritual discouragement.[3]

**Would you give some examples of a guilty conscience which God does not inspire? Can a person really feel crushing disapproval and yet be blameless before God?**
Categorically, yes! I served for a decade in the Division of Child Development at Children's Hospital of Los Angeles. We saw children throughout the year who were victims of various metabolic problems, most of which caused mental retardation in our young patients. Furthermore, most of these medical problems were produced by genetic errors—that is, each parent contributed a defective gene at the moment of conception which resulted in an unhealthy child being born. When a mother and father realized that they were individually responsible for the distorted, broken, intellectually damaged child before them, the impact was often disastrous. A sense of guilt swept over some parents in such enormous quantities that the family was destroyed by its impact.

Now, it is obvious that God is not the author of this kind of disapproval. He knows—even better than we—that the grief-stricken parents did not intentionally produce a defective child. Their genetic system simply malfunctioned. Certainly our merciful Creator would not hold them responsible for a consequence which they could not have anticipated or avoided. Nevertheless, guilt is often unbearable for parents who hold *themselves* personally responsible for unavoidable circumstances.

Parenthood itself can be a very guilt-producing affair. Even when we give it our best effort, we can see our own failures and mistakes reflected in the lives of our children. We in the Western world are extremely vulnerable to family-related guilt. One mother whom I know walked toward a busy street with her three-year-old daughter. The little toddler ran ahead and stopped on the curb until her mother told her it was safe to cross. The woman was thinking about something else and nodded in approval when the little child asked, "Can I go now, Mommy?"

The youngster ran into the street and was struck full force by a semitrailer truck. The mother gasped in terror as she watched the front and back wheels of the truck crush the life from her precious little girl. The hysterical woman, screaming in anguish and grief, ran to the road and gathered the broken remains of the child in her arms. She had killed her own daughter who depended on her for safety. This mother will *never* escape the guilt of that moment. The "video tape recording" has been rerun a million times in her tormented mind—picturing a trusting baby asking her mother if it was safe to cross the street. Clearly, God has not placed that guilt on the heartbroken woman, but her suffering is no less real.

I could give many other examples of severe guilt which were seemingly self-inflicted or imposed by circumstances. Clearly, at least in my opinion, guilt is not necessarily reflective of God's disapproval.[4]

**Would you explain your statement that a sense of guilt is sometimes inspired by Satan?**

Second Corinthians 11:14 indicates that Satan presents himself as "an angel of light," meaning he speaks as a false representative of God. Accordingly, it has been my observation that undeserved guilt is one of the most powerful weapons in the devil's arsenal. By seeming to ally himself with the voice of the Holy Spirit, Satan uses the conscience to accuse, torment, and berate his victims. What better tool for spiritual discouragement could there be than feelings of guilt which cannot be "forgiven"—because they do not represent genuine disapproval from God?

The Bible describes Satan as being enormously cunning and vicious. He is not at all like the comical character depicted in popular literature, with a pitchfork and pointed tail. He is a "roaring lion, seeking whom he might devour"; in fact, he is a threat even to those whom God has elected and received as His own. Thus, it has been my observation that Satan does not give up on the committed Christian—he merely attacks from a different direction. One of those directions is undeserved and irrational guilt.[5]

**Would you describe more completely the nature of the conscience and how it functions? You implied earlier that a person's sense of guilt is dependent, in part, on what he was taught in childhood. Is that correct?**

The subject of the conscience is an extremely complex and weighty topic. Philosophers and theologians have struggled with its meaning for centuries and their views have been characterized by disharmony and controversy from the beginning. Since I am neither a philosopher nor a theologian, I am keenly aware of the deep water in which we tread and have attempted to focus my views on the psychological aspects of the topic.

Concerning influences of childhood instruction on the conscience, the great German philosopher, Immanuel Kant, strongly opposed that concept. He stated unequivocally that the conscience was *not* the product of experience but was an inherited capacity of the soul. I believe most child psychologists today would disagree with Kant on this point. A person's conscience is largely a gift from his parents—from their training and instruction and approval and disapproval. The way right and wrong are taught throughout the first decade of life will never be completely forgotten—even though it may be contradicted later.[6]

**That obviously places a tremendous responsibility on us as parents, doesn't it?**

The proper "programming" of the conscience is one of the most difficult jobs associated with parenthood, and the one that requires the greatest wisdom. Fifty years ago, parents were more likely to produce excessive guilt in their children. Now, I feel, we have gone much too far in the other direction—in some cases teaching that nothing is sinful or harmful.[7]

**You have shown that some guilt does not come from the judgment of the voice of God. In other words, one can feel guilty when he is innocent before God. Now, how about the opposite side of that coin. Does the absence of guilt mean we are blameless in the sight of the Creator? Can I depend on my conscience to let me know when God is displeased with me?**

Apparently, not always. There are many examples of vicious, evil people who seem to feel no guilt for their actions. We can't know for sure, of course, but there is no evidence that Adolf Hitler or Joseph Stalin experienced any serious measure of self-condemnation toward the end of their lives, despite the torment they inflicted on the world.

My point is that the voice of disapproval from within is a fragile thing in some people. It can be seared and ignored until its whisper of protest is heard no longer. Perhaps the most effective silencer for the conscience is found in widespread social opinions. If everybody is doing it—the reasoning goes—it can't be very harmful or sinful.

One study revealed that a very large percent of today's college students now feel it is OK (i.e., not guilt producing) to have sexual intercourse with someone they have dated and "like a lot." One quarter of all individuals of college age have shared a bedroom with a member of the opposite sex for three months or more. You see, if these same "liberated" young people had participated in that kind of sexual behavior twenty years ago, most of them would have had to deal with feelings of guilt and remorse. Now, however, they are lulled into a false sense of security by the fact that their behavior is "socially acceptable." Individual guilt is partially a product of collective attitudes and concepts of morality, despite the fact that God's standards are eternal and are not open to revision or negotiation. His laws will be in force even if the whole world rejects them, as in the days of Noah.

I am saying that the conscience is an imperfect mental faculty. There are times when it condemns us for mistakes and human frailties that can't be avoided; at other times it will remain silent in the face of indescribable wickedness.[8]

**What am I to do with my conscience, then? Is it to be ignored altogether? Does God not speak through this mental faculty?**

Let's turn to the Scripture for answers to those questions. Direct reference is made to the conscience in dozens of passages throughout the Word. I have listed a few of those references, as follows, where the Bible refers to a—

"weak conscience" 1 Corinthians 8:7
"defiled conscience" Titus 1:15
"conscience void of offense" Acts 24:16
"pure conscience" 1 Timothy 3:9
"good conscience" Acts 23:1; Hebrews 13:18
"conscience seared with a hot iron" 1 Timothy 4:2
"testimony of our conscience" 2 Corinthians 1:12
the "answer of a good conscience toward God" 1 Peter 3:21

We simply cannot deny the existence of the conscience or the fact that the Holy Spirit influences us through it. Especially pertinent to this point is Romans 9:1, "I am speaking the truth as a Christian, and my own conscience, enlightened by the Holy Spirit, assures me it is no lie" (NEB).

Another Scripture which puts the conscience in proper perspective is found in Romans 2:14, and is quoted as follows:

> When the gentiles, who have no knowledge of the Law, act in accordance with it by the light of nature, they show that they have a law in themselves, for they demonstrate the effect of a law operating in their own hearts. Their *own consciences endorse the existence of such a law, for there is something which condemns or excuses their actions (Phillips, emphasis added).*

There it is in definite terms. The conscience is a reality, and the Holy Spirit makes use of it. On the other hand, the conscience has been shown to be unreliable on occasions. That contradiction poses a difficult dilemma for us as Christians; we must learn to separate the true from the untrue, the real from the imagined, the right from the wrong. How can we discern, for sure, the pleasure and displeasure of our loving God when the voice from within is somewhat unpredictable?[9]

**You are obviously not suggesting that we ignore our consciences altogether, are you?**

Most certainly not. As we have seen, the conscience is often specifically illuminated by the Holy Spirit and we *must* not disregard His leadings. My words to this point could offer ammunition for the confirmed rationalizer who wants to do his own thing anyway. However, my purpose is not to weaken the importance of the conscience, but rather to help us interpret its meaning more effectively.

Guilt is an expression of the conscience which is a product of our emotions. It is a *feeling* of disapproval which is conveyed to the rational mind by what we might call the "Department of the Emotions." Working steadily in the Department of the Emotions is the "Internal Committee on Ethics and Morality"—a group of stern little fellows who review all of our actions and attitudes. Nothing that we do escapes their attention, and they can be most offensive when they observe a difference between the way things are and the way they ought to be. However, the condemnation that they issue (and even their approval) is subject to error; they are biased by what they have seen and heard, and they sometimes make mistakes. Therefore, before the judgment of the Committee of Ethics and Morality is accepted as Truth, it must be tested within two other "departments" of the mind. The emotion of condemnation cannot be ignored, but it shouldn't be allowed to stand unchallenged, either.

Thus, a *feeling of guilt* must be referred to the "Department of the Intellect" for further evaluation and confirmation. There it is tested against rational criteria: What does my pastor recommend? What does my own judgment say about the rightness or wrongness of the behavior in question? Is it reasonable that God would hold me responsible for what I've done or thought?

And, of course, the ultimate standard on which guilt is evaluated must be the holy Scripture. What does the Bible say on the matter? If it is not directly mentioned in the Word, what underlying principle is implied? In this way, guilt is evaluated for its validity according to the intellectual process of reason.

There will be times when guilt will originate not in the emotions, but in the intellect itself. Suppose a person is studying the Bible and reads Jesus' words, "All liars will have their place in the lake of fire." He immediately remembers his distorted income tax return, and the numerous "white lies" he has told. The matter is instantaneously referred to the "Department of Emotions" and guilt ensues.

But there is a third division of the mind which must review the decisions of the emotions and the intellect. It is called the "Department of the Will." This is a vitally important mental faculty, for it deals with the person's intent. I personally believe no guilt should be considered to have come from God unless the behavior was an expression of willful disobedience.

Remember Jesus' words as he hung in agony on the cross, while being mocked by the Roman soldiers who put him there. He looked down at them and said, "Father, forgive them." We might ask "Why are they not to blame?" and hear His reply, "they *know not* what they do." Jesus did not hold them accountable for the most evil crime in history, because the perpetrators were ignorant of their wrongdoing.

It is with great comfort that I rest in that same relationship with God. I am certain that there are times when I do the opposite of what He wants. In my humanness—in my partial understanding—I undoubtedly fall short of His best for my life. But I believe that my merciful Father judges me according to the expression of my will. When He has told me what He requires and I refuse to obey, then I stand without excuse before Him.

When we are genuinely culpable before God Almighty, guilt will be validated by all three "departments" of the mind. In some ways, they operate as a system of "checks and balances"—as we intended for the executive, legislative, and judicial branches of the U.S. Government. Each division interacts with the work of the other two and keeps them from gaining unhealthy predominance.[10]

# SECTION 32

# INTERPRETATION OF IMPRESSIONS

**Whenever I want to know the will of God in a particular matter, I wait for Him to make me feel positive or negative about it. Do you think that is an effective method of discerning the "mind of God"?**

Determining the will of God by means of feelings or impressions always reminds me of the exciting day I completed my formal education at the University of Southern California and was awarded a doctoral degree. My professors shook my hand and offered their congratulations, and I walked from the campus with the prize I had sought so diligently. On the way home in the car that day, I expressed my appreciation to God for His obvious blessing on my life, and I asked Him to use me in any way he chose. The presence of the Lord seemed very near as I communed with Him in that little red Volkswagen.

Then, as I turned a corner (I remember the precise spot), I was seized by a strong impression which conveyed this unmistakable message: "You are going to lose someone very close to you within the next twelve months. A member of your immediate family will die, but when it happens, don't be dismayed. Just continue trusting and depending on me."

Since I had not been thinking about death or anything that would have explained the sudden appearance of this premonition, I was alarmed by the threatening thought. My heart thumped a little harder as I contemplated who might die and in what manner the end would come. Nevertheless, when I reached my home that night, I told no one about the experience.

One month passed without tragedy or human loss. Two and three months sped by, and still the hand of death failed to visit my family. Finally, the anniversary of my morbid impression came and went without consequence. It has now been more than a decade since that frightening day in the Volkswagen, and there have been no catastrophic events in either my family or among my wife's closest relatives. The impression has proved invalid.

Through my subsequent counseling experience and professional responsibilities, I have learned that my phony impression was not unique. Similar experiences are common, particularly among those who have not adjusted well to the challenge of living.

For example, a thirty-year-old wife and mother came to me for treatment of persistent anxiety and depression. In relating her history she described an episode that occurred in a church service when she was sixteen years old. Toward the end of the sermon, she "heard" this alarming message from God: "Jeanie, I want you to die so that others will come to Me."

Jeanie was absolutely terrified. She felt as though she stood on the gallows with the hangman's noose dangling above her head. In her panic, she jumped from her seat and fled through the doors of the building, sobbing as she ran. Jeanie felt she would commit a sin if she revealed her impression to anyone, so she kept it to herself. For fourteen years she has awaited the execution of this divine sentence, still wondering when the final moment will arrive. Nevertheless, she appears to be in excellent health today, fourteen years later.

From these examples and dozens more, I have come to regard the interpretation of impressions as risky business, at best.[1]

**Are you saying that God does not speak directly to the heart—that all impressions are false and unreliable?**
Certainly not. It is the expressed purpose of the Holy Spirit to deal with human beings in a most personal and intimate way, convicting, directing and influencing. However, some people seem to find it very difficult to distinguish the voice of God from other sounds within.[2]

**Do some of those "other sounds" represent the influence of Satan?**
Yes. That is why he is described in profoundly evil terms in the Bible, leaving little room for doubt as to his motives or nature. His character is presented as wicked, malignant, subtle,

deceitful, fierce, and cruel. He is depicted as a wolf, roaring lion, and a serpent. Among the titles ascribed to Satan are these: "Murderer," "Dragon," "Old Serpent," "Wicked One," "Liar," "Prince of the Devils," and more than twenty other names which describe a malicious and incomparably evil nature.

These scriptural descriptions of Satan are written for a purpose: we should recognize that the "Father of Lies" has earned his reputation at the expense of those he has damned! And there is no doubt in my mind that he often uses destructive impressions to implement his evil purposes.[3]

**You said your premonition of impending death occurred while you were praying. Is it really possible for Satan to speak in the midst of an earnest prayer?**
Was not Jesus tempted by Satan while He was on a forty-day prayer and fasting journey in the wilderness?

Yes, the devil can speak at any time. Let me go a step further: harmful impressions can bear other earmarks of divine revelation. They can occur and recur for months at a time. They can be as intense as any other emotion in life. They can be verified by Christian friends and can even seemingly be validated by striking passages of Scripture.[4]

**Are some impressions and feelings of our own making?**
In a way, they all are. By that I mean that all of our impulses and thoughts are vulnerable to our physical condition and psychological situation at any given moment. Haven't you noticed that your impressions are affected by the amount of sleep you had last night, the state of your health, your level of confidence at that time, and dozens of other forces which impinge upon your decision-making processes? We are trapped in these "earthen vessels," and our perception is necessarily influenced by our humanness.[5]

**I have sometimes wondered if my impressions don't obediently tell me what I most want to hear. For example, I felt greatly led to take a new job that offered a higher salary and shorter working hours.**
That reminds me of the minister who received a call to a much larger and stronger church than he ever expected to lead. He

replied, "I'll pray about it while my wife packs."

It is very difficult to separate the "want to" from our interpretation of God's will. The human mind will often obediently convince itself of anything in order to have its own way. Perhaps the most striking example of this self-delusion occurred with a young couple I later counseled, who had decided to engage in sexual intercourse before marriage. Since the young man and woman were both reared in the church, they had to find a way to lessen the guilt from this forbidden act. So, they actually got down on their knees and prayed about what they were going to do, and received "assurance" that it was all right to continue![6]

**I heard a man say that he dreamed he should marry a certain woman. Does God ever speak to us in that way through dreams today?**

I don't know. He certainly used this method of communicating in Old Testament times; however, it appears to me that the use of dreams has been less common since the advent of the Holy Spirit, because the Spirit was sent to be our source of enlightenment. (See John 16.)

Even in prior times, Jeremiah called dreams "chaff" when compared to the Word of God. Personally, I would not accept a dream as being authentic, regardless of how vivid it seemed, until the same content was verified in other ways.[7]

**What do you mean by having the "content verified in other ways"?**

I mean that the "direction" given to me in a dream should be supported by other pieces of information that I would receive. For example, suppose I dream that I am called to Africa as a medical missionary. Before I start packing, I should consider some other factors: Am I qualified by training, experience, interests? Have there been any direct invitations or opportunities presented?

John Wesley wrote in the nineteeth century, "Do not hastily ascribe things to God. Do not easily suppose dreams, voices, impressions, visions, or revelations to be from God. They may be from Him. They may be nature. They may be from the Devil. Therefore, believe not every spirit, but 'try the spirits whether they be from God.'"[8]

**What is the purpose of dreams, from a scientific and psychological point of view?**
Dreams appear to have two basic purposes: they reflect wish fulfillment, giving expression to the things we long for; and second, they ventilate anxiety and the stresses we experience during waking hours. They also serve to keep us asleep when we are drifting toward consciousness. Dreams are being studied at length in experimental laboratories today, although their nature is still rather poorly understood.[9]

**If what we feel is so unreliable and dangerous, then how can we even know the will of God? How can we tell the difference between the leadings of the Holy Spirit and subtle, evil influences of Satan himself?**
Let's look to the Scripture for a word of encouragement:

Concerning Christ's power to help in time of temptation: "Because he himself suffered when he was tempted, he is able to help those who are being tempted" (Heb. 2:18 NIV).

Concerning the power of God to convey his will to us: "And this is my prayer. That the God of our Lord Jesus Christ, the all-glorious Father, will give you spiritual wisdom and the insight to know more of him: that you may receive that inner illumination of the spirit which will make you realize how great is the hope to which he is calling you—the magnificence and splendour of the inheritance promised to Christians—and how tremendous is the power available to us who believe in God" (Eph. 1:16-19 Phillips).

Concerning the power of God over Satan: "You, my children, who belong to God have already defeated them, because the one who lives in you is stronger than the anti-Christ in the world" (1 John 4:4 Phillips).

Concerning the divine promise to lead and guide us: "I will instruct thee and teach thee in the way which thou shalt go: I will guide thee with mine eye" (Psa. 32:8 KJV).

In paraphrased form, these four Scriptures offer these promises:

1. Jesus was tempted by Satan when He was on earth, so He is fully equipped to deal with him now on our behalf.
2. "Inner illumination" and "spiritual wisdom" are made available to us by the God who controls the entire universe.
3. Satan's influence is checkmated by the omniscient power of God, living within us.

4. Like a father leading his trusting child, our Lord will guide our steps and teach us His wisdom.

These four Scriptures are supported by dozens more which promise God's guidance, care, and leadership in our lives.[10]

**Then how do you account for the experiences of those Christians who grope with uncertainty in the darkness and eventually stumble and fall? How do you explain incidents whereby Satan traps them into believing and acting on his lies?**

The Scripture, again, provides its own answer to that troubling question. We are told in 1 John 4:1: "Don't trust every spirit, dear friends of mine, but test them to discover whether they come from God or not" (Phillips). A similar commandment is given in 1 Thessalonians 5:21: "Prove all things; hold fast that which is good" (KJV). In other words, it is our responsibility to "test" and "prove" all things—including the validity of our impressions. To do otherwise is to give Satan an opportunity to defeat us, despite the greater power of the Holy Spirit who lives within. We would not have been told to test the spirits if there were no danger in them.[11]

**By what means can I "test" my own feelings and impressions? What are the steps necessary to "prove" the will of God?**

The best answer I've read for those questions was written in 1892 by Martin Wells Knapp. In his timeless little booklet entitled *Impressions*, he described those impulses and leadings that come from above (from God) versus those that originate from below (from Satan). Just as the Holy Spirit may tell us by impressions what His will is concerning us, so also can our spiritual enemies tell us by impressions what their will is. And unfortunately, there is often a striking resemblance between the two kinds of messages. According to Knapp, one of the objectives of Satan is to get the Christian to lean totally on his impressions, accepting them uncritically as the absolute voice of God. When this occurs, "the devil has got all he wants."

When seeking God's will, Knapp recommends that each impression be evaluated very carefully to see if it reflects four distinguishing features:

*Scriptural.* Is the impression in harmony with the Bible?

Guidance from the Lord is *always* in accordance with the Holy Scripture, and this gives us an infallible point of reference and comparison.

The most important aspect of this first test is that *the entire Bible be used* instead of the selection of "proof texts" or "chance texts." A reader can find support for almost any viewpoint if he lifts individual verses or partial phrases out of context.

*Right.* Knapp's second test of impressions involves the matter of rightness. "Impressions which are from God are always right," says Knapp. "They may be contrary to our feelings, our prejudices and our natural inclinations, but they are always right. They will stand all tests."[12]

I am acquainted with a family which was destroyed by an impression that could not have passed the test: Is it right? Although there were four little children in the home, the mother felt she was "called" to leave them and enter full-time evangelistic work. On very short notice, she abandoned the children who needed her so badly, and left them in the care of their father who worked six and seven days a week.

The consequence was devastating. The youngest in the family lay awake at night, crying for his mommy. The older children had to assume adult responsibilities which they were ill prepared to carry. There was no one at home to train and love and guide the development of the lonely little family. I simply cannot believe the mother's impression was from God because it was neither scriptural nor "right" to leave the children. I suspect that she had other motives for fleeing her home, and Satan provided her with a seemingly noble explanation to cover her tracks.

As Knapp said, "Millions of impressions, if compelled to answer the simple question, 'Are you right?' will blush and hesitate and squirm, and finally in confusion, retire."

*Providential.* In explaining the importance of providential circumstances, Knapp quoted Hannah Whitall Smith, writing in *The Christian's Secret of a Happy Life:*

> If a leading is from the Holy Spirit, "the way will always open for it." The Lord assures us of this when he says: "When he putteth forth his own sheep, he goeth before them, and the sheep follow him: for they know his voice" (John 10:4). Notice here the expression "goeth before" and "follow." He goes before to open the way, and we are to follow in the way thus opened. It is never a sign of divine

> leading when a Christian insists on opening his own way, and riding roughshod over all opposing things. If the Lord goes before us He will open all doors before us, and we shall not need ourselves to hammer them down.

*Reasonable.* The Apostle Paul referred to the Christian life as a "reasonable service." Accordingly, the will of God can be expected to be in harmony with *spiritually enlightened judgment.* We will not be asked to do absurd and ridiculous things which are devoid of judgment and common sense. Knapp said, "God has given us reasoning powers for a purpose, and he respects them, appeals to them, and all of his leadings are in unison with them."[13]

**Of Knapp's four criteria, "providential circumstances" seems hardest to apply. Can you give an example?**
Personally, I have come to depend heavily on providential circumstances to speak to me of God's will. My impressions serve as little more than "hunches" which cause me to pay closer attention to more concrete evidence around me. For example, in 1970 my wife and I considered the wisdom of selling our house and buying one better suited to the needs of our growing family. However, there are many factors to consider in such a move. The lifestyle, values, and even the safety of a family is influenced by the neighborhood in which it resides. I felt it would be foolish to sell our home and buy a new one without seeking the specific guidance of the Lord.

After making the possibility a matter of prayer, I felt I should offer our house for sale without listing it with a realtor. If it sold I would know that God had revealed His leading through this providential circumstance. For two weeks a For Sale sign stood unnoticed in the front yard. It didn't attract a single call or knock on the door, and my prayer was answered in the negative.

I took down the sign and waited twelve months before asking the same question of the Lord. This time, the house sold for my asking price without a nickel being spent on advertising or real estate fees. There was no doubt in my mind that the Lord had another home in mind for us.[14]

**How do you know that the sale of your house was not explained by economic circumstances or simply by the fact that an interested buyer came along? Can you say,**

**definitely, that God determined the outcome?**
Matters of faith can never be proved; they always have to be "the substance of things hoped for, the evidence of things not seen" (Heb. 11:1). It would be impossible to make a skeptic acknowledge that God influenced the sale of my house, just as the same unbeliever would doubt my conversion experience wherein I became a Christian. You see, it was not the unadvertised sale of my house that convinced me that God was involved in the issue—it was that I met with Him on my knees in prayer and asked for His specific guidance and direction. I have reason to believe that He cares about me and my family, and hears me when I ask for His leadership. Therefore, my interpretation of the event is based not on facts but on faith. Spiritual experiences must *always* rest on that foundation.[15]

**Will there be times when the application of Knapp's four tests still leaves a Christian in a state of doubt about the leadings of the Lord? Or does a committed Christian always know precisely what God wants of him?**
Your question is one which is rarely confronted in books dealing with the will of God, but I feel we must meet it head-on. I believe there are times in the lives of most believers when confusion and perplexity are rampant. What could Job have felt, for example, when his world began to crack and splinter? His family members became sick and died, his livestock was wiped out, and he was besieged by boils from the top of his head to the bottom of his feet. But most troubling of all was his inability to make spiritual sense of the circumstances. He knew he hadn't sinned, despite the accusations of his "friends," yet, God must have seemed a million miles away. He said at one point, "Oh, that I knew where to find God—that I could go to his throne and talk with him there" (Job 23:3 TLB). "But I search in vain. I seek him here, I seek him there, and cannot find him. I seek him in his workshop in the North, but cannot find him there; nor can I find him in the South; there, too, he hides himself" (Job 23:8, 9 TLB).

Was this experience unique to Job? I don't think so. In my counseling responsibilities with Christian families, I've learned that sincere, dedicated believers go through tunnels and storms, too. We inflict a tremendous disservice on young Christians by making them think only sinners experience confusion and depressing times in their lives.

We must remember that God is not a subservient genie who comes out of a bottle to sweep away each trial and hurdle which blocks our path. Accordingly, He has not promised to lay out an eight-year master plan that delineates every conceivable alternative in the roadway. Rather, He offers us His will for *today* only. Our tomorrows must be met one day at a time, negotiated with a generous portion of faith.[16]

**Are you saying there will be times in a Christian's life when God's will and actions may not make sense to him?**
Yes, and I regret the shallow teaching today which denies this fact. We are told in the Book of Isaiah, "For my thoughts are not your thoughts, neither are your ways my ways, saith the Lord" (55:8 KJV). Furthermore, the Apostle Paul verified that we "see through a glass darkly." In practical terms, this means that there will be times when God's behavior will be incomprehensible and confusing to us.[17]

**Are we to conclude, then, that there are occasions when we will pray for the will of God to be known, and yet we may "hear" no immediate reply?**
I think so, but I'm also convinced that God is as close to us and as involved in our situation during those times when we feel nothing, as He is when we are spiritually exhilarated. We are not left to flounder. Rather, our faith is strengthened by these testing periods. The only comforting attitude to hold during these stressful times is beautifully summarized in 2 Corinthians 4:8-10:

> We are pressed on every side by troubles, but not crushed and broken. We are perplexed because we don't know why things happen as they do, but we don't give up and quit. We are hunted down, but God never abandons us. We get knocked down, but we get up again and keep going. These bodies of ours are constantly facing death just as Jesus did; so it is clear to all that it is only the living Christ within [who keeps us safe] (TLB).[18]

**I know many people who make their financial decisions on the basis of astrology. Even their business dealings are influenced by their horoscopes. Will you comment on the practice of astrology and whether there are any scientific facts to support it?**

Of all the social developments occurring in recent years, none reveals our spiritual poverty more than the current devotion to astrology. I have been amazed by television personalities, politicians, and millions of American young people. Even France's former president, Georges Pompidou, admitted in a press conference that he consulted his astrologer before making important speeches or state decisions.

How ridiculous to think that Adolf Hitler, Queen Elizabeth, Harry Truman, William Shakespeare, Bing Crosby, Willy Mays, Ho Chi Minh, Golda Meir, and I should have everything in common because all of us were born under the sign of Taurus! How stupid to suppose that the success of our business ventures, our health, and even our sex lives are predetermined by the position of the stars and planets on the day of our births! Yet, there are more than 10,000 astrologers currently working in the United States, offering advice on everything from business deals to the compatibility of a man and his dog.

There is not a scrap of scientific evidence to support the validity of such illogical and atheistic notions. In fact, it was an all-knowing astrologist who advised Hitler to attack Russia—his biggest mistake! Nevertheless, millions of believers consult their horoscopes to obtain daily truth and wisdom.

I was recently introduced to a famous Hollywood actor while we sat waiting to appear on a television talk program. My wife was with me to observe the interview, and the actor commented on her attractiveness. He said, "I'll bet you are a Sagittarius, because most pretty girls are born under that sign." I was so appalled by the silliness of his statement that I felt obliged to challenge what he said. Trying not to insult his intelligence (which was difficult), I asked him if he had made any effort to prove his hypothesis. I pointed out how simple it would be, for example, to check the birth date of every girl entered in next year's Miss America or Miss Universe contest. I soon learned that the best way to end a conversation with an astrologist is to begin talking about scientific evidence.

In 1960, the world's astrologers announced that the worst combination of planetary influences in 25,000 years would occur that year. Seven of the nine planets were to appear in a line, which meant bad news for Mother Earth! Indian soothsayers were going crazy in sheer fright, and American skygazers were predicting everything from the drowning of California to the cataclysmic end of the world. But the fateful day came and went, of course, with no more disasters than on any other day. The astrologers had overlooked one fundamental fact: Man's destiny is not controlled by the planets. Both man and the heavenly bodies are under the indisputable authority of Almighty God!

When astrological advice is broadcast on radio or television stations, the announcers often repeat a disclaimer, saying they are not attempting to foster a serious belief in astrology and are providing the horoscopes for fun and entertainment. How about it, then? Is astrology just an amusing pastime for our enjoyment? What about those millions of Americans who depend on the stars to provide direction and meaning each day? Isn't it better that they believe in this myth than to believe in nothing at all? Should we foster a tolerant attitude toward astrology, or should it be seen as an insidious philosophy to be opposed wherever possible?

A widely quoted psychiatrist recently professed that he urges his patients to depend on their astrologers, even though he admits that their predictions are scientifically worthless. I couldn't disagree more totally! Astrology is not only mythical nonsense, but it is dangerous to those who accept its tenets. One serious concern is that it offers a substitute for rational judgment and wisdom. A young man or woman, for example, may choose a marital partner on the basis of compatibility of their charts, without proper regard for the lifetime implications of their decision. Others postpone or disregard needed action because of the "do nothing" advice printed in their horoscopes. There is no way to estimate how many important decisions are based on the stars each day, undoubtedly having a profound impact on family, business, and even governmental affairs. How risky it is to determine one's destiny by the flip of a fickle coin! The naive believer exchanges his understanding of the facts, his common sense, his experience, and his better judgment for a "know all—tell all" pulp magazine of forecasts. He reminds me of a man confidently leaning against the wind while standing on top of a ten-story building. His body is seemingly held in check as he teeters precariously over the edge of the structure. But sooner or later, the gusts will slacken and the man will suddenly plunge downward in panic. Likewise, the astrology convert is leaning against an apparition which cannot possibly hold him securely in place. Sooner or later, when troubling and fearful circumstances beset him (as will come to everyone), he will reach frantically for something stable and firm to grasp. But he will find little support in the myth and superstition on which he has been leaning. Please believe me when I say I am personally and professionally acquainted with individuals who have taken that frightening plunge. Some fun! Some entertainment![19]

**Why do you suppose so many highly educated and intelligent people are willing to follow their horoscopes, when astrology is so baseless and unsupportable?**
There are, I feel, three answers to that question:

1. In recent years, a tremendous spiritual vacuum has occurred in the lives of many people who previously believed in God. Now that their God is dead, they are desperate for a substitute who can offer some measure of meaning and purpose to life.

Accordingly, someone has said, "Superstition is the worm that exudes from the grave of a dead faith." In other words, human beings *must* have something in which to believe, and in the absence of a meaningful faith in God, reliance is placed in superstitious nonsense.

2. Astrology is the only "religion" which imposes no obligation on its followers. One does not have to go to church for it, pay tithes to it, obey it, sing praises to it, be moral and honest for it, or sacrifice for it. And certainly, its followers need not carry a cross nor die in its cause.

All one must do is read and believe the words of its self-appointed priests in the daily newspaper. (Or perhaps pay $3.75 for a supersignificant, individualized horoscope, autographed personally by an IBM computer!)

3. It would be unwise to underestimate the real force behind the current astrological interest; it is clearly the tool of Satan himself. Whenever astrologists do predict events accurately, it is because of the demonic insights of God's greatest adversary.

This is not merely my opinion on the subject, which isn't very important. It is clearly the viewpoint of God Himself, as expressed repeatedly in His Holy Word. The following two quotations from *The Living Bible* serve to summarize his commandments to us regarding the practice of astrology and sorcery:

> Hear the word of the Lord, O Israel: Don't act like the people who make horoscopes and try to read their fate and future in the stars! Don't be frightened by predictions such as theirs, for it is all a pack of lies (Jer. 10:1-3 TLB).
>
> Call out the demon hordes you've worshiped all these years. Call on them to help you strike deep terror into many hearts again. You have advisors by the ton—your astrologers and stargazers, who try to tell you what the future holds. But they are as useless as dried grass burning in the fire. They cannot even deliver themselves! You'll get no help from them at all. Theirs is no fire to sit beside to make you warm! And all your friends of childhood days shall slip away and disappear, unable to help (Isa. 47:12-15 TLB).[20]

# SECTION 33

# MID-LIFE AND BEYOND

**Most of your books and talks are directed to younger wives and mothers. But we middle-aged women have problems, too. I've survived most of the stages of life you describe, including menopause, but now I need help in knowing how to grow old gracefully. I don't want to become a boring, sour old woman. Would you offer a few suggestions that will help me avoid some of the problems that are characteristic of post-retirement age?**

There are at least four dangers to be circumvented. Let me discuss them briefly.

First, avoid the pitfall of *isolation*. Reuben Welch has written a book entitled, *We Really Do Need Each Other*, and he's absolutely right. Isolation is a bad thing; it ruins the mind. As you grow older, do not allow yourself to withdraw within the four walls of your house and cut yourself off from people. Keep up your social life even when the easiest thing to do is stay at home. Call your friends; they're probably lonely, too. Get involved with people. And remember, loneliness is not something others do to you; it is usually something you do to yourself.

Second, avoid the pitfall of *inactivity*, which is a common trap for the elderly. I once flew into Chicago very late at night and found that the hotel had rented my reserved room to someone else. The manager was obligated to help me find accommodations, but every hotel was full. Finally, he located a room in a facility for the elderly. My brief experience in that converted condominium was enlightening—and depressing. The following morning when I came down to breakfast, I saw four or five hundred elderly people sitting in the huge lobby. Most were silent—neither talking nor interacting. They weren't even reading newspapers. Most were sitting with their heads down, either nodding off to sleep or just staring into space. There was no activity—nor involvement—no interchange between people. How sad it seemed to see so many lonely human beings in one another's company, yet each was lost in his own thoughts. Inactivity and its first cousin, loneliness, are dangerous *enemies* of the elderly.

Third, avoid the pitfall of *self-pity*—an attitude that can kill its victim, quite literally. Those who yield to it are listening to Satan's most vicious lie. Instead of internalizing remorse, I suggest that you begin giving to others: bake something, send flowers, write a card. Get into the world of other people and develop a ministry of prayer for those around you.

Fourth, avoid the pitfall of *despair*. Many elderly people slip into the habit of thinking, "I'm getting old. There's nothing ahead but death . . . life is over." This hopelessness is especially unwarranted for the Christian, who must always be *future-oriented*. The real beauty of Christianity lies in the assurance of the world beyond this one where there will be no pain or suffering or loneliness.

This hope for the after-life was expressed to me in a beautiful way by my father, shortly before his death. We were walking on a country road, talking quietly about life and its meaning. He then made a comment about eternal life that I will never forget. He said when he was a young man, the possibility of a future heavenly existence was not a matter of great value to him. He had enjoyed his youth, and the thought of life beyond the grave was like a pearl that was crusted over with scales and grime. The beauty of the pearl was assumed but not apparent or realized. But as he grew older and began to experience some of the inconvenience of aging, including a serious heart attack and assorted aches and pains, the encrustations fell from the pearl of eternal life, one by one. Then it shone more brilliantly, more prized than any other possession in his grasp.

My father has now achieved that pearl which gave such meaning to his earthly existence . . . even in the winter of his life. Thankfully, the same blessed hope is available to every one of God's children, including you and me![1]

**Would you describe the physical changes that occur with the aging process?**

The decline in old age is not just a sudden deterioration of all systems at the same level and at the same rate. There is an order of deterioration under normal circumstances; that is, if there is not some disease factor that changes it. This is the normal process of aging:

The first thing to be diminished is the perceptual or sensory contact with the outside world. The lens of the eye loses its ability to contract and focus, so we wear bifocals to give us both distant and close vision. Cataracts further damage clarity of vision in some cases.

The conduction of sound is lessened by a wearing away of the three little bones in the ear, so we don't hear quite as well as we did before. Higher pitches are the first to go, then we lose perception at the lower ranges of sound. The taste buds in the mouth and tongue atrophy, so nothing tastes quite as good as it did previously. There's not the joy in eating that we once had. The sense of smell is diminished, which also makes food less tasty, since much of the satisfaction in eating is actually derived from its pleasant odor. There's a dryness and hardening of the skin, which decreases the sense of touch. So all of the five senses are diminished and become less capable of detecting information and relaying it to the brain.

Later, we experience a change in motor activity, the ability to move efficiently. The first to diminish is control of fingertips, followed by less dexterity of the hand, then wrist, elbow, and shoulder. The lessening of coordination moves from the extremities inward toward the center of the body. That's why the shaky writing of an older person reveals his age.

Next, changes take place in the cardiovascular system. The fat in and around the heart forces it to work harder to accomplish the same purpose. When a person over-exerts, it requires longer to return to his normal rate of circulation. A gradual stiffening of the arteries also adds to the cardiac strain. Cholesterol collects in the arteries and constricts the flow of blood, which can lead to heart attacks, strokes, and other cardiovascular disorders. Furthermore, the autonomic nervous system no longer regulates the body's processes efficiently, exacerbating such problems as poor circulation.

Reproductive activity ceases—at about forty-five years of age in women and fifty or sixty years in men. Life no longer trusts us with its most precious gift of procreation.

To summarize, these are the major areas of change that occur in the process of aging: first, we experience perceptual deterioration, and second, the body undergoes a motor deterioration, that is, physical changes relating to movement. If life continues beyond that point, a decline in mental alertness may occur.[2]

**Is it inevitable that sexual desire must diminish in the fifth, sixth, and seventh decades of life?**

There is no organic basis for women or men to experience less desire as they age. The sexual appetite depends more on a state of mind and emotional attitudes than on one's chronological age. If a husband and wife see themselves as old and unattractive, they might lose interest in sex for reasons only secondary to their age. But from a physical point of view, it is a myth that menopausal men and women must be sexually apathetic.[3]

**What does a woman most want from her husband in the fifth, sixth, and seventh decades of her life?**

She wants and needs the same assurance of love and respect that she desired when she was younger. This is the beauty of committed love—that which is avowed to be a lifelong devotion. A man and woman can face the good and bad times together as friends and allies. By contrast, the youthful advocate of "sexual freedom" and non-involvement will enter the latter years of life with nothing to remember but a series of exploitations and broken relationships. That short-range philosophy which gets so much publicity today has a predictable dead-end down the road. Committed love is expensive, I admit, but it yields the highest returns on the investment at maturity.[4]

SECTION 34

# DR. DOBSON TALKS ABOUT FAMILIES

Reprinted in the following section is an interview with James Dobson conducted by the editors of *Christian Herald* magazine, and originally published in its July-August, 1979 issue. (Used by permission.)

## A CONVERSATION WITH DR. JAMES DOBSON, ONE OF AMERICA'S FOREMOST FAMILY EXPERTS

**Dr. Dobson, is there a comprehensive Christian formula for solving family problems?**

Albert Einstein spent the last thirty years of his life in a gallant attempt to formulate a unifying theory that would explain all dimensions of physics, but he never succeeded. Likewise, I doubt if the human personality will ever be reduced to a single understanding. We are far too complex to be simplified in that way. From another perspective, however, there is one "formula" that applies to all human relationships, and of course I'm referring to the four-letter word called *love*. Conflicts seem to dissolve themselves when people live according to 1 Corinthians 13 (avoiding boastfulness, irritability, envy, jealousy, selfishness, impatience, rudeness, etc.). The ultimate prescription for harmonious living is contained in that one chapter, and I doubt if any new "discovery" will ever improve on it.

**Practically speaking, what does that mean? For example, how does that formula apply to kids who constantly fight and argue?**

I'm convinced that many of the emotional problems suffered by some adults can be traced to the viciousness and brutality of siblings and peers during their early home experiences. Self-esteem is a fragile flower, and can easily be crushed by ridicule and mockery occurring routinely between children. But it need not be so. One of the primary responsibilities of parents and teachers (especially those within the Christian faith) is to teach children to love one another. It can be done. Most boys and girls have a tender spirit beneath the unsympathetic exterior. Adults who take the time to cultivate that sensitivity can create a genuine empathy for the handicapped child, the overweight child, the unattractive child, the retarded child, or the younger child. But in the absence of that early instruction, a hostile competitiveness often emerges which can become a barrier to serving Christ later in life.

**In other words, you see this empathy as an important element in early Christian training?**
Yes, Jesus gave the highest priority to the expression of love for God and for our neighbor, yet we often miss this emphasis in Christian education. For example, many Sunday schools diligently teach about Moses and Daniel and Joseph, but permit a chaotic situation to exist, where their cavorting students are busily mutilating one another's egos. In the absence of strong, adult leadership at this point, Sunday school can become the most "dangerous" place in the child's week. I would like to see teachers spring to the defense of a harassed underdog, and in so doing, speak volumes about human worth and the love of Jesus.

**There are those who fear you are too authoritarian. They feel that following your principles too closely will create too much dogmatism, and that the world already has too many people who are, in effect, mini-dictators. How do you answer that criticism?**
Naturally, I don't believe that criticism is justified. I have gone to great lengths in all my books to warn parents of the dangers of being harsh and oppressive with their children. One of those books, *Hide or Seek*, is dedicated in its entirety to the fragile nature of a child's spirit. Nowhere in my writings will you find a recommendation that mothers and fathers disregard the feelings of their boys and girls, or that they use excessive punishment for childish behavior. What I said is that I believe in parental leadership—that children should be taught to respect the benevolent authority of their parents and teachers. If that makes me authoritarian, then so be it. All I can say in response is that my own children live in an atmosphere of freedom which

is made possible by *mutual* respect between generations. That two-sided coin is clearly supported in the Scripture which instructs children to obey their parents and then warns parents not to provoke their children to wrath. I like that combination.

**How much of a problem is physical chemistry in the feeling cycles we go through? Do they sometimes affect our moral judgments? How do we reconcile these factors with God's demands on our lives? Or put it this way: Isn't it easier to behave better some days than others?**
Aren't you asking, "How can God hold us accountable for obedience and compliance when some individuals are apparently not in control of their actions?" Quite honestly, that question has troubled me until recently. The hyperactive child, for example, is often more rebellious and willful than the boy or girl who is calm and serene. How will his defiant nature affect his future relationship with God? What about the sexual deviate who was warped by emotional turmoil during the formative years? What exceptions does God make for the person whose parents specifically taught him immoral and atheistic concepts at home? How about the woman who abuses her child during the stresses of premenstrual tension? What about the person you've described who is possibly driven by chemical forces we don't even comprehend medically?

These issues defy human interpretation, although they no longer distress me from a theological point of view. I have concluded that an infinite God who rules the vast universe is capable of judging those exceptional individuals in a way that will be infinitely just. It is not my business to decipher God's system of evaluation, any more than I can comprehend other aspects of His divine nature. His ways are higher than my ways, and His thoughts are higher than my thoughts. Isn't that why the Bible commands us not to judge one another? We are obviously not equipped to handle the assignment. All I know is that the Lord has required trust and obedience from *me*; as to the reactions of my fellow man I hear Him saying, "What is that to thee? Follow thou Me!"

**Do you lend any credence to bio-rhythm theories?**
We are biochemical beings, and our bodies definitely operate according to regular patterns and rhythms. A woman's

reproductive system functions on a twenty-eight-day cycle, for example, and there appear to be less obvious patterns in men. Men *and* women also experience "circadian" rhythms or twenty-four-hour oscillations that account for the stresses of "jet lag" among travelers who interfere with their internal clocks. Unfortunately, this chemical understanding has motivated yet another phony theory about the human body and its "fate." Several books on bio-rhythms have led to the notion that the date of one's birth can be used to calculate good days and bad days during adult years. There is not a scrap of evidence to support such a claim.

**You don't quote much from the Bible in your counseling materials. Is there a reason why you don't cite the Scriptures more frequently?**
Most of my books and tapes were prepared while I have been on the staff of Children's Hospital of Los Angeles and the University of Southern California School of Medicine. This required me to obtain approval from a critical publications committee which reviews everything written by the professional staff. In order to obtain their sanction, I was obligated to take a very casual approach to the Christian application in my books. I now believe the Lord actually motivated this "soft sell" style, because my writings have found a measure of acceptance among those who would not read a more traditional Christian book. Whether right or wrong, however, I've had little choice in the matter. Let me say for the record that all of my views are consistent with my understanding of the Scriptures, and whether or not references are provided, the Bible is my standard.

**It's often said that part of the motivation for the study of psychology is that the person wants to know himself or herself. Do you feel you know yourself pretty well? What are the things you need to keep working on?**
I'm still getting acquainted with myself and will probably work on that project until I die. And I endure a generous assortment of flaws and shortcomings that I wish I could correct. For example, there's an adolescent characteristic called "ego needs" which surfaces every now and then. I also have to struggle with self-control and self-discipline like everyone else. Nevertheless, God accepts my imperfections and is helping me deal with the changes He requires.

**Relative to your arguments about lack of self-esteem, don't you think the Bible in its teaching on original sin says we are inferior?**
Absolutely not! We are made in the image of God Himself. He said each of us is worth more than the possession of the entire world, and because of that significance, Jesus was not embarrassed to refer to His followers as brothers. We are, therefore, members of the family of God, which is exclusive company. I believe the Bible teaches that we are to walk humbly before God, "esteeming others higher than ourselves," without groveling in self-doubt and despair. Nowhere do I find a commandment that I am to hate myself and live in shame and personal disgust. However, unfortunately, I know many Christians who are crushed with feelings of inferiority, and some have been taught this concept of worthlessness by their church.

**Do you feel that biblical principles and psychological principles (the latter drawn from experience, empirical data, etc.) can be complementary?**
Dr. Gary Collins sees modern psychology based on five suppositions which are humanistic and atheistic in substance. They are empiricism, reductionism, relativism, determinism, and naturalism. If that statement is accurate, and I agree that it is, then a Christian psychologist must reject a certain portion of the training he receives in university programs. I have certainly had to do that. But in its place has come a wealth of information about human nature which originated with the Creator of mankind. The Bible offers us a "manufacturer's manual" which I have found to be absolutely valid in the psychology it presents. But to answer your question more directly, there are many instances where traditional psychological understandings are perfectly consistent with biblical teaching.

**On what key points do Christian psychologists differ today?**
Therapists differ regarding methods of treatment, as do specialists on parenting techniques. I would like to point out, however, that *every* profession is characterized by similar differences in opinion. The Supreme Court often splits 5 to 4 on the issues it considers. And physicians disagree on almost every concept in medicine, although their patients are typically

unaware of the conflict. It is reasonable, therefore, that psychologists—even Christian psychologists—would draw different conclusions about the complex human mind. Until our knowledge of behavior is more complete, there will continue to be differences of views among behavioral scientists.

**Would you encourage young people to think of psychology as a strategic vocation from a Christian perspective?**
Psychology offers a unique opportunity for a person to be of service as a disciple of Christ. Remember that people usually seek professional help at a time of stress when they are looking for answers, and when they are open to new solutions and alternatives. They have reached a point of vulnerability when the right advice can be very helpful and the wrong counsel can be devastating. I have found it rewarding in my practice to represent the Christian view of marriage, morality, parenting, and honesty, while respecting the right of the individual to make his own choice. What I'm saying is that Christian psychology is a worthy profession for a young believer to pursue, *provided* his own faith is strong enough to withstand the humanistic concepts to which he will be exposed in graduate school. If he begins to compromise on his fundamental beliefs, he could easily become a liability and a hindrance to the Christian faith.

# FINAL COMMENT

As I indicated in the introduction, my purpose in preparing this book has been to provide practical, "how to" advice regarding the everyday problems of family living. Moreover, I wanted to arrange the items in a format that would be easily accessible to those with specific needs or concerns. Having completed that assignment in the form of over four hundred questions and answers, I would like to conclude by explaining why such a book was thought to be needed, and finally, what philosophy underlies the recommendations expressed.

When a baby was born during the 1800s or before, his inexperienced mother was assisted by many friends and relatives who hovered around to offer their advice and support. Very few of these aunts and grandmothers and neighbors had ever read a book on child-rearing, but that was no handicap. They possessed a certain folk wisdom which gave them confidence in handling infants and children. They had a prescribed answer for every situation, whether it proved to be right or wrong. Thus, a young woman was systematically taught how to "mother" by older women who had many years' experience in caring for little people.

With the disappearance of this "extended family," however, the job of mothering became more frightening. Many young couples today do not have access to such supportive relatives and friends. They live in a mobile society wherein the next-door neighbors are often total strangers. Furthermore, their own mothers and fathers may live in far-away Detroit or Dallas or Portland (and might not be trusted even if they were available to help). Consequently, young parents often experience great anxieties over their lack of preparation for raising children. Dr.

Benjamin Spock described their fears in this way: "I can remember mothers who cried on the morning they were to take their baby home. 'I won't know what to do,' they wailed."

This anxiety has brought parents rushing to the "experts" for information and advice. They have turned to pediatricians, psychologists, psychiatrists, and educators for answers to their questions about the complexities of parenthood. Therefore, increasing numbers of American children have been reared according to this professional consultation during the past forty years. In fact, no country on earth has embraced the teaching of child psychology and the offerings of family specialists more than has the United States.

It is now appropriate that we ask, "What has been the effect of this professional influence?" One would expect that the mental health of our children would exceed that of individuals raised in nations not having this technical assistance. Such has not been the case. Juvenile delinquency, drug abuse, alcoholism, unwanted pregnancies, mental illness, and suicide are rampant among the young, and continue their steady rise. In many ways, we have made a mess of parenthood! Of course, I would not be so naive as to blame all these woes on the bad advice of the "experts," but I believe they have played a role in creating the problem. Why? *Because in general, behavioral scientists have lacked confidence in the Judeo-Christian ethic and have disregarded the wisdom of this priceless tradition!*

It appears to me that the twentieth century has spawned a generation of professionals who felt qualified to ignore the parental attitudes and practices of more than 2,000 years, substituting instead their own wobbly-legged insights of the moment. Each authority, writing from his own limited experience and reflecting his own unique biases, has sold us his guesses and suppositions as though they represented Truth itself. One anthropologist, for example, wrote an incredibly gallish article in *The Saturday Evening Post*, November 1968, entitled, "We Scientists Have a Right to Play God." Dr. Edmund Leach stated,

> There can be no source for these moral judgments except the scientist himself. In traditional religion, morality was held to derive from God, but God was only credited with the authority to establish and enforce moral rules because He was also credited with supernatural powers of creation and destruction. Those powers have now been usurped by

> man, and he must take on the moral responsibility that goes with them.

That paragraph summarizes the many ills of our day. Arrogant men like Edmund Leach have argued God out of existence and put themselves in His exalted place. Armed with that authority, they have issued their ridiculous opinions to the public with unflinching confidence. In turn, desperate families grabbed their porous recommendations like life preservers, which often sank to the bottom, taking their passengers down with them.

These false teachings have included the notions that loving discipline is damaging, irresponsibility is healthy, religious instruction is hazardous, defiance is a valuable ventilator of anger, all authority is dangerous, and so on and on it goes. In more recent years, this humanistic perspective has become even more extreme and anti-Christian. For example, one mother told me recently that she works in a youth project which has obtained the consultative services of a certain psychologist. He has been teaching the parents of kids in the program that in order for young girls to grow up with more healthy attitudes toward sexuality, their fathers should have intercourse with them when they are twelve years of age. If you gasped at that suggestion, be assured that it shocked me also. Yet this is where moral relativism leads—this is the ultimate product of a human endeavor which accepts no standards, honors no cultural values, acknowledges no absolutes, and serves no "god" except the human mind. King Solomon wrote about such foolish efforts in Proverbs 14:12: "There is a way which *seemeth* right unto a man, but the end thereof are the ways of death" (KJV, emphasis added).

Now, admittedly, the answers to questions provided in this book also contain many suggestions and perspectives which I have not attempted to validate or prove. How do these writings differ from the unsupported recommendations of those whom I have criticized? The distinction lies in the *source* of the views being presented. The underlying principles expressed herein are not my own innovative insights which would be forgotten in a brief season or two. Instead, they originated with the inspired biblical writers who gave us the foundation for all relationships in the home. As such, these principles have been handed down generation after generation to this very day. Our ancestors taught them to their children who taught them to their children, keeping the knowledge alive for posterity. Now, unfortunately, that understanding is being vigorously challenged in some circles and altogether forgotten in others.

Therefore, my purpose in preparing this book has been to verbalize the Judeo-Christian tradition and philosophy regarding family living in its many manifestations. And what is that philosophical foundation? It involves parental control of young children with love and care, a reasonable introduction to self-discipline and responsibility, parental *leadership* which seeks the best interest of the child, respect for the dignity and worth of every member of the family, sexual fidelity between husbands and wives, conformity with the moral laws of God, and it attempts to maximize the physical and mental potential of each individual from infancy forward. That is our game plan. That is the common thread which links 400 widely divergent issues and concerns discussed throughout the pages of this book.

If the objectives cited above could be boiled at extreme temperatures until only the essential ingredients remained, these four irreducible values would survive unscathed:

1. A belief in the unestimable worth and significance of human life in all dimensions, including the unborn, the aged, the widowed, the mentally retarded, the unattractive, the physically handicapped, and every other condition in which humanness is expressed from conception to the grave.
2. An unyielding dedication to the institution of marriage as a permanent, life-long relationship, regardless of trials, sickness, financial reverses or emotional stresses that may ensue.
3. A dedication to the task of bearing and raising children, even in a topsy-turvy world that denigrates this procreative privilege.
4. A commitment to the ultimate purpose in living: the attainment of eternal life through Jesus Christ our Lord, beginning within our own families and then reaching out to a suffering humanity that does not know of His love and sacrifice. Compared to this overriding objective, no other human endeavor is of any significance or meaning whatsoever.

The four corners of this Christian perspective have been under severe assault in recent years, yet the philosophy will remain viable for as long as mothers and fathers and children co-habit the face of the earth. It will certainly outlive humanism and the puny efforts of mankind to find an alternative.

# NOTES

**Key to Abbreviations**

DD– *Dare to Discipline,* Kingsway Publications 1971. Published in the USA by Tyndale House Publishers. Copyright © Tyndale House Publishers 1970.
DWYC– *Discipline While You Can,* Kingsway Publications 1978. Published in the USA by Tyndale House Publishers under the title *The Strong-Willed Child.* Copyright © Tyndale House Publishers 1978.
EM– *Emotions: Can You Trust Them?,* Hodder & Stoughton 1982. Published in the USA by Regal Books. Copyright © Regal Books 1980.
HS– *Hide or Seek,* Hodder & Stoughton 1982. Published in the USA by Fleming H. Revell Co. Copyright © Fleming H. Revell Co. 1974, 1979.
MMW– *Man to Man about Women,* Kingsway Publications 1976. Published in the USA by Tyndale House Publishers under the title *What Wives Wish Their Husbands Knew about Women.* Copyright © Tyndale House Publishers 1975.
PA– *Preparing for Adolescence,* Kingsway Publications 1982. Published in the USA by Vision House Publishers. Copyright © Vision House Publishers 1978.
STMW– *Straight Talk to Men and their Wives,* Hodder & Stoughton 1981. Published in the USA by Word Books. Copyright © James C. Dobson 1980.
FF– *Focus on the Family* cassette tapes (not available in the United Kingdom).

Please note that page numbers refer to the American editions of the books and are slightly different from the British numbering.

Section 1
**Life in the Family**
1. DWYC 9, 52
2. DD 126
3. DD 95, 96
4. DWYC 160, 161
5. DWYC 27, 28
6. HS 70, 71
7. DD 185
8. FF *Questions Parents Ask Most Frequently about Rearing Children*
9. DWYC 162, 163
10. STMW 78, 79
11. HS 64, 65
12. FF *How to Save Your Marriage*
13. MMW 166, 167
14. DD 118-121
    DWYC 222
15. STMW 79-81
16. MMW 105-108
17. DWYC 8

Section 2
**Spiritual Training of Children**
1. DD 179-181
2. DWYC 57
3. STMW 75, 76
4. DWYC 171, 172
5. FF *The Spiritual Training of Children*
6. DWYC 174
7. STMW 73-75
8. DD 187, 188
9. HS 72, 73
10. DWYC 56
11. DWYC 141
    FF *The Single Parent*
12. DWYC 117
13. DD 43-46
14. STMW 146
15. DD 185, 186
16. HS 129
17. DD 181
18. STMW 81-85

Section 3
**Education of Children**
1. DD 162
2. DD 163, 164
3. HS 102, 103
4. DD 182, 183
5. DD 96, 97
6. DD 104, 105
7. DD 79-81
8. DD 164-166
9. DWYC 185
10. DWYC 185, 186

Section 4
**Learning Problems in Childhood**
1. From the *APA Monitor* (American Psychological Association), vol. 7. no. 4, 1976.
2. DWYC 48-50
3. DWYC 161
4. DD 137

5. DD 159, 160
6. DD 136, 137
7. DD 139, 140
8. DD 160
9. DD 140, 141
10. DD 144, 145
11. DD 146-148
    HS 100
12. HS 103
13. DD 148
14. Further explanation of immediate reinforcement is provided on p. 236 in this book.
15. DD 150-152
16. DWYC 158-160

Section 5
**Sex Education at Home and School**
1. DD 181, 182
2. DD 170, 171
3. DD 171
4. DD 175, 176
5. HS 133
6. DD 171-173
7. HS 141
8. HS 139, 141
9. DD 182

Section 6
**The Discipline of Infants and Toddlers**
1. DWYC 19
2. DWYC 40
3. DWYC 39
4. DD 90
   DWYC 39, 40
5. DWYC 41, 42
6. DWYC 42, 44, 45, 50
7. DWYC 70, 71
8. DWYC 66, 67
9. FF *To Spank or Not to Spank*
10. DWYC 47, 48
11. DD 61, 62
12. STMW 58-60, 70
13. DWYC 52
14. DWYC 53
15. DD 52, 53

Section 7
**Understanding the Role of Discipline**
1. HS 96, 97
2. DD 52
3. DD 62
4. DD 33
5. DWYC 182, 183
6. DD 25-27
7. DD 31
8. DWYC 30
9. DD 55, 56
10. DWYC 16-18
11. DWYC 65, 66
12. DWYC 176, 177
13. DWYC 177, 178
14. DWYC 179, 180
15. DWYC 180, 181
16. DWYC 181, 182
17. DD 46
18. DD 222-224
    DWYC 171

Section 8
**The "How To" of Discipline**
1. DWYC 31-33
2. DWYC 76-78
3. DWYC 78, 83, 84
4. DWYC 24, 25
5. DD 34
6. DWYC 68
7. DWYC 26, 27
8. DWYC 99-101
9. DD 188, 189
10. DWYC 23
11. DWYC 115, 116
12. HS 98
13. DD 62
14. HS 98, 99
15. DWYC 57-60
16. DWYC 67, 68

Section 9
**Spankings: When, How, and Why**
1. Marguerite and Willard Beecher, *Parents on the Run: A Commonsense Book for Today's Parents* (Crown Publishers Inc., 1955) pp. 6-8
2. SWC 73-76
3. John Valusek, *Parade Magazine,* February 6, 1977, n.p.
4. HS 95
5. DWYC 34-38
6. DWYC 33, 46, 47
7. DD 52
8. DD 58, 59
9. DWYC 61
10. DWYC 203-205

Section 10
**The Source of Self-Esteem in Children**
1. HS 20
2. HS 23-25
3. MMW 36, 37
4. HS 34, 40
5. HS 25, 26
6. HS 31, 32
7. HS 40, 41
8. HS 77, 78
9. HS 45-47
10. HS 48, 49
11. HS 13, 60, 61
12. HS 59, 60
13. MMW 60
14. HS 169, 170

Section 11
**Developing Self-Esteem in Children**
1. HS 80, 81
2. HS 163-165
3. HS 83
4. HS 83, 84
5. HS 89-91
6. DWYC 87, 88
7. HS 97
8. HS 97
9. HS 85
10. HS 85, 86
11. HS 86
12. HS 92, 93
13. HS 86-88
14. HS 68, 69
15. HS 75
16. HS 182, 183
17. HS 71, 72
18. HS 78
19. HS 78, 79
20. Morton Edwards, ed., *Your Child from 2 to 5,* pp. 182-184.
21. DWYC 88-92
22. HS 176-179

Section 12
**Parental Overprotection**
1. DD 47, 48
2. HS 107
3. HS 105, 106, 109
4. Domeena C. Renshaw, M. D., *The Hyperactive Child* (Nelson-Hall Publishers, 1974), pp. 118-120.
5. DWYC 216, 217
6. HS 108
7. HS 108, 109
8. DWYC 219-222

Section 13
**Sibling Rivalry**
1. DWYC 126, 127
2. Beecher, op. cit.
3. DWYC 127, 128

4. DWYC 128, 130
5. DWYC 130
6. DWYC 133-135
7. DWYC 131-133
8. HS 88, 89
9. DWYC 135, 136
10. DWYC 135
11. HS 67, 68

Section 14
**Teaching Children to Be Responsible**
1. DWYC 25, 26
2. DWYC 163, 164
3. DD 53, 54
4. HS 69
5. DWYC 61, 62
6. DWYC 113-115
7. DWYC 69
8. DD 63-68
9. DWYC 136
10. DD 71, 72
11. DD 73, 74
12. DD 74-77
13. DD 88-90
14. DD 78, 79
15. DD 84
16. DD 78, 84-86

Section 15
**Hyperactivity in Children**
1. DWYC 145-147
2. DWYC 147, 148
3. DWYC 148
4. DWYC 149
5. DWYC 150
6. DWYC 150
7. DWYC 151
8. DWYC 151, 152
9. DWYC 153
10. DWYC 152, 153
11. DWYC 154
12. DWYC 155
13. DWYC 155, 156
14. Renshaw, op. cit., 118-120
15. DWYC 156-158
16. DWYC 160

Section 16
**Coping with Adolescence**
1. HS 122
2. HS 122-125
3. PA 70, 71
4. HS 88
5. HS 138
6. HS 125
7. HS 128
8. HS 139
9. HS 115, 116
10. DWYC 190-192
11. HS 79, 80
12. DWYC 193, 194
13. HS 152-154
14. DWYC 197-202
15. DD 90, 91
16. DWYC 223
17. DD 181
18. HS 84, 85
19. DD 196
20. DD 194, 195
21. HS 161, 162
22. HS 129

Section 17
**Questions from Adolescents**
1. PA 49
2. PA 69, 70
3. PA 28-31
4. PA 35, 36
5. PA 66-71
6. PA 71-77
7. PA 79
8. PA 79-86
9. PA 87, 88
10. PA 88-90

Section 18
**Self-Esteem in Adulthood**
1. HS 20, 21
2. MMW 25-28
3. HS 149
4. HS 52
5. MMW 128, 129
6. MMW 37, 40
7. HS 104, 105
8. MMW 22, 23
9. MMW 37-39
10. MMW 40, 41
11. HS 145, 146
12. HS 147, 148
13. HS 146, 147
14. HS 184-187

Section 19
**A Christian Perspective on Anger**
1. EM 9-11
2. EM 85
3. EM 85, 86
4. EM 87, 88
5. EM 91
6. EM 92
7. EM 92
8. EM 92-95
9. EM 101, 102
10. EM 103, 104
11. DWYC 108-111

Section 20
**Romantic Love**
1. MMW 88-90
2. MMW 90, 93
3. PA 106, 107
4. MMW 99
5. MMW 102, 103
6. MMW 93, 94

Section 21
**Conflict in Marriage**
1. STMW 92-94
2. MMW 76, 77
3. MMW 78-80, 82
4. MMW 82-84
5. STMW 125, 126
6. MMW 163
7. STMW 110, 111
   MMW 179-181
8. STMW 106-108
9. STMW 108, 109
10. STMW 101-103
11. STMW 108-110

Section 22
**The Homemaker**
1. STMW 151, 152
2. MMW 153
3. STMW 152, 153
4. STMW 154, 155
5. STMW 158
6. MMW 165, 166
7. Urie Bronfenbrenner, "The Origins of Alienation", *Scientific American*, August 1974, p. 57.
8. STMW 88
9. Copyrighted by Mary Bourgoin.

Section 23
**Depression in Women**
1. MMW 15
2. MMW 22
3. MMW 41
4. MMW 18, 19
5. HS 70, 73
   DD 219-221
6. MMW 51-54
7. EM 118, 119
8. HS 148
9. STMW 188, 189

Section 24
**Understanding Premenstrual Tension**
1. *Premenstrual Tension* (cassette)
2. STMW 163
3. MMW 151, 152

4. *Psychology Today* (Davis Publishing Co.) February 1972.
5. STMW 164
6. MMW 152
7. STMW 164, 165 MMW 153 *Premenstrual Tension* (cassette)
8. *Premenstrual Tension* (cassette)
9. *Premenstrual Tension* (cassette)
10. MMW 155
11. MMW 155, 156
12. MMW 155

Section 25
**Coping with Menopause**
1. *The Thirty Critical Problems* (cassette)
2. *The Thirty Critical Problems* (cassette)
3. MMW 147, 148
4. *The Thirty Critical Problems* (cassette)
5. *Hormone Imbalance in Mid-Life* (cassette) MMW 155
6. MMW 154
7. MMW 153, 154

Section 26
**Male and Female Uniqueness**
1. STMW 165
2. STMW 165-167
3. MMW 64
4. MMW 117, 118
5. MMW 114-116
6. *Family Life*, February 1971, vol. 31, no. 2.
7. MMW 130-133

Section 27
**The Meaning of Masculinity**
1. STMW 64, 65
2. STMW 168
3. STMW 191
4. STMW 51, 52
5. STMW 71-73
6. DWYC 45
7. STMW 65, 66
8. STMW 174
9. STMW 173, 174
10. STMW 174-177, 179
11. STMW 180, 181
12. STMW 180
13. STMW 139, 140

Section 28
**Adult Sexuality**
1. MMW 120, 121
2. MMW 121, 122
3. MMW 116, 117
4. MMW 126, 127
5. MMW 127, 128
6. MMW 125, 126
7. MMW 129
8. MMW 124, 125
9. MMW 122, 123
10. MMW 96, 97
11. MMW 96, 98
12. STMW 117, 118
13. STMW 118, 119
14. MMW 130
15. STMW 121, 122
16. FF *The Lure of Infidelity*
17. MMW 130
18. DWYC 226-230

Section 29
**Homosexuality**
1. HS 140
2. HS 140, 141
3. HS 141
4. *Cosmopolitan*, June 1974.
5. MMW 141, 142

Section 30
**Television and Violence**
1. HS 73, 74
2. FF *The Impact of TV on Young Lives*
3. FF *The Impact of TV on Young Lives*
4. HS 165, 166
5. DWYC 122, 123

Section 31
**Understanding Guilt**
1. STMW 76, 77
2. EM 18
3. EM 21
4. EM 21, 22
5. EM 22-24
6. EM 33, 34
7. EM 34
8. EM 24-26
9. EM 26, 27
10. EM 27-30

Section 32
**Interpretation of Impressions**
1. EM 113-115
2. EM 115
3. EM 115, 116
4. EM 116
5. EM 117, 118
6. EM 118
7. EM 119
8. EM 119, 120
9. EM 120
10. EM 120, 121
11. EM 121, 122
12. This and following quotes are from *Impressions*, Martin Wells Knapp (Revivalist Publishing, 1892).
13. EM 122-125
14. EM 125, 126
15. EM 126, 127
16. EM 128, 129
17. EM 130
18. EM 131
19. MMW 108-111
20. MMW 111, 112

Section 33
**Mid-Life and Beyond**
1. FF *The Impact of Aging* MMW 175, 176
2. FF *The Impact of Aging*
3. MMW 129
4. MMW 176

# QUESTION INDEX

SECTION 1 **LIFE IN THE FAMILY**


1. Can you give my husband and me a foundational philosophy that will guide our parenting efforts with our new baby? *21*
2. How much work should children be required to do? *22*
3. Should parents force a child to eat? *23*
4. What do you think of the phrase, "Children should be seen and not heard"? *23*
5. Would you go so far as to apologize to a child if you felt you had been in the wrong? *23*
6. Is it possible to forecast a child's future character and personality traits from an early age? *24*
7. How do you feel about having a family council where each member of the family has an equal vote on the decisions affecting the entire family? *24*
8. Should I punish my child for bed-wetting? *24*
9. How would you deal with a bed-wetting six-year-old boy? *25*
10. My wife and I are extremely busy. Do you agree with us that the quantity of time spent with kids is unimportant, but it's the quality that matters? *26*
11. We are also very busy and live a hectic lifestyle. What effect does that rapid pace have on a family? *27*
12. How can we begin to slow the pace and put a sense of togetherness into our family life? *28*
13. When I try to reserve time for my family I feel guilty for not giving more time to my church. How do I deal with that? *29*
14. We can't spend a lot of money for vacations and hobbies. Can you suggest some simple traditions that will appeal to small children? *30*
15. Can traditions be useful in teaching spiritual values as well? *32*
16. What would you do if your eighteen-year-old son decided to become a social dropout and run away from home? *32*
17. Does your home always run smoothly? Do you ever feel like a failure as a father? *34*
18. Our financial problems get more frustrating every day. Do you have any suggestions? *35*
19. Considering how difficult it is to be good parents, why should anyone want to have children? *37*


SECTION 2 **SPIRITUAL TRAINING OF CHILDREN**


20. Should a child be allowed to "decide for himself" on matters related to his concept of God? Aren't we forcing our religion down his throat when we tell him what he must believe? *41*
21. My wife and I don't feel that it is enough to pray each night with our young child and have him attend Sunday school each week. What more can we do to ensure his religious development? *42*
22. We feel family devotions are important, but our youngsters seem bored and squirm when the Bible is being read. What do you suggest? *42*
23. How is the concept of God established in the mind of the child? *43*
24. What is the most critical period in the spiritual training of young children? *43*

25. Many people believe that children are basically "good." Do you agree? *44*
26. What does it mean to "train up a child in the way he should go"? What should be taught in his first seven years — the "prime time" for religious training? *44*
27. My four-year-old is constantly bullied by her peers. As a Christian parent, what should I tell her about defending herself? *46*
28. Do you think children between five and ten should be allowed to listen to rock music? *47*
29. How can I help my child develop wholesome, accepting attitudes toward people of other racial and ethnic groups? *48*
30. Shouldn't the church be doing something to help the single parent? *48*
31. My husband and I are missionaries and have been assigned to a remote area where the nearest boarding school is 200 miles away. Would you recommend we keep our children with us or send them away to school? *49*
32. What is your view of materialism in the life of a child? *51*
33. How can I teach my children Christian attitudes toward possessions and money? *53*
34. Do you think war toys are damaging to children? *54*
35. All of a sudden our teenager seems to be rejecting her Christian beliefs. What should be our attitude and approach in response? *54*
36. At what age should a child be given more freedom of choice regarding his religious beliefs and practices? *55*
37. Can you offer some guidelines regarding how a parent can help his children cope with death? *55*

SECTION 3 **EDUCATION OF CHILDREN**

38. I've read that it is possible to teach four-year-old chiildren to read. Should I be working on this with my child? *63*
39. Do you think it is a good idea to eliminate report cards and academic marks in the classroom? *63*
40. Do you ever favor removing a child from one school and transferring him to another? *64*
41. Do you think religion should be taught in the public schools? *65*
42. Why do elementary, junior high, and even high school students tend to admire the more strict teachers? *65*
43. I teach junior high science and my students don't come prepared. I lend them materials but I never get them back. What do you suggest? *66*
44. Do you think it would be useful to reinstate the traditional rules and regulations in the schools concerning dress, hair, and grooming? *67*
45. I teach a wild fifth-grade class. Can you offer some tips that will help me gain control of my students? *67*
46. If after three months we forget 80 percent of everything we learn, what good is academic "learning"? *68*
47. The children who attend our church tend to be rather wild, and consequently, the classes are chaotic. Is this characteristic of most church school programs? *70*
48. Why do you think our Sunday schools are so lax and permissive, and what can we do about it? *70*

SECTION 4 **LEARNING PROBLEMS IN CHILDHOOD**

It is true that you can increase the mental abilities of your child by stimulating him during the early years? If so, how can I do this with my baby? *75*
50. My six-year-old son is not medically hyperactive but he can't stay in his seat. Now he's having learning problems. What should I do? *76*
51. Does the "late bloomer" eventually catch up with his class academically? *78*
52. If age is such a poor factor to use in determining classroom readiness, why do schools use it exclusively to indicate when a child will enter kindergarten? *78*
53. We have a six-year-old son who is also a late bloomer, and he is having trouble learning to read. Can you explain the link between his immaturity and this perplexing learning problem? *78*
54. What is a "slow learner"? *79*
55. What causes a child to be a slow learner? *80*
56. What special challenges might a slow learner face at school? *80*
57. Is retention in the same grade advisable for any child, other than the late bloomer? How about the slow learner? *81*
58. If retention and summer school do not solve the problems of the slow learner, what can be done for these children? *81*

59. Do slow learners and mentally retarded children have the same needs for esteem that others have? *83*
60. Will you define the term "classic underachiever"? *84*
61. What solution would you offer for the problem of underachievers? *84*
62. My child has a visual-perceptual problem. What should be the attitude of a parent toward a child who fails year after year? *86*

SECTION 5 **SEX EDUCATION AT HOME AND SCHOOL**
63. When do children begin to develop a sexual nature? Does this occur suddenly during puberty? *91*
64. Who should teach children about sex and when should that instruction begin? *91*
65. Neither my husband nor I feel comfortable about discussing sex with our children. Must we force ourselves to do it? *92*
66. Do you believe in the "double standard," whereby girls are expected to remain virgins while boys are free to experiment sexually? *92*
67. Our child is eleven and we haven't gotten around to sex education. Is it too late, or is there still time to prepare her for adolescence? *92*
68. What should I talk about when I discuss sex with my preteenager? *93*
69. How do you feel about sex education in the public schools, as it is typically handled? *93*
70. Do you agree that good sex education will reduce the incidence of promiscuity and sexual irresponsibility among teenagers? *94*
71. How do you feel about the teaching of traditional male and female roles to children? *95*
72. Do you think coed dorms and unrestricted visiting hours on college campuses promote more healthy attitudes toward sex? *95*

SECTION 6 **THE DISCIPLINE OF INFANTS AND TODDLERS**
73. Do you believe that children are born as "blank slates," being devoid of personality until they interact with their environment? *99*
74. If children do differ in temperament, are some babies more difficult to care for than others? *100*
75. What kind of discipline is appropriate for my six-month-old son? *101*
76. My baby cries whenever I put her down and my doctor says it's because she wants my attention. I can't hold her all day — how can I make her less fussy? *101*
77. Describe the best approach to discipline a one-year-old child. *103*
78. Are the "terrible twos" really so terrible? *104*
79. We have an extremely defiant child who we have disciplined as well as possible. But I still feel guilty and defeated when he defies and disobeys us. Why? *105*
80. My mother-in-law feels our twenty-four-month-old son should already be toilet trained. Should we spank him for soiling his pants? *106*
81. My two-year-old will not be quiet in church even though he knows he ought to be. Should I spank him? *106*
82. At what age could you expect a child to sit quietly in church? *107*
83. How can I make our toddler leave our expensive trinkets and china alone? *107*
84. When should the toddler be subjected to mild punishment? *108*
85. My three-year-old daughter throws temper tantrums in stores when she doesn't get her way. I don't want to punish her in front of all those people, and she knows it. What should I do? *108*
86. Other than infrequent spankings, what disciplinary techniques do you suggest for a disobedient toddler? *110*
87. My three-year-old son climbs out of bed even while I'm standing there telling him to stay put! What can I do? *110*
88. We do not feel we have the right to discipline our adopted child, since we are not his real parents. Are we doing right? *111*

SECTION 7 **UNDERSTANDING THE ROLE OF DISCIPLINE**
89. Why is there so much confusion on the subject of discipline today? Is it really that difficult to raise our children properly? *115*
90. Permissiveness is a relative term. Please describe its meaning to you. *116*
91. Do you think parents are now beginning to value discipline more? Is the day of permissiveness over? *116*
92. Will an undisciplined preschooler continue to challenge his parents during the latter years of childhood? *117*

93. My first year as a teacher was a disaster. Since then, I've learned that children can't accept love until they have tested the strength and courage of their teachers. Why is this true? *117*
94. Some parents feel guilty about demanding respect from their children because it could be an underhanded way of making themselves feel powerful and important. What do you think? *118*
95. Don't parents have an equal responsibility to show respect for their children? *119*
96. What goes through the mind of a child when he is openly defying the wishes of his parent? *119*
97. Could you explain further why *security* for the child is related to parental discipline and structure? *120*
98. If children love law and order, why doesn't my son respond better to me when I talk reasonably with him about his misbehavior? Why do I have to resort to some form of punishment to make him listen? *121*
99. If our goal is to produce children with *self*-discipline and *self*-reliance, how does your approach to external discipline get translated into internal control? *122*
100. What do you think about "Parent Effectiveness Training"? *123*
101. Dr. Gordon says that we should treat our children with the same respect that we do our adult friends. Would you comment on this? *124*
102. Dr. Gordon equates parental "power" with parental authority. Do you agree? *125*
103. What do you think about Gordon's suggested use of "I" messages versus "you" messages in moments of conflict? *125*
104. Do you make weighty decisions on behalf of your kids with unshakable confidence? How do you know what's best for them? *126*
105. Would you compare the authoritarian and the permissive approaches to child rearing, then describe their effects on children? *127*
106. On what scriptural references do you base your philosophy of discipline, especially your understanding of the will and the spirit? *128*

SECTION 8 **THE "HOW TO" OF DISCIPLINE**

107. Give me a step-by-step set of instructions that will help me discipline properly. *133*
108. How can I deal with my strong-willed child's misbehavior without hurting his self-concept? *135*
109. How can I shape my nine-year-old son's will without damaging his spirit? *136*
110. *Can* a strong-willed child be made to smile and give and cooperate? If so, how is that accomplished? And is her future gloomy? *136*
111. Does all unpleasant behavior result from deliberate defiance? *138*
112. I allow my six-year-old to talk back and call me names because I feel he needs this emotional outlet. Do you agree? *138*
113. How should I respond if my child says, "I hate you!" when he is angry? *139*
114. What is the most common error made by parents in disciplining their children? *140*
115. What place should fear occupy in a child's attitude toward his mother or father? *141*
116. Do other parents of strong-willed children suffer from feelings of guilt and self-doubt like I do? *142*
117. Why do I find it easier to say "no" to my children than to say "yes"? *142*
118. Our neighbor children are bratty and disrespectful but I don't feel I have the right to discipline them. How can I deal with this? *143*
119. My husband and I are divorced. How does this change the recommendations you've made about discipline in the home? *144*
120. How can I get my little girl out of a sour, sullen mood when she has not really done anything to deserve punishment? *144*
121. Our six-year-old makes the entire family miserable with his sour disposition. How should I deal with him? *145*
122. My four-year-old tried to convince me that he had seen a lion in the backyard. I want him to be truthful. Should I have spanked him for telling this lie? *148*
123. How can I know when to ignore a misbehavior and when to confront my child? *148*

SECTION 9 **SPANKINGS: WHEN, HOW, AND WHY**

124. As an advocate of spankings, aren't you contributing to the incidence of child abuse? *153*
125. What is your rationale for the use of corporal punishment? Doesn't it teach children to hit and hurt others? *155*
126. Can you provide some "ground-rules" for the use of corporal punishment with a strong-willed toddler? *158*

127. How long do you think a child should be allowed to cry after being punished or spanked? *160*
128. Is spanking ineffective with some children? *160*
129. Is my ten-year-old too old to be spanked? *161*
130. I would like to hear your views about disciplining a teenager. *161*

SECTION 10 **THE SOURCE OF SELF-ESTEEM IN CHILDREN**
131. Why are feelings of inadequacy and inferiority so prevalent among people of all ages at this time? *165*
132. When evaluating human worth, what characteristics rank the highest to us? *165*
133. How do feelings of inferiority get started? *166*
134. Why are people more conscious of their physical flaws and inadequacies today than in the past? What accounts for the "epidemic" of inferiority which you described? *167*
135. How does a child learn to assess himself and others on the basis of physical attractiveness? *168*
136. What role do teachers play in emphasizing the importance of physical attractiveness? *169*
137. What are the prospects for the very pretty or handsome child? *170*
138. What do teenagers most often dislike about themselves? *170*
139. What ranks second to physical attractiveness in the "system" of evaluating human worth? *171*
140. Most children leave school feeling stupid. Would you explain why this attack on self-worth affects so many kids today? *172*
141. It is obvious that you think the attitudes and reactions of parents play a key role in the self-esteem of children. *173*
142. What are some of the factors that hinder parents from building their children's self-esteem? *173*
143. What is the source of self-esteem? *174*
144. What other influences besides beauty and intelligence contribute to the child's level of self-confidence? *175*
145. What values do you suggest I teach to my children in place of beauty, brains, and materialism? *176*

SECTION 11 **DEVELOPING SELF-ESTEEM IN CHILDREN**
146. What can I do to help my nine-year-old daughter who lacks confidence and self-respect? *179*
147. Can you explain the process of compensation? How does it relate to feelings of low self-esteem? *180*
148. What is the *best* source of compensation for boys in this culture? *181*
149. How can I as a parent decide what skill my son should develop? Shouldn't that choice be left to him? *182*
150. What happens when a child is so different from the group that he cannot compete, no matter how hard he tries? *182*
151. Do you agree that adults should attempt to intercede when a child is being attacked by his peers? *183*
152. You implied that the "middle child" has greater problems with low self-esteem. *184*
153. What can I do to help my middle child who suffers from low self-esteem? *184*
154. My son is an outstanding gymnast. Yet he performs terribly when competing before judges. Why does he fail during the most important moments? *185*
155. My twelve-year-old goes blank when asked to recite something in front of a crowd. Why does his mind "turn off" when he's under pressure? *186*
156. What can I do to help him? *186*
157. What kinds of homes produce children with a high degree of self-confidence? *187*
158. I tell my son that it isn't important what he looks like or how intelligent he is. What matters is the person inside. Do you agree with this approach? *187*
159. Is it harmful to laugh and tease each other within the family? *189*
160. My twelve-year-old is embarrassed about the size of her nose and she always talks about it to her friends. What should I do? *190*
161. How can I begin bracing my daughter for the esteem problems and social pressure she is likely to face as a teenager? *190*
162. Why are you critical of "Barbie" doll products? *192*
163. How should I respond to my depressed child after he has been ridiculed and hurt by neighbor children? *193*
164. Am I wrong to make my daughter wear her hair the way I want it? *193*

165. What suggestions do you have for parents of adopted children regarding the questions and special problems that will arise? *194*
166. What important changes could be made in our culture to produce a higher percentage of emotionally healthy children and adults? *197*

SECTION 12 **PARENTAL OVERPROTECTION**
167. Is it possible to love a child too much? *203*
168. What happens to a child whose parents are overprotective and fail to assign appropriate responsibility to their child? *203*
169. Alert me to the key elements of the dependency trap. *204*
170. Please explain and elaborate on your statement, "All of life is a preparation for adolescence and beyond." *205*
171. My mother waited on me hand and foot when I was a child, and I would feel guilty if I didn't serve the needs of my kids as well. Do you really think it is in their best interest for me to do less for them? *206*
172. Why is it so difficult for mothers to grant independence and freedom to their kids? *207*
173. I sense that letting go is one of the most important responsibilities parents face. *208*
174. What do you do when your child of eighteen or twenty years makes choices quite different from what you had hoped? *210*

SECTION 13 **SIBLING RIVALRY**
175. Do all parents struggle with sibling rivalry or does the conflict between my children result from failure on my part? *217*
176. What causes sibling rivalry? *218*
177. If jealousy is so common, then how can parents minimize it between siblings? *218*
178. Should parents discourage healthy competition in order to minimize the jealousy factor between children? *220*
179. If my children fight in order to attract my attention, how should I respond? *220*
180. My children continue to fight even though I've been fair with them and have given them no reason to resent one another. What can I do? *221*
181. The younger of my two very bright daughters refuses to apply herself in school. Why would this be? *223*
182. I thought you would be interested in an improvement I made on a reward system you suggested in an earlier book. *224*
183. We are planning our family very carefully, and want to space the children properly. Is there an ideal age span that will bring greater harmony between them? *224*
184. Our three-year-old son shows signs of jealousy toward our new baby. Please suggest some ways I can ease him through this period of adjustment. *225*

SECTION 14 **TEACHING CHILDREN TO BE RESPONSIBLE**
185. What is the distinction between a child's willful defiance and mere childish irresponsibility? *229*
186. How should parents deal with childish irresponsibility when it involves neither defiance nor passive aggression? *230*
187. Do you think a child should be required to say "thank you" and "please" around the house? *231*
188. My ten-year-old is very irresponsible and I often lose my patience with him. Am I damaging his self-esteem by these outbursts? *231*
189. Isn't it possible to create a spoiled brat by offering him too many words of praise? *232*
190. How can I acquaint my junior higher with the need for responsible behavior throughout his life? *232*
191. Each morning I end up screaming at my daughter in order to get her to meet the bus on time. Tell me how I can get her moving without this emotion every day. *233*
192. My eight-year-old puts his milk glass too close to his elbow when eating. Yesterday he spilt it again and I spanked him. Should I have reacted more patiently? *235*
193. My two adopted daughters have many sloppy habits. How can I teach them to take responsibility for themselves like other children their ages? *236*
194. Isn't the parent manipulating the child by the use of rewards and punishment? *237*
195. Using rewards to influence my kids seems like bribery to me. What do you think? *237*
196. If rewards are not a form of bribery, then what does constitute an inappropriate gift? *238*
197. Do rewards *have* to be in the form of money or toys? *239*
198. I gave each of our sons a sucker and they stopped throwing temper tantrums. Is this an example of using the Law of Reinforcement properly? *241*

199. My daughter constantly whines. How can I break her of this habit? *242*
200. Isn't the system of extinction used to help smokers and overeaters break their habits? *243*
201. My child is afraid of the dark. Can the principle of extinction be helpful in overcoming this fear? *243*

SECTION 15 **HYPERACTIVITY IN CHILDREN**

202. What is hyperactivity and what causes it? *247*
203. How can damage to brain tissue cause frantic activity in a child? *248*
204. How can anxiety or emotional problems cause hyperactivity? *248*
205. How early can the problem be identified? *249*
206. Is there a "normal" hyperactivity? *249*
207. How can I tell whether my child is normally active or genuinely hyperactive? How can I decipher whether it is the result of emotional or physical impairment? *249*
208. What role does nutrition play? *250*
209. How common is hyperactivity? *250*
210. Do other mothers sometimes resent their hyperactive child too? *250*
211. What other problems does the hyperactive child face? *251*
212. What are the solutions? *252*
213. Won't the long-term use of medication increase the possibility of my child becoming a drug user? *252*
214. Do medications solve all the problems? *252*
215. How does the parent "discipline" a hyperactive child? *253*
216. What does the future hold? *255*

SECTION 16 **COPING WITH ADOLESCENCE**

217. What else besides the essentials of reproduction and sex education should I tell my preteenager? *259*
218. What are the other major developments which I should prepare him to experience? *259*
219. My thirteen-year-old lies around the house and sleeps half a day on Saturday. Is this typical of early adolescence? How should I deal with this laziness? *261*
220. My daughter has no need for a bra but insists she have one because most of her friends do. Should I give in? *262*
221. Our teenage daughter demands that her sisters leave while she dresses. I think this is silly, don't you? *262*
222. What accounts for the fact that children seem to be growing up at a younger age today? *263*
223. My teenager seems to be ashamed to be seen with me. Is this normal? Should I resist or accept it? *263*
224. Must I act like a teenager in order to show my adolescent that I understand him? *264*
225. How can I teach my fourteen-year-old the value of money? *264*
226. What is the most difficult period of adolescence, and what is behind the distress? *265*
227. Will my junior higher grow out of his low self-esteem? *266*
228. Why are so many adolescents angry at their parents and family? *267*
229. I still have to impose some limits and discipline on my hostile teenager don't I? *268*
230. What do you think causes my teenage son to isolate himself from his peers? *269*
231. How am I to handle my fourteen-year-old son who is in a period of rebellion like nothing I've ever seen? *270*
232. What would you do to encourage the cooperation of my fifteen-year-old who deliberately makes a nuisance of himself? *273*
233. My fourteen-year-old daughter wants to date a seventeen-year-old boy. I don't feel good about it? What should I say to her? *274*
234. What should be my attitude toward my unmarried daughter whom I just discovered to be three months pregnant? *274*
235. I hate my son's hobby of animal collecting. What should I do? *275*
236. Why do teenagers take drugs when they know it is harmful? Are they merely the victims of "pushers" who get them hooked on narcotics? *275*
237. What should parents look for as symptoms of drug abuse? *275*
238. Do you think better education is the answer to the drug abuse problem? *276*
239. How can I help my child withstand the pressure of adolescent conformity to drug use and sexual immorality? *276*
240. Are adults also vulnerable to group pressure and conformity? *276*
241. I've heard different opinions about the dangers and safety of marijuana usage. What are the facts? *277*

242. How can I recognize the symptoms of marijuana use in my sixteen-year-old son? *278*
243. How do you feel about the mothers of elementary and high school students being employed outside the home? *279*

SECTION 17 **QUESTIONS FROM ADOLESCENTS**

244. I am a teenager and I want to look and dress just like all my friends. My parents tell me I should be an individual and be willing to be different, but I just can't do it. Do *you* understand? *283*
245. What causes pimples and what can I do about them? *283*
246. I'm thirteen and I feel miserable about myself. Is there anything I can do? *284*
247. Can you help me learn how to influence people and make them like me? *285*
248. My dad says my body will soon change a lot. I don't understand. Would you fill me in? (Male) *286*
249. I'm an eleven-year-old girl. What physical changes can I expect to take place? *288*
250. I'm thirteen-and-a-half and I haven't started to change yet. Is there anything wrong with me? (Male) *291*
251. I want to know more about making babies and all that stuff. *292*
252. What are wet dreams that I hear other boys talking about? (Male) *296*
253. Is there anything else I need to know about growing up that I haven't thought to ask? *29*

SECTION 18 **SELF-ESTEEM IN ADULTHOOD**

254. If I understand your writings correctly, you believe a majority of Americans experience low self-esteem to one degree or another. Assuming that to be true, what are the *collective* implications of that poor self-concept? *301*
255. Why is low self-esteem so prevalent among women today? Why is this more common now than in the past? *301*
256. Then low self-esteem among women is still greatly influenced by the same physical factors they worried about when they were younger? *302*
257. How does the self-esteem of men differ from women in regard to the influences of "beauty" and "brains"? *303*
258. My husband's teasing about my body makes me disinterested in sex. Why can't I just ignore his comments when I know he doesn't mean to hurt me? *303*
259. I have never felt attractive to the opposite sex. Does this explain my extreme modesty? *304*
260. What part does intelligence play in the self-esteem of adults? *304*
261. Can you describe what a person goes through when he feels inadequate and inferior? *305*
262. Why would my friend feel guilty and personally responsible when her husband lied and deceived her and ran off with a younger girl? *305*
263. I know a woman who has a terrible inferiority complex and unintentionally drives people away. How can I help her without making her feel even worse about herself? *307*
264. The psychiatrist I went to for treatment of my problem with low self-esteem wasn't helpful and didn't seem to care. How would *you* approach a patient with my kind of problem? *307*
265. I am *not* coping so well with the problems of self-doubt. What encouragement can you offer? *309*
266. I am handling my own inadequacies pretty well and now feel ready to take more steps toward self-confidence. What do you recommend? *310*
267. How do you scripturally defend your position of building self-esteem in children when the Bible specifically condemns an attitude of "pride"? *310*

SECTION 19 **A CHRISTIAN PERSPECTIVE ON ANGER**

268. How can we as Christians be expected to remove the common response of anger from our personalities? *315*
269. Is all anger sinful? *316*
270. Is it possible to prevent all feelings of anger? *316*
271. Doesn't the Bible take an absolute position on the subject of anger? *317*
272. Under what circumstances is anger sinful, in your opinion? *317*
273. Are you saying that being "right" on an issue does not justify a wrong attitude or behavior? *318*
274. Is anger evil even if it is held inside and never revealed? *318*
275. Can you harmonize the scientific understanding of the need to vent anger with the scriptural commandment to be "slow to wrath"? *318*

276. I had tried to make friends with a very ill-disposed neighbor when she "told me off" one day about something she obviously misunderstood. I was hurt and reacted with irritation. Now I feel bad about it. What should have been my reaction? *320*
277. What do you say to people who try not to, but continuously lose their temper? Is it possible for them to learn self-control? *320*
278. Why does my kid *try* to upset me when he knows I love him? *321*

SECTION 20 **ROMANTIC LOVE**
279. Do you believe love at first sight occurs between some people? *327*
280. Do you believe real love can easily be distinguished from infatuation? *327*
281. Does God select one particular person for each Christian to marry? *328*
282. Do you believe that genuine love between a husband and wife is permanent, lasting a lifetime? *329*
283. I'm nineteen and know that some awful circumstances occur in marriage. So why should I bother to marry at all? *329*
284. Should happily married husbands and wives be able to live without fighting one another? *329*

SECTION 21 **CONFLICT IN MARRIAGE**
285. What is *the* most common marital problem you hear about in your office? *333*
286. Can you help me effectively communicate my needs to a husband who's willing to learn about our differences? *335*
287. Are you suggesting that a woman should crawl on her belly, begging her master for a pat on the head? *336*
288. My husband seems totally disinterested in me and treats me rudely in public. I've begged him to love me, but I feel I'm losing him. What can I do to save my marriage? *338*
289. My wife and I love each other but our relationship has become stagnant recently. How can we escape this deadening lifestyle and enrich our marriage? *340*
290. My husband is a good man but he *cannot* comprehend my emotional needs. What do you suggest I do? *340*
291. Explain what you mean by developing a healthy "perspective" on marriage. *341*
292. My husband will *always* be unromantic and uncommunicative. Is divorce the answer? *343*
293. Why are men so insensitive to women's needs today despite the effort made to communicate and educate? *345*
294. Are you saying that I am responsible to help meet my wife's emotional needs, too? *346*
295. What effect does the breakdown in friendship and camaraderie between women have on marriages? *347*

SECTION 22 **THE HOMEMAKER**
296. Why is the role of homemaker and mother so often disrespected in our culture? *351*
297. Have TV and movie producers *deliberately* attempted to destroy or change the traditional role of American women? *351*
298. What has been the result of this feminine sex-role revolution and where are we headed from here? *352*
299. Should we all be locked into traditional male and female sex roles, whether we choose them or not? Should women be expected to bear children whether they want to or not? *354*
300. What answer do you give those who say being a mother and a housewife is boring and monotonous? *355*
301. How do you feel about mothers being employed outside the home, especially when it's not financially necessary? *355*
Editor's note: An article written by a working woman who examines her dual role as mother and employee begins on page *361*.

SECTION 23 **DEPRESSION IN WOMEN**
302. Is depression more common among men or women? *367*
303. When women get depressed, what specific complaint or irritant is most commonly related to the condition? *367*
304. My wife has been severely depressed for nearly three months. What kind of treatment or therapy would you recommend for her? *368*
305. Why do I feel depressed after every holiday? *368*
306. How can I slow down from a life of "routine panic"? It takes every minute of the day (and night) to care for my children and meet the needs of our family! *369*

307. My wife often gets depressed when she can't keep up with the children and the housework. I'm too busy also, but what can I do to help her cope? *370*
308. I notice that spiritual discouragement and defeat are much more common when I am tired than when I am rested. Is this characteristic of others? *371*
309. Are children typically vulnerable to parental discouragement and depression? *372*
310. Can you explain why so many Americans express a dissatisfaction with life, despite our affluency? *372*

SECTION 24 **UNDERSTANDING PREMENSTRUAL TENSION**

311. Is the moodiness I feel before my menstrual periods something that all women suffer? *377*
312. Describe the mood fluctuations that are associated with the menstrual cycle each month. Is this chemical influence evident at times other than during or before a period? *377*
313. Can you explain why I experience the greatest feeling of inadequacy and inferiority during the "premenstrual" phase? *378*
314. How do we know that the symptoms of premenstrual tension (PMT) are not merely psychological? *379*
315. Each month I find myself suffering from low self-esteem and general anxiety even though I know my depression is the result of physiological conditions. How can I do a better job of coping with the menstrual cycle? *380*
316. Will you offer some advice to my husband about the physiological problems I experience? *380*
317. Why are some women more prone than others to have unpleasant symptoms? *382*
318. Can I help relieve the symptoms by eating right? *382*
319. Is PMT similar to menopause in emotional characteristics? *383*
320. When my wife is suffering from PMT, why does she become even more irritable when I tell her everything isn't as bad as it seems? *383*
321. Do women who take "the pill" fluctuate emotionally? *384*

SECTION 25 **COPING WITH MENOPAUSE**

322. The children are gone and my husband and I are finally free to travel. But I'm always tired and sometimes just want to cry. Do you think I could be losing my mind? *387*
323. Can you give me a simple definition of menopause? *387*
324. Do all women feel as miserable as I do when menopause occurs? *388*
325. What are the primary symptoms of hormone imbalance during menopause? *388*
326. I'm only thirty-seven but I'm having some of the symptoms of menopause. Surely I'm too young, don't you think? *389*
327. I'm going through menopause now. Will it ever end? Will I feel like my old self again someday? *390*
328. Why do some women make it through menopause without the need for estrogen replacement therapy? *390*
329. Is there a "male menopause" comparable to what is experienced by women? *390*

SECTION 26 **MALE AND FEMALE UNIQUENESS**

330. How do men and women differ emotionally? *405*
331. Could you describe some of the more *subtle* ways males and females are unique? *405*
332. Would you explain differences between the way men develop self-esteem and the way women do? *407*
333. Is the felt need for sex the same in both males and females? *408*
334. Could you summarize the major differences in sexual desire and preferences between males and females? *408*
335. Besides the differences related to reproduction, could you list the other *physical* characteristics of males and females? *409*

SECTION 27 **THE MEANING OF MASCULINITY**

336. It is apparent from reading your book, *Straight Talk to Men and Their Wives*, that you are a strong advocate of masculine leadership at home. What response do you offer to activist women who would consider this view to be chauvinistic and archaic? *415*
337. Do you not favor a 50-50 arrangement on husband-wife interaction? *416*
338. Do you agree that American men should learn to loosen the rein on their emotions? *417*

339. What do you feel is a father's number one priority? *417*
340. Should I wait for my husband to accept spiritual leadership in our family or should I assume this responsibility when he doesn't? *418*
341. I keep hearing that it is unwise to get too carried away with the successes of your kids, but I can't help it. Is it wrong for me to feel a sense of fatherly pride when my son succeeds in basketball? How can I not *care* about the quality of his performance? *420*
342. How do you feel about the importance of a father's involvement in the discipline of preschool children? *421*
343. My children respond to a word or frown from my husband but I have to scream and threaten. Why is this true? *421*
344. What is the "mid-life" crisis that many men experience? *422*
345. When does this occur and how universal is it among men? *422*
346. What does a man experience during a full-fledged mid-life crisis? *423*
347. What causes this period of trauma and how can I head it off? *425*
348. I'm undergoing a mid-life crisis. Will I always be this depressed and miserable? *426*

SECTION 28 **ADULT SEXUALITY**
349. Why are some men and women less sensual than others? *431*
350. My wife is in therapy for depression caused from very little sexual desire. Can you help me understand better what she is feeling? *432*
351. Will you explain why failure to understand sexual uniqueness can produce a continual state of marital frustration and guilt? *433*
352. I find that I am easily distracted during intimate moments, especially by the fear of being overheard by the kids. This doesn't seem to bother my husband at all. Am I being foolish to worry about such things? *434*
353. My husband and I don't get to bed until nearly midnight each evening and then I'm too tired to get into love making. Is there something unusual or wrong that I can't respond? *435*
354. My husband and I never talk about the subject of sex, and this is frustrating to me. Is this a common problem in marriage? *435*
355. Would you say that *most* marital problems are caused by sexual difficulties? *436*
356. Is it possible for my wife to enjoy our sexual relationship when she rarely experiences orgasms? *437*
357. Explain why the sexual revolution has resulted in a higher incidence of certain physical problems. *437*
358. Why do you believe that the sexual revolution has the power to destroy us as a people? *438*
359. Why do you think the sexual behavior of people is related to the strength and stability of their nation? I don't see how those two factors are connected. *438*
360. How common is the desire for extramarital sexual encounters in men, even among those who remain faithful to their wives? *440*
361. What is the primary motivation that would cause a spouse to "cheat"? *441*
362. What role does the desire for sex play in influencing marital infidelity? *442*
363. After two or three years, what happens to those who become involved in affairs in order to deal with their unmet needs? *442*
364. Have you found that even professing Christians are being caught in the trap of marital infidelity? *443*
365. Is it true that some women fail to enjoy sex because of weakness of the muscular structure in the pelvic region? What can be done about it? *443*
366. From a Christian perspective, what is your view of abortion on demand? *444*

SECTION 29 **HOMOSEXUALITY**
367. What causes homosexuality? *451*
368. What is the most common home environment of a future homosexual? *451*
369. What can parents do to prevent homosexuality in their children? *451*
370. What should be the Christian's attitude toward homosexuality? *452*
371. What is the responsibility of the person who wants to be a Christian but struggles with homosexual attractions? *453*
372. What is bisexuality and why are we hearing so much about it now? *453*

SECTION 30 **TELEVISION AND VIOLENCE**
373. What is your view of TV, generally? Should parents regulate what children watch? *457*

374. Wouldn't it just be better to get rid of our TV set until after our children are grown? *458*
375. How can we control television without resorting to dictatorial rules and regulations? *458*
376. What can we do about the violence and decadence of television? *459*
377. How do you explain our predisposition to killing and acts of violence in the Western culture? *459*
378. What do you think can and should be done about the violence in our society and the forces which propel it? *461*

SECTION 31 **UNDERSTANDING GUILT**

379. Is there anything we can do about our past failures as parents, even though our children are grown? My wife and I are new Christians and realize that we raised our kids by the wrong principles. *465*
380. As a psychologist, would you explain what the conscience is and how it works in the mind? *466*
381. Do guilt feelings always contain a message of disapproval from God? *466*
382. Can a person suffer from a guilty conscience which God does not inspire? Would you give some examples? *467*
383. Would you explain your statement that a sense of guilt is sometimes inspired by Satan? *468*
384. Would you describe the nature of the conscience and how it functions? Does a person's childhood teachings affect his sense of guilt? *468*
385. That obviously places a tremendous responsibility on us as parents, doesn't it? *469*
386. Does the absence of guilt mean we are blameless in the sight of the Creator? Can I depend on my conscience to let me know when God is displeased with me? *469*
387. What am I to do with my conscience, then? Is it to be ignored altogether? Does God not speak through this mental faculty? *470*
388. You are obviously not suggesting that we ignore our consciences altogether, are you? *471*

SECTION 32 **INTERPRETATION OF IMPRESSIONS**

389. Do you think an effective method of discerning the "mind of God" is to wait for Him to make me feel positive or negative about a particular matter? *477*
390. Are you saying that God does not speak directly to the heart — that all impressions are false and unreliable? *478*
391. Do some of those "other sounds" represent the influence of Satan? *478*
392. Is it really possible for Satan to speak in the midst of an earnest prayer? *479*
393. Are some impressions and feelings of our own making? *479*
394. I have wondered if my impressions don't obediently tell me what I most want to hear. *479*
395. I heard a man say that he dreamed he should marry a certain woman. Does God ever speak to us in that way through dreams today? *480*
396. What do you mean by having the "content verified in other ways"? *480*
397. What is the purpose of dreams, from a scientific and psychological point of view? *481*
398. How can we tell the difference between the leadings of the Holy Spirit and the subtle, evil influences of Satan himself? *481*
399. Then how do you account for Christians who grope blindly or fall into Satan's traps and believe his lies? *482*
400. By what means can I "test" my own feelings and impressions and "prove" the will of God? *482*
401. Of Knapp's four criteria, "providential circumstances" seems hardest to apply. Can you give an example? *484*
402. How can you say definitely that God, rather than circumstances, determined the outcome of the sale of your house? *484*
403. Will the application of Knapp's four tests always prove conclusive? *485*
404. Are you saying there will be times in a Christian's life when God's will and actions may not make sense to him? *486*
405. Will there be occasions, then, when we will pray for the will of God to be revealed, and yet we may "hear" no immediate reply? *486*
406. Will you comment on the practice of astrology and whether there are any scientific facts to support it? *487*
407. Why do so many highly educated people follow their horoscopes when astrology is so unsupportable? *489*

SECTION 33 **MID-LIFE AND BEYOND**


408. I've survived everything so far, but I don't want to become a sour old woman. Would you offer a few suggestions that will help me avoid some of the problems characteristic of post-retirement age? *493*

409. Would you describe the physical changes that occur with the aging process? *494*

410. Is it inevitable that sexual desire must diminish in the fifth, sixth, and seventh decades of life? *496*

411. What does a woman most want from her husband in those last decades of her life? *496*


SECTION 34 **DR. DOBSON TALKS ABOUT FAMILIES**


412. Is there a comprehensive Christian formula for solving family problems? *499*

413. How does that formula apply to kids who constantly fight and argue? *499*

414. Do you see this empathy as an important element in early Christian training? *500*

415. How do you answer the criticism that your principles are too authoritarian? *500*

416. How much of an effect does our physical chemistry have on our feeling cycles? Or put it this way: Isn't it easier to behave better some days than others? *501*

417. Do you lend any credence to bio-rhythm theories? *501*

418. Is there a reason why you don't cite the Scriptures more frequently in your materials? *502*

419. Do you feel you know yourself pretty well? What things do you need to work on? *502*

420. Relative to your arguments about lack of self-esteem, don't you think the Bible in its teachings on original sin says we are inferior? *503*

421. Can biblical principles and psychological principles be complementary? *503*

422. On what key points do Christian psychologists differ today? *503*

423. Would you encourage Christian young people to pursue the field of psychology as a profession? *504*